School of American Research
Advanced Seminar Series

DOUGLAS W. SCHWARTZ, GENERAL EDITOR

Ancient Civilization and Trade

ANCIENT CIVILIZATION AND TRADE

EDITED BY

JEREMY A. SABLOFF

AND

C. C. LAMBERG-KARLOVSKY

3549

A SCHOOL OF AMERICAN RESEARCH BOOK

UNIVERSITY OF NEW MEXICO PRESS · Albuquerque

Foreword

"Commerce is the great civilizer. We exchange ideas when we exchange fabrics."—R. G. Ingersoll

The importance of trade has long been part of our economic philosophy, but, as Ingersoll has suggested, trade also carries with it a crossfertilization of ideas. Only recently, however, has trade's dynamic role in the growth of early civilizations begun to be a matter of detailed interest to the anthropologist. The papers in this volume examine this intriguing subject from the vantage points of archaeology, economics, social anthropology, and cultural geography. The chapters are beautifully balanced; we have conceptual and analytical presentations on the one hand, and case studies pointing to broader considerations on the other. Together they provide an excellent insight into the role of trade in the growth of civilization, and the problems surrounding the study of this relationship.

Colin Renfrew's lead article provides an excellent conceptual framework for the total volume, weaving central-place theory, the concepts of early state modules, information flow, and a typology of modes of trade and their evolution into a provocative discussion of the development of early civilization.

George Dalton follows with a valuable and stimulating analysis of Karl Polanyi's consideration of long-distance trade. In addition, Dalton provides an excellent short background on the history of economic anthropology and its basic questions, offering an overview of its paradigms and the current status and the changing universe of economic anthropology in relation to Polanyi's contributions. In essence, Dalton lays a base for the development of a new paradigm in economic anthropology.

Karl Polanyi's article, published posthumously, on trade and the trader follows with a masterly and systematic review of the classes of trade, kinds of goods, categories of traders, motives, and transport, and the "two-sidedness" of the institution of trade. Malcolm Webb examines the change from the chiefdom to the state. His most useful review of the origins of the state—using the examples of Egypt, lower Mesopotamia, the Indus and Yellow river valleys, highland Mesoamerica, and coastal Peru—puts particular emphasis on military conquest and population growth in relation to trade. K. C. Chang examines certain procedural and conceptual problems relating to trade as seen through the material remains of the Shang civilization. Gregory Johnson uses fourth millennium Uruk Period Mesopotamian material to provide an important discussion of locational analysis and central-place theory as analytical tools for the archaeological investigation of local exchange systems.

C. C. Lamberg-Karlovsky examines the modes of exchange and production of the resource chlorite (steatite) in early third millennium Mesopotamia in terms of access, time-space systematics, supply and demand, quantitative control, and place and mode of production activities. This analysis of a single exchanged material provides a view of the complexity the archaeologist faces in dealing with a prehistoric trade situation. Jeremy Sabloff and David Freidel look at another aspect of the trade facilities that expedite the transfer of goods, using as a case study a trading center off the coast of Yucatán on the island of Cozumel. William Rathje then views this same situation from the point of view of general systems theory to hypothesize trends in resource management and production-distribution systems.

All of these papers, as Robert McC. Adams suggests in his overview, do illustrate the search for new formulations and analytical approaches that were part of a "highly exploratory symposium." This volume does indeed forcefully record that "trade has become a . . . productive focus for research on the development of ancient complex societies."

Douglas W. Schwartz

School of American Research

Preface

This volume is a result of a School of American Research Advanced Seminar held in Santa Fe from October 28 through November 2, 1973.

The participants included Robert McC. Adams; K. C. Chang; Gregory A. Johnson; C. C. Lamberg-Karlovsky, cochairman; William L. Rathje; Colin Renfrew; Jeremy A. Sabloff, cochairman; Malcolm Webb; Paul Wheatley; and Henry Wright. All these participants, with the exceptions of Adams and Chang, circulated their papers in advance of the seminar. Revised versions of these papers appear in the present volume. Adams and Chang served as discussants and wrote their papers after the completion of the seminar. George Dalton was unable to attend but circulated his paper prior to the seminar. Professor Dalton also obtained the previously unpublished paper of the late Karl Polanyi. Through the kindness of Ilona Polanyi and Professor Dalton, this paper has been included in this volume. Finally, because of problems with his computer programs, Professor Wright unfortunately was unable to include his paper here. It is to be hoped, however, that he will be able to rectify this situation in the near future so that his important and stimulating work on computer simulations of trade can be read by the profession as a whole.

The possibility of holding an advanced seminar on ancient civilization and trade was first suggested to J. A. Sabloff by Dr. Douglas W. Schwartz, director of the School of American Research, in the spring of 1972, while he was visiting the excavations of the Cozumel Archaeological Project in Mexico. The project, which is directed by Sabloff and

W. L. Rathje, is concerned principally with understanding the role of long-distance trade in the development of ancient Maya civilization. Dr. Schwartz noted that the Cozumel Project's general interests were becoming widespread and that it might be worthwhile and productive to bring together a group of archaeologists who shared these interests, along with scholars who had backgrounds in cultural geography and economics, to discuss new research directions in archaeological studies of trade and ancient civilizations. Back at Harvard University, Sabloff found that C. C. Lamberg-Karlovsky, whose long-term project at Tepe Yahya in Iran was investigating the role of long-distance trade in cultural developments from ancient Mesopotamia to the Indus area, also had been considering organizing a conference on archaeological trade studies. After discussion of their mutual plans, they decided to pool forces and jointly organize an advanced seminar on ancient trade.

The success of the seminar was due to the efforts of many people. In particular, the enthusiasm, generosity, and support of Doug Schwartz made the seminar and this volume possible. The friendliness of many members of the School of American Research also helped make the stay of the seminar's participants in Santa Fe very pleasant. David Noble and Jeton Brown made all the arrangements which enabled the seminar to flow so smoothly. Last, but certainly not least, the cheerful service and aid of Ella Schroeder and the staff at the seminar house was greatly appreciated by all the participants.

To conclude, it is hoped that the papers in *Ancient Civilization and Trade* will give the reader a useful view of different archaeological approaches to the study of trade. Varied methodologies for investigating trade are illustrated, and the theoretical significance of studies of trade is explored. In addition, a number of dynamic roles that trade and trading networks may have played in the growth of civilizations are illuminated. If this work leads to a greater appreciation of the potential importance and utility of research on ancient trade and helps to stimulate new, imaginative, and innovative studies of trade, then the editors and all the participants will feel well rewarded.

Jeremy A. Sabloff

C. C. Lamberg-Karlovsky

Contents

Figures

Figures

Tables

PART I

INTRODUCTION

1

Trade as Action at a Distance: Questions of Integration and Communication

COLIN RENFREW

University of Southampton

In recent years, trade has become one of the principal foci of archaeo-logical research. There are two reasons for this. The first is pragmatic: trade can be studied. The objects of trade, or at least the imperishable ones, can frequently be found, modern analytical techniques allow the determination of the source, and quantitative methods inspired by geog-raphy permit generalizations about distribution patterns. The second reason is theoretical: in the past, the development of human culture and cultures has often been seen primarily in material terms (subsistence, technology, economy—for instance by Childe) or primarily in spiritual terms (social relations, religion, knowledge of the world—for instance by Frankfort). Recently the relationship between these two arbitrarily separated areas has been more fully appreciated, as we have become aware of their total and integral interdependence.

Trade is an activity which closely relates these two groups of subsystems; it requires organization as well as commodity, and it implies criteria of value and measure. The crucial importance of the study of trade today is that it offers a practical way of investigating the organization of society in social terms as well as purely in economic ones.

Trade, a term synonymous with exchange, has been defined as "the mutual appropriative movement of goods between hands" (Polanyi 1957:266). The movement need not be over any great distance, and may operate within social or spatial units (internal trade) or between them, across cultural boundaries (external trade). In what follows, the notion of *movement*, in the sense of change of location, is crucial as the generator of spatial distribution. And *between hands* introduces at the outset the theme of human interactions.

This is why trade offers one of the most convenient approaches to the origins of civilizations or of states. For however these terms are defined, they imply an organization, a specialized administration, which regulates human activities both in terms of procurement (movement of goods including raw materials) and of social relations (human encounters with exchange of information and goods). "The essence of a social system is interdependence, and the essence of interdependence is men's investment of themselves in other men" (Coleman 1963). The degree of organization and its evolution, and of the evolution of civilization itself, may be understood in the light of the exchanges within a civilization. In this chapter I should like to examine more closely some of these interactions, of which trade is among the most important, and to suggest that we have not yet understood their complexity, nor the range of interpretive uses to which the archaeological record may be put.

In the first part of what follows I shall outline a general approach to civilizations and their formation, and discuss the role of interactions within and between them. The second part of the chapter is concerned with the pragmatic archaeological problems involved in the study of trade.

4

INTERACTION AND ORGANIZATION

Trade as Local Interaction

Marcel Mauss (1954) was the first fully to stress that in circumstances of relative self-sufficiency, many exchanges of goods take the form of gifts, and that such gifts have far more than a purely economic significance. They are social acts, prestations, in which the material aspect may have a subsidiary importance. Anthropologists from Malinowski to Sahlins have held this view, stressing the embeddedness of the economy within a social matrix among communities of band or tribal organization. An exchange of goods in such communities is primarily an act reinforcing a social relationship, and material exchange is an important aspect of the adjustment of the individual's relationship with others in his social environment, and in the adjustment of the band's or tribe's relationships with its neighbors.

Sociologists have taken the idea of exchange further to describe all interpersonal contacts, viewing all social behavior as an exchange of goods, nonmaterial as well as material (Homans 1958). In this perspective, the cohesiveness of a group, defined as anything that attracts people to take part in a group, is a value variable, referring to the degree of reinforcement that people find in the activities of the group. Communication or interaction is seen as a frequency variable: a measure of the frequency of emission of valuable and costly verbal behavior. The more cohesive a group is, and the more valuable the sentiment or activity the members exchange with one another, the greater the frequency of interaction among its members.

The anthropologist studying trade can profit from this approach, although he will interpret value rather differently and will broaden the discussion from the primarily verbal interactions which the sociologist may have in mind. For all human action may be viewed at a distance as exchange, both of material and of nonmaterial goods. We can measure the intensity of the interaction either in terms of frequency, as Homans suggests, or in terms of quantity of goods transferred. This is a simple enough concept for material goods, a more difficult but potentially useful one in the field of information. When the exchange habitually takes place at a specific location, we may describe that location as

5

a central place, which will then take on a special significance for the cohesiveness of the group.

Let us for the moment divide the totality of "goods" exchanged over a given period into material goods (among which "energy"—i.e., work or services—is here included) and information, defined as a constraint or stimulus upon present or future behavior. The total interaction, A, between two individuals is then the sum of the exchanges of goods, G, and information, I.

$$A = A_{12} + A_{21} = G_{12} + G_{21} + I_{12} + I_{21}$$

And the total interactions in a group of N individuals is

$$A = \Sigma A_{ij} = \Sigma G_{ij} + \Sigma I_{ij}$$

This approach leads us to contrast two extremes: exchange of goods without a wide range of accompanying information, and exchange of information without goods. The first is clearly the intention of "silent trade" (although even here information bearing on the future conduct of the trade itself is transmitted, for instance in the acceptance or not of the goods laid out). It is also a feature of market trade, where contacts can be at their most impersonal. The second extreme applies to any contact which we may identify as purely social or purely religious, although on examination many which we might so describe involve the exchange of material goods.

Information is not being used here in the special sense used in information theory. Yet the observation holds in that sense also. For quantity of information there indicates the magnitude of the set of possibilities of different messages: information conveyed is not an intrinsic property of the individual message. As Weaver (1949:12) remarks, "The word information relates not so much to what you *do* say, as to what you *could* say." In this special sense the silent trade and its modern equivalent, the supermarket, are also devices which restrict information.

For the archaeologist, the study of trade is central to the study of society because of the association of goods and information in most exchanges, an aspect of the embeddedness of the economy. Indeed, one might go a step further and claim that this association of material and social, of goods and information, this embeddedness, is the *normal* state of society, that is to say the basis upon which human interaction functions in the absence of special mechanisms. From this standpoint the introduction of money and the use of markets are devices of some sophistication to allow the separation of functions, a differentiation overcoming the "normal" association or embeddedness. Coinage is a further sophistication, as are deferred payment, credit facilities, and the like. The associative embeddedness can only be avoided by the formulation of specific rules and conventions, both in the economic field and in the socioreligious one, where the renunciation of material things allegedly practiced in some sectarian groups completes the dissociation, with separate renditions on the one hand to God and on the other to Caesar or to Mammon.

It is appropriate now to set these interactions in spatial terms. In a uniform plain, with a dispersed settlement pattern, we can visualize each nuclear family as a point. If his home is fixed and his economy sedentary, the movements of the individual may be restricted to forays of a few kilometers' distance. Since the plain is uniform he may have minimal contact with his neighbors in adjacent territories. Such an individual or family, living alone, independent and self-sufficient, isolated from other humans, is the antithesis of civilization. Our interest is in the interactions that can make this individual, without change of local residence, a part of a functioning civilization. (Sedentary settlement is here under discussion: the position of mobile groups, including nomads and transhumant pastoralists may require a different treatment. For convenience a sedentary settlement will be defined as one in which no less than 90 percent of the annual man nights of the population are spent at home, in the permanent residence, or in fields not more than a few kilometers from it.)

This picture of minimum interaction is the very antithesis of civilization. Nor is the presence or absence of dispersed or agglomerate settlement in itself the crux of the matter. For agglomerate settlement does not in itself define civilization, although it must bring with it some measure of interaction. Indeed, we can visualize an agricultural population, every family of which is entirely self-supporting, in which the houses are clustered. This is in fact approximately the case in many early farming villages, some of which reach almost urban size without reflecting an urban organization. Çatal Hüyük is an example. The size of such

7

communities is limited by two parameters: the carrying capacity C (expressed as number of persons per unit area) and the maximum distance from the center of land that is farmed, given the available transport facilities. The maximum population P is $320\ R^2C$, where R is in kilometers and C in persons per hectare. A radius of 5 km. and Allan's figure of 0.5 for C in modern Anatolia (Allan 1972:225) gives a notional population of 4,000. This figure is indeed exceeded by the agricultural "towns" of southern Italy (Chisholm 1968:114), and both early neolithic Jericho and Çatal Hüyük may have housed comparable populations. There is no justification for taking a population figure of this order as an indication in itself of civilization or of cities: degree of interaction is not determined by population density or size of settlement unit, although both are among the determining factors.

High population need not be permanently associated with a central place, and indeed at periodic central places there is frequently no population. The Siassi-Gomlongon market described by Harding (1967:150) is at one extreme here; purely religious centers, such perhaps as Stonehenge, are at the other; and between is the whole range of periodic tribal central places which are distinct from residential locations. Residential locations can of course themselves be periodic central places; examples are the circulation markets of the Yoruba or in China, or at the other extreme and in our own society, a circus traveling from village to village.

These different interactions or exchanges, with their flow of goods and of information, are what remove the individual in his Crusoe-like isolation, suggested above, from a condition of brute independence, making him part of a functioning society of a kind we term civilization, with a high degree of interaction and specialization.

It was Karl Polanyi who made a fundamental distinction, about human affairs in general as well as about the economy, when he isolated for discussion both reciprocity and redistribution. Their importance can be tabulated as follows:

Perspective	Reciprocity	Redistribution
Configuration	Symmetry	Centricity
Geographical	No central place	Central place
Affiliation	Independence	Central Organization
"Solidarity" (Durkheim)	Mechanical	Organic

Reciprocity can of course work as a distributive mechanism, even with specialist manufacture. If we imagine village A making water jars and fine pottery, village O producing fibers and poultry products, and village Z salt, flowers, and maize we can imagine each exchanging its products for those produced by the other. If the number of production points is N, each producer will need to visit or be visited by $(N - 1)$ village representatives from other villages to effect full distribution, with a consequential $\dfrac{N.N - 1}{2}$ journeys.

If, on the other hand, a system of redistribution operates, and one village functions as a central place as well as a small production location, inhabitants of the surrounding villages will have to travel only to the central one, and its inhabitants will not need to travel at all, so that the total of journeys will be $N - 1$. (fig. 1). As the number of participating production centers increases and also the proportion of the

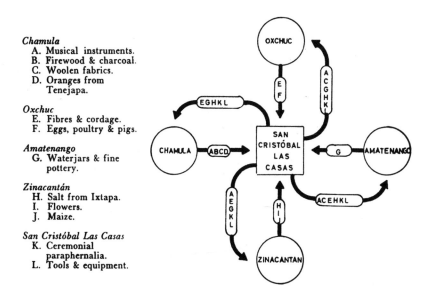

Chamula
  A. Musical instruments.
  B. Firewood & charcoal.
  C. Woolen fabrics.
  D. Oranges from
     Tenejapa.

Oxchuc
  E. Fibres & cordage.
  F. Eggs, poultry & pigs.

Amatenango
  G. Waterjars & fine
     pottery.

Zinacantán
  H. Salt from Ixtapa.
  I. Flowers.
  J. Maize.

San Cristóbal Las Casas
  K. Ceremonial
     paraphernalia.
  L. Tools & equipment.

FIGURE 1. TRANSFER OF GOODS BY REDISTRIBUTION. In spatial terms this does not differ from market exchange, and the example is based on the market center of San Cristóbal las Casas, south Mexico. Reproduced from Siverts (1969).

produce of each that is exchanged, the institution of the central redistributive agency becomes overwhelmingly more efficient in terms of transport cost.

This, then, is a purely economic reason for the emergence of central places as the exchange of goods develops. In cases where there is also marked local diversity, with ecological variations within the region, a desire to obtain the products of a neighboring niche will inevitably promote exchange, which in turn will favor the development of central places.

The counterpart of the exchange of goods, namely the exchange of information, is no less important. And underlying any analysis of human society must be the recognition that public meetings take place in nearly all cultures, whether or not they are viewed as adaptively useful in stimulating solidarity and in reducing conflict. One convenient solution is for meetings to take place at each village in succession, which brings some of the benefits of centricity without long-term loss of symmetry. This solution has indeed been adopted by many band and tribal societies, of which the Kyaka of New Guinea are a good example (Bulmer 1960). But the provision of an impressive permanent facility for the occasion, such as a magnificent temple, becomes prohibitively expensive if it has to exist at each settlement. Again a central place is an obvious solution, this time for the exchange of information.

Just as craft specialization offers advantages in quality of product and in economics of scale, so specialization in communication, by priests and leaders controlling a central administration, is efficient and offers an attractive product. These full-time specialists at the center of redistribution are paid for by the goods of those who come to interact: it is an exchange of information against material goods. Redistribution is therefore simply an exchange of this kind, which, like the exchange of purely material goods, operates most efficiently at a central place.

This perspective allows us to see market exchange, Polanyi's third category along with reciprocity and redistribution, more clearly. For market exchange, seen in spatial terms, does not differ from redistribution. Indeed, figure 1, used above to illustrate redistribution, is taken from an article on market exchange in south Mexico (Siverts 1969:106), and the central place is not a redistribution center but the market of San Cristóbal las Casas in Chiapas. The difference, of course, is that accompanying the exchange, in the case of redistribution, is a central organization within whose functioning the economic function is embedded. In the physical sense, redistribution implies the physical reception and disbursement of the goods by the central authorities and hence the provision of considerable storage facilities, as in the Minoan-Mycenaean palaces (Renfrew 1972:291–97). But increasingly sophisticated devices make possible a system of redistribution, involving the bulk of the produce not consumed by the producer, without its physical possession—first by nominal possession, although not under the direct control of the central authority, and then by more complicated accounting procedures. There is thus some formal equivalence between redistribution and market exchange which may make it difficult to distinguish between them in archaeological terms.

Moreover, Polanyi did not sufficiently stress that all marketing implies some kind of order, of security—ultimately, indeed, in the case of permanent markets, of jurisdiction. So that while the economic activity is to the fore, there *is* a social relationship (although not necessarily much active interaction) between those exchanging and the central authority ordering the central place. In this sense, market exchange may be regarded as redistribution with a dissociation of the central authority from the material transaction. Market exchange cannot take place without such order, either reigning precariously as in some tribal market exchange, or maintained by central authority, itself normally sustained by taxation (a monetary form of redistribution). The position of the port of trade, originally discussed by Polanyi and more recently by Rathje and Sabloff (cf. Rathje and Sabloff 1972; Sabloff et al. 1973), is an interesting one, for where the trade is at a level of fairly sophisticated market exchange, order is maintained by what may be viewed as reciprocity.

The foregoing discussion makes clear why there can be no civilization without permanent central places. The city has been well described as a "communication engine," and this description applies as much to low-population central places, such as some of those of Egypt or Mexico, as to great cities like Warka or Tenochtitlán. In studying the origins of civilization we are considering the rise of such central places. The consideration of exchange, of both information and material, reveals why population size is a secondary parameter.

In this section the rise of civilization has been equated with the devel-

11

opment of interpersonal interactions among the population of an area, many of these persons being necessarily at a distance from each other. It has been suggested that with the development of such interactions central places arise and that these need not be large centers of population. Before examining alternative models for the formation of civilization, it will be useful to consider some features of the spatial organization of many early civilizations.

The Administrative Module in Early Civilizations

A permanently functioning central place is a feature of every civilization. The central place may also be a major population center, or it may not have a large resident population. It serves as a focus for the material and informational exchanges that make up the interactions characteristic of civilization, and the permanent existence of the central place and its function as such is one of the features distinguishing civilizations from chiefdom societies, such as those of Polynesia. For even in the most stable of these chiefdoms, with a center functioning as the permanent seat of a chief, the central place actually operated as a major redistributive center—for both material and social exchange—only on one or two occasions during the year. (The ceremonial center of Mu'a in Tonga is a good example [McKern 1929:95], for major redistribution took place there only on one or two occasions during the year, notably at the great *inasi*, the annual first-fruits ceremony.)

I would like to suggest that in most, possibly in all, early civilizations a pattern can be discerned which has not clearly been distinguished hitherto. Perhaps this is because it is a spatial pattern, while the state and civilization (and even urbanism) are generally defined in terms of human specialization and organization, rather than spatially. But of course spatial order is an inescapable aspect of all organization, and the rise or origin of civilization can profitably be considered in terms of the genesis of that spatial organization. The recognition of this general pattern allows a discussion of the question which is not predicated upon an analysis of "cities" or "urban centers," since the central places in question are not necessarily of a character which would universally be accepted as urban. A firm distinction must be made here between the "civilization"—viewed as a "culture" (possessing a distribution in space

12

and time) of a certain complexity—and the organizational units ("states") which comprise it.

1. In most, perhaps all, early civilizations there function a number of autonomous central places which, initially at least, are not brought within a single unified jurisdiction. It is such autonomous territorial units, with their central places, which together constitute what we would all term a civilization. They may be recognized as iterations of what I propose to call the *early state module* (ESM).

If the territorial extent of any early civilization is marked on a map, the higher-level organization pattern will take the configuration seen in figure 2—fairly evenly spaced autonomous central places set in territories

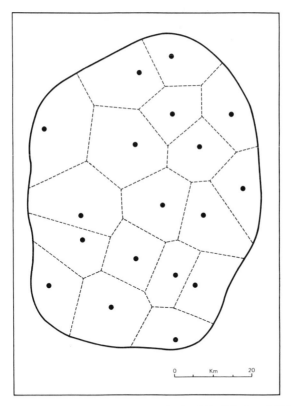

FIGURE 2. IDEALIZED TERRITORIAL STRUCTURE OF EARLY CIVILI-ZATIONS, showing the territories and centers of the ESMs within the civilization (i.e., area of cultural homogeneity).

13

which may notionally be indicated by means of Thiessen polygons. At the level of the early civilization or early state, these are the largest central places found. And when archaeologists claim to speak of the origins of early civilizations, they are usually found to be speaking of the development of these ESMs and of the less permanent and less active central places which preceded them. A central place, as considered here, is not, of course, merely an agglomeration of population; indeed its population may be small. This point is considered further in the next section.

2. The early state module apparently falls within a restricted size range. Frequently the modular area is approximately 1500 sq. km. with a mean distance of about 40 km. between the central places of neighboring modules. Special environmental or social factors may reduce this distance to about 20 km., while intervening parcels of uncultivable land may increase it to at least 100 km.

3. Many early civilizations comprise, before subsequent unification, about 10 of such early state modules, although the number may vary by a factor of at least 2, and cases are known where the number is higher.

Mycenaean Greece may be taken by way of example (fig. 3). The results of site survey (Hope Simpson 1965) indicate 14 palaces or major fortresses, of which perhaps 2 (Gla and Mideia) may not have been permanently occupied. Unweighted Thiessen polygons (Dirichlet regions) have been drawn to show the notional boundaries of the ESMs. Taking only adjacent territories (with a common terrestrial boundary), the centers have a mean separation of 76 km., partly in consequence of the rugged terrain between some of them. Minoan Crete offers a similar picture (Renfrew 1972:258), with a mean separation of 35 km., but the restricted size of the island allows room for only 5 or 6 palaces. In both cases the terrain imposes severe restrictions on the spatial distribution.

The pattern is seen again in the Maya area (fig. 4) where, in the southeast Petén, Hammond (1972:784) has identified "realms" (ESMs) approximately 1600 sq. km. in area. In Mesopotamia a similar modular organization can be identified; here the predynastic and early dynastic city-states are the central places of the modules, of which more than a dozen have been identified. A similar pattern may be recognized among the Hausa states of northern Nigeria (Magobunje 1968:51, fig. 3). For classical Greece, Doxiadis (1971) has proposed an area of 1471 sq. km.

14

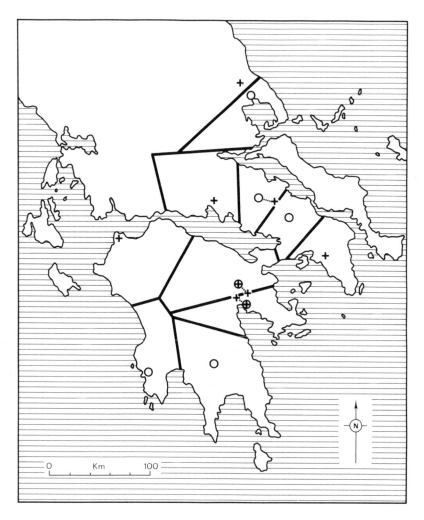

FIGURE 3. THE EARLY STATE MODULE IN MYCENAEAN GREECE, showing palaces (circles), major strongholds (crosses), and hypothetical territorial boundaries.

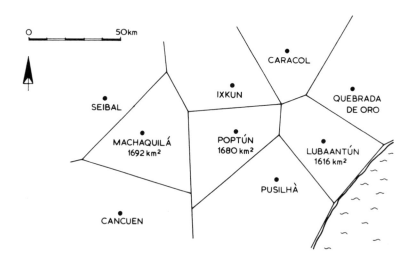

FIGURE 4. THE EARLY STATE MODULE IN THE MAYA LOWLANDS: realms in the southeastern Petén. Reproduced from Hammond (1972).

for the territory of a city-state. Early Etruria (fig. 5) offers another instance of an arguably "pristine" civilization, which emerged into history as a hegemony of 12 city-states. The mean distance between neighbors (with common terrestrial boundaries) is 56 km. Egypt, of course, is something of an exception to this schema, since the Nile imposes a linear arrangement, and little is known of the settlement pattern or administrative organization before the unification at the outset of the Old Kingdom. The discussion here, furthermore, is restricted to sedentary agricultural societies; more mobile units are discussed later.

The possibility of some uniformity in the size and spacing of these ESMs is particularly interesting, since the central places of one civilization are evidently different in size from those of another, as are the population densities. Brush and Bracey (1955) have, however, made a similar observation, although at a lower administrative level, in their comparisons between modern southwestern Wisconsin and southern England, where they found a spacing of about 21 miles between higher-order centers, about 7 miles between lower-order ones, and about 5 miles between the lowest-order centers. The interest here lies not in the abso-

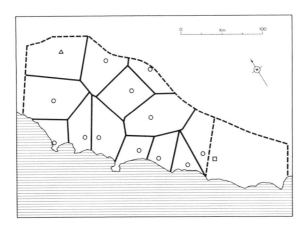

FIGURE 5. THE EARLY STATE MODULE IN ETRURIA: the 12 cities of ancient Etruria (circles) with hypothetical territorial boundaries. Rome is indicated by a square and Fiesole by a triangle.

lute figures but in the existence of modular units which appear in this case also to be of the same order in quite unrelated rural regions.

Settlement hierarchies have been recognized in a number of early civilizations, but the mean distances between adjacent centers of autonomous units have not been reported. Hodder (1972), writing of the hierarchy of settlement in Roman Britain, reports a distance of 6.5 miles between minor settlements, of 13 miles between major unwalled settlements, and 26 miles between walled settlements. His interest, however, is in the Roman period, and not in the pre-Roman Iron Age, when south Britain was composed of effectively autonomous tribal units. The Roman cantonal capitals approximate those of the previous period, and using Rivet's map (1964, fig. 9) I have calculated the mean distance between centers with common territorial boundaries in south Britain. For this purpose a line was drawn between the Wash and the Bristol Channel, and all civitates or *coloniae* south of the line, other than London and Glevum, were included. This gave a mean distance of 52 Roman miles, or approximately 76 km. Iron Age Britain was not of course organized at the state level, but it has been widely recognized that the major hill forts and oppida were central places which one might term proto-urban, although the Roman conquest radically altered the course of subsequent development. It would be particularly interesting to know how this mean distance changes during the transition from chiefdom to early state; my suspicion is that it decreases more often than it increases. I have not attempted any detailed cross-cultural survey of early civilizations that would test the extent to which (a) the cellular pattern of ESMs and (b) their modular size are universal. But certainly many other early instances could be found: Wheatley and Chang have both (in seminar comments) discussed the spatial organization of Shang China in this way, and the forerunner of the Hittite Empire is amenable to similar treatment.

If this concept of ESM is accepted, it throws into relief a much-neglected feature of early civilizations. For while the external, long-distance trade of such civilizations is much discussed, and the internal trade, within the modules—that is to say the redistributive organization, with some residue of reciprocal exchange—has been well considered, the flow of goods and information *between* the ESMs, what we may term the *intermediate trade*, is rarely discussed. Yet this is the exchange whose effect must have been to produce and maintain the uniformity of culture or civilization as a whole. This question of uniformity or similarity has never been adequately considered for the state or civilization level of organization. D. L. Clarke (1968: chap. 9) has given an interesting discussion of spatial similarity patterns among tribes, but nowhere in the literature is there a careful investigation of the exchange mechanisms underlying them, other than vague reference to "pan-tribal sodalities" and the like.

Here one aspect of exchange must be discussed for its substantial impact on information flow: exogamy with respect to the territorial unit. There is no doubt that the most influential form of interaction at a distance takes place when the "distance" is permanently negated by change in place of residence. This simple truth underlies much older migrationist reasoning, but only in a few studies, such as those of Deetz (1965) and Hill (1966), has it been applied to a "steady state" situation. One can see that any perceived division into "them" and "us" is likely to lead, within the restrictions of the society's marriage rules, to a higher degree of intermarriage among "us" and hence a greater information flow, leading to an effective, operational difference in the culture of "them" and "us" which will reinforce the perceived distinction. The extent to which ESMs function as exogamous entities is relevant, therefore, to an understanding of the homogeneity of the culture of the ESMs within the civilization as a whole, although it does not diminish the significance of other kinds of exchange.

The initial autonomy of the ESMs implies that trade between them will be reciprocal, primarily between the major central places. Indeed, when there is a shift from reciprocity to redistribution, implying the emergence of a higher-order central place, the civilization is consequently unified to form an empire. Alternatively, when the reciprocity breaks down, giving rise to hostility, unification may again be the consequence. This is the phenomenon implied in Julian Steward's term "Era of Cyclical Conquests" (Steward 1955:196). (Attack from outside may bring a measure of unification, very much like that seen in a segmentary lineage system [Bohannan 1954].) On occasion such unification processes have been identified with state formation itself (c.f. Krader 1968: chaps. 3, 5, and 6), but there is in such cases a confusion between organization and perceived ethnic identity over a wide area. My focus here is on aspects of organization and interaction without which no civilization or state can function, and on sedentary rather than nomad societies.

The ESM for various early civilizations clearly falls within a limited size range, and the maximum distance from center to territorial boundary must be related to the means of transport available. For the Etruscan city territories the maximum is about 50 km.; for the Mycenaean centers, with their uncultivable intervening terrain, about 70 km. In none of the early civilizations we are discussing was the horse widely used (although horses were ridden in Etruria); the ox-drawn cart was significant in some. So the boundaries of the module were generally no more than one or two days' march from its center. The distance from chief center to boundary for a civilization-empire could clearly be much larger, and effective military control must have been a crucial factor, implying a military hierarchy, with local governors and often local garrisons, and with the development of the totalitarian structure that some authors consider typical of the state. I suggest, however, that effective control—if less obviously militaristic—will have come first at ESM level.

The exchange situation implied by this model is seen in figure 6. Within an ESM, the internal exchange is by redistribution with some

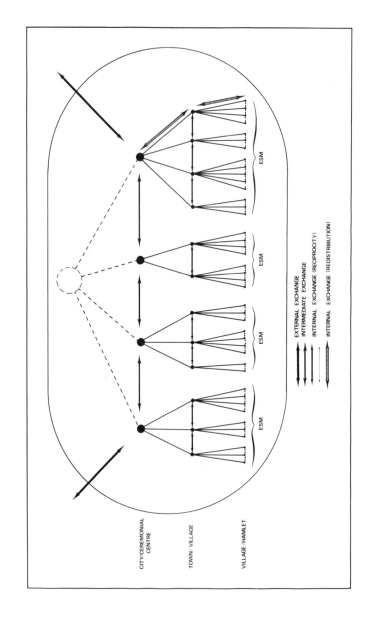

FIGURE 6. MODES OF EXCHANGE FOR AN EARLY CIVILIZATION, indicating the place of the ESMs within it and the scope of internal, intermediate, and external trade. Dotted lines indicate the organizational unification occurring when the ESMs of the civilization merge to form a single empire or civilization-state.

reciprocity (redistribution including the possibility of market exchange). Among ESMs there is intermediate exchange on a basis of reciprocity. And between ESMs and the outside world there is external exchange. Dotted lines indicate the possibility of the amalgamation of the ESMs into an empire, with the development of a higher-order central place (or the emergence as such of the center of one of the ESMs).

Trade as Remote Interaction

The archaeologist has traditionally been interested in trade less for its role in the internal organization of society than for its importance as a proof of "diffusion." The frequent and widespread use of the term *diffusion* is open to objection not so much because it is not appropriate (although this has been the case in a large number of misguided applications) as because it does not, as used by the archaeologist, have any explanatory content. Archaeologists generally use it to mean simply that contact with areas outside the system may be documented, and that, on the assessment of the observer, "independent invention" is to be denied. Rarely is the nature of the contact analyzed or any consideration given to what "invention" would mean in the context, whether "independent" or not. The term *diffusion*, used in this general sense, is best avoided.

Diffusion as a spatial process has been analyzed usefully by geographers (e.g. Hägerstrand 1967), and their work no doubt still offers many insights for the archaeologist. In their analysis, however, they are generally required to assume precisely those matters which, for the prehistoric case, are here in question: how the diffusion process works, in personal as well as spatial terms; the homogeneity or lack thereof of the spatial field; and precisely what is being diffused.

The interactions associated with exchange within the system, specifically within the ESM, have already been mentioned, with redistribution taking a major part (with or without the agency of market exchange), reciprocity a subsidiary position, and marriage exchange a significant role. Intermediate exchange between ESMs, but within the culture or civilization, still awaits adequate analysis. But again marriage exchange must be an important factor. It is now exchange across the boundaries of the culture or civilization—external exchange—that concerns us.

Our interest is in the effects of this exchange upon a culture which, in terms of organization, of hierarchy, of volume of internal exchange, is *less* highly differentiated than its neighbor. The possible effects of the internal organization arising with the development of an export trade are indicated in the next section; our interest focuses here not so much on purely economic organization as on the effects upon the system of the flow of information reaching it from its more highly organized neighbor, the process numbered 6, *Emulation,* below (p. 33).

It should be explained at this point that exchange between major regions with very different resource patterns has not been singled out for special mention. For I take it as axiomatic that any early civilization must control, normally within its boundaries, such resources as are altogether essential for its survival. In cases where there is a very heavy interdependence between them, developments may occur as in process 3, *Intraregional Diversity* (p. 29 below), and the boundaries of the civilization may develop (as a consequence of the strong interactions between the regions) so that the ecological diversity is an internal one.

Our interest in remote interactions was well expressed by Flannery (1972:135): "It might provide a great deal of unexpected fun if future studies used such exchange as a window into each society's explosively evolving ability to collect and process information about neighboring societies."

Exchange of goods between A and B through intermediary or intermediaries C can effect the transmission of information in three ways:

1. *Commodity.* The traded material itself, at its place of receipt, and independent of the means by which it reached that place, may convey meaning. In information theory terms it can be both signal and message (whether or not the transmitter or the receiver had a prior intention of transmitting or receiving). In what it *is,* if this is something new, it is a message with appreciable semantic content. A cup made of gold, to a person who has not previously seen gold, imparts information about the world. From the standpoint of the receiver it is a message.

Secondly the object itself may function as signal, which requires decoding before yielding any recognizable semantic content. Let us take as an example here the remarkable steatite carvings of Tepe Yahya (Lamberg-Karlovsky 1972b). In the hands of a person (destination) who is familiar with the symbolism involved, these carvings are, for instance, religious scenes making sense to a participant in Sumerian civilization: he can decode the signal. In the hands of someone who does not have the code, they are just odd carvings.

The extent to which meaning and hence information is conveyed by objects is a complicated one. The complexity arises, as so often in the attempt to apply information theory in an unrestricted human context, because many channels of communication are in operation, and more are continually being opened. The process does not easily lend itself to analysis, since the bandwidth can never be regarded as fixed.

Objects themselves, in isolation, can convey information, and this process is precisely what Kroeber (1940) meant by the term "stimulus diffusion."

2. *Association with commodity.* Inherent in the act of exchange between intermediary C and recipient B is a complex of mutual understandings, which have to be common to B and C and which will be conveyed from B to C or vice versa before the transaction can be completed. Some, in turn, may have been transmitted to C on the occasion of his interaction with A. These understandings include concepts of number and of unit of measure (weight, capacity, and so forth), as well as the means of measuring these (scales, graded capacities, and the like). Inherent in the exchange is the very concept of exchanging the two commodities in question, as well as the valuation systems by which quantities are established. (Here, after all, was what motivated much of early European trading endeavor in the Middle Ages: the search for El Dorado, where the streets would be paved with gold bricks, was the search for a land not only with a supply of the desired commodity but also with a favorable value system.) Accompanying the exchange also may be the concept of currency, and possibly some system of recording. It is within this constellation of information types that the regulating effect of exchange over the supply of desired commodities operates (Wright and Zeder in press; Rappaport 1967).

Accompanying the exchange, moreover, even in a "silent trade" situation, are modes of communication formally extraneous to it. The dress of the intermediary, the form of transport he uses, and other features all offer channels of potential communication.

3. *Verbal exchange.* The intermediary C can tell the recipient B what

he knows of A and of his culture. A large quantity of information can be transmitted in this way.

The trade situation is an exchange situation, and an exchange situation is an information flow situation. For this reason the analogy seen in figure 7 between a communication system (Weaver 1949) and a trading system is only in part analogy; in part it is descriptive. The reciprocal nature of all trade and exchange is indicated, or more strictly the cyclical nature.

The enormous complexity of the communication of information during trading exchanges makes it understandable that in the past the whole process has been swept under the carpet by using the term *diffusion*. Progress, however, will only come when different categories of information, conveyed by different channels, are distinguished.

Alternative Models for Civilization Formation

The origin of the early civilization or the state, whatever its subsequent career, has been identified above with the emergence of early state modules, each with a stratified organization for exchange. This central place exchange, and the permanency and permanent functioning of the central places, underlie the interdependence of ESM society, in contrast to the relative independence of local units linked only by reciprocal exchanges.

One obvious concomitant of central places, not yet discussed here, is *central persons*. These are the individuals upon whom the exchange of goods and of information focuses. The hierarchy of central places thus carries with it a hierarchy of central persons, who may themselves be singled out by great prestige and wealth. While this may be the case, however, it is not a necessary part of their function (even if display, sumptuary rules, and conspicuous consumption often have an adaptive role in facilitating that function). Archaeologists often assume that a pronounced hierarchy of personal wealth and conspicuously asserted prestige is a necessary accompaniment of early civilizations. This, however, is not so. In both the Greek city-states and Republican Rome, a different set of values soon developed—although it could be argued

24

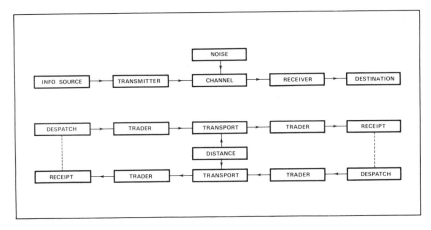

FIGURE 7. EXCHANGE AS INFORMATION FLOW: the structural homology between the transmission of a signal and the trade of goods.

that these democratic, antiroyal values were not a feature of the first emergence of the ESM.

I have often thought how singular the Indus Valley civilization is in this respect. For it possesses very large urban centers with a rectangular layout more impressive than any in Early Dynastic Mesopotamia, and worthy of comparison with Teotihuacán. The centers have "citadels" with large granaries which were clearly the nub of a complex redistributive exchange system. A range of traded materials is seen. Yet nowhere, on the basis of the archaeological record at present available, is there the superabundant personal wealth so characteristic of the early civilizations of Egypt, Mesopotamia, and China. Nor has there been found the exceedingly complex and monumental religious symbolism characteristic of the Mesoamerican early state modules. Nor yet, despite the existence of a script, is there the vainglorious assertion of personal power, expressed in colossal monuments of inscription, that we see in Egypt and Mesopotamia. The Harappan civilization does not reveal to the world any Ramses, any Hammurabi, nor yet any Gudea of Lagash. Indus exchange evidently functioned without such emphatically assertive statements about the prestige and power of the central person.

I should like to identify now six different *processes* which may lead to the formation of central places serving ESMs. In most real instances a number of these processes will be in operation, but they can be separately distinguished. Indeed, different "mixes" of these processes can be seen to generate a typology of early centers which approximates the range recognized by archaeology today. All of these processes center upon exchange "at a distance"—at a central place—whether of information or of goods. The first three involve internal exchange, and only one of these calls for marked ecological diversity within the ESM. The three processes of internal exchange will first be outlined.

ENDOGENOUS GROWTH

1. *Social and religious exchange predominating.* With an initial distribution of dispersed settlement in farmsteads, hamlets, or small villages, a *periodic* central place emerges, for seasonal ceremonies related either to the identity of the community (i.e. the common affiliation of the participants), in some cases focusing on the person of the chief, or to projections of the seasonally changing world, or both. The Kyaka meetings of New Guinea are instances of such functioning at tribal level, and nearly all chiefdoms have such periodic central places. Mention has already been made of Mu'a on Tongatapu, which was the scene of the annual presentation of first fruits to the Tu'i Tonga. Sahlins and others have stressed the material redistribution of such occasions, which was certainly impressive, but an annual feast can have little long-term impact on subsistence. The importance of the occasion was in terms of information—as a meeting. The ceremonial center of Orongo on Easter Island is particularly interesting because the business of awaiting the migratory arrival of the sacred bird necessitated the prolonged occupation of the site. It seems likely that some of the central places of the British Neolithic (Renfrew 1973) were periodic central places of this kind.

At the point that such a periodic central place becomes a permanent central place, the territorial unit may be regarded as an ESM. It is not sufficient, however, that the location be inhabited throughout the year; it must continue to fulfill its central function as well. And the specialists who control that function must be full-time specialists. This implies, of course, that the exchange includes a measure of foodstuffs and other goods to sustain these central persons, in return for the information they impart.

A multiplier-effect interaction is here possible between the subsistence and projective systems. For the calendric expertise offered at the central place may be of real significance in the scheduling of subsistence activities in relation to the seasons, and the successful development of the subsistence subsystem may thus be linked to that of the projective one.

Naturally such central places become the foci also of other types of exchange. Yet the process described may be seen in operation. I suspect that this exchange model is applicable to a number of Mesoamerican developments. Prototypes for the ESM center are to be seen in many chiefdom periodic central places. The population of the central place on this model need be very small—little larger than that of the various residence units which it serves.

2. *Population agglomeration and craft specialization.* On this model, the population accumulation, at a local agricultural village/town location, of an agglomerate population distribution makes possible economies of scale. It was indicated above that in parts of the Old World, villages of up to 4,000 persons are possible, without any of these being supported in exchange for the discharge of central-person functions. In reality, of course, 4,000 persons living together at one location do interact and do participate in exchanges, even if theoretically they could live as independently as if their settlement pattern were dispersed.

Population size itself may lead to the development of specialist occupations—potter, leather worker, weaver, and so forth—so that the society becomes differentiated, and a redistributive system develops. This is possible without any marked ecological diversity in the territory.

With the emergence of a redistributive system, some central regulation or control is likely to develop. And this can actively *organize* aspects of the specialization. For instance, irrigation works can be regulated centrally with far greater efficiency than that of persons acting together on an essentially reciprocal basis of mutual agreement.

As the benefits of specialization are seen, the center becomes a point of attraction for a larger territory and can act as an exchange center for goods made elsewhere. For instance, if one neighboring village is effective at pottery manufacture, and another at weaving, the center will become the locus of exchange of these products (fig. 1).

It should be noted that specialization of this kind need not rely in any way upon diversity of resources; it can arise simply from the local development, over a long period, of specialist skills. For instance, in the well-organized—but not central place–based—trading system of the Vitiaz Strait, the production of some goods is, of course, environmentally determined. For other products, however, this is not so. "For example, Sio lacks neither the resources nor skills required to produce mats, ornaments of cowrie shell, and tambu shell as sago. Why import these goods from Siassi?" (Harding 1967:54).

An answer to this question can be offered at several levels. At that of personal motivation may be the desire for prestige through the ownership of goods, which are obtained through successful trade. Wright and Zeder (in press) have stressed a suggestion by Rappaport (1967) that the real, operative function of the trade of some "ritual" artifacts may be to regulate exchange systems of goods essential to the maintenance of life. Harding's question may perhaps be answered along these lines. In any case, devices such as those described by Harding and Rappaport do ensure the existence of a permanent trade at a tribal level, rather than the periodic exchange occurring in the earlier stages of model 1 above.

The central place of the ESM likewise regulates such exchange, whether or not by the use of prestige commodities. In the long term it is to the advantage of a village entirely independent in terms of subsistence commodities and with a temporary sufficiency (or "surplus") of others to go on trading. For to fail to do so would endanger the survival of trading partners who are not self-sufficient in subsistence terms and would hence jeopardize the long-term supply of the imports currently in surplus.

Of course in most real cases prestige commodities will also be involved, their prestige deriving from an ascribed value in the social or projective subsystem. The case which does not rest heavily on prestige commodities is, however, worth stressing so that the validity of this second model can be recognized, even if it usually works in association with other processes.

Prototypes for such ESM centers may be recognized in such early population centers as Jericho and Çatal Hüyük. The central-place activities here outlined, in the absence of ecological diversity, are very much those of classical central-place theory.

3. *Intraregional diversity.* Consider a region no more than 1,000 sq. km. in area with four subregions, in each of which the same four different crops may be grown but with differing yields per unit area. Suppose that each subregion can grow one of these crops with a higher yield per unit area than the three other subregions. Clearly it is possible for an individual in one region to live independently and have a supply of all four crops, homegrown. His total yield, however, will be increased if he can specialize in the one crop at which he is most efficient and exchange a portion of his harvest for supplies of the other three crops.

The advantages of redistribution over reciprocity, in terms purely of efficiency, as indicated above, when a large proportion of the total per capita produce is to be exchanged, are considerable. In such a case a redistributive center is to be expected, located at or near the point of intersection where three of the four, or if possible all four, subregions meet.

The same arguments apply with even greater force when key resources are very highly localized, as in the case of metals, precious stones, and other minerals.

These ecological circumstances thus favor the development of a major exchange center, the subsistence subsystem developing a multiplier effect with the communications subsystem. Flannery and Coe (1968) have described this process in their discussion of the development of social organization in symbiotic areas of ecological diversity. I have similarly stressed the crucial significance for early Aegean civilization of Mediterranean polyculture (Renfrew 1972:297–307). The development of viticulture and the cultivation of the olive made effective what was formerly only a potential diversity in the environment, and led in the third millennium B.C. to the formation of small proto-urban settlements, which were succeeded in the second millennium by the palace centers of the Minoan-Mycenaean civilization (fig. 3). Yet the population of many of the ESM central places was no larger than Early Neolithic Çatal Hüyük.

These three entirely endogenous processes can be imagined as working in isolation, but in reality each carries with it something of the others. The process of city formation in terms primarily of these three processes is seen schematically in figure 8. The starting point is a small, noncentral place with small population—a hamlet. The three processes are seen at work, generating (1) a proto-urban center indicating a periodic central place (Stonehenge, perhaps); (2) a center of population with few urban functions (such as Jericho); and (3) a redistribution locus regulating intraregional diversity (such perhaps as Early Bronze Age Lerna in the Aegean, with the central store, the House of the Tiles, and associated sealings).

If these processes continued unchecked they would reach more extreme situations (now shown on fig. 8). For instance, process 1 would result in colossal ceremonial centers without any sizable permanent population or any significant role as an exchange center for goods. Probably Monte Albán or Angkor Wat come as close as any human center to this extreme. Process 2 would result in massive urban centers of population, with limited social or religious significance and without much local diversity. The Indus Valley cities could be caricatured to fit this role, but there is probably no real case to fit it. Process 3 would result in centers for local redistribution, or in markets, which have only a low population and little symbolic or socioreligious function. Again it would be difficult to find real cases to fit this extreme—ports of trade are excluded here since they do not exist until well after the development of ESMs. But one of the main points of the earlier argument was that redistributive functions imply central persons, and hence usually social actions centered upon them.

Figure 8 indicates six paths by which the three notional forms of urban center which reflect the working of two of these processes may be reached. The circle labeled 1 + 3 designates those centers where redistribution and social and religious functions take place but which have a limited permanent population. This is the well-known phenomenon of "civilization without cities," where the degree of urbanization (calculated on the basis of the number of "urban" dwellers) is much lower than in an agglomerate population distribution whose centers nonetheless lack urban functions.

The final stage envisaged is the emergence of the city with its full complexity. In reality few cities have emerged without a contribution

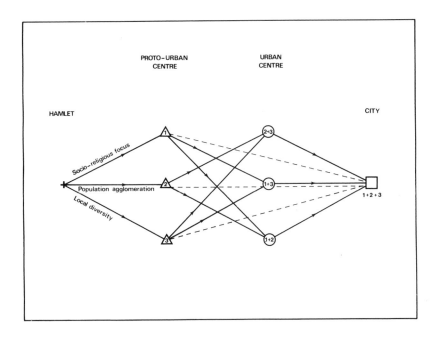

FIGURE 8. ALTERNATIVE PATHS FOR THE FORMATION OF THE UR-BAN CENTER AND THE CITY. Three processes, all endogenous, are singled out: increase of population, exchange arising from local diversity, and the development of a social or religious focus. In each case the proto-urban center will be of a different type. The city is always the product of the operation of all three processes.

from all three processes, and ultimately the systemic model which considers all three at a time, mutually operating, is closer to reality. To distinguish discrete paths, as in figure 8, may not be entirely warranted, but it does allow a typology of central places to arise, generated by the varying operation of these processes.

In discussing such endogenous change, no mention has been made of the operation of external trade or of other input from outside the civilization territory. Yet external factors can play a significant role in morphogenesis without making the process itself an exogenous one; an exogenous civilization, that is one that is secondary or derived, can only arise through contact with an existing earlier civilizaton. But neither

31

external trade nor conflict at the borders of the civilization need imply contact of this kind. Such factors are:

(a) External trade. When conducted with *less* centralized communities, external trade may nonetheless play a significant role: the goods traded may be such as will readily appear prestigious within the civilization boundary. Central persons who control the supply of these goods may thus achieve added power and status. This is not, however, the process described by Flannery (1968), where trade was heightening a hierarchy of a *less* ordered society, in trading contact with a *more* highly ordered one. And in the instance from the central Maya lowlands discussed by Tourtellot and Sabloff (1972), it was again supposed that a ranked society emerged, partially as a consequence of trade in prestige goods, these being supplied by a more highly ranked society whose values were in some way adopted along with the goods.

(b) Hostilities. Armed conflict has not been considered here as a major process leading to the formation of central places. It may indeed favor aggregation behind a wall, as at Jericho, but that is little more than a preliminary for process 2. A Çatal Hüyük or a Jericho need display no more than a mechanical solidarity. Similarly, conflict on the fringes of the civilization may act in this way as an agglomerative factor, but this need not imply that the external disruptive force is as organized as the culture under attack.

EXOGENOUS GROWTH

There are three evident ways in which civilization can grow up in a region as a consequence of interaction with an existing, more highly structured civilization nearby.

4. Urban imposition. As noted earlier, one of the most efficient forms of communication among humans is change of location. When this is accompanied by armed conflict, the entire information-carrying system of one area can be imposed upon the other. This may not result in instant urbanization, but centralizing processes can then be initiated which will be self-sustaining. The Roman conquest of the British Isles is a good example. The early Roman centers were primarily military, but they soon developed the other features of centrality described. Even after three centuries of continuous functioning, however, they collapsed when the external contact with Rome came to an end.

5. Implantation. A colonial enclave is conceived here as an intrusive community—one whose inhabitants are foreigners with respect to their neighbors—which continues to interact strongly with its parent community. A major component of this interaction is frequently an intensive trade. This intensive trade has a major effect on the activities of the indigenous inhabitants, amongst whom an economic organization develops with increasingly more intensive interactions. This can lead to the development of civilization without any extensive adoption of the technology, customs, or beliefs of the colonial newcomers.

6. *Emulation.* External trade brings exotic prestige artifacts which confer status on those individuals controlling the supply. A prominent hierarchy can thus emerge in what was formerly only a partly stratified society. In this case the society supplying the goods is already highly organized and stratified, and with the goods comes information, a set of values and social procedures which are more readily adopted because of the sophistication of the source society's products and the prestige in which they are held. This process had been admirably described by Flannery (1968) and by Tourtellot and Sabloff (1972). It contrasts with the process of external trade (a) discussed above, for there the information component of the exchange was not a significant one. Here, ideas, values, and technological innovations are being transmitted from the parent society. This is the process which earlier writers termed *diffusion.*

In reality, once again, processes 5 and 6 are not readily separable. For in most real cases, the structurally significant economic effects (of 5) are indeed accompanied by the adoption of the technology and values of the more "advanced" colonists (of 6). Yet the processes can usefully be distinguished.

Gordon Childe, the most systematic and persuasive advocate of "diffusion" in recent decades, used a compound of these two processes, which I have termed *implantation* and *emulation,* to explain the diffusion of civilization in the Old World outside the "primary centers" of Egypt, Mesopotamia, and the Indus. His argument is so coherent that it is worth repeating at length (Childe 1936:169–70):

But once the new economy had been established in the three primary centres it spread thence to secondary centres, much like Western capitalism spread to colonies and economic dependencies. First on the borders of Egypt, Babylon and the Indus valley—in Crete and the Aegean islands, Syria, Assyria, Iran and Baluchistan—then further afield, on the Greek mainland, the Anatolian plateau, South Russia, we see villages converted into cities and self-sufficing food-producers turning to industrial specialisation and external trade. And the process is repeated in ever widening circles around each secondary and tertiary centre. . . . The second revolution was obviously propagated by diffusion; the urban economy in the secondary centres was inspired or imposed by the primary foci. And it is easy to show that the process was inevitable. . . . In one way or another Sumerian trade and the imperialism it inspired were propagating metallurgy and the new economy it implies. . . . These secondary and tertiary civilisations are not original, but result from the adoption of traditions, ideas and processes received by diffusion from older centres, and every village converted into a city by the spread became at once a new centre of infection.

This is a powerful model, an evocation of the way a new, secondary civilization can be "called into being" (Childe 1958:163) through trading contact with an existing primary civilization. The distinction between the purely economic effects and the impact of new activities and ideas has been drawn above. The latter will be examined further in the next section. The magnitude of this impact in some cases cannot be denied, although the mechanisms are sorely in need of elucidation so that the meaningless term *diffusion* can be circumvented.

At this point, however, what must be stressed is that Childe was demonstrably wrong in many of his applications of this impressive model. Elsewhere (Renfrew 1972) I have established at length that the situation in the Aegean was almost the converse of the one which Childe described, and that the Aegean civilization must be explained primarily in local terms. More recently, the widespread application of his model to other aspects of European prehistory has been criticized. In my view, the distinctions which in practice have been drawn between many "primary" or "pristine" civilizations, and others which are supposedly "secondary" or "derived," are totally without value. Many discussions of the origins of civilization have been cripplingly limited in scope by their restriction to some received list of *the* five or six, or whatever, "primary" civilizations. I do not doubt, as the preceding discussion will have shown, that the origin of some civilizations can be seen as fundamentally modified through contact with another civilization. But with the exception of a few recent writings about Mesoamerica, there has been no adequate attempt to consider mechanism, or to set up valid criteria by which "primary" and "secondary" can be distinguished. If *total* absence of contact were a condition for primacy there would only be two "primary" civilizations in the world, or perhaps only one, and the course of Human History would be very much as Elliot Smith, with his Egypto-centric belief in the absolute primacy of a single civilizing center, described it (1930).

Trade and the Culture System

Civilization implies the development of a highly structured and differentiated society, with specialist production (craftsmen), a permanent controlling organization disposing of a significant proportion of produce (government), and a developed, explicit set of shared beliefs (cognitive structure), sometimes with large aggregations of population. (Partial or periodic manifestation of these features is characteristic of chiefdom society.)

Complex societies of this kind cannot be characterized in terms of a single variable, whether it relates to population, subsistence (e.g., irrigation), technology, social organization (e.g., palaces), or the cognitive structure (e.g., writing). In much of what I have written above, human culture is being viewed from the standpoint of trade. The choice of perspectives for the investigation of culture change is, of course, entirely up to us, but when all the variables in the inquiry are interdependent, to single out any one for heuristic purposes as the independent variable is obviously arbitrary. To do so, however, need not imply any reliance on monocausal explanations, and I suggest that it is useful to have in mind some general model of society to cope with its multivariate complexity. At present a systems model does allow a rounded, qualitative view, and the framework offers the possibility of eventual quantification.

The spatial boundaries of the culture, archaeologically defined, or in some cases the boundaries of the administrative module, are convenient bounds for the system. Its components are the persons within the unit, the artifacts they use, and those elements of the "natural" environment with which they interact. (The natural environment is included: to regard the human population alone as constituting the system enforces a needless division between "man" and "nature," making any ecological approach difficult.)

The culture may arbitrarily be divided into subsystems defined by human activities. Each individual operates simultaneously in several subsystems. The following have been used in an analysis of the prehistoric Aegean (Renfrew 1972) and are generally applicable:

subsistence subsystem
technological subsystem
social subsystem
symbolic or projective subsystem
trade or communication subsystem

Using such a model, population and population density do not constitute a subsystem, but are parameters of state, relevant to all the subsystems.

The stable persistence of the system through time, with limited change in the values of the state variables of the subsystems, is the consequence of negative feedback. Human culture is largely conservative in nature, and the stability of the system may consequently be described in terms of homeostasis.

Growth and culture change, however, cannot adequately be described in these terms, simply as homeostatic responses to change outside the system, as participants at an earlier School of American Research seminar have erroneously held (Hill 1970). Culture change involves fundamental and irreversible changes in structure, and the process of morphogenesis cannot be explained simply by means of negative feedback. On the contrary, growth cycles imply positive feedback, so that the growth is sustained. The term *multiplier effect* has been proposed for the positive mutual interaction between subsystems which alone can result in growth and in the deep structural changes involved in such basic transformations as the genesis of cities or the emergence of civilization.

This general model for the growth of civilization is relevant here in offering an insight into the importance of trade in early civilizations. For it emphasizes that trade will only be a major force for change if it enters into this kind of positive relationship with another subsystem of the society.

Both the explanation offered by Flannery (1968) for the growth of trade between the Olmec and the Valley of Oaxaca and the analysis by Tourtellot and Sabloff (1972) of the development of trade in the Maya lowlands can be seen in these terms. In each case the interaction between the two subsystems produced coupled development through the multiplier effect.

It is important to note that such interaction is possible only when the traded commodity achieves a value or importance in the social system, often in terms of prestige. This is an instance of the symbolic equivalence of material and social values (Renfrew 1972:496–500) which lies at the root of many applications of the multiplier effect. For not all trade works this way. The obsidian trade in the Aegean, for instance, involved transport by sea already in the seventh millennium without striking social consequence, and declined dramatically when a more useful and more prestigious commodity—bronze—came into use.

Through the operation of the "law" of supply and demand, an equilibrium will normally be reached whereby the flow of a given commodity settles down to a stable rate. The development of a social system is just one of the ways, however, by which sustained growth in the volume of trade may occur. Multiplier-effect interaction can occur with other subsystems: in the third millennium Aegean, the technological interaction was particularly strong. There the innovation of bronze metallurgy (which did not take place overnight, and can itself be analyzed in these terms) naturally resulted in a trade in bronze goods. The bronze trade did not, however, stabilize at a given level, with a steady supply of daggers or axes. For at each stage the increasing flow of trade, related to increasing production, seems to have produced a spin-off of innovation. The new forms of artifact thus produced (such as metal vessels and swords) became new commodities for trade without necessarily competing with the older ones. Again, the increasing bulk of material manufactures seems to have led both to economies of scale and to further technological innovation. A period of technological and commercial growth ensued which lasted for well over a millennium (fig. 9) and terminated only when other factors (probably demographic and social) brought about a system collapse and the Greek Dark Age.

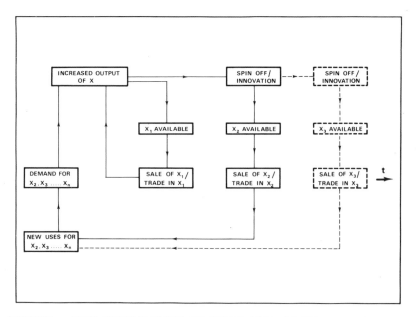

FIGURE 9. THE DEPENDENCE OF SUSTAINED GROWTH UPON THE INTERACTION BETWEEN SUBSYSTEMS: the multiplier effect. In this example growth in trade is related to technological innovation, and vice versa. (Note that *demand* and *new uses* relate also to the social subsystem.)

In general terms, therefore, the importance of trade for the development of early civilization will be understood fully only in the context of its impact upon other subsystems of the culture system.

QUESTIONS OF ARCHAEOLOGICAL ANALYSIS

Hypothetical analyses such as those drawn in the last section, and considerations of information flow, can be of practical use to the archaeologist only if they allow him to seek and find (or disconfirm) patterns among the real data. Progress has been made in this direction; there is scope for much more.

Documentation of Action at a Distance

The most striking advance of the past decade in the study of trade has been the development of characterization studies reliably establishing, by scientific means, the source of traded materials found far from their origin. Generally speaking, this can most readily be accomplished for minerals, but techniques exist also for organic products such as amber (by infrared absorption spectroscopy: Beck et al. 1965) and marine shells (by oxygen isotope analysis: Shackleton and Renfrew 1970). In general, however, the spatial discrimination that can be achieved by these means for plant and animal products is no finer than the spatial discrimination arising from their differential distribution in different ecological zones or niches. The most obvious such ecological distinction is sea versus land, allowing firm although rather unspecific conclusions to be drawn from marine finds on land.

Among the discriminatory methods listed in an earlier survey (Renfrew 1969) were examination of thin sections by the petrological microscope, X-ray diffraction, trace-element analysis by optical spectroscopy, trace-element analysis by X-ray fluorescence spectroscopy, and trace-element analysis by neutron activation. Other well-established methods are atomic absorption spectroscopy and analysis by gamma-ray backscatter. Descriptions of these and other techniques will be found in the periodical *Archaeometry*.

Other characterization methods recently employed include fission track analysis (Durrani et al. 1971), cathode luminescence (Renfrew and Peacey 1968), Mössbauer spectrography (Pires-Ferreira 1973), and mass spectrometry for metal isotopes (Brill and Wampler 1967).

Among important recent developments based on existing methods have been the characterization of traded objects in the Pacific area (Ambrose and Green 1972) and the much more systematic and effective use of petrological methods (including heavy mineral analysis) to study early ceramics (Peacock 1970).

Finally, the use of explicitly statistical procedures to handle the results of these analyses (e.g. Newton and Renfrew 1970) has made the resulting discrimination both finer and more reliable. In some fields, however—for instance the characterization of metals by trace-element analysis—problems of interpretation sometimes make the results of doubtful validity.

Spatial Analysis

Until recently the effect of different modes of exchange upon spatial distribution of traded goods has been neglected. In consequence, the possibility of learning about exchange modes from the archaeological distributions recovered has not been explored.

There are three obvious complications. The first is that only some classes of traded commodity are sufficiently durable or distinguishable to be reflected as such in the archaeological record. A trade in slaves, for instance, would be extremely hard to detect.

Secondly, the distributions recovered come in the form of what is found—that is to say in the form of materials that left the trading system. The record covers either use of the goods resulting in burial or loss of goods resulting in burial. The archaeologist studying trade is thus in the same position as the archaeologist using frequencies of tools recovered to gauge frequencies of utilization (cf. Binford 1973). Archaeological recovery results from the ancient civilization's failure to keep things and is therefore not a direct measure of frequency of use. Burial of goods with the dead will, of course, normally be a deliberate act, but does not necessarily give a representative inventory of the full range of the dead person's possessions.

Thirdly, a spatial distribution of finds never represents a situation at a single point in time. It represents a series of events over a definite time span; it is a palimpsest of activities.

All these restrictions imply that the archaeologist cannot use the geographical techniques of locational analysis unthinkingly, despite their potential value. On the other hand, the presence of more than one characterizable commodity within a trading network offers a much wider range of approaches. The work of G. A. Wright (1969), H. T. Wright (1972), and Pires-Ferreira (1973) makes pioneering steps in this promising direction.

One of the problems bearing on the analysis of trading distribution is that it must be quantitative in nature, and this places greater weight on the recovery techniques of excavators than many are able to sustain.

For instance, no meaningful figure for the absolute weight of a commodity found at a site or part of a site, whether expressed in weight or in weight per unit volume, can be given without an efficient sieving (screening) procedure. Recent studies have shown how vulnerable such results are to variations in mesh size. An alternative is to use dimensionless quantities—i.e., ratios (for instance sherds of one fabric per 1,000 sherds recovered, or number of pieces of obsidian against number of flint)—in the hope that recovery of the two classes compared will be efficient or inefficient to approximately the same degree.

MODES OF TRADE: SPATIAL ASPECTS

In what has been said so far a number of different modes of exchange are implied, each differing as to where the transfer of goods takes place, and between whom. Our interest here is in the extent to which they may differ in *operational* terms, that is to say in their impact upon the flow and distribution of goods, and hence upon the pattern of artifacts discovered. An implicit and dangerous assumption here, already questioned above, is that there is a close linear relationship between intensity of use at a location and intensity of loss or burial and hence of archaeological discovery. This proposition certainly does not hold good in all cases, but I am using it as a simplifying assumption here. In all real cases it requires investigation.

In figure 10 an attempt is made to indicate the spatial implications of ten of the various modes of trade frequently discussed by archaeologists and anthropologists. The purpose of this classification is not to set up a typology for its own sake but to clarify the implications of some of the concepts in use and to examine how they differ in spatial terms. The modes of exchange to be distinguished are:

1. Direct access. *B* has direct access to the resource at *a* without reference to A. If a territorial boundary exists, he can cross it with impunity. There is no exchange transaction.
2. Home-base reciprocity. *B* visits A at A's home base (*a*), and exchanges the special product of *b* for that of *a*.
3. Boundary reciprocity. A and B meet at their common boundary for exchange purposes.
4. Down-the-line trade. This is simply reduplicated home-base or

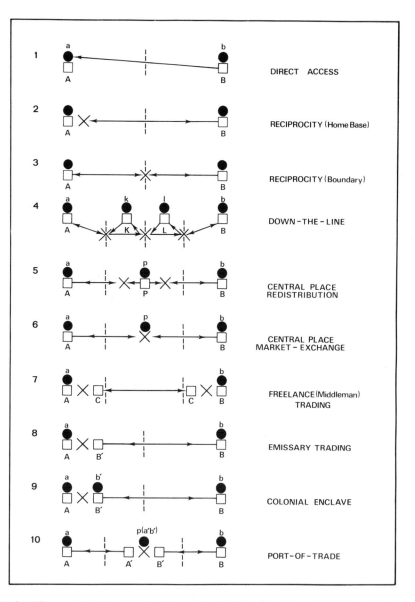

FIGURE 10. MODES OF TRADE AND THEIR SPATIAL IMPLICATIONS.
Circles *a* and *b* indicate respectively the point of origin and the place of receipt of
the commodity, squares *A* and *B* the person at the source and the recipient. Circle *p*
is a central place, square *P* a central person. Exchange transactions are indicated by a
cross, and territorial boundaries by a broken line.

boundary reciprocity, so that the commodity travels across successive territories (k, l) through successive exchanges.

5. Central place redistribution. A takes his produce to p and renders it to P (no doubt receiving something in exchange, then or subsequently). B takes his produce to p and receives from P some of A's produce.

6. Central-place market exchange. A takes his produce to p and there exchanges it directly with B for produce from b. The central person P is not immediately active in this transaction.

7. Middleman trading. The middleman C exchanges with A at a and with B at b. C is not under the control of A or B.

8. Emissary trading. B sends his emissary B', who is his agent and under his jurisdiction, to a to exchange goods with A.

9. Colonial enclave. B sends his emissaries B' to establish a colonial enclave b', in the close vicinity of a, in order to exchange with A.

10. Port of trade. Both A and B send their emissaries A' and B' to a central place (port of trade) which is outside the jurisdiction of either.

It should be noted that under 7, 8, 9, and 10, place b is itself likely to be a central place, since organization of this kind implies that place b will operate a distribution system for some of the goods acquired, although the mechanism implies that place a is not within the jurisdiction of its own system of redistribution.

Five of these modes, numbers 4, 7, 8, 9, and 10, transport goods over very great distances.

Although there is no prescription which says that one of these modes will develop from or give rise to another, the sequence as listed can be an evolutionary one. Mode 1 is a very simple one, where A does not have territorial jurisdiction over the produce in his own neighborhood. It has been suggested that the early obsidian trade of the island of Melos in the Aegean was of this kind (Renfrew, Cann, and Dixon 1965). Strictly this is not trade or exchange, but simply transportation.

As soon as the people at place a were prepared to assert their right to locally produced materials, mode 1 would develop into mode 2. There are many ethnographic instances of inhabitants of one village visiting another for the purpose of trade. It may be more satisfactory that an intermediate place be chosen (cf. Harding 1967:150), in which case mode 3 applies.

When the produce acquired by the people of *b* is further exchanged with their other neighbors (down the line), mode 4 applies. It has been suggested that the obsidian trade in the Near East was of this form (Renfrew, Dixon, and Cann 1968).

As discussed earlier, central-place trade is in some senses more efficient than reciprocal trade. Regional diversity, for example, will favor the development of a redistributive system (mode 5). With the development of more sophisticated exchange mechanisms, including money, the exchange becomes less embedded, less integrally related to the social organization. This differentiation allows the growth of market exchange (mode 6).

The increasing importance of long-distance trade, and the increasing bulk, implies that mode 4, with its many changes of hands, is inefficient. The number of changes of hands can be reduced if one carrier or middleman has the means of transport (and can assure security over intermediate territories) to cover the entire intervening distance between *a* and *b* (mode 7). Both security and transport are facilitated by riverine or marine travel, and waterborne trade was a favorite mode for ESMs. Trade between the Aegean and the East Mediterranean in Middle Minoan times may have been of this kind (Renfrew 1972:468–70), as was the trade in Homeric times described by Hesiod (Knorringa 1926: 2–15).

The increasing external trade of ESMs made desirable a closer control over the activities of traders, so that much of the trade became state organized (mode 8). This was apparently the mode which developed in early dynastic Mesopotamia (Mallowan 1965). As the bulk of trade increased and the power of the ESM was assimilated within the greater power of the empire capital, remote trading stations could be set up, colonial enclaves in a distant land (mode 9). The famous Assyrian settlement at Kültepe in Cappadocia is a well-known example. Finally, at this much more highly organized level, where we are speaking of exchange between ESMs or empires, higher-order central places again emerged, analogous in some ways to mode 6. But in mode 10 we are dealing with long-distance trade between more powerful and highly organized units, so that the port of trade has its own special characteristics (cf. Revere 1957; Chapman 1957).

In historical terms it is probably fair to present this as a possible evolutionary sequence. In terms of interaction, however, some modes allow a much greater flow of information than do others. For instance, in spatial terms there is a close formal similarity between modes 2, 9, and 10. In each case persons from *b* travel to *a*. These persons will learn far more about *a*, and communicate it to *B* more efficiently, than under any other mode. Moreover, in mode 9, the population of *a* stands to learn much more about the culturally patterned activities of *b* from the colonial population living at *b'*.

There is likewise a formal similarity between modes 3, 6, and 10, where the exchange takes place on the borders of or outside the territories of both *a* and *b*. As indicated earlier, the silent trade (which operates under mode 3), market exchange, and the port of trade are all devices which maximize the flow of goods while minimizing the flow of information that accompanies the exchange.

These different modes of trade are distinguished here in spatial terms. But there are, of course, other criteria indispensable to the generation of an adequate typology of trading types.

In the first place, absolute distance and the transport facilities available are of central relevance. Marine trade virtually excludes certain modes, such as mode 4, and it is a truism that rivers or seas, or indeed deserts, may be regarded either as barriers or as easy channels of communication according to the transport available.

The distinctions made here carry with them some implications for the organization of the trade, but none for the nature of the commodity carried. It may be transported in bulk or in smaller quantities; it may be productive, in the sense of facilitating subsistence or technology, or unproductive (this is the same distinction as that drawn by Tourtellot and Sabloff [1972] but avoids the paradox of using *functional* as the antithesis of *useful*). It may be destined for circulation freely or only among a segment of the recipient population; and it may or may not have ascribed to it high value, or confer prestige upon its owners.

This last is an important distinction, since in a society where currency is not used in all cases, it may be that certain classes of goods are not exchanged for other classes. Such distinctions apply even in our own monetized society: invitations to certain social functions may not be acquired even in exchange for dollars. Certainly in Britain the sale of honors, such as peerages, for mere money, even in large quantities, has always been deplored, and occasional suggestions that such traffic has taken place have been met with passionate denials. These are different "spheres of conveyance." Firth (1939:340) describes three "spheres of exchange" among the Tikopia, and Malinowski (1922) earlier indicated the different commodities appropriate to the kula (ceremonial) and *gimwali* (barter) exchanges of the Trobriand Islanders. Evidently these different kinds of exchange involve not only different goods, but also different exchange partners at different distances and differing attendant circumstances governing the flow of information in the exchange.

The information-minimizing aspects of some modes of trade have already been emphasized. It is clear also that the number of exchange transactions between A and B has an attenuating effect on the flow of information between them: each intervening exchange transaction is a source of "noise."

The distinctions drawn here, carrying with them certain spatial implications, should to some extent be reflected in archaeologically recoverable artifact patternings. The next sections make some suggestions in this direction.

RECIPROCITY

The obsidian trade in the Near East has been examined spatially in terms of distribution (Renfrew, Dixon, and Cann 1968), and Ian Hodder of the University of Cambridge is currently making quantitative studies of the distribution of other commodities traded in early times. The Near Eastern obsidian showed that within a "supply zone" radius of 200 or 300 km. from the source, the proportion of obsidian in the total chipped stone industry fell only gradually, to a figure above 80 percent. The suggestion offered to explain this was that mode 1 was in operation, or mode 2, or 3 *within* a culture region; this is conceived as an internal trade with high frequency of interaction. Outside this radius, in the contact zone, the proportion fell off rapidly, falling to around 0.1

percent at a radius of 600 km. The device of plotting the percentage on a logarithmic scale (the distance remaining linear) showed the fall-off to be exponential (fig. 11).

It was further suggested that this pattern was the result of down-the-line trade, mode 4, the result of a large number of exchanges. It can be shown (Renfrew 1972:466) that precisely this distribution, described by the formula $y = k^{x/l}.N$, will occur with a village spacing of l, where y is the percentage of obsidian in the chipped stone industry received at distance x from the edge of the supply zone, N the proportion at the edge of the supply zone, and k the proportion of that which it receives passed on by each village. However, a regular spacing of villages or exchanges is not a necessary part of the theory; the crux of the theory is a long series

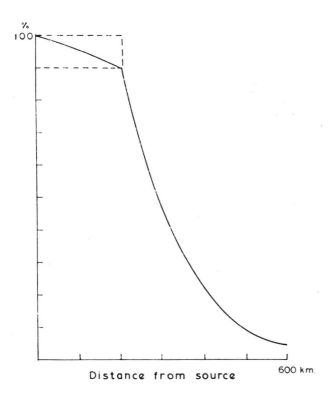

FIGURE 11. DOWN-THE-LINE TRADE: fall-off in abundance of commodity with distance from source.

of successive exchanges of material from a point source. Comparable distributions for coins have been obtained using the theory of random flights (Hogg 1971). In both cases, however, reciprocal exchange as shown in mode 4 is envisaged. An excavation at any location should thus yield a lower proportion of the traded commodity than at any point closer to the source. Points equidistant from the source should have the same proportion, thus maintaining the symmetry which Polanyi suggested was a basic feature of reciprocity.

CENTRAL-PLACE REDISTRIBUTION

The existence of a central place will fundamentally distort this picture. For if we make the necessary assumption that the quantity recovered at any location bears some regular relationship to the quantity passing through it, the high intensity of interaction at a central place destroys this symmetry, producing the centrality which Polanyi recognized in central places, and which, as I have suggested above, is also a feature of places of market exchange.

If the vertical axis in figure 12 now indicates total quantity recovered, rather than proportion, the asymmetry surrounding the central place at location B is clearly seen. This corresponds to modes 5 and 6. Indeed figure 12 could be modified so that, within the territory served by the central place, the fall-off with increasing distance from it could be exponential but much less steep than the generally prevailing fall-off. (It should be noted, however, that the *proportion* of the commodity under consideration recovered at the central place will be higher in this way only if that commodity is more intensively traded there than elsewhere with respect to the commodities with which it is compared. This assumption may well hold when the commodity is brought by long-distance trade and the others are widely and locally produced.)

FREE-LANCE TRADE

Spatial analysis can be expected to reveal a futher trading mechanism: free-lance (middleman) trading. For the effect of a middleman trader is to make much more affect the distribution of the commodity than would affect it under down-the-line reciprocal exchange, *within the locus*

48

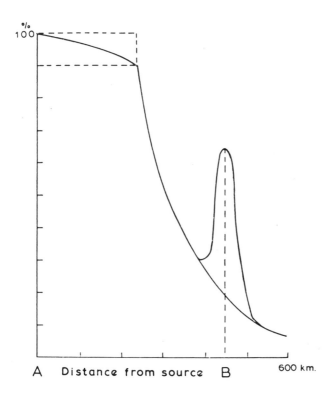

FIGURE 12. DIRECTIONAL TRADE (redistribution): fall-off in abundance with distance from source.

of his activity. Any middleman has an effective area of operation, outside of which he does not normally travel. Within this area, in the absence of any preferential service for central places, the fall-off of the commodity with distance from source will be much less rapid (fig. 13, where point C represents the outer boundary of the region served by the trader). This corresponds to mode 7.

These suggestions, at least in favorable cases, allow the distinction of modes 2, 3, and 4 from modes 5 and 6, and of both these groups from mode 7. Modes 8–10 and the distinction between modes 5 and 6 will be considered in the next section. (Mode 4 is, of course, simply the aggregation of repeated transactions of the type seen in modes 2 and 3: I see no way of distinguishing archaeologically between 2 and 3 if the place of

49

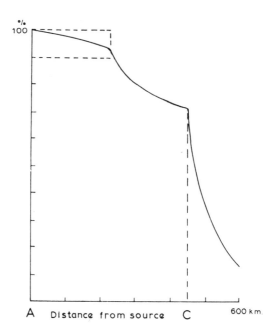

FIGURE 13. FREE-LANCE TRADE: fall-off in abundance with distance from source.

exchange under 3 is always a different one.) Mode 1 could presumably be recognized by the dearth at place *b* of objects originating at place *a*, since the transaction works only to the favor of *a*.

Once again, no consideration has been given here to the nature of the commodity traded or the manner of the exchange. I have suggested, however (Renfrew 1972:467), that goods carrying high prestige or value and exchanged reciprocally under mode 4 may in fact produce a distribution differing in one respect from figure 11 (fig. 14). In such "prestige chain" exchange the effective parameter *l* is lengthened, and the fractional parameter *k* is closer to unity. In the first place, the transfer of prestige goods often takes place between specific notable persons, and it is likely that exchange partners at this level will, on the average, reside a greater distance apart than the average for ordinary (*gimwali*) exchange. Secondly, these goods are not expended or utilized in daily life but are frequently handed on in subsequent exchanges—Malinowski's fundamental point about the kula ring. Both these effectively in-

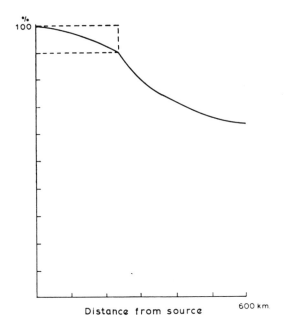

FIGURE 14. PRESTIGE-CHAIN TRADE: a modification of down-the-line trade (see fig. 11).

crease k to a figure nearer unity. This has the result of making the exponential fall-off more gradual, and thus of increasing the detectable range of travel of the goods. It seems likely that the great distances reached by the Spondylus trade of neolithic Europe (Shackleton and Renfrew 1970) were the consequences of the prestige-chain variant of mode 4.

Evidence of Organization

The most neglected feature of prehistoric trade is organization, in its nonspatial aspects. Not until the emergence of written records in Meso-potamia and Crete, which give explicit (cognitively predigested) informa-tion on this count, has the evidence been systematically exploited by archaeologists. So it is that, despite the thousands of seals and hundreds of sealings from Crete and mainland Greece which archaeologists have studied from the standpoint of typology and style, there remains to be written an article systematically considering their use and the implications they hold for the organization of Minoan society. I suspect that the same applies for the numerous cylinder seals found in Mesopotamia dating from as far back as predynastic times.

The two obvious fields of investigation are central places of exchange and central authority. The former may in themselves be difficult to recognize, but clearly large storehouses offer prima facie evidence of redistribution—as indeed does any evidence from craft specialization. The investigation of large storehouses necessitates excavation at a particular spot within the settlement, so that negative evidence has little force. Craft specialization, however, may be deduced from a wide range of artifacts. Craft specialization in itself, and the extent to which it can be inferred from specific products, is another of the much-neglected fields of prehistoric research.

Fortunately, however, size of settlement is not independent of centrality, although, as discussed above, they are very far from the same thing. Archaeologists are now starting to study spatial distributions of settlements with particular reference to their size and the existence of fortifications (e.g., Hodder and Hassall 1971), and such studies can certainly give evidence for the existence of central places. In doing so they need not imply any adherence to "Central Place Theory" in its more abstruse forms, where a determination to find hexagons where none exist approaches the fervor of Ptolemaic astronomers adding epicycles to "save the Phenomena" of the celestial spheres. As Hodder justly remarks (1972:889): "It is the various characteristics of spatial behaviour that underlie the model that are really being considered." Evidently the study of settlement distribution can give clues about the organization of trade, even if these will need corroboration by other evidence of organization and by the traded goods themselves.

Central authority, crucial to the understanding of trading organization, may be revealed in the first place by any insignia or symbols of authority. Seals, sealings, and bullae fall in this class. Wright (1972) based his rejection of the hypothesis that interregional exchange alone causes state development on the find of a bulla at his site in levels prior to those indicating a transformed exchange network. His major conclusion is no doubt correct, as indeed may be his interpretation of the crucial bulla; my point is simply to emphasize its critical value and, indeed, the value of all such finds, which reveal the informational component of the exchange.

A further field, sadly neglected by economic anthropologists, is the archaeological evidence for currency. Recent studies have at last begun to study minted coinage from the anthropological rather than the numismatic standpoint (Collis 1971). The presence of coins in a civilization is a crucial one, and Collis has shown convincingly in one case that while gold and silver coinage might there have had a prestige value, being employed in conditions of reciprocity, a bronze coinage was employed for market exchange. I think one can risk the generalization that the existence of any low-denomination coinage, used within the jurisdiction of the issuing authority, is an indication of market exchange. Indeed Polanyi, with his skepticism concerning early market exchange in the Old World, very nearly implied the converse, that there was no market exchange without coinage. Certainly market exchange would be unthinkable without some established currency.

Evidence for Information Flow

In this chapter an attempt has been made to stress the importance of trade within the broader meaning of the term *exchange*. All interactions imply information flow, so that continuous spatial distributions of any class of artifact imply repeated interaction and effective information flow. In the past, artifact counts at different locations have been used to give a measure of "similarity" between them. Yet this lumping together of features implies a holistic approach to culture, and there is a risk that to lump all interactions together as an exchange of "information" falls into the same error. For unlike the cyberneticist or the information theorist, the archaeologist must ask, "Information about what?" One of the most significant contributions to archaeology in the past two decades has been Lewis Binford's investigation of this question (cf. Binford 1972:329–41); indeed, all his work could be regarded as just this: the examination of the significance of artifact variability. When we are examining the emergence of early civilizations, therefore, it is particularly relevant to ask wherein lies the unity of the particular civilization which justifies the use of the term *civilization*. And when using Joseph Caldwell's helpful term *interaction sphere* (1964) we must ask what kind of interaction this embraces, and what it includes.

The consequence of this line of thought is that it will be profitable to examine—together with the distribution of traded materials documenting commodity exchange—the distribution of stylistic and symbolic materials indicating information exchange. In terms of the discussion here, the former should extend across cultural boundaries, the latter be more intense within them. Finds like the steatite carvings of Tepe Yahya (Lamberg-Karlovsky 1972a, 1972b) take on a crucial significance, since they document an exchange both of commodity (originating near that site) and of information (apparently originating in Mesopotamia). If the information did originate in Mesopotamia, I wonder whether the exchange had any great relevance for the emergence of civilization (itself here conceived as an exchange organization) *within* Mesopotamia; clearly it has many implications for Iran. Can this have been trade of mode 9—was there a Sumerian colony at Yahya? If not, how do we explain Sumerian symbolism on its products?

Attention to the role of trade in early civilization has so far focused upon three areas—Mesopotamia, Mesoamerica, and the Aegean—and the present volume reflects these interests. But what about the Indus, Egypt, China, and Peru? And what indeed of those second-class citizens, separate but not equal, the "secondary" civilizations? If our interest is in the working of culture process, why arbitrarily exclude a major part of the available sample? In each case it is the nature of the interactions between members of the civilization which is crucial, whatever the influence of outside forces upon these internal interactions. Trade, because it is at once the motive and the indication of such interactions, offers a most promising field for their investigation.

References

ADAMS, R. M.
1966   *The Evolution of Urban Society* (Chicago: University of Chicago Press).

ALLAN, W.
1972   "Ecology, Techniques and Settlement Patterns," in *Man, Settlement and Urbanism*, ed. P. J. Ucko, R. Tringham, and G. W. Dimbleby (London: Gerald Duckworth & Co.).

AMBROSE, W. R. AND R. C. GREEN
1972   "First Millennium B.C. Transport of Obsidian from New Britain to the Solomon Islands," *Nature* 237:31.

BECK, C. W., E. WILBUR, S. MERET, M. KOSSOVE, AND K. KERMANI
1965   "The Infrared Spectra of Amber and the Identification of Baltic Amber," *Archaeometry* 8:96–109.

BINFORD, L. R.
1972   *An Archaeological Perspective* (New York: Seminar Press).
1973   "Interassemblage Variability—the Mousterian and the 'Functional' Argument," in *The Explanation of Culture Change: Models in Prehistory*, ed. C. Renfrew (London: Gerald Duckworth & Co.).

BRILL, R. H. AND J. M. WAMPLER
1967   "Isotope Studies of Ancient Lead," *American Journal of Archaeology* 71:63–77.

BRUSH, J. E. AND H. E. BRACEY
1955   "Rural Service Centres in Southwestern Wisconsin and Southern England," *Geographical Review* 45:558–69.

BOHANNON, P.
1954   "The Migration and Expansion of the Tiv," *Africa* 24:2–16.

BULMER, R.
1960   "Political Aspects of the Moka Ceremonial Exchange System among the Kyaka People of the Western Highlands of New Guinea," *Oceania* 31:1–13.

CALDWELL, J. R.
1964   "Interaction Spheres in Prehistory," in *Hopewellian Studies*, ed. J. R. Caldwell and R. L. Hall. Illinois State Museum Papers 12, no. 6.

CHAPMAN, A.
1957   "Port of Trade Enclaves in Aztec and Maya Civilizations," in *Trade and Market in the Early Empires*, ed. K. Polanyi, C. M. Arensberg, and H. W. Pearson (New York: Free Press).

CHILDE, V. G.
1936   *Man Makes Himself* (London: Franklin Watts).
1958   *The Prehistory of European Society* (Harmondsworth, Eng.: Penguin Books).

CHISHOLM, M.
1968   *Rural Settlement and Land Use* (London: Methuen & Co.).

55

CLARKE, D. L.
1968 *Analytical Archaeology* (London: Methuen & Co.).

COLEMAN, J. S.
1963 "Comment on the Concept of Influence," *Public Opinion Quarterly* 27:63–82, quoted by W. Buckley, *Sociology and Modern Systems Theory* (Englewood Cliffs, N. J.: Prentice-Hall), p. 139.

COLLIS, J. R.
1971 "Markets and Money," in *The Iron Age and Its Hill-Forts*, ed. D. Hill and M. Jesson (Southampton, Eng.: Southampton University Archaeological Society).

DEETZ, J.
1965 *The Dynamics of Stylistic Change in Arikara Ceramics*, Illinois Studies in Anthropology 4 (Urbana: University of Illinois Press).

DOXIADIS, C. A.
1971 "Ancient Greek Settlements," *Ekistics* 182:4–21.

DURRANI, S. A., H. A. KHAN, M. TAJ, AND C. RENFREW
1971 "Obsidian Source Identification by Fission Track Analysis," *Nature* 233:242–45.

ELLIOTT SMITH, SIR G.
1930 *Human History* (London: Jonathan Cape).

FIRTH R.
1939 *Primitive Polynesian Economy* (London: Routledge & Kegan Paul).

FLANNERY, K. V.
1968 "The Olmec and the Valley of Oaxaca: A Model for Interregional Interaction in Formative Times," in *Dumbarton Oaks Conference on the Olmec*, ed. E. P. Benton (Washington, D. C.: Dumbarton Oaks Library).
1972 "Evolutionary Trends in Social Exchange and Interaction," in *Social Exchanges and Interaction*, ed. E. N. Wilmsen. University of Michigan Museum of Anthropology, Antholopological Papers no. 46 (Ann Arbor).

FLANNERY, K. V. AND M. D. COE
1968 "Social and Economic Systems in Formative Mesoamerica," in *New Perspectives in Archaeology*, ed. L. R. Binford and S. R. Binford (Chicago: Aldine Atherton).

HÄGERSTRAND, T.
1967 *Innovation Diffusion as a Spatial Process* (Chicago: University of Chicago Press).

HAMMOND, N. D. C.
1972 "Locational Models and the Site of Lubaantún, A Classic Maya Centre," in *Models in Archaeology*, ed. D. L. Clarke (London: Methuen & Co.).

HARDING, T. G.
1967 *Voyagers of the Vitiaz Strait* (Seattle: University of Washington Press).

HILL, J. N.
1966 "A Prehistoric Community in Eastern Arizona," *Southwestern Journal of Anthropology* 22:9–30.
1970 "School of American Research Advanced Seminar," *American Anthropological Association Newsletter* 13.

HODDER, I. R.
1972 "Locational Models and Romano-British Settlement," in *Models in Archaeology*, ed. D. L. Clarke (London: Methuen & Co.).

HODDER, I. R. AND M. HASSALL
1971 "The Non-random Spacing of Romano-British Walled Towns," *Man* 6:391–407.

HOGG, A. H. A.
1971 "Some Applications of Surface Fieldwork," in *The Iron Age and Its Hill-Forts*, ed. D. Hill and M. Jesson (Southampton, Eng.: Southampton University Archaeological Society).

HOMANS, G. C.
1958 "Social Behavior as Exchange," *American Journal of Sociology* 63:597–606.

HOPE SIMPSON, R.
1965 *A Gazetteer and Atlas of Mycenaean Sites*. Institute of Classical Studies, Bulletin Supplement 16 (London).

KNORRINGA, H.
1926 *Emporos, Data on Trade and Trader in Greek Literature from Homer to Aristotle* (Amsterdam: Hakkert).

KRADER, L.
1968 *Formation of the State* (Englewood Cliffs, N.J.: Prentice-Hall).

KROEBER, A. L.
1940 "Stimulus Diffusion," *American Anthropologist* 42:1.

LAMBERG-KARLOVSKY, C. C.
1972a "Trade Mechanisms in Indus-Mesopotamian Interrelations," *Journal of the American Oriental Society* 92:222–29.
1972b "Tepe Yahya 1971, Mesopotamia and the Indo-Iranian Borderlands," *Iran* 10:89–100.

MCKERN, W. C.
1929 *Archaeology of Tonga*, Berenice P. Bishop Museum Bulletin 60.

MAGOBUNJE, A. L.
1968 *Urbanization in Nigeria* (London: University of London Press).

MALINOWSKI, B.
1922 *Argonauts of the Western Pacific* (London: Routledge & Kegan Paul).

MALLOWAN, M. E. L.
1965 "The Mechanics of Trade in Western Asia," *Iran* 3:1.

MAUSS, M.
1954 *The Gift* (London: Cohen).

MEADOW, R. H.
1971 "The Emergence of Civilisation," in *Man, Culture and Society*, ed. H. L. Shapiro (Oxford: Oxford University Press).

MEIER, R. L.
1962 *A Communications Theory of Urban Growth* (Cambridge, Mass.: M.I.T. Press).

NEWTON, R. G. AND C. RENFREW
1970 "British Faience Beads Reconsidered," *Antiquity* 44:199–206.

57

OPPENHEIM, A. L.

1954 "The Seafaring Merchants of Ur," *Journal of the American Oriental Society* 74:6–17.

PEACOCK, D. P. S.

1970 "The Scientific Analysis of Ancient Ceramics—A Review," *World Archaeology* 1:375–89.

PIRES-FERREIRA, J. W.

1973 "Formative Mesoamerican Exchange Networks" (Ph.D. dissertation: University of Michigan).

POLANYI, K.

1957 "The Economy as Instituted Process," in *Trade and Market in the Early Empires*, ed. K. Polanyi, C. M. Arensberg, and H. W. Pearson (New York: Free Press).

RAPPAPORT, R. A.

1967 *Pigs for the Ancestors* (New Haven: Yale University Press).

RATHJE, W. L.

1971 "The Origin and Development of the Lowland Classic Maya Civilization," *American Antiquity* 36:275–85.

1973 "Models for Mobile Maya," in *The Explanation of Culture Change: Models in Prehistory*, ed. C. Renfrew (London: Gerald Duckworth & Co.).

RATHJE, W. L. AND J. A. SABLOFF

1972 "Ancient Maya Commercial Systems: A Research Design for the Island of Cozumel, Mexico." Paper read at the annual meeting of the American Anthropological Association, Toronto, December 1972.

RENFREW, C.

1969 "Trade and Culture Process in European Prehistory," *Current Anthropology* 10:151–69.

1972 *The Emergence of Civilisation* (London: Methuen & Co.).

1973 "Monuments, Mobilisation and Social Organisation in Neolithic Wessex," in *The Explanation of Culture Change: Models in Prehistory*, ed. C. Renfrew (London: Gerald Duckworth & Co.).

RENFREW, C., J. R. CANN, AND J. E. DIXON

1965 "Obsidian in the Aegean," *Annual of the British School of Archaeology at Athens* 60:225–47.

RENFREW, C., J. E. DIXON, AND J. R. CANN

1968 "Further Analysis of Near Eastern Obsidians," *Proceedings of the Prehistoric Society*, 34:319–31.

RENFREW, C. AND J. S. PEACEY

1968 "Aegean Marble—A Petrological Study," *Annual of the British School of Archaeology at Athens* 63:45–66.

REVERE, R. B.

1957 " 'No Man's Coast': Ports of Trade in the Eastern Mediterranean," in *Trade and Market in the Early Empires*, ed. K. Polanyi, C. M. Arensberg, and H. W. Pearson (New York: Free Press).

RIVET, A. L. F.
1964 *Town and Country in Roman Britain* (London: Hutchinson Publishing).

ROWLANDS, M. J.
1973 "Modes of Exchange and the Incentives of Trade with Reference to Later European Prehistory," in *The Explanation of Culture Change: Models in Prehistory*, ed. C. Renfrew (London: Gerald Duckworth & Co.).

SABLOFF, J. A., W. L. RATHJE, D. A. FREIDEL,
J. G. CONNOR, AND P. L. W. SABLOFF
in press "Trade and Power in Postclassic Yucatán: Initial Observations," in *Recent Research in Mesoamerican Archaeology* (London: Gerald Duckworth & Co.).

SAHLINS, M.
1972 *Stone Age Economics* (Chicago: Aldine Atherton).

SHACKLETON, N. AND C. RENFREW
1970 "Neolithic Trade Routes Re-aligned by Oxygen Isotope Analysis," *Nature* 228:1062–65.

SIVERTS, H.
1969 "Ethnic Stability and Boundary Dynamics in Southern Mexico," in *Ethnic Groups and Boundaries*, ed. F. Barth (London: George Allen & Unwin).

STEWARD, J.
1955 *Theory of Culture Change* (Urbana: University of Illinois Press).

STRUEVER, S. AND G. L. HOUART
1972 "An Analysis of the Hopewell Interaction Sphere," in *Social Exchange and Interaction*, ed. E. Wilmsen. University of Michigan Museum of Anthropology, Anthropological Papers no. 46 (Ann Arbor).

TOURTELLOT, G. AND J. A. SABLOFF
1972 "Exchange Systems among the Ancient Maya," *American Antiquity* 37:126–35.

WEAVER, W.
1949 "The Mathematics of Communication," *Scientific American* 181:11–15.

WHEATLEY, P.
1971 *The Pivot of the Four Quarters* (Edinburgh: Edinburgh University Press).

WOOD, W. R.
1972 "Contrastive Features of Native North American Trade Systems," *University of Oregon Anthropological Papers* 4:153–69.

WRIGHT, G. A.
1969 *Obsidian Analyses and Prehistoric Near Eastern Trade: 7500 to 3500 B.C.* University of Michigan Museum of Anthropology, Anthropological Papers no. 37 (Ann Arbor).

WRIGHT, H. T.
1972 "A Consideration of Interregional Exchange in Greater Mesopotamia: 4000–3000 B.C.," in *Social Exchange and Interaction*, ed. E. Wilmsen. University of Michigan Museum of Anthropology, Anthropological Papers no. 46.

WRIGHT, H. T. AND M. A. ZEDER
in press "The Simulation of a Linear Exchange System under Equilibrium Conditions." Forthcoming paper.

PART II

THEORETICAL BACKGROUND

2

Karl Polanyi's Analysis of Long-Distance Trade and His Wider Paradigm

GEORGE DALTON

Northwestern University

"He who only knows his own subject does not know that either."
—S. R. Steinmetz

"History [of science] suggests that the road to a firm research consensus is extraordinarily arduous."
—Thomas Kuhn

"In a subject where there is no agreed procedure for knocking out errors, doctrines have a long life."
—Joan Robinson

"Everything that can be said can be said clearly."
—Ludwig Wittgenstein

SEVERAL PRELIMINARY MATTERS

This is an expository paper, an attempt to express clearly what we already know and to clarify what today is still difficult or unresolved. I have learned over the last fifteen years that in writing on topics for which scientific experiment, mathematical model, or statistical measurement cannot be employed, exposition is indeed difficult. When one is confined to words, one must very consciously choose words very carefully. One must also illustrate general statements with examples drawn from the real world, quote what one wants to criticize (rather than attribute positions to opponents, thereby risking unconscious distortion of what opponents are actually saying), and contrive diagrams, charts, or analogies to say the same thing more than once.

I have several reasons for not restricting myself in this paper to Polanyi's analysis of long-distance trade. One cannot understand his treatment of external trade without understanding other parts of his conceptual scheme, such as the internal organization of early and primitive economies and the inappropriateness of conventional economics as a universal frame of reference for all economies.[1] I shall have to demonstrate this quite explicitly. In doing so, I shall try to find fresh ways to explain Polanyi's work.

In the writings of Polanyi and his associates, long-distance trade under early state conditions is more fully analyzed and illustrated with examples than any other single topic: chapters, 2, 3, 4, 5, 7, 8, 9, and 13 of *Trade and Market* are devoted wholly or partly to external trade; so too a journal article (1963) and a book (1966) by Polanyi, a survey article by Leeds (1961), and part of a long article by Humphreys (1969) assessing Polanyi's work. It may be of use to archaeologists if I consider other economic institutions and the meanings of several theoretical concepts mentioned but not so extensively considered by the Polanyi group.

It is now sixteen years since *Trade and Market in the Early Empires* was published. During those years, a good deal of analytical writing as well as fresh ethnographic, historical, and archaeological description has been forthcoming. It seems sensible to refer to recent work whenever it contributes explanations of interest to archaeologists and anthropologists concerned with economy.

Archaeologists, historians, and social anthropologists who want to understand the economies of the societies they are professionally concerned to analyze have to acquire what I shall call (following Kuhn [1970]) an economic "paradigm": a theoretical framework, a language of concepts to interpret the actual economies of time and place they study. Polanyi's is only one of several economic paradigms that exist. I shall have to mention some of the others to show how Polanyi's differs.

I am told that archaeology is changing in two ways. First, archaeologists themselves are bringing to bear new physical, chemical, and statistical techniques of analysis, or they are engaging the technical expertise

64

of consulting physical scientists who analyze the properties of bones, stones, earth, flora, and shells in ways that create more usable data for the archaeologist. Carbon dating, flotation processes, and computers allow more precise establishment of facts, provide methods to extract more information from materials recovered, and permit special sorts of numerical analysis.

The second sort of innovation is conceptual rather than technical. Archaeologists are asking new questions, or, in expressing their dissatisfaction with old answers, seeking new answers to old questions about social organization, economy, polity, and culture, questions of a sort that ordinarily interest social anthropologists and historians. In short, archaeologists are looking for new theories and concepts capable of powerful explanation of the societies, economies, and polities they unearth: "Archaeology gives the appearance of being in a crisis . . . there is a strong reaction within the discipline against the familiar excursions into prehistoric religion, economics, or art appreciation that are neither grounded in, nor controlled by, theory or adequate knowledge" (Finley 1971:169).

It strikes me that technical and conceptual changes are also influencing subjects close to archaeology (for example, the economic history of early medieval Europe), and subjects much more distant from archaeology (such as modern economics). Medieval economic and social historians are also acquiring fresh data in addition to the written sources upon which they have traditionally relied: sunken ships, coin hoards, and burial remains dug up by archaeologists; linguistic analysis of place names; and photography from airplanes to reveal early field systems used in farming and the location of village settlements which have disappeared. The French historians, I believe, began some time ago to study village-level demographic and social history in order to estimate the size of peasant households and of village population changes, studies of a sort which the British now also undertake. Indeed, witchcraft in early Europe has again become a respectable topic for historians; in 1972 Marc Bloch's old work on the magical power of medieval kings to heal was finally translated into English. In the long run, it seems, we are all sociologists: "Research into [monetary and nonmonetary] payments must . . . become a social study; and so indeed must all research work in economic history" (Bloch 1967:241).

Actually, some archaeologists and historians of medieval Europe are changing their economic viewpoint in the same way. They no longer implicitly assume that economic organization, whether prehistoric or medieval, in Mycenaean Greece or in Charlemagne's France, is simply some crude commercial variant of our own twentieth-century economy, to be interpreted in the terms of "supply," "demand," "price," "buying," "selling," and "capital" that economists since David Ricardo have contrived for industrial capitalism (see Finley 1957; Grierson 1959).[2]

PARADIGMS IN ECONOMIC ANTHROPOLOGY: UNDER WHICH LYRE?

This section describes the range of topics considered in economic anthropology and the sorts of theory so far contrived to analyze its component segments. We shall see that Polanyi's theory relates to only one segment of economic anthropology and see also why theory in economic anthropology is difficult to create and why at present theory is not unified and not widely shared.

I have said repeatedly in print that the theoretical portions of economic anthropology are only beginning to be formulated systematically. I am now convinced that the clearest way to explain this point is to use the terminology of Kuhn.[3]

As used by Kuhn, *paradigm* is a stronger concept than the term *theory*. A paradigm provides a theoretical framework, a vocabulary of conceptual terms, and, in some sense, a picture inside of one's head about the nature of the real-world activities to be analyzed. A new paradigm redefines the scope of the subject and points up the most interesting problems to be solved. A paradigm, then, is a deep and important theory which renovates a field of study. Not only Copernicus, Newton, and Einstein, but also Ricardo, Marx, Weber, Freud, and Keynes were makers of paradigms: deeply persuasive theoretical constructs which illuminated some portion of reality in a new way. Their concepts and analytical conclusions, moreover, were adopted, refined, and extended by those who followed as the best approach to investigating some range of processes and problems newly revealed, partially formulated, or finally solved by the inventor of the paradigm. Persons in the same subject adhering to different paradigms choose somewhat different problems to

66

address and use different conceptual terms in their analyses. They also arrive at different analytical conclusions about real-world activities and institutions.

Paradigms are extremely important to physical and social scientists because paradigms provide satisfactory explanations of the physical, chemical, biological, or social processes they spend their professional lives trying to understand. It is not fanciful to suggest that a paradigm is like a professional religion: it is the theoretical framework inside one's head used to make deep sense of the segment of the world one is professionally concerned with. Indeed, what differentiates the chemist from the anthropologist from the economist is the paradigm each has professionally acquired (and also what Kuhn calls his "disciplinary matrix"), his theories and methods:

> . . . I take [paradigms] to be universally recognized scientific achievements that for a time provide model problems and solutions to a community of practitioners. . . . paradigms provide scientists not only with a map but also with some of the directions essential for map-making. In learning a paradigm the scientist acquires theory, methods, and standards together, usually in an inextricable mixture. Therefore, when paradigms change, there are usually significant shifts in the criteria determining the legitimacy both of problems and of proposed solutions. (Kuhn 1970:viii, 109)

Kuhn's points require qualification for economic anthropology because Kuhn is dealing with theory in physical sciences. Physics and chemistry differ in several important ways from subjects like economic anthropology.

(1) There are many more physicists and chemists doing research than there are anthropologists. And physical science is more uniform internationally than anthropology, a subject influenced, for example, by each nation's colonial experience.

(2) Physics and chemistry are older subjects than anthropology, which means that paradigms were established much earlier. This is a very important matter because it means, for example, that Einstein's work published in 1905 and after was addressed to solving problems or explaining anomalies that an already-established paradigm could not solve or explain, something that was immediately recognized by a number of physicists brought up on the old paradigm. But in a new, small,

and esoteric subject like economic anthropology, there were no strongly established paradigms when Polanyi wrote, no theoretical frameworks elaborately spelled out and widely shared; there were only bits of theory, partial paradigms, and few adherents to each because there were so few doing research in the subject (see, for example, Herskovits 1952). It is difficult to name more than a half-dozen anthropologists, who, in 1957, had a specialist's interest in economic anthropology—say, more than half of whose publications were in economic anthropology. And the few anthropologists interested in economy were not really in professional touch with the archaeologists and the economic historians of early societies who had similar interests.

Polanyi's work did not contradict any theory strongly and widely held by economic anthropologists (such as "formal economics"). In 1957 there was no strongly held theory of any sort in economic anthropology. Rather, there was an awareness that two unsolved problems existed: (i) Primitive and peasant economies both resembled and differed from industrial capitalism. But how anthropologists could cope with the systematic presentation of these similarities and differences was not clear (see, for example, Goodfellow 1939; Firth 1951: chap. 4). (ii) The second unresolved problem was rather complicated: How, if at all, could anthropologists make use of the elaborate corpus of conventional economics to interpret the primitive economies of the Trobriand Islanders and Tikopians? Firth (1929a; 1929b: chap. 1) had been aware of both problems as early as 1929, and indeed attempted to solve them over the next forty years, without, I think, succeeding. He is still ambivalent about the role to be played by conventional economics in economic anthropology (see Firth 1967; 1972). Herskovits too wrestled with these problems in 1940 and 1952 without solving them.

Polanyi attempted to solve both problems. His "substantive" definitions of the terms *economic, external trade, money,* and *market* indicated the *similarities* among primitive, archaic, and modern economies. His "formal" definitions of these terms indicated their special meanings in industrial capitalism. His "institutional" definitions indicated the *differences* between aboriginal and developed–industrial market economies by showing the special forms money, markets, and external trade took in aboriginal economies. Throughout these presentations, Polanyi argued forcefully against the use of market theory to analyze nonmarket economies. The formalist writers (for example, LeClair 1962; Cook

68

1966) did not state their formalist positions until after Polanyi wrote. It was Polanyi and his associates they were reacting to.

(3) Physicists and chemists specialize much more than do anthropologists. It is not common for many anthropologists to work precisely on the same problem or process, say, the nature of foreign trade in aboriginal economies.

(4) There is a much greater need for economic anthropologists to incorporate theory and factual information from other subjects, such as early economic history and recent economic development, than there is for physical scientists to incorporate outside theory and facts.

(5) Physical scientists, and, to a lesser extent, economists, use several research methods not at all employable in anthropology, such as controlled experiments and mathematical models, although anthropologists have recently begun to employ one such technique, statistical enumeration. Demonstrable proof of theory, therefore, is easier to establish in physical science and in economics than it is in verbal subjects. This complicated matter of methodology requires additional explanation.

Theories, concepts, methods, paradigms are to be judged by the explanatory power of the conclusions they reach about real-world activities and processes. The theories of Einstein and Keynes were powerful because their concepts allowed them to explain important physical and economic processes that could not be as satisfactorily explained without their theories. In short, paradigms are like mousetraps: we decide which of two mousetraps of different design is superior by choosing the one that catches most mice. Effectiveness in use is the paramount criterion, not strength of materials or elegance of design. In social science, effectiveness in use means explanatory power demonstrated to the satisfaction of the professional audience (Kuhn's "scientific community"):

> Paradigms gain their status because they are more successful than their competitors in solving a few problems that the group of practitioners has come to recognize as acute. . . . After the discovery had been assimilated, scientists were able to account for a wider range of . . . phenomena or to account with greater precision for some of those previously known. . . . As in political revolutions, so in paradigm choice—there is no standard higher than the assent of the relevant community (Kuhn 1970:23, 66, 94).

The scientific community's assent is obtained by demonstrating the explanatory power of a paradigm. In economic anthropology, this means the explanation of external trade, primitive valuables, bridewealth, palace economies, and such.

One's ability to persuade professional colleagues of the superiority of one's new theory in any subject—physics, economics, anthropology—depends to a great extent on the methods of proof conventionally used in that subject, its "disciplinary matrix"—in short, the methodology available to it. "Soft" subjects, such as political history, literary criticism, and much of cultural anthropology, are soft because they are confined to verbal analysis only. Persons doing research in such subjects frequently are polarized permanently; that is, they commonly adhere to markedly different theories. (Actually, in Kuhn's view, such subjects are not sciences because, since they have no strong and widely shared paradigm, theoretical progress is not evident; they are in a "pre-paradigm" condition.)

In contrast, physics is a "hard" subject, in the sense that persuasive proofs can be adduced to support new paradigms because controlled experiment, mathematical equation, precise measurement, and statistical quantification can be employed to prove theory. Closer to home, economics is "harder" than the other social sciences. Paradigms in economics, such as those contrived by Ricardo, Marshall, Keynes, and Samuelson, come to be widely shared among economists because mathematical model, statistical quantification, and policy application to real-world problems of unemployment, development, and inflation are usable in economics (note that policy application is another way of proving theory).

I might point out that it was impossible to construct a satisfactory national Graduate Record Examination in anthropology because the subject is so variously taught in American universities. Anthropology is so variously taught for two reasons: There is an enormous range of specific research specialties engaged in by archaeologists, physical anthropologists, and cultural anthropologists. And in many branches of anthropology there are no strong and therefore widely shared paradigms. What is true for economic anthropology seems, then, to characterize other branches of anthropology as well: an absence of systematically formulated theory so persuasive as to be widely shared among anthropologists.

Any theory or paradigm in any subject has three very closely related components: (1) the specific real-world processes, situations, or events the theory is designed to analyze (that is, designed to reach conclusions about); (2) the special concept it employs; and (3) the analytical or explanatory conclusions it arrives at. A theory is essentially the way the concepts (2) are used to explain the real-world processes (1). A theory, moreover, can always be stated in terms that provide answers to specific questions. Keynes's theory, for example, answered the question, "What causes short-run fluctuations in national income, output, and employment in the highly developed, industrial capitalist economies of Western Europe and North America of the 1930s"? The real-world process he analyzed was national income determination and its fluctuation in the special set of industrial capitalist economies. The special concepts he employed were (among others) "marginal propensity to consume," and "liquidity preference"; and the most important of his several analytical conclusions was that Britain and the United States in the 1930s were inherently unstable because the private market sector contained no mechanism to assure automatically that all goods produced at full employment would be bought. The same holds true for Polanyi or any other creator of theory. His paradigm also comprises a special set of real-world processes, special concepts, and analytical conclusions reached by using the concepts to analyze the processes.

Economic anthropology considers village-level economies of bands, tribes, and peasantries on all the continents and inhabited islands of the world in three historical time periods of utterly different length. It also considers the economic sectors special to larger-scale economies and societies—for example, the palace economies and foreign trade sectors of chiefdoms and state systems such as kingdoms and empires. Let us call the oldest or the earliest subset "aboriginal" or "traditional" or "indigenous" or "precolonial" economies:[4] the Kwakiutl Indians of the northwest coast of America before the white man arrived; the Inca before the Spanish arrived; village and rajah India before the British arrived. These are usually called, rather loosely, "primitive" or "peasant" economies. I would suggest, incidentally, that the village and state sectors of the economies of Western Europe up to 1200 or 1300 A.D., Japan up to about 1600 A.D., and China up to about 1800 A.D., belong in the same category of traditional or aboriginal economies.[5]

Now things become rather complicated and I have had to contrive table 1 to help convey my meaning. This first subset of aboriginal-

TABLE 1
BANDS, TRIBES, PEASANTRIES, AND STATES
IN AFRICA, LATIN AMERICA, THE MIDDLE EAST, ASIA,
NORTH AMERICA, THE CARIBBEAN, AND OCEANIA
STUDIED BY ANTHROPOLOGISTS

		Aboriginal	*Colonial*	*Postcolonial*
Paradigms, Partial Paradigms, and Bits of Theory		(Existing and changing over millennia)	(1500–1950 A.D.)	(Since 1950 A.D.)
	Static:	Marxian Economics		
		Formal Economics		
		Substantivist Economics		
				Macro (Nation) and Micro (Village)
	Dynamic:	Marxian	Marxian	Marxian
		Energy/Evolution	Energy/Evolution	Energy/Evolution
		Contact/Subjugation	Acculturation	Macrodevelopment
		Diffusion	Applied anthropology	Macromodernization
		Multiplier effects (Renfrew 1972)	Culture contact	Differentiation/ Integration
			Dualism	Cumulative Causation
			Agricultural involution	Microdevelopment
				Micromodernization

traditional or precolonial economies on all the world's continents and inhabited islands existed and changed over millennia. According to the classification I employ here, we would include the economy of any society of interest to archaeologists; any of interest to historians and anthropologists before European colonial incursion into Africa, Asia, Latin America, the Caribbean, and the Middle East; and, for the portions of the world that were not colonized in modern times (Japan, Europe), before modernization and economic development began (see Dalton 1972).[6] Archaeologists, anthropologists, and historians of preindustrial economies anywhere in the world have a common interest in aboriginal economies.

Two kinds of theoretical questions are put to aboriginal economies:

static and dynamic questions (see table 1). By static I mean questions relating to the organization or performance of an economy at one point in time: for example, how foreign trade was organized by the Maya in the period immediately preceding the Spanish conquest; or what the role of cattle as primitive valuables was in the Nuer of the 1930s. By dynamic I mean questions relating to the strategic causes or important consequences of change—in this case, of course, change under aboriginal, precolonial conditions: for example, the causes and consequences of settled agriculture, or of the emergence of civilization (Renfrew 1972), or of the decline of early empires (Cipolla 1970).

There are at present three contending paradigms used to analyze aboriginal economies under static conditions:

(1) The formal economics of conventional price theory, with its market terminology of *price, capital, economizing, maximizing, scarcity, choice, rationality, decision making,* and such (see LeClair and Schneider 1968). To use formal price theory to interpret aboriginal economies is to stress the similarities between them and modern capitalism.[7] Those who adopt the paradigm of formal economics to analyze aboriginal economies do so because they regard economic "scarcity" as universal, and "choice making" and "economizing" or "maximizing" as universally necessary. They assume that all economies, therefore, work like market systems and are usefully described in market terminology. They put economists' questions to aboriginal economies: How do persons in primitive economies "maximize"? (Cancian 1966; Burling 1962). How do they decide between alternative economic activities? (Ortiz 1967).

(2) The second paradigm, used by some economic historians (Kosminsky 1956), archaeologists (Childe 1936), and anthropologists (Wolf 1966), to analyze aboriginal economies at one point in time, is Marxian, which is not nearly as elaborate a paradigm as formal price theory. Marx was principally concerned with nineteenth-century industrial capitalism. His remarks about aboriginal economies were fragmentary (see Marx 1964): "Now it is generally agreed that Marx and Engels' observations on pre-capitalist epochs rest on far less thorough study than Marx's description and analysis of capitalism. Marx concentrated his energies on the study of capitalism, and he dealt with the rest of history in varying degrees of detail, but mainly in so far as it bore on the origins and development of capitalism" (Hobsbawm 1964:20).

Marxian categories relating to aboriginal economies consist of only a few concepts, like "surplus" and "exploitation"; who owns the means of production and how labor is organized in any economy are regarded as crucially determinative for social and political organization. The Marxian paradigm regards class conflict between owners and nonowners as endemic. Marx employed a sixfold evolutionary classification of economic systems, the first three classes of which refer to aboriginal economies: primitive communism; slavery; feudalism; preindustrial and then industrial capitalism; industrial socialism; industrial communism. Marxians address such questions as, How do owners and rulers extract economic "surplus" from rank-and-file workers? Economic anthropologists use Marxian concepts most frequently in discussing peasant economies (Wolf 1966); they do not seem to use them in discussing aboriginal bands and tribes.

(3) The third paradigm is Karl Polanyi's formulation of concepts and conclusions taken from Weber, Maine, Tönnies, Menger, Bücher, Thurnwald, and Malinowski, and, I believe, significantly extended and made systematic by himself. The terms used are *reciprocity, redistribution, (market) exchange, special-purpose money, administered trade, port of trade, operational device,* and others. Polanyi's paradigm stresses the differences between aboriginal economies and modern capitalism, and shows how economic organization in aboriginal economies is socially controlled by polity, kinship, religion, and the like.[8]

Polanyi argued repeatedly against the employment of formal economics as a universal paradigm. He deliberately intended his own paradigm to displace market economics in the static analysis of aboriginal economies.[9] More accurately, perhaps, he intended to solve the problems that had been raised by Firth (1929: chap. 1) and Herskovits (1940; 1952) by explaining why formal economics is not usefully applicable to nonmarket economies, and by showing how one can take account of both the similarities and the differences between aboriginal economies and modern industrial capitalism. Polanyi's paradigm at the time of his death in 1964 was by no means a finished scheme of analysis. Rather, it was an important beginning, and it continues to be extended and clarified by others, including Bohannan (1959; 1960), Sahlins (1965; 1972), Neale (1971), and myself (Dalton 1971a; 1971b; 1971c).[10]

One reason, then, why the theoretical portions of economic anthropology are only at the beginnings of systematic formulation is that three rather different paradigms, partial paradigms, and bits of theory contend at present for professional acceptance in the static analysis of aboriginal economies. Polanyi's theory, moreover, is still being extended (which, incidentally, is quite in keeping with Kuhn's remarkable description of the sequential development of new paradigms). Most anthropologists, perhaps, would still consider that the question of which theory is best to explain which economic sectors in which aboriginal economies is yet to be firmly settled (see Dalton 1969).

We are far from exhausting the subject matter of economic anthropology and the need for theoretical constructs. There are also the dynamic aspects of aboriginal economies—a matter, of course, of special interest to archaeologists: What were the strategic causes and important consequences of deep change in aboriginal economies and societies? How did larger-scale stratified civilizations emerge from smaller and simpler societies? How did empires arise and decline? Please note that neither formal economics (price theory) nor Polanyi's substantive economics provides a theory of change under aboriginal conditions. Both are concerned exclusively with static structure and performance, the actual organization of the Tiv, Nuer, Inca, Maya, or Trobriands as these economies functioned at specific (precolonial) dates.

For the dynamic aspects of aboriginal economies, there were—until Renfrew's recent book (1972)—several partial paradigms and bits of theory.[11] Most seem to stress economic and technological change as the prime movers in aboriginal societies; such theorists include the Marxians, Wittfogel, and the Energy/Evolutionists (White 1949: chap. 13). Thurnwald (1932), however, has a different sort of theory. He suggests that larger-scale socially stratified societies and economies came into being under aboriginal conditions through culture contact, military conquest, and political reorganization of the conquered. The result is some variant of a feudal system or a state system, with the conquering elite forming an aristocratic or upper stratum economically, as well as militarily and politically (see for example Oberg 1940). This larger-scale linking up of different ethnic groups rearranges labor allocation and increases the economic specialization of the different ethnic components of what is now one larger system, as, for example, with the caste-jajmani stratification of traditional village India (see Neale 1957a). The newly amalgamated and newly stratified society is now technologically more diverse, because each component ethnic group brings its own technology into the new and larger society.[12]

Aside from static structure and dynamic change in aboriginal economies, there are two other broad segments of economic anthropology, both concerned principally with dynamic matters.[13] One concerns the same set of bands, tribes, peasantries, and kingdoms as they underwent economic, technological, social, cultural, and political change under historically recent European colonization, that is, since 1500 A.D.; the other is concerned with change since 1947: very recent postcolonial economic development and cultural modernization in the entirely new historical context of newly created nation-states—India, Nigeria—beginning to construct nationally integrated economies and polities.

For economic change under colonial and then postcolonial conditions, we have no strong paradigms. The Marxians and the Energy/Evolutionists do have general or universal dynamic theories; that is, they purport to explain deep change under all historical conditions, aboriginal, colonial, and postcolonial.[14] For change under colonial conditions, we have in addition to the Marxians and the Energy/Evolutionists many bits of theory, each of which analyzes some aspect of change under some sort of colonial situation in some part of the world: acculturation (Herskovits 1938), culture contact (Mair 1957; Wilson and Wilson 1954), applied anthropology (Spicer 1952), dualism (Boeke 1942), and agricultural involution (Geertz 1963).

Why is there no strong paradigm for economic and social change under recent colonial conditions? The short answer would emphasize three points: (1) The postcolonial period, except in Latin America, began only in 1947. It is not yet, I think, commonly understood that postcolonial national and village development differs sharply from the economic and social change that took place under colonial conditions. (2) There was extreme variability in the types of aboriginal economies and societies that were colonized: bands, tribes, and peasantries in North, Central, and South America, Asia, Africa, Oceania, and the Middle East; Eskimos and Kwakiutl, Tiv, Ashanti and Bantu, Inca, Maya, and Aztec, Asian Indian villages and states—and many more—all were colonized. (3) The impacts of European colonization on aboriginal societies differed utterly: the Spanish, the Portuguese, the Dutch, the English, the French, the Germans, the Americans (who themselves were colonized until 1776), all colonized. The Caribbean Indians and the Indians of Latin America were colonized early, the Highlanders of New Guinea late. Europeans settled in large numbers in North, Central, and South America and South Africa, but not in West Africa or parts of Asia. Around 1500, when the Spaniards colonized Central and South America, the Spanish themselves were barely out of feudalism and the industrialization of Spain was centuries in the future; in contrast, the British colonized parts of West Africa after 1875, when the British themselves had been industrializing for a century.

We have no strong paradigm for economic and social change under recent colonial conditions.[15] We do have the components out of which a paradigm can be made: excellent descriptive accounts and some theoretical insights and conceptual terms which can be fashioned into a mosaic of unified theory to make deep sense out of variability.[16]

So, too, for postcolonial village change in the new context of national (or macro) economic development and cultural modernization. Despite the newness of the subject, excellent components for a strong paradigm already exist for reasons that are clear: Processes of acculturation and applied anthropology under colonial conditions were studied by a relatively small number of social anthropologists; in contrast, postcolonial macrodevelopment, microdevelopment, and modernization are studied by an international army of economists, sociologists, political scientists, and psychologists, as well as by anthropologists. Important insights into Third World national and village development today are being provided by writings on the historical development of the industrialized countries of Britain, Western Europe, Japan, and Russia (see, for example, Landes 1969; Kuznets 1966; Gerschenkron 1962; 1968; 1970; Smith 1959). Some recent theoretical work is addressed to the complicated interaction processes of economic development and social change: Smelser (1963) on "differentiation" and "integration"; Myrdal (1957) on "cumulative causation"; Epstein (1962; 1973) on the different social consequences following from different sorts of economic innovations at the village level in South India; Hagen (1962) on the enormously difficult topic of how personality formation affects the emergence of entrepreneurial capacities in colonized peoples; Adelman and Morris (1967) on the use of statistical techniques to show how economic and social change mutually affect each other.[17]

To summarize the points stressed in this section on paradigms in economic anthropology: It is necessary to see the full scope of the subject, the enormous range of economies considered, economies existing in utterly different historical conditions, and the welter of paradigms (e.g., price theory), partial paradigms (e.g., Marx), and bits of theory (e.g., acculturation) so far contrived, in order to understand the difficulties encountered in creating theory. It is also necessary to see the reasons why at present a unified theory of economic anthropology does not exist.

Four large subfields make up the subject, each of which requires its own theoretical framework: (1) the organization and performance of aboriginal village-level economics of bands, tribes, and peasantries, and the the elite and state levels of kingdom and empires; (2) economic and social change under aboriginal conditions; (3) economic and social change under historically recent conditions created by the European colonization of Africa, Asia, Latin America, Oceania, the Caribbean, and the Middle East; (4) postcolonial economic development and cultural modernization of village communities within newly created nation-states.

For each of these four subfields in economic anthropology there is a literature of empirical description and theoretical analysis written by archaeologists, historians, economists, sociologists, and others. One must draw on this literature as well as on the ethnographic and theoretical writings of anthropologists in order to construct paradigms in economic anthropology.[18]

For aboriginal economies under static conditions, we have three contending paradigms, only one of which (the formal economics of neoclassical price theory) is highly elaborated. Marxian theory as it relates to aboriginal economies is very sketchy (only a few concepts and generalizations are given). Polanyi's paradigm is still being clarified (as, indeed, I am trying to do in this present paper) and extended, for example, to include aboriginal peasantries. For aboriginal economies undergoing change, we have several partial paradigms—sketchy theories, really—except for Renfrew's recent and more comprehensive theory. For economic change in the Third World under European colonial conditions, we have a half-dozen or more bits of theory, but no strong paradigm. Nor do we yet have a strong paradigm for the very recent situation of microdevelopment, that is, village-level transformation within newly formed nation-states instituting regional and national programs of industrialization, education, and such. For colonial change and postcolonial development, however, there exist very important theoretical components for constructing paradigms.

POLANYI'S STATIC PARADIGM FOR ABORIGINAL ECONOMIES[19]

The published work of Polanyi and his associates consists of two parts: theory and its application to actual economies of time and place. "A new theory is always announced together with applications to some concrete range of . . . phenomena; without them it would not be even a candidate for acceptance" (Kuhn 1970: 46). The theoretical part, in turn, has two components: a positive paradigm for the analysis of non-market aboriginal economies—what Polanyi called institutional analysis; and a negative critique, an elaborate explanation of the unsuitability of formal economic theory as a universal paradigm for all economies of record.

Polanyi and his associates apply their own positive theory to sectors, processes, and institutions of actual economies, and, while doing so, continually illustrate the inappropriateness of formal price theory to analyze those aboriginal economies they are writing about. The subjects of their works include external trade and internal economic organization in eighteenth-century Dahomey (Arnold 1957a;b; Polanyi 1966) and in the prehistoric Middle East (Polanyi 1957a; Oppenheim 1957); ports of trade in the Eastern Mediterranean (Revere 1957); the internal economic organization of villages in parts of traditional India (Neale 1957a); preconquest Aztec-Maya long-distance trade (Chapman 1957); marketplaces in precolonial Berber Highlands (Benet 1957); the usage of primitive valuables in parts of Africa and Oceania (Bohannan 1959; Dalton 1965); kinds of marketplaces and market transactions in aboriginal and colonial Africa (Bohannan and Dalton 1962); variants of reciprocity in aboriginal bands and tribes (Sahlins 1965).

Every essay in *Trade and Market* repeats Polanyi's strong negative message: what primitive and archaic economies were *not*. They were not early market variants of nineteenth- and twentieth-century capitalism. Indeed, Polanyi's first book, *The Great Transformation* (1944), and an article written shortly thereafter, summarizing the main themes of the book, "Our Obsolete Market Mentality" (1947), are principally concerned to show the historical uniqueness of nineteenth-century capitalism, the real-world economic system for which conventional price theory was invented (and the system against which Marx was reacting).

Polanyi's strong critique of formal economics—maximizing, economizing, scarcity, the uncritical use of supply-and-demand concepts to characterize any economy—evoked several sharp rejoinders, resulting in what is inelegantly called the "formalist-substantivist controversy."[20] Two aspects of this controversy are particularly revealing: the formalists do not take issue with Polanyi's positive paradigm—reciprocity, redistribution, ports of trade, and such—about which they say almost nothing. Their concern, rather, is to dispute Polanyi's negative critique of formal price theory as a universal paradigm (see, for example, LeClair and Schneider 1968). The second revealing feature is the vituperative language used by some of the formalists, a sure sign that a clash over paradigms is taking place. For example, Cook (1966) calls Polanyi and me romantic, unscientific antiquarians, ignorant of economics, with a curious interest in "moribund" or "extinct" economies (that is, aboriginal economies, the ones archaeologists and ancient historians study). Here is a nosegay:

> The present critique is intended . . . [to elaborate] . . . the thesis that the substantivists' intransigency concerning the cross-cultural applicability of formal economic theory is a by-product of a romantic ideology rooted in an antipathy toward the "market economy" and an idealization of the "primitive". . . . given the fact that marketless subsistence economies are rapidly disappearing as ethnographic entities, being displaced by market-influenced or -dominated transitional and peasant economies, it seems rather pointless to persist, as Dalton does, in concocting tortured arguments in defense of a theory [Polanyi's] which was designed specifically for the analysis of these moribund types of economies (i.e., substantive economic theory). (Cook 1966: 323–25)

Another anthropologist, who himself has never written on the theoretical issues separating the formalists and the substantivists,[21] nevertheless finds it therapeutic to dismiss Polanyi and the rest of us in language whose only virtue is that it is barely audible because it is spoken from such an enormous height:

> From the beginning the substantivists (as exemplified in the justly famous works of Polanyi and others) were heroically muddled and in error. It is a tribute to the maturity of economic anthropology that we [*sic*] have been able to find precisely in what the error consisted in the short space of six years. The paper . . . written by Cook [1966] when he was a graduate student neatly disposes of the controversy. I did not think it necessary [in Nash 1966] to regale readers with the history of error. [In social science] . . . it is virtually impossible to down a poor, useless, or obfuscating hypothesis, and I expect that the next generation of creators of high-level confusion will resurrect, in one guise or another, the substantive view of the economy (Nash 1967:250).[22]

Heated disputes between social scientists or between historians are always about one of two things: *policy* (how should we change the real world?) or *paradigms* (how should we analyze the real world?). This one, of course, is about paradigms: What is the most useful theoretical framework of questions to ask, processes to study, concepts to use, in order to arrive at deep understanding of aboriginal economies?

The Subjects of Polanyi's Paradigm

Which real-world economies and which sectors, transactions, processes, and institutions in those economies is Polanyi's paradigm designed to analyze? Polanyi is concerned with the sociology of economic institutions—foreign trade, money—for those aboriginal economies in which markets are not dominant, that is, aboriginal bands, tribes, and the economic sectors of early state systems:[23]

> . . . the study of the economy in early societies comprises several related empirical fields: *primitive societies*, mainly kinship organized, non-literate; *archaic societies*, as a rule literate, practicing plow agriculture, but not using money widely as a means of [commercial or market] exchange. . . . The third overlapping field is *antiquity* which includes both societies of the primitive and archaic types as well as "modern" societies, i.e., such as widely employ money in [commercial or market] exchange. (Polanyi Mimeo. no. 1: 11).

Polanyi considered the internal organization of such economies and their foreign trade, as well as what we now call the "subsistence sector" (the acquisition, production, and disposition of foodstuffs and other ordinary goods) and the "prestige sector" (the transaction of valuables such as kula bracelets, cows as bridewealth, and such). He concentrated particularly on what he regarded as three very important institutions: markets, monetary objects (including primitive valuables), and foreign trade. These exist in a wide variety of past and present economies and so are capable of detailed comparison and contrast.

One of his central concerns was to show how, in aboriginal economies, external trade, local marketplaces, and money usages had independent origins and independent organization, that is, were not fused as they are in modern capitalism. There is a dynamic component to Polanyi's work, but it has to do with the institutions of external trade, money, and markets, rather than with change over time in entire economies or economic systems; and so his dynamic component does not fit neatly into table 1. He thought that a major problem in the economic history of Europe was to come to understand how external trade became overwhelmingly private commercial or market trade, how monetary objects overwhelmingly came to be used as means of commercial exchange, and how market transactions came to be dominant and integrative, regionally and nationally as well as internationally; hence his concern with the rise of market economy in *The Great Transformation*, a book linked in several ways to his later work on aboriginal economies.

I use the phrase "sociology of economic institutions" to characterize Polanyi's work because his continuing concern is to show that in the absence of market dominance (and therefore the absence of modern market exchange money as the prevailing kind, as well), the production and distribution of ordinary and prestige goods in aboriginal economies is socially controlled; that reciprocal transactions are rooted in social symmetry; that redistributive transactions are rooted in political centrality; that aboriginal economies are Gemeinschaften; that just as land tenure in aboriginal Africa (Bohannan 1960) and Melanesia (Malinowski 1935) are direct expressions of lineage affiliation, so too are all important allocations and transactions of natural resources, labor, and goods direct expressions of political, kinship, or religious institutions.[24]

82

Polanyi's Analysis of Long-Distance Trade

Concepts and Terminology

The concepts used by any theorist rivet our attention on the processes to be analyzed (and point as well to the conclusions to be reached). Concepts are the link between the real-world processes and the analytical conclusions about them the theory is designed to produce. When Srinivas, for example, contrived the concept "Sanskritization," he compressed into a single fabricated word an analytical conclusion about a real-world process: In sharply stratified Hindu India, upward mobility of lower caste groups is achieved by their emulation of the practices and values of higher castes. So too Marx's "exploitation" and "surplus value," Freud's "Oedipus complex," and Keynes's "marginal propensity to consume." Concepts are crucial ideas expressed in words and are an integral part of any theory designed to analyze any real-world process in any subject.

Some of Polanyi's concepts are simple and easily understood; some are more complicated and difficult. The simple concepts are terms he used for tangible objects or narrowly defined or quite specific institutions and practices, such as *operational device, port of trade, administered trade,* and *sorting.* The difficult concepts are the terms he used for broad institutions and practices whose specific forms vary in different societies such as *reciprocity, redistribution,* and *special-purpose money.*

Polanyi uses three sets of concepts, "substantive," "formal," and what he called "institutional" terms. The substantive meanings of *economic, external trade, money,* and *market* indicate what all economies, all sorts of foreign trade, all sorts of money, and all sorts of markets have in common. Here, Polanyi meant to call attention to the similarities among all economies. The formal meanings of these terms indicate their special organization and functioning in modern capitalism, that is, national industrial economies integrated through markets. The institutional terms relate especially (but not exclusively) to the forms money, markets, and external trade take in nonmarket aboriginal economies.

Polanyi meant by the "substantive definition of *economic,*" then, material provisioning, that is, what all economies have in common. Any society, past or present, has an economy of some sort in the sense of systematic arrangements to provide its people with food and shelter and to provide goods and services to sustain community life—defense, warfare, religious practice, marriage, and so forth. All economies bear a family resemblance because they all provision people living in communities. In their provisioning, they all use natural resources, human labor, technology (that is, tools and knowledge about producing goods or using the physical environment), and they all employ some range and forms of institutional practices, that is, man-made conventions and rules, such as foreign trade, monetary objects, and, frequently, markets of some sort.

The mere presence of a practice like foreign trade does not tell us anything interesting about an economy, because foreign trade was carried on in various ways for different purposes in many differently organized economies. Today, the USSR and the United States both engage in foreign trade (and both use monetary objects and marketplaces) despite their being differently organized economies. But *how* foreign trade is organized in each, the *range* and *kinds* of imports and exports involved, the *quantitative importance* of foreign trade in each, these sensitively reflect the internal organization of each economy (as well, incidentally, as its achieved level of economic development; see Kuznets 1966).

This simple example of the United States and the USSR yields several general points of importance to Polanyi's concepts and mode of analysis: (1) Like warfare, language, and the family, foreign trade, monetary objects, and markets are institutions widely present in utterly different societies. (2) But foreign trade, money, and markets vary enormously in how they are organized, what specific purposes or functions they serve, and how important they are. (3) In any economy—the Maya just before the Spanish conquest, the Trobriand Islands of Malinowski's day, the United States at present—the organization of foreign trade, its purposes, its quantitative importance are all direct consequences of the internal organization of that specific economy. Foreign trade, monetary objects, and markets do not have an independent existence; their organization and importance are determined by the internal organization of the economies, societies, and polities in which they function. (So too for religion, the family, warfare, and other institutions present in widely differing societies.)

For the Maya, Trobriands, and the United States, then, *economic* means material provisioning, that which is necessary to sustain individual physical existence and community life. The substantive meaning of *external trade* is the peaceful acquisition of goods from a distance by trading other goods for them in any of several ways. The substantive meaning of *money* is quantifiable objects used in specific sociological (e.g., bridewealth) or economic (provisioning) situations to perform any (not necessarily all) of four functions or operations: (commercial or noncommercial) payment, exchange, hoarding, or the use of monetary units as a standard of accountancy.[25] The substantive meaning of *market* is a site where buyers and sellers meet to buy and sell at prices formed in various ways.

Now for the "formal" meanings of these terms, the meanings they have come to have in formal economics, the subject invented to analyze the highly developed, nationally and internationally integrated industrial capitalism of the nineteenth and twentieth centuries in Britain, Western Europe, and America.[26] European mercantilism from 1400 to 1750 and the Industrial Revolution that followed created this "market economy"; and a century of price theory, from Ricardo's *Principles* in 1817 to Joan Robinson's *Imperfect Competition* in 1932, concentrated on the minute functioning of markets:

> Economic analysis [price theory] is a derivation of formal economics, itself a branch of logic dealing with rules that govern behavior in scarcity situations, i.e., situations of choice induced by insufficiency of means; while substantively, economics deals with the causal dependence of man upon his natural and social environment for the material means of his existence. The value of economic analysis as a discipline lies primarily in the intellectual mastery of the phenomena of a market-structured economy; the importance of economics in the substantive sense, in its [presently] sub-organized state hardly deserving the name of a discipline, is given by the knowledge it conveys of the human economy in its anthropological, historical, comparative, and developmental aspects (Polanyi Mimeo. no. 2: 3).

Industrial capitalism is the system under which we American and West European archaeologists, historians, and anthropologists live, in the same sense, of course, that Christianity and democracy are the religious and political systems under which we live. Capitalism, obviously, is the economic system we are most familiar with, just as English is the language we are most familiar with. I belabor the obvious for two reasons, one psychological, the other semantic. Living in a market system means that we all do fieldwork in it every day, as buyers, savers, investors, wage earners, and so on. Because of its ingrained familiarity to us, our own market economy becomes a kind of unconscious model of "the" economy, and the Maya and the Trobriand Islanders are then perceived by some as being merely early or crude commercial variants—Model T's —of our own market-dominated economy. This unconscious (or at least, unexamined) predisposition to perceive early economies as simplified versions of our own—and money, markets, and external trade wherever they occur as simplified versions of our own—is what Polanyi called the "economistic prejudice."

Our own economic vocabulary, moreover, is also the most familiar one to us. We associate the word *money* not with cowrie or pig-tusks, but with dollars, sterling, or francs. We associate *foreign trade* not with the kula circuit, but with private U.S. firms importing Volkswagens and exporting farm machinery.

Money, markets, and foreign trade are subjects of enormously elaborate analysis by economists, who, up to the 1930s, were concerned exclusively with their organization and functioning under market or capitalist institutions.[27] Formal economics is a powerful paradigm for the analysis of money, markets, external trade, and much else *in our own system*, a system in which our money, markets, and foreign trade are intimately linked together, and in which all express our dominant and integrative mode of transaction or organization, market exchange (see Polanyi 1944).

Markets in modern capitalist economies are local, regional, national, and international; there are markets for labor, natural resources, consumption goods, specialist services, capital goods, finance, and transportation. Money income is required to live; every income recipient receives income in the form of money wage, rent, profit, or interest, the amount of which depends on the money prices of the labor, specialist service, or inanimate property the income recipient owns. Production depends on money profit; profit depends on two sets of money prices made in markets: the prices of labor and resources which form costs of production, and the sales price of the finished product. Markets are important in the sense that we all depend on them for livelihood. Most labor, natural resources, and produced goods are transacted through purchase and sale in markets. Indeed, with us, even gifts are usually gifts of goods first purchased on markets, and all levels of government acquire the goods and services they dispense by first buying them on markets.

In a market system, both the substantive and the formal meanings of *economic* apply: *economic* takes on its double meaning of "provisioning" by "economizing," whether it is a consumer maximizing utility by carefully buying consumption goods, or a producer maximizing profit or minimizing costs of production. To "economize" is to do a cost-benefit comparison in order to choose an outcome which is the best available, a maximum. Cost-benefit comparisons to choose maximizing outcomes also occur in a wide variety of "noneconomic" (nonprovisioning) situations, for example, in games such as chess and poker where the rules of the game specify options available, as prices do in markets, and the maximizing goal is to win; also in war, where the aim is to win with the least expenditure of our army's lives. Polanyi called all such situations "the logic of rational action" to emphasize two points: that economizing can occur in scarcity situations other than material provisioning through markets; and that the least ambiguous meaning of the treacherous term *rational* is economizing, that is, a cost-benefit calculation to achieve a preferred goal with the least expenditure of means.

Economizing is of superb relevance to market economies, as, indeed, the detailed elaboration of price theory shows. Consumers and producers are confronted with many alternatives among which to choose; precise calculation is possible because all labor, resources, and goods bear money prices, and material livelihood, material security, and social position are achieved through economizing choice. The market society makes material acquisition very important to the participants.

Money in a market system has special characteristics (Polanyi's formal definition of money). First, it is what Polanyi called, unhappily, "general-purpose money." This is not a good phrase because it does not immediately convey the meaning he intended: that in France, Britain, or America, anything which can be paid for in money, or any commercial or noncommercial obligation that can be discharged in money, can be paid for or discharged with the *same* money—francs, sterling, or dollars. We buy goods with dollars (means of commercial exchange); we pay debts for past purchases of goods with dollars (means of commercial payment); we pay traffic fines in dollars (means of noncommercial payment); we pay taxes in dollars (also noncommercial payment—in this case, means of redistributive payment); we save dollars (hoarding, in Polanyi's terms). Dollars are used as units of account to measure all sorts of fees, assessments, emoluments, tithes, and obligations.

Polanyi did not mean by general-purpose money what at least one anthropologist has wrongly attributed to him: that everything in a market society is purchasable or all debts of whatever sort dischargable with money. If we are convicted for murder, we cannot discharge the obligation by a cash payment; rather, we "pay our debt to society" by going to jail or worse. We may have to pay cash fees to acquire Ph.D. degrees and Phi Beta Kappa keys; but the cash fees are not a sufficient condition for acquiring them. Ours is a general-purpose money in two senses: (a) commercial exchanges and payments are made in dollars (e.g., buying goods), and some noncommercial payments are made in dollars (e.g., politically induced payments, such as paying fines and taxes); (b) a single sort of money, dollars, performs all four monetary uses of payment, exchange, hoarding, and accounting. These characteristics of dollars, francs, and sterling are a direct expression of our market dominance and market integration. Our money is what it is because our market system is what it is.[28]

> Once money as a means of [market] exchange is established, the practice of [monetary] payment spreads far and wide. For with the introduction of markets as the physical locus of exchange [of labor, land, and goods] a new type of obligation comes into prominence as the legal residue of transactions. Payment [of money] appears as the counterpart of some material advantage gained in the transaction. Formerly [that is, in aboriginal economies] a man was made to pay taxes, rent, fines, or blood-money. Now he pays for the goods he bought. Money is now means of [noncommercial] payment [of taxes and fines] *because* it is means of [market] exchange [of labor, land, and goods]. The notion of an independent origin of [noncommercial] payment [of taxes, fines, bloodwealth] fades, and the millennia in which it sprang not from economic [provisioning] transactions, but directly from religious, social, or political obligations, are forgotten (Polanyi 1968:183).

Polanyi's formal definition of external trade is, of course, a description of its special organization in a national market economy dealing internationally with other national market economies, as with modern Europe and America. Where markets dominate domestically, foreign market trade dominates as well.

(1) Foreign commercial trade is essentially like domestic commercial trade. Goods move between London and New York for the same economic reasons (economic in both senses, provisioning and economizing) that goods move between New York and San Francisco, namely for regional comparative advantage expressed in cheaper money prices. Almost all the goods and services commercially imported by an industrial capitalist country are capable of being produced by that importing country. Goods are imported *not* because they are unavailable at home, but because they are either cheaper abroad or because our households and business firms prefer the foreign to the domestic good. America produces cars, wine, and cheese; it also imports them.

(2) Commercial foreign trade is a continuous, not a sporadic, activity, a regular business rather than an occasional expedition. Goods and services move internationally twenty-four hours a day and are bought and sold internationally by ordinary commercial firms. Polanyi stressed the point that in market economies, to export is regarded as more important than to import. During the preindustrial capitalist period called mercantilism, and then under industrial capitalism, a "favorable" balance of payments means to export more than a nation imports.

(3) An enormous range of goods and services is purchased and sold internationally: consumers' goods (wheat, fish) and producers' goods (tractors and trucks), services (insurance, transportation) and prestige goods (diamonds); goods used by households (cars), by business firms (computers), and by government (military aircraft). Although land and factories cannot be moved internationally, their ownership can, through foreign investment. Not only is the range of goods and services traded enormous—thousands of different items—but the economic (provisioning) importance of international trade to developed capitalist countries is also enormous. As table 2 shows, it is typical in recent years for the yearly exports plus imports of a capitalist country to be equal to 40 percent or more of its gross national product.

(4) The extent, variety, and importance of commercial international trade and investment between national market economies requires linked

TABLE 2

PROPORTIONS OF FOREIGN TRADE TO GROSS
NATIONAL PRODUCT IN DEVELOPED COUNTRIES
IN A POST–WORLD WAR II YEAR

	Exports plus Imports as % of GNP
Countries in descending order of GNP	Commodities and services
1. United States	9.6
2. United Kingdom	41.7
3. France	26.5
4. West Germany	44.5
5. Canada	40.4
6. Japan	27.3
7. Australia	33.6
8. Belgium	65.5
9. Sweden	55.4
10. Netherlands	96.8
11. Switzerland	60.6
12. Denmark	67.3
13. Norway	88.7
14. New Zealand	53.0
15. Luxembourg	161.5

Source: Kuznets (1966: 301)

monetary systems. In the nineteenth and early twentieth centuries, this
was provided by the gold standard (for details, see Polanyi 1944: chaps.
6, 16; Dalton 1974: chap. 1).

We shall see that none of these distinguishing characteristics of external trade carried on commercially by market economies typically
holds true for nonmarket aboriginal economies, whose external trade
Polanyi described as gift trade, or reciprocity, and as (politically) administered trade.[29]

Finally, we come to the institutional concepts, that special set of
terms Polanyi contrived to analyze socioeconomic processes, transactions, and sectors, especially (but not exclusively) in aboriginal economies, and which he used to delineate the differences between aboriginal
economies and modern market economies.

Terms such as *subsistence economy, primitive economy, communal, collectivistic, status society, precapitalist,* and *Gemeinschaft* tell us only one thing: the economy being labeled is not one in which markets are dominant and integrative. But the Soviet Union today, the Trobriand Islands yesterday, the Maya five hundred years ago, the medieval European manor a thousand years ago, and, apparently, Mycenaean Crete thirty-five hundred years ago were all nonmarket economies. In short, terms like *subsistence economy* and *communal* do not specify modes of transaction, types of organization, or the exact workings of monetary, market, or foreign trade institutions. Polanyi set out to specify these processes.

Reciprocity, redistribution, and market exchange. These very broad categories are used by Polanyi to characterize transactions at different levels and in different sectors of the same economy—village and state, internal and external, subsistence and prestige—and also to refer to transactions in utterly different economies: aboriginal bands, tribes, and peasantries; industrial capitalist and industrial communist economies.

> Reciprocity relates the corresponding members of symmetrically placed groups; redistribution relates members of a group to a center towards which and from which the goods and services move, physically or dispositionally. . . . [Market] exchange as a dominant form of integration is present only in societies where the economic process is instituted through a self-regulating system of price-making markets (Polanyi Mimeo. no. 1: 13).

> These patterns [of integration (reciprocity, redistribution, and market exchange)] do not—and this should be stressed—supply us with a classification of economic systems as a whole; rather the co-existence of patterns notably of reciprocity and redistribution is common. Also, markets, which do not integrate the economy, may fit into either pattern. And any of the patterns may predominate, reflect the movements through which land, labor, and the production and distribution of food are merged into the economy. But other patterns may obtain alongside the dominant one in the various sectors of the economy [e.g., internal and external sectors] and at varying levels of its organization [i.e., household, village, state] (Polanyi 1968:331).

All production processes—hunting, gathering, fishing, herding, farming, mining, manufacture—require transactions of labor, natural resources, and produce (and therefore involve reciprocity, redistribution, or market exchange). If we asked questions about labor and land allocation, work organization, and the disposition of produce in an aboriginal farming economy such as Malinowski's Trobriands (1922; 1935), our answers would indicate that variants of reciprocity were the most important organizational principles there (but not the only ones), just as market exchange is in modern capitalism.

There are four points of special importance about Polanyi's patterns of integration (which I prefer to call simply "modes of transaction"): (1) There are many variants of reciprocity, redistribution, and market exchange. (2) Typically, any economy uses more than one because these terms characterize transactions at all levels of economy (household, village, state), in different sectors (internal and external, subsistence and prestige), and in different lines of production (agriculture, fishing, herding, construction). (3) The kinds of money or valuables and the kinds of external trade that are employed in any economy are direct and sensitive expressions of the dominant internal mode or modes of transaction in that economy. (If we have reason to believe that long-distance trade among the preconquest Maya was differently organized from our own international market trade, it was because Maya internal economic organization was differently organized from U.S. domestic economy.) (4) Modes of transaction are also directly related to political organization, social organization, and culture. That is, bands, tribes (with and without central government), and peasantries differ from one another with regard to a set of economic, social, and political institutions. I shall explain each of these points briefly.

It is easiest to see how a single mode of transaction varies in its actual institutionalization by referring to the economy we are all familiar with: our own. Like reciprocity and redistribution, market exchange is also a broad category. In the economy of the United States, *market* refers to a place of final sale, such as a retail store, and to the transactional principle of purchase and sale at money price regardless of the place of final sale (the real estate market or the wheat market). Economists distinguish finely among types of markets—what laymen would call different industries—depending on the number of producers in each and how close or substitutable or interchangeable the commodity produced is;

markets in pure competition, differentiated oligopoly, and monopoly are examples of different market situations (out of a dozen or more that bear separate names).

Reciprocity and redistribution are also broad categories within which there are different types and variants. And they too describe land and labor allocation as well as the disposition of goods produced—that is, production as well as distribution or exchange. Sahlins (1965) described very clearly how reciprocal transactions differ with social distance and with the type of good or service involved. No similar work has yet been published describing varieties of redistribution.[30]

Polanyi used the term *redistribution* in general and special senses. Its general meaning refers to the economic sector of any centralized polity: chiefdom, kingdom, empire, modern capitalist state, or modern communist state. In this general sense, redistribution entails obligatory payments of any sort—cash or kind, labor or goods, foodstuffs or valuables—to central political authority, which uses the money, goods, or labor for the maintenance of political (or religious) leaders and their entourage of retainers, and also to provide some range of public works and community services (roads, defense, dispute settlement).

> Redistribution obtains with a group to the extent in which the allocation of goods (including land and natural resources) is collected in one hand and takes place by virtue of custom, law, or *ad hoc* central decision. In this way the reuniting of divided labor is achieved. Sometimes it simply amounts to storage-cum-redistribution. It occurs for many reasons and on all levels [household, band, village, state], from the primitive hunting tribe to the vast storage systems of ancient Egypt. With a hunt, any other method of distribution would lead to disintegration of the horde or band, since only "division of labor" can ensure results in a hunt. In large countries differences of soil and climate may make the reuniting of labor necessary; in other cases it is caused by discrepancy in point of time, as between the harvest and consumption. Methods of collection may differ widely. From a simple pooling of catch or game to elaborate methods of taxation in kind, various devices are met with (Polanyi 1951: chap. 4).

A special variant of redistribution that interests historians and archaeologists occurs in aboriginal "palace economies," in which obligatory taxes, rents, and tributes in kind, mostly composed of staples, are

93

paid into a royal storehouse or magazine and disbursed as rations to palace retainers, craftsmen, functionaries, and sometimes to the populace at large. The political center collects, stores, and pays out (redistributes) goods, which means, incidentally, that keeping records becomes important.[31] Here is Finley's characterization of the economic (provisioning) and social stratification implications of the Linear B Mycenaean tablets deciphered by Ventris and Chadwick (1956):

> At least this much deducible from the tablets: that the palace records embraced agriculture and pasturage; a great range of specialized productive processes; stores of goods of a variety and number which point well beyond the mere consumption needs of the palace narrowly conceived (even allowing for extensive waste and conspicuous display); and a numerous personnel hierarchically ordered from "slaves" to the king at the top, each stratum connected in the actual texts with either a function (including military and religious as well as "economic") or a holding of land, or both (Finley 1957:135).

Typically, any economy employs more than one mode of transaction. In the United States, remarkable for the extent of dominance of market exchange, there is a relatively large redistributive sector of taxes to and disbursements by government, and a smaller sector of gift exchange between kin and friends (the latter being small also in the sense of not being tied to livelihood, but rather to occasional ceremonial expression). There are also modern variants of reciprocal long-distance trade between governments, as with lend-lease during the Second World War.[32]

Figure 15 portrays sectors and levels of an economy in an aboriginal state. By *level* I mean a social grouping of characteristic size located in a specific place: household level, village level, state level. Note how elastic our English word *economy* is. In English we can talk of the economy of the household, the economy of the village or tribal segment, the economy of the palace or the state/governmental level or sector, or the national economy or the international economy. It should not surprise us to find reciprocal exchanges within lineage, village, or tribal segments— for example, reciprocal work parties harvesting everyone's crops in turn— but market or commercial exchanges of produce between villages.

For any level of economy, we can talk about transactions internal and external to it; such a phrase as "the external trade sector at the village level" (or at the state level) then becomes meaningful. All this verbiage

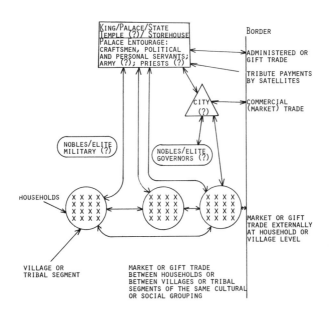

FIGURE 15. LEVELS AND SECTORS OF AN ECONOMY IN AN ABORIG-INAL STATE.

Levels and Sectors
Household economy/village economy elite economy/palace economy/city economy.
Obligatory payments upward by villages to elite and/or king.
Obligatory public services downward from elite and/or king to villages.
External trade (and tribute) transactions between palace and other kings.
External trade between households or between villages of same culture.
External trade between households or between villages of different cultures.
City transactions with palace, nobles, villages, and outside world.

Variants
King sometimes has his own source of income—demesne, estate, plantation—usually along with obligatory receipts from subjects.
Role of cities varies (in some aboriginal states there are none). Some are principally religious or military establishments with supporting entourages (e.g., of craftsmen); some are principally commercial; some combine several functions.
Roles and locations of nobles-elite-military vary.
Extent of political centralization/decentralization varies.
Organization of both agricultural and other economic activities (e.g., mining) varies.

and definition mongering is necessary to achieve clarity because real-world economies and societies are complicated: there are in fact households, villages, and palaces; bands, tribes, and peasantries; internal and external transactions; land, labor, and tools; purchases, gifts, tax and tribute payments; subsistence and prestige goods, luxuries and treasure, foodstuffs and valuables.

Polanyi's concepts and analytical conclusions can be used to construct models to show the systematic relationships between economic, political, and social organization; that is, to show how they fit together in aboriginal societies. In this chapter, whose length is already great, I can only sketch in by way of one illustration these congruences, correlations, or functional relationships between types of economic, political, and social organization.[33]

Why didn't the traditional peasants of Europe, Asia, and the Middle East have potlatch, kula, bloodwealth, and primitive valuables (such as Yap stones or pig tusks)? The short answer is because traditional peasants had states, formal social stratification (castes, feudal rankings), marketplaces, commercial money, or world religion. The aboriginal Kwakiutl and Trobrianders, who did have potlatch, kula, bloodwealth, and primitive valuables, did not have states, formal social stratification, market dependence, commercial money, or world religion. Theirs were stateless, Big Man, nonmarket systems. These sets of political, social, and economic institutions go together, something which can be appreciated only when the meaning and usage of primitive valuables (as special-purpose money) is understood, because the acquisition and disbursement of primitive valuables is a vital part of the social and political organization of tribes without rulers and without dominant markets.

Special-purpose money. Polanyi distinguished between general-purpose and special-purpose money because he wanted to distinguish between francs (or sterling or dollars) as they are used in modern, national, market economies, and primitive monies, such as pig tusks, cowrie, brass rods, Yap stones, and such, as they are used in aboriginal nonmarket economies.[34]

At this point I must remind the reader that I am considering aboriginal economies, their organization *before colonization* began with serious European commercial penetration and political control of Latin America around 1500, and the rest of the Third World later. One of

96

several reasons why it has been so difficult to create a theory of primitive money is that most of the anthropological data on primitive money were gathered by fieldworkers *late in the colonial period*. At that time francs and sterling were importantly present in the same economies in which aboriginal raffia cloth (Douglas 1958), fathoms of bird feathers (Davenport 1961), and copper shields (Codere 1951) were also importantly present; the usage of the primitive monies, however, had already been seriously affected by the presence of the modern European money.[35]

I now prefer to divide Polanyi's special-purpose money into two classes, *primitive money* and *primitive valuables*. Both were alike in their limited or special usage compared to dollars or francs. That is, primitive money and primitive valuables were not general-purpose money in two senses: They did not usually enter into both market and nonmarket transactions, and they did not have the full set of usages that dollars have, that is, means of (commercial and noncommercial) exchange, payment, hoarding, and a standard for accountancy. Typically, they served only one or two of these uses in either the market or the non-market sector.

Primitive money, such as cowrie, twists of wire, iron hoes, and slabs of salt, consisted of divisible and relatively uniform objects used in ordinary commercial purchase and sale in the market sector of aboriginal economies in which variants of reciprocity and redistribution were usually more important modes of transaction. These primitive monies were usually confined to petty, marketplace transactions of foodstuffs and other ordinary consumption goods and small tools, whereas land, labor, and the bulk of livelihood were acquired in ways not requiring the transaction of primitive monies. (For illuminating examples from medieval Europe, see Bloch 1967: chap. 8.)

By primitive valuables I mean the kula bracelets of the Trobrianders (Malinowski 1922), the large stones used on Yap (Einzig 1948), cows among the Nuer (Lewis 1973), pigs and pearl shells in the Highlands of New Guinea (Strathern 1971), and the like. As physical objects, primitive valuables are much less uniform and less easily divisible than primitive money. Primitive valuables usually have individual names and pedigrees; they are not anonymously interchangeable units. Usually they are ranked or classed, each grade of valuable being used as means of noncommercial payment in a special range of social and political transactions and events, such as bridewealth, bloodwealth, fines, reparation, sacrifice. Primitive valuables appear in stateless societies having economies in which markets (and therefore, commercial money) are either absent, or, if present, restricted to a narrow range of goods—petty markets. The primitive valuables are not used for commercial purchase.[36]

The acquisition and noncommercial payment of primitive valuables occurs within a "prestige" sphere, the exact nature of which, I believe, differs sharply between aboriginal stateless societies and aboriginal state societies. For clarity, I shall call *primitive valuables* those which appear in stateless societies, and *treasure* that which appears (usually, but not exclusively) in state societies. In aboriginal stateless societies, the primitive valuables are the means of acquiring superior political, military, judicial, and religious roles in the form of Big Man status, prerogatives, power, and an entourage of followers. In aboriginal state systems, social organization seems invariably to be stratified sharply into castes or classes. Superior political, military, judicial, and religious roles are formally organized and conferred; the treasure items play different roles here, in their elite circulation. Polanyi provides important clues in the disentangling of these complicated matters, in his several writings on the noneconomic origins of primitive money and on how monetary devices affect status and state-building in aboriginal societies. Here is one example:

> Treasure [and, I would add, primitive valuables] makes the round of the Trobriand Islanders in the Kula ring. In early Greece it circulates among gods, kings, and chiefs either against other prestige goods or items of honor, power, and safety. This made for an *élite circulation of treasure*, as it might be called. Prestige goods, such as precious metals, ivory, slaves, horses, change hands only against each other, i.e., in a closed circuit. A primitive people, such as the Tiv, practice an equivalency exchange in prestige goods. So called *leiturgies* in classical Greece provided public services at the cost of the wealthy citizen, who was expected to supply the service, at his own expense, as an honorific obligation. . . . Prestige factors of one sort or another show up in primitive and early state alike. They shall serve as illustrative material for the problems of transition between tribal and state society (Polanyi Mimeo. no. 1:17–18).

Equivalencies. Equivalency is a "substantive" term for a general set of things, one of which, in the "formal" sense, is a market price. Polanyi contrived this awkward term to avoid calling them all prices because of the ingrained market connotation of the word *price*. What he meant by equivalencies was prices or exchange ratios formed other than by market forces. The specific equivalencies uppermost in his mind were those used in palace economies whose storehouses received taxes and tribute in kind (barley, wool, oil, wine). Here, the political authority may stipulate, say, a barley-to-wine ratio (equivalency) of four bushels of barley equals one gallon of wine, and then accept wine instead of barley as taxes, at the discretion of the payer. Equivalencies, then, are substitutable goods in prescribed proportions. Note that an early meaning of a fungible good is one for which something else may be substituted in payment to fulfill an obligation. Another equivalency is the frequently mentioned (but rarely explained) practice in aboriginal economies of a container exchanged for that which fills it up; a clay pot exchanged for the amount of beer which fills the pot. Here is Polanyi on equivalencies:

> We find *equivalencies* established for a number of *standardized staples* by custom, statute or proclamation; these also occur, as [noncommercial] exchange equivalents, in primitive communities such as the Tikopia or the Tiv. Under archaic conditions, equivalencies indicate the amount of staples of different kinds that can be substituted—not exchanged—for each other in the payment of taxes and rent, or, the other way [i.e., in receiving from the center] when claiming one's rations or wages in kind. Where reciprocity relations obtain, equivalencies may indicate adequacy of the return gift rather than [arithmetic] equality. . . . Equivalencies underlay various important devices employed in *staple finance*, i.e., the carrying on of operations "in kind" on a large scale such as planning, budgeting, balancing, accounting, and clearing, unavoidable in the practice of state or temple economies under archaic conditions (Polanyi Mimeo. no. 1:16–17).

Operational devices. Xerxes had no Xerox, but nevertheless had administrative operations to perform, so he had to employ scribes who used operational devices for "planning, budgeting, balancing, accounting, and clearing" of various sorts, to record state decisions and to keep accounts and calculate receipts and disbursements. Polanyi used the term *operational device* to point up the variety of accounting, census-

99

taking, and record-keeping devices reported in the literature, a matter obviously important in palace economies and all governmental redistributive sectors. These devices are functionally equivalent to what modern societies do through their use of literacy and of money as a standard for accounting, double-entry bookkeeping, and calculating machines of different sorts.[37] The abacus, quipo strings (used by the Inca), and census by pebble count in eighteenth-century Dahomey are examples; also in Dahomey the remarkable device, used to record, witness, and remember, of having female counterparts to all male palace and military officials, the female rememberer always being present when her male counterpart was transacting business with the king (see Polanyi 1966: 54–56). William the Conqueror's Domesday Survey of 1086 was also a remarkable operational device, an early equivalent of national income accounting, contrived to estimate the taxable capacity of England.

In *Dahomey and the Slave Trade* (1966), Polanyi speculated on matters of direct interest to this symposium, namely the emergence of civilization from smaller, less differentiated social groupings, emphasizing economic techniques of statecraft, such as operational devices and ports of trade required to carry out those economic activities of the state that Polanyi called (internal) redistribution and (external) administered trade:

> It seems probable . . . that the accomplishment of literacy as a criterion of civilization should be dropped in the light of highly stratified societies that banned the art of writing for religious, political, or economic reasons, preferring isolation to undesirable culture contact. The Ashanti and Dahomeans come to mind. How were their accomplishments in war, or in trade and currency, compatible with illiteracy? The answer lies in a forgotten phase of civilization which we might call "operational," owing to the gadgets by means of which complex mechanical and organizational feats may be performed without a conceptualization of the successful process. Some early states—prototypes of archaic society—may have emerged from primitivism precisely by virtue of operational devices, of which elaborate pebble statistics or differentiated numeration systems are a sample. There were in Dahomey, for example, the two ways of counting—the one applying to cowrie money, the other to . . . all other things. These devices were an advance in communication comparable to I.B.M., which also results in replacing and surpassing thought by mechanism (Polanyi 1966:xx–xxi).

LONG-DISTANCE TRADE

It may very well be easier to understand aboriginal long-distance trade in 1973 than it was to understand it in 1873, the heyday of laissez-faire capitalism in Europe and America. In the last fifty years, new forms of international gift and state trading have appeared, modern variants of Polanyi's reciprocal and administered trade: trade within the Soviet bloc and between communist and capitalist countries; bilateral trade agreements and special-purpose monetary devices used in international trade in Hitler's Germany just before the war; lend-lease during the war; and the Marshall Plan and development aid since the war. And even where ordinary, private international market trade continues to dominate, it is now most frequently politically controlled market trade: tariffs, import quotas, embargoes on exports of military goods, subsidies to domestic export industries, and the like. These, of course, are the international trade equivalents of the domestic market controls that have proliferated as part of the welfare state (for example agricultural price supports, minimum wage legislation, and price controls in inflation).[38]

It is a mark of the power of nineteenth-century market institutions and of classical and neoclassical economic theory that the model or norm of foreign trade we all carry in our heads is purely commercial trade between private enterprises run by private merchants responding as buyers and sellers to private supply-and-demand forces in internationally linked markets using internationally linked money and price systems. We have only recently begun to see how many other sorts of foreign trade there were. Indeed, if foreign trade of the strictly private market sort that dominated nineteenth-century international capitalism was the sort found in aboriginal economies, then archaeologists and economic anthropologists could use ready-made the formidable array of concepts and conclusions created by foreign trade theorists from Ricardo to Harry Johnson. But even as late as 1776 Adam Smith devoted a third of his long book to arguments against mercantilism, an elaborate system of politically controlled commercial foreign trade:

> By the 8th of Elizabeth, chap. 3, the exporter of sheep, lambs, or rams, was for the first offence to forfeit all his goods for ever, to suffer a year's imprisonment, and then to have his left hand cut off in a market town, upon a market day, to be there nailed up; and for

the second offence to be adjudged a felon, and to suffer death accordingly. To prevent the breed of our sheep from being propagated in foreign countries, seems to have been the object of this law (Smith 1776:612–13).

I need hardly tell archaeologists that external trade is a very old and widespread practice (see Clark 1965). Actually, I do not know of an economy which did not practice external trade of some sort. If foreign trade is not literally ubiquitous or universal, it is almost so.

Some common characteristics of external trade under aboriginal conditions: Typically, it was not a massive activity involving large quantities and wide varieties of imports and exports necessary for everyday livelihood (nothing like foreign trade today). Long-distance trade was difficult and dangerous, partly due to the limitations of early technology (the design of boats and knowledge of navigation), and partly due to the risks of travel among strangers. The difficulties, distances, and dangers meant that early trade was typically carried out by group expeditions armed for protection, or traveling under the protection of kings or temples on whose behalf the traders traded and whose emblem they displayed. Usually, security was further assured by trading with foreigners with whom some special political, treaty, tribute, or social relationship already existed (as with kula partners abroad who provided hospitality and protection for their trading guests, or the elaborate device of the port of trade with its specialized facilities and containment of visiting traders). Trade expeditions or voyages were seasonal and sporadic, not continuous activities.

All this meant that the goods sought abroad were unusually important and unavailable at home; thus the stress on elite or treasure goods—slaves, spices, weapons. It was the desire for specific imports and not the economic (provisioning, income- or livelihood-earning) need to export that motivated early trade. Most trade consisted of the procurement of a few desired items from a distance; export goods were necessary to acquire imports.

Ports of trade and kula partnerships meant social control over trade. The strangers who come to trade with us must be controlled because they may be dangerous: they may carry infectious diseases, infectious ideas, or malicious intent (for example, they may be spies, or come with the intent to enslave us). Or the goods they carry may be dangerous to us unless controlled (weapons, for example). Here is a translation of some mid-seventeenth-century decrees of Imperial China, regulating the movement of foreigners and their goods, but also protecting them and assuring them fair treatment:

> . . . In the Shun-chih period (1644–1661) it was fixed that after foreign countries bringing tribute to Court have come to the capital and their rewards have been distributed to them, a market may be opened in the Residence for Tributary Envoys, either for three days or for five days. . . . The Board of Ceremonies shall communicate with the Board of Revenue which shall ahead of time detach [Treasury Overseers] to do the receiving and buying. When the despatch in reply has passed through the Board (of Ceremonies) then they shall issue a notice (of the opening of the market) and despatch officials to superintend it. They shall give orders for just and fair trade. It is altogether prohibited to collect or buy works of history. As to black, yellow, purple-black, large flowered, Tibetan, or lotus satins; together with all forbidden implements of war, salpetre, ox-horn, and such things—all shopmen and hongists shall bring their goods to the Residence (for sale) and exchange them justly and fairly.
>
> Dying-cloth, thin silk, and such goods shall be handed back within fixed limits. If there are any who buy on credit and intentionally delay (payment), cheating or seeking "squeeze," with the result that the foreigners wait a long time, they together with those who trade with them in private, will be condemned; and will be put in the cangue for one month in front of their shops. If there are foreigners who purposely violate the prohibitory regulations and secretly enter people's houses to trade, the goods dealt in privately will be confiscated. In the case of those [foreigners] who have not yet been given their (imperial) rewards (i.e., gifts) [in return for the tribute brought to the Chinese Emperor], there will be a consideration of a proportional diminution.
>
> All soldiers and commoners inside or outside the Residence [for Tributary Envoys] or neighboring it on any side, who on behalf of foreigners deal in prohibited goods, will be condemned to the cangue for a month, and banished to the border for military service for life. If there are those who take contraband implements of war, copper or iron, or such things, and sell them to foreigners to get a profit, according to the law for taking military implements out of the border in secret and thereby revealing affairs (of military im-

portance), the ringleaders' heads will be cut off and exposed as a warning to the multitude. At the time of trade, the Board of Ceremonies will issue a notice giving such official information.

It also proposed and imperially sanctioned that when a foreign merchant's vessel returns to its country, in addition to contraband goods, it shall not be allowed to take people of the interior (i.e., Chinese passengers), nor to export secretly such things as big beams, iron nails, oil, or hemp for making ships. Of rice and grain it may only take (enough for) provisions; it is not allowed to carry more. When trade is finished and it is time to return to their country, the Governor-General and Governor concerned shall select and depute virtuous and able officers who shall make a strict examination and put a stop to smuggling (Fairbank and Têng 1941:167–68).

The remarkable cases of "silent trade," in which the two trading sides never come face to face, is an extreme example of the fear of foreigners who come to trade, but the willingness nevertheless to trade with them because of the desire for the goods the foreigners bring. Trade is also controlled because the foreigners may belong to an economic system organized differently from ours—just like American trade with China today—which means that special agreements must be reached on what goods are to be traded and under what specific terms of trade. Such arrangements over terms of trade are also necessary whenever there is no international currency in use.

In sum, long-distance trade under aboriginal conditions was usually very different from modern commercial international trade. It was not a reflection of cost differentials; rather, goods were sought abroad that were not obtainable at home. It was not a continuous activity, but consisted rather of sporadic expeditions. It was typically confined to relatively few goods and there was no monetary standard linking together the different domestic systems of the traders (as was the case with our gold standard). Usually each side traded goods for other goods or for treasure that was not ordinary commercial money.[39] Except for specialist trading peoples like the Phoenicians and the Hausa, trade was rarely basic to livelihood. To import, not to export, was the prime impetus.

How can a government, palace, or king, under early state conditions, acquire goods from a distance? There seem to be six ways:

(1) By raid and plunder—war booty and ransom. "Better raid than

trade" was not an uncommon aboriginal point of view. To raid is manly, and, if successful, cheap; one doesn't have to give anything in return for what one gets. The Vikings did rather well in Ireland, England, France, Sicily, and elsewhere; piracy too is an old institution.

(2) By receiving tribute in kind or treasure from a weaker satellite, client-state, vassal kingdom, or satrapy. Danegeld to pay off the Vikings was an improvement from the viewpoints of both payer and receiver over the bloody raids that preceded it. It was also an extreme variant of tribute—an extortion really. Imperial emperors in China and kings in Africa regularly received various sorts of tribute payments from satellites. In early state societies, borders were frequently demarcated by taxes giving way either to tribute or to hostility. To "pay tribute" is to pay respect, to display deference, to give an earnest of peaceful intentions, and to placate the distant and more powerful sovereign in the hope that peace will continue to prevail. Tribute—of which there are several variants—is usually a respectful bribe paid in treasure or elite goods.

Tribute sometimes accompanies trade as a sort of entrance fee to elicit permission to trade, which, at the same time, declares the peaceful intentions and deference of the tribute payers. Here I again quote at length from an excellent and important article which deserves careful study by anyone interested in the nature of foreign trade in early states and empires (Fairbank and Têng 1941). It describes the salient characteristics of the tributary system during the Ch'ing dynasty of the Manchus (1648–1912) conducted with several dozen states and tribes. The article translates and analyzes many official documents relating to such tribute payments and also to the foreign trade which accompanied tribute. All but one of the quotations to follow are from the 110-page article by Fairbank and Têng (1941). The final quotation is from a shorter version of the article (Fairbank 1942), which adds to the longer article an interpretation of the demise of the tributary system. See also Yü (1967).

> . . . (1) that the tributary system was a natural outgrowth of the cultural preeminence of the early Chinese, (2) that it came to be used by the rulers of China for political ends of self-defense, (3) that in practice it had a very fundamental and important commercial [that is, foreign trade of some sort] basis, and (4) that it served as the medium for Chinese international relations and diplomacy.

It was, in short, a scheme of things entire, and deserves attention as one historical solution to problems of world-organization (Fairbank and Têng 1941:134).

. . . Chinese superiority over the barbarians had a cultural rather than a mere political basis; it rested less upon force than upon the Chinese way of life embodied in such things as the Confucian code of conduct and the use of the Chinese written language; the sign of the barbarian was not race or origin so much as non-adherence to this way of life. From this it followed . . . that those barbarians who wished to "come and be transformed" (lai-hua) and so participate in the benefits of (Chinese) civilization, must recognize the supreme position of the Emperor; for the Son of Heaven represented all mankind, both Chinese and barbarian, in his ritual sacrifices before the forces of nature. Adherence to the Chinese way of life automatically entailed the recognition of the Emperor's mandate to rule all men. This supremacy of the Emperor as mediator between Heaven and Earth was most obviously acknowledged in the performance of the kowtow, the three kneelings and nine prostrations to which European envoys later objected. It was also acknowledged by the bringing of a tribute of local produce, by the formal bestowal [by the Emperor] of a seal, comparable to the investiture of a vassal in medieval Europe, and in other ways. Thus the tributary system, as the sum total of these formalities, was the mechanism by which barbarous non-Chinese regions were given their place in the all-embracing Chinese political, and therefore ethical, scheme of things (Fairbank and Têng 1941:137–39).

In the intercourse between the Chinese state and the barbarians, commercial [i.e., foreign trade of some sort] relations became inseparably bound up with tributary. Trade was conducted by barbarian merchants [i.e., traders of some sort] who accompanied the tributary envoy to the frontier or even to the capital; sometimes it was conducted by the members of the [tribute] mission itself. That tribute was a cloak for trade has been a commonplace [in China] ever since merchants [i.e., traders of some sort] from the Roman orient arrived in China in 166 A.D. claiming to be envoys of Marcus Aurelius (Fairbank and Têng 1941:139).

Fairbank and Têng point out that although the barbarians (including the Europeans who came to China) may have viewed tribute payments as a sort of entrance fee to get on with the real business of foreign trade, the Chinese did not so view it. They quote T. F. Tsiang, "China and European Expansion," *Politica* 2, no. 5 (March 1936):3–4, as follows:

> If [foreign] relations there had to be, they must be of the suzerain-vassal type, acceptance of which meant to the Chinese acceptance of the Chinese ethic on the part of the barbarian. . . . It must not be assumed that the Chinese Court made a profit out of . . . tribute. The imperial gifts bestowed in return were usually more valuable than the tribute . . . Chinese statesmen before the latter part of the nineteenth century would have ridiculed the notion that national finance and wealth should be or could be promoted by means of international trade. On China's part the permission to trade [symbolized by the Chinese Court's acceptance of the tribute offering] was intended to be a mark of imperial bounty and a means of keeping the barbarians in the proper state of submissiveness . . . (Fairbank and Têng 1941:140).

Fairbank touches on a point of interest to this symposium by showing the connection between foreign trade and the decline of Imperial China, whose traditional tributary system could not cope with the massive commercial foreign trade the powerful capitalist barbarians of mid-nineteenth-century Europe and America insisted on bringing to China:

> . . . it seems anomalous that foreign trade could be considered in Chinese theory to be subordinate to tribute, but so it was. It was officially regarded as a boon granted to the barbarian, the necessary means to his sharing in the bounty of China and nothing more. No doubt this quixotic doctrine reflected the anti-commercial [anti-market] nature of the Chinese state, where the merchant was low in the social scale and beneath both the farmer and the bureaucrat who lived off the produce of the land. It was strengthened perhaps by the self-sufficiency of the empire which made supplies unnecessary from abroad. At all events, it was the tradition that foreign trade was an unworthy object for high policy, and this dogma was steadily reiterated in official documents down into the nineteenth century. Meanwhile foreign trade developed and grew ever larger within its ancient tributary framework.
>
> This brings us to a paradox in the history of modern China and one of the fundamental reasons for the collapse of the Confucian state. Trade and tribute in the Confucian view were cognate aspects of a single system of foreign relations. The important thing to the rulers of China was the moral value of tribute. The important thing for the barbarians was the material value of trade. The rub came when the foreign trade expanded and finally in some cases eclipsed tribute entirely, without changing the official myth. Tribute continued to dominate Chinese official thought after trade had begun to predominate in the practice of Chinese foreign relations.

In the modern period the Confucian bureaucracy tried to treat the new trading nations of the west as mere tributaries. Naturally they failed, being incapable of changing their immemorial theory to fit a new situation. The paradox in this tragedy lies in the fact that the new situation to which the Chinese government could not adjust itself had been created largely by the maritime trade of Chinese merchants. China had been for too long a continental empire, accustomed to relations across a land frontier. Her new maritime relations caught her unprepared and destroyed her ancient defense, the tributary system (Fairbank 1942:139).

(3) By receiving taxes in kind, labor, treasure, or anything else movable, from regionally distant and ecologically different constituencies over which the king had jurisdiction. The Inca (S. F. Moore 1958), the Lozi king (Gluckman 1943), and the king of Dahomey (Polanyi 1966: 44–49) received regularly scheduled taxes in kind from their regional constituencies. What the constituencies received in return from the king varied greatly. Most frequently, perhaps, they received military protection against outsiders, punishment of capital crimes by central authority, and emergency food in time of famine from official storehouses. (Much work remains to be done on variants of redistribution.)

It is not misleading to regard trade as an alternative to raid, tribute, and taxation as a method to acquire goods from a distance: "Reciprocity and redistribution were the dominant forms of integration in archaic Greece. Insofar as war, piracy, and raiding did not perform the functions of trade, i.e., insofar as trade was peaceful, it was mainly *gift-trade* between kings and chiefs" (Polanyi Mimeo. no. 3:29).

> The basis of the regime of the Spanish Conquest was the usurpation of political power and economic control achieved through military victory. Deliberately, the Spaniards utilized those of the aboriginal institutions that would further their own ends, attempted to destroy those which opposed their objectives, and let those disintegrate for which they had no need. Accordingly, they utilized such aboriginal institutions as the ancient system of tributes and status, slavery, forced labor tenantry, and cacao bean money. However, temples were demolished, idols smashed and religious codices burned. As to [indigenous] long-distance trade, they had no use for it and allowed it to disintegrate. They had other means of acquiring goods; during the Conquest by plunder and confiscation, later by tribute and in the markets (Chapman 1957:119; see also p. 122).

108

Polanyi contrasted external trade with raid, tax, and tribute by defining trade as a peaceful, two-sided exchange of goods. Raid is not peaceful, and tax and tribute transactions are not necessarily two-sided. There are, then, three characteristic forms of external trade, each of which has several variants:

(4) Gift exchange (reciprocity) between rulers (see Grierson 1959); at the local village level, reciprocal trade between kin groups or individual trade-partners (Malinowski 1922; Thomson, 1949; Clark 1965).

(5) Commercial (market) foreign trade, controlled or uncontrolled.

(6) Politically administered trade, elaborately analyzed by Polanyi and his associates.

CONCLUSION

The organizers of this symposium asked me to do two things: to explain Polanyi's analysis of long-distance trade and to write on anything else that might be of interest to archaeologists studying the economic aspects of early societies.[40]

To explain Polanyi's analysis of long-distance trade I have had to consider his wider theoretical system—his paradigm. To explain his paradigm I have had to describe the full scope of economic anthropology and therefore mention other bits of theory, partial paradigms, and paradigms which are variously employed by anthropologists, archaeologists, historians, economists, and others, to analyze static and dynamic aspects of aboriginal, colonial, and postcolonial economies.

Neither Polanyi nor anyone else has yet produced a general or universal paradigm for economic anthropology and early economic history. Polanyi had no theory of change under aboriginal conditions (although he said some interesting things about the two sets of aboriginal social and political conditions under which feudalism appears; see Polanyi 1971a).[41] He had no theory of change under colonial conditions (although he had some insights into the negative consequences for colonized peoples of European commercial trade practices; see Polanyi 1944: chap. 13 and its appendix). He had no theory of development and modernization, that is, Third World change under postcolonial conditions, a very new subject.

With regard to aboriginal economies, he did not himself explicitly consider village-level peasant economies (other than his occasional remarks on "householding"). Nor did he systematically consider the influence or role of physical environment and technology on economy. And he did not concern himself with aboriginal economic performance, that is, quantifiable output, its total amount, composition, and fluctuation. All these, I believe, are interesting areas of research for economic anthropology and are what I have in mind in saying that Polanyi's work is an important beginning, not a finished system of analysis.

If we are to judge Polanyi's theory by its explanatory power when put to use, what can be claimed for it? What are his analytical conclusions? To say that Polanyi's theory is more informative than formal (or Marxian) economics in the analysis of aboriginal economies is to say two things: (1) *Polanyi's theory answers some specific questions or solves some specific problems better.* For example, why did Trobriand Islanders engage in long-distance kula trade? I hesitate to speak for the formalists, but I would guess they would answer, "to maximize prestige" (much as U.S. businessmen maximize profits); or they would say that kula trade was simply an elaborate cover for the commercial trade that accompanied it. It was such a cover, but it was much more. Polanyi's theory (in my view, of course) leads to a deeper explanation: To acquire kula valuables in an aboriginal stateless society is to acquire the tangible means to make status payments and thereby acquire superior community roles (Big Man positions) and an entourage of followers. (And, of course, it is the audience of economic anthropologists who will assess the analytical conclusions and the evidence each theory adduces to support them.)

(2) The second way in which Polanyi's theory is more effective in the analysis of aboriginal economies is that *it concerns itself with a different and more revealing set of real-world structures and processes— different questions and problems—than does formal (or Marxian) economics.* This is the heart of the matter. Formal economics is designed to analyze market activities in modern industrial capitalism. Nonmarket activities (which nevertheless provision the community), government, religion, kinship, social organization, and social stratification are outside its sphere of analytical interest. Occasionally, a Veblen or a Galbraith complains that too much is being left out, and attempts an offbeat sort of socioeconomic analysis to show how current happenings of impor-

tance—affluence, the political and military implications of advanced technology—can be explained by going outside conventional economics to include social and political institutions. Economists respond by saying that Galbraith's stuff is interesting, but it is not economics. They are right. But Galbraith's stuff is nevertheless important.

Polanyi, like Galbraith, is asking a different set of questions from those formal economics permits one to ask. Polanyi's contribution was to contrive a paradigm for the socioeconomic organization of aboriginal bands and tribes and for the internal and external sectors of early state systems. He showed how the organization and functions of monetary objects, markets, and foreign trade systematically vary with the type of domestic economy and society in which they appear.[42]

Polanyi also shows the essential similarities among aboriginal economies in their social control over economic activities ("embeddedness" of economy in society, in his phrase). In so doing he points up the core of interest shared by archaeologists, economic anthropologists, and economic historians. It is easy for me to infer from his work what he himself obviously practiced but never spelled out in detail: that there is a subject to be studied consisting of aboriginal economies— that is, economies which are neither industrialized nor organized by market institutions—*wherever they occur*. It is encouraging to see archaeologists (for example, Renfrew 1972) making intelligent use of Polanyi's ideas and of other writings in economic anthropology.

There is a related subject consisting of the modern transformation of such aboriginal economies, the coming of land and labor markets, modern money, machines, and nation-states, *wherever they occur*. It is also encouraging to see development economists making intelligent use of economic anthropology (e.g., Adelman and Morris 1967). Indeed, economic historians of modern Europe and even economic theorists are now asking big historical and sociological questions, such as why Europe —rather than the impressive aboriginal civilizations of China or the Middle East—was the first to industrialize? (See Landes 1969:chap. 1; Kuznets 1966:chaps. 1, 10; Hicks 1969.) Unquestionably, Polanyi and the rest of us substantivists are the beneficiaries of a good deal of serendipity; social science trends together with real-world events create more and more interest in the workings of nonmarket economies and in the connections between economic and social organization.

Polanyi's conceptual distinctions and their application to specific aboriginal economies of time and place make it possible for us to unlearn the model of market economy as a universal referent. It was not an eccentric obsession on his part to hammer away at "formal" economics as a universal paradigm and at the special and linked form that commercial money, external commercial trade, and national markets took in nineteenth-century capitalism. To understand the economies—or sectors, such as foreign trade—of the Trobriand Islands and the Maya, one has to unlearn Robbins's *The Nature and Significance of Economic Science* and, indeed, Samuelson's *Principles,* which are about national and industrial market economies, and nothing else. Here, Polanyi confers a general perspective on the richness, diversity, and ingenuity of economic institutions in early societies that is in sharp contrast with the ethnocentric view of them as crude market links leading up to the modern market economy. Like our own, aboriginal economies provisioned their people and also made use of foreign trade and, frequently, some sort of money and marketplace. But the absence of national market integration, market money, and machine technology—the dominant characteristics of modern capitalism—meant that aboriginal economic organization was fundamentally different from ours, and so too their organization of foreign trade, money, and markets.

One final word: We archaeologists, anthropologists, and historians of primitive and early economies are dealing with subjects very much in need of theoretical formulation. Intelligent men still disagree utterly in their interpretations of the basic functioning of economies remote from our own. I recommend to all of us three books, none of which was written with us in mind, but all three of which, I think, contain important messages for us: Watson's *The Double Helix,* Kuhn's *The Structure of Scientific Revolutions,* and Wittgenstein's *Philosophical Investigations.*

Watson's may be regarded as a footnote to Kuhn's book because it illustrates (inadvertently) *one* of the reasons for heated controversy between colleagues disputing paradigms. Watson's unintended message for us is that even scientists who do work of first-order importance are capable of petty professional jealousy, naked professional vanity, and a pushy concern that their professional achievements in creating or extending paradigms be properly recognized and praised. It is uncomfortably true that the National Academy of Sciences is not far from Watergate.

Kuhn's book, itself a history-of-science paradigm describing the way physical science theories get born, mature, and are killed off, contains several messages for us. I could easily string together a dozen or more quotations from Kuhn which quite accurately characterize the sequential reactions to Polanyi's work, reactions by adherents and opponents. To anyone like myself who has tried to clarify and extend Polanyi's paradigm, Kuhn's book comes as a revelation because of the remarkable clarity and precision with which it describes what one has been up to all these years and why, indeed, one's writings are reacted to so differently by professional colleagues.

Wittgenstein's message to us is the need to be consciously aware of the meanings of the words we use if we are to avoid using concepts which inhibit the construction of theories capable of deep explanation of the real-world processes we analyze. I have yet to see a Marxian define *exploitation* in such a way that it does not fit the Soviet Union as well as the United States. The concept of economic "surplus" as that which causes aboriginal change is a superficial notion whose employment obscures the varied and complicated events that actually cause change (see the much more persuasive composite theory put forth by Renfrew 1972: chap. 21). The formalists' use of the term *maximizing* has become a reassuring ritual to them, a fingering of their conceptual beads, as it were. It is now so trivially used as a definitional identity as to mean nothing more than what people actually do, regardless of what they actually do. *Barter*, when meant as "moneyless transaction," nevertheless conveys to the reader the economists' meaning of "moneyless market exchange," and so kula and potlatch, when called barter, become transmogrified into ordinary commercial exchange. So too for *bride-price*.[43] All this is quite important, especially to the traditionally minded economic anthropologists and historians, those who do not use numbers in their writings, only words. Grahame Clark says it all very well:

> A basic condition for understanding the past is to avoid applying categories of thought and shades of meaning inappropriate to the period under review. This applies with special force to the study of the prehistoric past, by definition the phase of history most remote

from the present and for this very reason most likely to be misunderstood. . . . much of the controversy between those who write about prehistoric trade and those who deny its existence is semantic: it arises from the different meanings they attach to the word trade. If one takes a definition of trade proper to a society with an advanced division of labor and an economy based on money—if one chooses, for example, to define trade as an activity carried on by a class of traders for financial gain, it is understandable that no evidence for trade can be found in societies functioning at a simpler level, societies in which there is a bare minimum of specialization and to which the notion of profit in the sense we understand it may be quite foreign. Yet, if one sees it as, in the last resort, no more than the peaceful and systematic exchange of goods, one has no difficulty in recognizing that trade of a kind is practiced among even the most primitive societies known to ethnologists; and, by implication, one is entitled to seek for traces of it in the archeological record of history (Clark 1965:1).

NOTES

1. Note that when Polanyi (1960) contributed a paper to a symposium of archaeologists, he too found it necessary to describe his wider conceptual system before getting down to the two specific topics that were the subjects of his paper.

2. Unhappily, not so for the relatively new subject of precolonial African economic history. With no proof at all, Gray and Birmingham (1970:10) equate copper crosses found in burial mounds with commercial money, and then equate commercial money with commercial trade: "And currency, of course, in turn suggests a commerce already decisively more significant than subsistence-oriented trade." They should read Grierson (1959) for alternative explanations.

Conventional economics also has undergone technical and conceptual changes since the Second World War (see Dalton 1974: introduction). Applied mathematics has virtually revolutionized economic theory; computers and the refinement of input-output measurement and national income accounting have vastly increased the quantity and quality of statistical information to make policy. New conceptual schemes are also being contrived in response to changes in the real-world economies of industrial capitalism (e.g., Galbraith 1968), industrial communism (e.g., Wilczynski 1972), and the newly developing nations of the Third World (e.g., Adelman and Morris 1967).

3. Sebastian Green of the University of Sussex, who has just returned from doing fieldwork in Peru, has written a paper explaining the formalist-substantivist controversy in economic anthropology in Kuhn's terminology: "The Formalist-Substantivist Controversy: a Clarification." I hope Green's paper will be published when he finds time to revise it. Here I merely pose the problem that Green's persuasive paper addresses. I am grateful to Green for showing me that the contentious theoretical issues in economic anthropology are to be most clearly explained in Kuhn's terms, and for

referring me to Loasby (1971), who also illustrates the power of Kuhn's terminology by using it to consider paradigms in conventional economic theory.

4. This, of course, is the only portion of economic anthropology of interest to archaeologists. The other two historical subsets, change under European colonial conditions created since 1500, and change under very recent postcolonial conditions, are of no interest to them.

A word of explanation about these historical demarcations: Economic anthropology is empirically rooted in those parts of the world which were colonized after 1500: Latin America, Africa, Asia, Oceania, the Caribbean, and the Middle East. I regard European colonization as a watershed change, that is, a deep change, as I do the coming of political independence after the Second World War. From my point of view, therefore, anthropologists are interested in precolonial (aboriginal), colonial, and postcolonial economies. Europe and Japan differ in two ways: They were not colonized in modern times, and they have achieved a level of economic development, industrialization, and cultural modernization altogether higher than the anthropological set of societies in what we now call the Third World. For analyzing peasant-village and state-elite sectors (or levels) in Europe and Japan, I find it useful also to employ three historical periods: traditional economy (roughly, up to 1300 A.D. in West Europe and 1600 A.D. in Japan), early modernization (between 1300 and 1900 in West Europe), and late modernization (since 1900). See Dalton (1972).

5. If I am told that anthropologists did not do fieldwork in these early European and Asian economies, I would reply that neither did they do fieldwork among the precolonial Kwakiutl, Inca, or village Indian economies whose social, political, and economic organization they nevertheless are professionally interested in reconstructing.

6. It is important to bear in mind that modern social anthropology—Morgan, Boas, Malinowski, Radcliffe-Brown—began during the colonial period. The ethnographies of Malinowski on the Trobriand Islands, Evans-Pritchard on the Nuer, and even much more recent work, e.g., the excellent book by Strathern (1971) on Highland New Guinea, are able to portray "aboriginal" economies and societies in a special sense: they had not yet been *deeply* changed by European colonial policies, institutions, or activities (such as Christianity, cash cropping, European schools). But the fieldwork itself, of course, occurred in the colonial period of the societies studied. Archaeologists are concerned with aboriginal economies throughout the millennia during which any information at all is available; social anthropologists, really, are concerned with the very late phase of their aboriginal periods, as well, of course, as with change under colonial and postcolonial conditions.

7. The principal classical and neoclassical contributors to microeconomics (price theory) were Ricardo, Mill, Marshall, Jevons, Menger, Clark, Chamberlin, and Robinson. Robbins (1935) gives an elementary formulation of the concepts of price theory. His book is frequently referred to by the formalist economic anthropologists. Recent expository and critical writings that bear on the "applicability" of formal price theory as a universal paradigm are those of Little (1950), Dalton (1961), and Loasby (1971). Loasby's paper is particularly illuminating because he employs Kuhn's terminology and insights concerning paradigms.

8. Note that Herskovits (1952), in what remains to this day the only extensive book-length treatment of economic anthropology—Belshaw (1965) and Nash (1966)

are 150-page surveys of parts of the subject—employs concepts from all three paradigms, formal, Marxian, and substantive economics.

9. Briefly, but distinctly, Polanyi also criticizes Marxian concepts as they are employed by archaeologists and anthropologists to analyze aboriginal economies. His point is that Marx erroneously generalized backward to early economies and forward to future economies what was true only for nineteenth-century industrial capitalism.

10. A book (Polanyi 1966) and two articles (Polanyi 1971a, 1971b) appeared posthumously. Mrs. Polanyi and Harry Pearson are preparing to publish two or more volumes of Polanyi's manuscripts and English translations of his early writings in German and Hungarian. It is a matter of deep personal and professional regret to me that Polanyi got such a late start in academic research and writing. He was born in 1886. The first of his three major works, *The Great Transformation*, was published in 1944 when he was fifty-eight. He began teaching economic history at Columbia in 1947 at age sixty-one, and had to retire from teaching in 1953, at age sixty-seven. His second big book (edited with Conrad Arensberg and Harry Pearson), *Trade and Market*, appeared in 1957, when he was seventy-one. Most of the research for *Dahomey and the Slave Trade*, 1966, was done in 1950. When I reread his published works and unpublished manuscripts, I am continually astonished at the number of suggestive insights that he had no time to develop, among them "operational devices" (to be mentioned later in this paper), "primitive feudalism and the feudalism of decay" (in Polanyi 1971a), "money and state-building" (Polanyi 1966; chap. 11; see also Vidal-Naquet 1972).

11. Almost certainly I will leave some out because I haven't encountered them in print. I have not myself done serious research on change under aboriginal conditions. All my published work is about the static structure and performance of aboriginal economies (e.g., Dalton 1962; 1965) and change under modern colonial and postcolonial conditions (e.g., Dalton 1971a: introduction).

12. Polanyi was impressed by Thurnwald's theory and devoted several lectures to it in his course at Columbia. The 1932 translation of Thurnwald into English is a selection from his five volume work *Die menschliche Gesellschaft*.

13. And neither of which, I think, is of direct interest to archaeologists; however I must sketch them in for the reader to appreciate the difficulties and complexities involved in creating theory in economic anthropology. What follows on change under colonial and postcolonial conditions is extremely compressed.

14. I do not think that universal theories of social change—theories which assert that a single factor, such as property ownership or technology, is the strategic prime mover under all historical conditions—are useful, for two reasons: (1) The forces of change in the precolonial, colonial, and postcolonial periods differ essentially. To be sure, in all three periods, economic, technological, social, political, and cultural changes occurred; but their quality was different. The coming of settled agriculture and, millennia later, the coming of industrialization are both economic and technological changes, but their consequences are utterly different. In the precolonial period, I think that famine, epidemic, warfare, and military conquest were more frequent inducers of deep change than were economic and technological innovations. (2) It has always seemed to me that biological evolution is a misleading model for social change because in all historical periods societies are subject to large external shocks

116

and idiosyncratic events and rulers. It is difficult to believe that the English, the French, and the Russian revolutions, Napoleon, Lenin, Stalin, Hitler, Roosevelt, and Mao Tse-tung, the American Civil War, and the First and Second World Wars were not important causes of deep change. In the course of writing this paper I have come across Renfrew's (1972) impressive analysis of the emergence of civilization in the Aegean. I note that his basic idea of subsystems mutually interacting to produce multiplier effects is also what one sociologically inclined development economist suggests for postcolonial development as "cumulative causation" and "spread effects." See Myrdal (1957) especially chaps. 1–3. See also Douglas (1962) and Epstein (1962; 1973) for empirical examples of cumulative causation.

15. For useful collections of case studies and bits of theory of change under colonial conditions, see Bohannan and Plog (1967), Wallerstein (1966), and Dalton (1971a).

16. Such a unified theory of change under colonial conditions would not be anything like the single-factor theories of change of Marx and the Energy/Evolutionists. Rather, it would include ideal types, such as those given by Balandier (1966) for the "colonial situation," and by Dalton (1969) for "degenerative change," "cash-income earning without development," and "microdevelopment"; models of "dualism" and of sequential change under colonial conditions, such as those given by Boeke (1942) and Geertz (1963) for Indonesia, and Wolf (1959) for Latin America, and the general economic case of dualism in Lewis (1954). Also, theoretical insights are to be had by putting specific questions to colonial situations: Why didn't commercial foreign trade and investment with Europe and America yield more development and modernization to the colonies? Some answers are to be found in Singer (1950), Watson (1958), and Myrdal (1957).

17. The works of B. Moore (1966) and of Hunter (1967; 1969) are more descriptive than explicitly theoretical; but both contain important insights into the historical and present-day processes of economic development and cultural modernization. For brief summaries of some of the work mentioned here, see Dalton (1971a: introduction; 1974: chap. 7).

18. In several of my writings and edited volumes I have tried to demonstrate the importance to economic anthropology of the work done by historians and other non-anthropologists. See Dalton (1967; 1971a; 1971b; 1971c; 1972; 1974).

19. In this section I shall treat as a single set of ideas Polanyi's writings, those of his *Trade and Market* associates, and the extensions, clarifications, and elaborations of Polanyi's work by Bohannan, Sahlins, Neale, and myself.

20. The two dozen or more articles and chapters relating to this controversy are listed in the bibliographical notes in Dalton (1971b; 1971c). A sampling of the mixed professional reactions to this controversy is reflected in the twenty-four brief comments accompanying Dalton (1969), and the further comments on the article by Frank (1970), a Marxist, and Dobyns (1971), from the viewpoint of acculturation and applied anthropology.

21. But whose superficial treatment of economic anthropology I strongly criticized in a review of his 150-page textbook purporting to survey what in the present paper (see table 1) is called the full gamut of aboriginal, colonial, and postcolonial economies. Nash's assessment of Polanyi and the substantivists was rather more favorable

before I reviewed his book. In Kuhn's terms, economic anthropology is still in the "pre-paradigm" stage: no one theory (in any of the branches of the subject) is so widely adhered to as to knock out its rivals; hence, vituperative disputes. "The pre-paradigm period, in particular, is regularly marked by frequent and deep debates over legitimate methods, problems, and standards of solution, though these serve rather to define schools than to produce agreement. . . . Furthermore debates like these do not vanish once and for all with the appearance of a paradigm. Though almost non-existent during periods of normal science, they recur regularly just before and during scientific revolutions, the periods when paradigms are first under attack and then subject to change." (Kuhn 1970:47–48).

22. And the Marxians, asking their single question—Is Polanyi good for the Revolution or bad for the Revolution?—decide he is bad (see Frank 1970). The egregious Harold Schneider, who in neither learning anything nor forgetting anything ensures that he is always on the cutting edge of retrogression, continues to make an industry out of attributing to Polanyi and me positions we never held (see, for example, Schneider 1969:89–91). It seems likely to me that the caustic language used by several anthropologists to heap scorn upon the writings of Polanyi and myself is due to the threats we pose to them: (1) We are economists, not anthropologists. I note that Bohannan and Sahlins are not vituperatively criticized, even though they share with me Polanyi's static paradigm for aboriginal economies. (2) Polanyi and I draw on empirical case studies and analytical writings outside of social anthropology—early European economic history, archaeology, comparative economic systems, economic development, agricultural economics—as well as the writings of anthropologists. (3) And, of course, to present a new paradigm is to challenge the one preferred by the users of the vituperative language. Eric Wolf reacts to my critique of his Marxian analysis of peasant economies (Dalton 1972) by calling it "muddle," "superannuated social Darwinism," "a rehash of stale concepts," and "ethnocentrism" (Wolf 1972: 410–11). In response to Nash's dismissal of us as "high level confusion," I mention that Polanyi's The Great Transformation, 1944, is now in its twelfth printing, has just been translated into French, and is being translated into Japanese and German; that Trade and Market in the Early Empires, 1957, has just appeared in paperback, and is about to appear in French translation; that Dahomey and the Slave Trade, 1966, has recently appeared in Hungarian translation and at present is being translated into Japanese; and that Polanyi's collection of essays, Primitive, Archaic, and Modern Economies, is being translated into French, Italian, Hungarian, and German. Nash's dismissal of Polanyi and his associates as "high level confusion," then, seems to have been a bit premature. From all this one learns the wisdom of the British aphorism "It is no use kicking against the pricks."

23. Polanyi himself never dealt explicitly with the village-level sector of aboriginal peasant economies beyond some sketchy remarks on "householding." He meant by "primitive" economies what anthropologists would call the precolonial economies of bands and tribes—the Arapesh of New Guinea, the Trobriand Islanders—whose economies are furthest removed from our own. He meant by "archaic" economies early state systems in which markets (and cash used as means of commercial exchange) were not importantly present. For these, he considered the economic aspects of the governmental sector and external trade, but not their village-level groupings. Neale (1957a) and I (Dalton 1972) have extended his analysis to such traditional, village-level peasant economies.

24. Polanyi understood that there were aspects of aboriginal economies he was not including in his analysis, such as ecology and technology: "Process and institutions together form the economy. Some students stress the material resources and equipment—the ecology and technology—which make up the process; others, like myself, prefer to point to the institutions through which the economy is organized" (Polanyi 1968:307). Neither did Polanyi include in his analysis of aboriginal economies matters relating to their productivity or measurable economic performance, that is, the amounts and variety of goods produced, the composition of total output, or fluctuations in output. He is concerned with "the institutions through which the economy is organized," principally in bands, tribes, and the governmental sector of early state systems. And, of course, the institutions of money, external trade, and markets, which he analyzed in detail.

25. Money, monetary objects, and valuables are especially important and especially complicated in aboriginal economies. Later in this chapter I shall suggest and then explain some terminological distinctions that help clarify the meaning of these terms and their specific organization and usage in very different economies: the distinctions between what I shall call "modern money," "primitive money," and "primitive valuables"; and the need to indicate the mode of transaction (reciprocity, redistribution, market exchange) for each. The mode of transaction indicates the purpose of the transaction in which the monetary object or valuable enters. See Dalton (1965; 1971d).

26. Let us simply call industrial capitalism in Europe and America since 1930 "welfare state capitalism," to differentiate it from the "laissez-faire capitalism" of the nineteenth century; for a detailed explanation of these distinctions, see Myrdal (1960); Dalton (1974: chaps. 1, 3, 5). Briefly, welfare state capitalism differs from laissez-faire capitalism in five ways: (1) Governments control a larger number of prices and markets to increase or stabilize the incomes of selected persons or groups, e.g., minimum wage laws, agricultural price supports. (2) Governments provide a wider range of free or subsidized services, e.g., education, health care and housing, and of transfer payments to the unemployed, the indigent, and the elderly. (3) Governments spend and tax a larger amount; these days, between 30 and 40 percent of gross national product. (Before 1914, in peace time it was under 10 percent.) (4) Governments take responsibility to contrive policy to assure satisfactory macroeconomic performance of the national economy, that is, deliberately to affect the level of employment, rate of growth, the price level, income distribution, and the balance of payments. Finally, (5) in most welfare state capitalist economies—particularly in England and Sweden—government owns a minor but significant amount of productive enterprise (railroads, coal mines, some manufacturing), usually less than one-third of all producing firms (as measured either by employment or the value of output as a fraction of total output).

27. Even today, something like 80 percent of American, British, and West European economists are concerned exclusively with modern capitalist economy. After 1928, when the Russian Communists began central planning, the subject of Soviet economy came into being (that is, as a university subject with courses, seminars, publications, and research specialists), and it grew with the establishment of a dozen more Communist economies in Eastern Europe, Asia, and Latin America after the Second World War. But it engages very few economists as a field for research and teaching. More are now engaged in economic development of the Third World, an

even more recent field in economics than Communist economies. It is perhaps worth mentioning to archaeologists that preindustrial economic history does not engage many economists either. Except for American Indians (studied by anthropologists), the U.S. had no "aboriginal" economy in the sense that France, England, and Japan in the year 900 A.D. had aboriginal economies. Overwhelmingly, Americans who specialize in economic history specialize in American economic history, and therefore have no professional interest in nonmarket economies. There are, of course, relatively few economic historians in any country having a professional interest in medieval economic history of Europe, or in earlier periods. Mainstream economics is about industrial capitalism today. Several eminent economists have recently begun to pay serious attention to preindustrial, nonmarket economies: see Kuznets (1966), Robinson (1970), Hicks (1969), Hagen (1962).

28. Therefore, wherever we find monetary objects or valuables *not* having the characteristics of dollars—kula bracelets, Yap stones, potlatch coppers—it is because markets are either absent, or, if present, petty; these primitive valuables play special social roles in economies (polities and societies) different from our own; so too where foreign trade is organized differently from our own.

29. The failure to appreciate the quantitative importance of domestic and international market trade that makes it sensible to call nineteenth- and twentieth-century European and American economies "capitalist" economies leads some economic historians (e.g., Pirenne 1914) to equate "capitalism" with the mere *presence* of domestic or foreign commercial transactions (no matter how narrow the range of items bought and sold, or how small the quantity of such market transactions); and so "capitalism" is seen wherever markets of *any* sort are present. But medieval England (Postan 1973), Bohannan's Tiv of the 1940s (Bohannan and Bohannan 1968), the United States in 1776 (and in 1973), and the USSR at present all contain markets, that is, ordinary purchase and sale transactions; the markets, however, are of utterly different sorts and of utterly different importance to their markedly different economies and societies.

30. I am presently engaged in doing such a piece of research.

31. As Polanyi indicates in the quotation just cited, a variant of redistribution occurs in hunting and gathering bands—stateless societies—in the form of sharing or pooling of the hunt or catch; in this sense of sharing among a small, intimate, local group, redistribution goes on within households in all sorts of old and new economies.

32. For examples of nonmarket transactions in modern economies today, see Dillon (1968) and Titmuss (1970).

33. For more detailed explanations, see Pearson (1957b), Polanyi (1968: chap. 12), and Dalton (1971d; 1972).

34. Empirical descriptions of primitive monies abound, e.g., Einzig (1948), Quiggen (1949). We have only recently, however, begun to construct a *theory* of primitive money. See Polanyi (1957; 1968: chap. 8), Bohannan (1959), Douglas (1958; 1967), Dalton (1965; 1966; 1971d), Lewis (1973).

35. Another reason why it has been so difficult to create a theory of primitive money is because it is so difficult to unlearn the paradigm or model of modern money. Economic anthropologists used sterling or francs as a model of "real" money, and any valuable which did not have the characteristics of sterling or francs was simply

judged not to be money; see, for example, Firth (1929a). Unhappily, those who used sterling as a model of real money did not then go on to say exactly why the kula valuables and potlatch coppers were important; *why* were they worth acquiring?

36. A widely reported exception is what Bohannan and I (1962) called "emergency conversion," usually a famine situation in which the primitive valuables (or, indeed, slaves or even children) are sold to strangers for food.

37. The identifying seals placed on vats of foodstuffs in storehouses are another example of an operational device (see Ventris and Chadwick 1956; Renfrew 1972). Unhappily, one rash interpreter of Mycenae interprets the vats of foodstuffs identified by seals as being in "the house of the merchant," thereby implicitly assuming the presence in Mycenae of commercial-market transactions (why else "merchant"?). There is not the slightest shred of evidence for such supposition. The vats identified by seals were in a storehouse of some sort; but why not a palace storehouse rather than "the house of the merchant"? Note that the emperor of China conferred seals on tributaries who came to China to trade. See Fairbank and Yêng (1941).

38. I am reminded that Polanyi's opening lecture, on the place of economies in societies, in the course of lectures he gave in General Economic History at Columbia in 1950, contained a similar theme, namely that the uncontrolled market model as a paradigm for all economies was being shaken by three happenings: (1) the writings of economic anthropologists, like Malinowski on the Trobrianders and Margaret Mead on the Arapesh of New Guinea; (2) mounting criticism of Marx's economic determination of history as a general theory; and (3) the recent momentous enlargement of political control in economies and societies between 1930 and 1950, i.e., central planning in Russia; the Nazi system in Germany; the American New Deal; the first Labor government in Britain.

39. I avoid using the term *barter* because it is used in two different meanings which must be kept distinct: a moneyless exchange or transaction of *any* sort; and a moneyless market exchange, which is what economists usually mean by barter, implicitly assuming by such usage that market exchange is the only known mode of transaction.

40. I do not think that Polanyi's work bears in any direct way on two of the problems of interest to this symposium: how ancient trade relates to the rise and fall of civilizations; and research strategies for archaeology. The closest he comes on the first problem, I believe, is in his remarks about archaic economic institutions and those operational devices special to aboriginal state systems, and in his economic embellishment of Thurnwald's analysis of the emergence of states from smaller, simpler, less stratified social groupings. One account of these matters appears in *Dahomey and the Slave Trade*, especially the introductory chapter called "Perspective," and chapter 11:

> The economist is indeed at a loss to account for the emergence in an early society of an effective demand of first magnitude for a means of currency as such. The notion that economic developments are mainly referable to what we have become used to calling "economic interests" is apt to be misleading. Rather, weighty events in the sphere of state-building and of economic organization may have accounted for the introduction of currency systems in West Africa. This may have been the source of the demand for money objects to be used as currency and consequently of the finance capable of supplying the purchasing

power for their acquisition. The economic historian may have to seek an explanation in the rise of new empires, or even in the need for a popular currency which would speed the functioning of local food markets. Cowrie legend seems to point in this direction. . . . The acting force that shaped and organized the economy was the state, in the person of the king. Food, money, and market are all statemade. . . . From Pharaonic Egypt and Babylon to the empires of the Niger, the state-building drive appears as a secular force within the sphere of economic organization. The factors that doubtless pressed toward statehood as such are a different matter. Together with the military factors, they belonged to the economic prehistory of the state. But once set on the course of state-building, the monarchy was engaged in the organizing of an army and its provisioning "in kind," the launching of a currency as an instrument of taxation, and the creating of markets [marketplaces] and of small change for the distribution of the food. This again involved state-made "equivalents" which determined the rate at which staples could be substituted for one another in the payment of taxes and in rationing [in the sense of paying out rations]. These performances of government concerning the economy are here recalled from previous chapters to provide a more realistic approach to the origin and functioning of the cowrie currency which was strung by the king's wives in Dahomey for the provisioning of the conquered peoples in the local food markets (Polanyi 1966:184, 186–7).

On the second problem of this symposium: I feel it to be unseemly for me to suggest research strategies to archaeologists. Rather, in this paper I have tried to explain the work done by Polanyi and his associates in the hope that our work might be of use in interpreting the economies of prehistory.

41. There is much more in his lecture notes and unpublished manuscripts about change under aboriginal conditions, but it is tentative, not nearly as elaborately spelled out as the work he published. Pearson (1957b) and I (Dalton 1960; 1963) severely criticize the theories of change under aboriginal conditions which attribute change to the appearance of economic "surpluses." In addition to Polanyi's short piece published posthumously, "Primitive Feudalism and the Feudalism of Decay" (which is spelled out at much greater length in his lecture notes), he published two other short accounts concerning change under aboriginal conditions, which were referred to in the previous footnote, on the roles of operational devices and of monetary institutions in the formation of states (see Polanyi 1966: "Perspective" and chap. 11, the latter of which is reprinted in his essays, *Primitive, Archaic, and Modern Economies*).

Polanyi makes another suggestion that may interest archaeologists and anthropologists who are concerned with the differences between a "civilization," a "primitive" society, and a "modern" society. What Polanyi called "archaic economic institutions," such as ports of trade and operational devices used in palace economies, are, I think, special to the early state systems that archaeologists call "civilizations." If Polanyi's point is empirically correct, then he has isolated an economic aspect of aboriginal civilizations not shared by primitive or modern societies:

The word "archaic" that was dropped from systematic anthropology as merely of esthetic and cultural connotation may have to be restored to denote a sociological phase intervening between the "primitive" and the "modern." But the historian will have to apply it with caution, if he is not to find himself entangled in a circular definition. The interconnected phenomena of state and economy, institution and society—each of them sometimes called archaic—lack an authentic priority to the claim of being the name-giving category. Not states and societies, not even economies as a whole should be regarded as archaic. We shall prefer the genetic approach describing as "archaic" those *economic institutions* which do not yet appear in primitive communities but are no longer found in societies where the use of money as a means of [market] exchange is already common (Polanyi 1966:xxxv; see also pp. 173–74).

42. Although *The Great Transformation* is principally devoted to the market organization of nineteenth-century capitalism, it contains much that is related to Polanyi's *Trade and Market*, and *Dahomey*, writings that engage the interest of archaeologists and anthropologists. For example, in *Trade and Market* and in several of his journal articles reprinted in *Primitive, Archaic, and Modern Economies*, Polanyi showed how, in aboriginal economies, monetary objects were used in noncommercial payments (such as bridewealth, bloodwealth, taxes, and tribute); also how aboriginal external trade was frequently organized as gift exchange and politically administered trade. *The Great Transformation* attempts to answer two big historical questions that Polanyi thought to be very important: How did early foreign trade become market trade? And how did early treasure and primitive valuables come to be market-exchange money? The answers are to be found in the economic history of Europe over the thousand years ending in the late eighteenth century, in the Industrial Revolution. Very elaborately, Polanyi shows how external trade, money, and markets originated independently of one another; then, how they became fused in the self-regulating market system—modern capitalism.

43. See Finley (1970) for a superb example of how the careful translation of key words is necessary to make sense of Aristotle's "economics."
One source of semantic ambiguity is that American and English writers attach different meanings to the same words without being aware that they are doing so. Most, but not all, Americans use *market exchange* and *commercial* as exact synonyms. Some British (and a few American) writers use the words *commerce* and *commercial* as synonyms for *trade*, thereby unintentionally converting all trade to market trade, without, apparently, being aware that there are nonmarket (noncommercial in the American sense) forms of trade, i.e., reciprocal and administered trade. Here is an example of British usage, *commercial* being used as a synonym for what I should prefer to call *trade of an unspecified sort*, in fourteenth- and fifteenth-century Africa: "The strictly commercial [i.e., trade of an unspecified sort] importance of copper is clearly seen at Ingombe Ilede. The cruciform ingots have remarkably similar weights; the trade wire is bent in standardized lengths, which obviously had an established value in long-distance trade circles" (Fagan 1970:33). On pages 37–38, Fagan uses *commercial* to mean *trade of an unspecified sort* five times. The result, inadvertently, is to suggest—surely not only to Americans—rampant market trade, when, in fact, the mode of transaction is entirely unknown, that is to say, it is entirely unknown whether it was gift trade, politically administered trade, or market (commercial) trade. Compare such usage with the careful terminology used by Clark (1965) analyzing quite similar transactions.

References

ADELMAN, I. AND C. T. MORRIS
1967   *Society, Politics, and Economic Development* (Baltimore: Johns Hopkins University Press).

ARNOLD, ROSEMARY
1957a "A Port of Trade: Whydah on the Guinea Coast," in *Trade and Market in the Early Empires*, ed. K. Polanyi, C. M. Arensberg, and H. W. Pearson (New York: Free Press).
1957b "Separation of Trade and Market: Great Market of Whydah," in *Trade and Market in the Early Empires*, ed. K. Polanyi, C. M. Arensberg, and H. W. Pearson (New York: Free Press).

BALANDIER, G.
1966   "The Colonial Situation: A Theoretical Approach," in *Social Change: The Colonial Situation*, ed. I. Wallerstein (New York: John Wiley & Sons).

BELSHAW, C. S.
1965   *Traditional Exchange and Modern Markets* (Englewood Cliffs, N.J.: Prentice-Hall).

BENET, FRANCISCO
1957   "Explosive Markets: The Berber Highlands," in *Trade and Market in the Early Empires*, ed. K. Polanyi, C. M. Arensberg, and H. W. Pearson (New York: Free Press).

BLOCH, M.
1967   "Natural Economy or Money Economy: A Pseudo-dilemma," in *Land and Work in Medieval Europe* (London: Routledge and Kegan Paul).

BOEKE, J. H.
1942   *The Structure of Netherlands Indian Economy* (New York: Institute of Pacific Relations).

BOHANNAN, P.
1959   "The Impact of Money on an African Subsistence Economy," *The Journal of Economic History* 19:491–503. (Reprinted in Dalton 1967.)
1960   "Africa's Land," *The Centennial Review* 4:439–49. (Reprinted in Dalton 1967).

BOHANNAN, P. AND L. BOHANNAN
1968   *Tiv Economy*. Northwestern University African Studies No. 20 (Evanston: Northwestern University Press).

BOHANNAN, P. AND G. DALTON (EDS.)
1962   *Markets in Africa*. Northwestern University African Studies No. 9 (Evanston: Northwestern University Press).

BOHANNAN, P. AND F. PLOG (EDS.)
1967   *Beyond the Frontier: Social Process and Cultural Change* (New York: Doubleday & Co.).

BURLING, R.

1962 "Maximization Theories and the Study of Economic Anthropology," *American Anthropologist* 62:802–21.

CANCIAN, F.

1966 "Maximization as Norm, Strategy, and Theory: A Comment on Programmatic Statements in Economic Anthropology," *American Anthropologist* 69:465–69. (Reprinted in LeClair and Schneider 1968.)

CHAPMAN, A. C.

1957 "Port of Trade Enclaves in Aztec and Maya Civilizations," in *Trade and Market in the Early Empires*, ed. K. Polanyi, C. M. Arensberg, and H. W. Pearson (New York: Free Press).

CHILDE, V. G.

1936 *Man Makes Himself* (London: Franklin Watts).

CIPOLLA, C. M. (ED.)

1970 *The Economic Decline of Empires* (London: Methuen & Co.).

CLARK, G.

1965 "Traffic in Stone Axe and Adze Blades," *The Economic History Review*, 18:1–28.

CODERE, H.

1951 *Fighting with Property: A Study of Kwakiutl Potlatching and Warfare, 1792–1930* (New York: J. J. Augustin).

COOK, C. S.

1966 "The Obsolete 'Anti-market' Mentality: A Critique of the Substantivist Approach to Economic Anthropology," *American Anthropologist* 68:323–45. (Reprinted in LeClair and Schneider 1968.)

DALTON, G.

1960 "A Note of Clarification on Economic Surplus," *American Anthropologist* 62:483–90. (Reprinted in Dalton 1971b.)

1961 "Economic Theory and Primitive Society," *American Anthropologist* 63:1–25. (Reprinted in LeClair and Schneider 1968; also in Dalton 1971b.)

1963 "Economic Surplus, Once Again," *American Anthropologist* 65:389–94. (Reprinted in Dalton 1971b.)

1965 "Primitive Money," *American Anthropologist* 67:44–65. (Reprinted in Dalton 1971b.)

1966 "Bridewealth versus Brideprice," *American Anthropologist* 68:732–38. (Reprinted in Dalton 1971b.)

1967 *Tribal and Peasant Economies* (New York: Doubleday & Co.).
(ed.)

1969 "Theoretical Issues in Economic Anthropology," *Current Anthropology* 10: 63–102. (Reprinted in Dalton 1971b.)

1971a *Economic Development and Social Change: The Modernization of Village*
(ed.) *Communities*. American Museum Sourcebooks in Anthropology Series (New York: Doubleday & Co.).

1971b *Economic Anthropology and Development* (New York: Basic Books).

1971c *Studies in Economic Anthropology* (Washington, D.C.: American Anthro-
(ed.) pological Association).

1971d "Traditional Tribal and Peasant Economies: An Introductory Survey of Economic Anthropology" (Reading, Mass.: Addison-Wesley Modular Publications).

1972 "Peasantries in Anthropology and History," *Current Anthropology* 13:385–415. (Reprinted in Dalton 1971b.)

1974 *Economic Systems and Society: Capitalism, Communism, and the Third World* (Harmondsworth, Eng.: Penguin Books).

DAVENPORT, W. H.

1961 "Primitive and Civilized Money in the Santa Cruz Islands," in *Symposium: Patterns of Land Utilization and Other Papers*, ed. V. E. Garfield. Proceedings of the 1961 Annual Spring Meeting of the American Ethnological Society (Seattle).

DILLON, W. D.

1968 *Gifts and Nations* (New York: Macmillan Co.).

DOBYNS, H. F.

1971 "On the Economic Anthropology of Postcolonial National Development," *Current Anthropology* 12:393–96.

DOUGLAS, M.

1958 "Raffia Cloth Distribution in the Lele Economy," *Africa* 31:109–22. (Reprinted in Dalton 1967).

1962 "Lele Economy Compared with the Bushong: A Study of Economic Backwardness," in *Markets in Africa*, ed. P. Bohannan and G. Dalton (Evanston: Northwestern University Press). (Reprinted in LeClair and Schneider 1968; also in Dalton 1971a.)

1967 "Primitive Rationing: A Study in Controlled Exchange," in *Themes in Economic Anthropology*, ed. R. Firth (London: Tavistock Publications).

EINZIG, P.

1948 *Primitive Money* (London: Pergamon Press).

EPSTEIN, T. S.

1962 *Economic Development and Social Change in South India* (Manchester, Eng.: Manchester University Press).

1973 *South India, Yesterday, Today, Tomorrow* (London: Macmillan & Co.).

FAGAN, B. M.

1970 "Early Trade and Raw Materials in South Central Africa," in *Precolonial African Trade: Essays on Trade in Central and Eastern Africa before 1900*, ed. R. Gray and D. Birmingham (London: Oxford University Press).

FAIRBANK, J. K.

1942 "Tributary Trade and China's Relations with the West," *The Far Eastern Quarterly* 1:129–49.

FAIRBANKS, J. K. AND S. Y. TÊNG

1941 "On the Ch'ing Tributary System," *Harvard Journal of Asiatic Studies* 6:135–247.

FINLEY, M. I.

1957 "The Mycenaean Tablets and Economic History," *Economic History Review* 10:128–41.

1970 "Aristotle and Economic Analysis," *Past and Present* 47:3–25.

1971 "Archaeology and History," *Daedalus* 100:168–86.

FIRTH, R.

1929a "Currency, Primitive," in *Encyclopaedia Britannica*, 14th ed. (London).

1929b *Primitive Economics of the New Zealand Maori* (Wellington, N. Z.: Routledge and Kegan Paul).

1951 *The Elements of Social Organization* (London: Watts).

1967 "Themes in Economic Anthropology: A General Comment," in *Themes in Economic Anthropology*, ed. R. Firth (London: Tavistock Publications).

1972 "Methodological Issues in Economic Anthropology," *Man* 7:467–75.

FRANK, A. G.

1970 "On Dalton's 'Theoretical Issues in Economic Anthropology,'" *Current Anthropology* 11:67–71.

FURNIVAL, J. S.

1948 *Colonial Policy and Practice* (Cambridge, Eng.: Cambridge University Press).

GALBRAITH, J. K.

1968 *The New Industrial State* (Boston: Houghton Mifflin Co.)

GEERTZ, C.

1968 *Agricultural Involution: The Process of Ecological Change in Indonesia* (Berkeley and Los Angeles: University of California Press).

GERSCHENKRON, A.

1962 *Economic Backwardness in Historical Perspective* (Cambridge, Mass.: Harvard University Press).

1968 *Continuity in History and Other Essays* (Cambridge, Mass.: Harvard University Press, Belknap Press).

1970 *Europe in the Russian Mirror* (Cambridge, Eng.: Cambridge University Press).

GLUCKMAN, M.

1943 "Essays on Lozi Land and Royal Property," in *Rhodes-Livingstone Papers*, No. 10.

GOODFELLOW, D. M.

1939 *Principles of Economic Sociology* (London: Routledge and Kegan Paul).

GRAY, R. AND D. BIRMINGHAM

1970 "Some Economic and Political Consequences of Trade in Central and Eastern Africa in the Precolonial Period," in *Precolonial African Trade: Essays on Trade in Central and Eastern Africa before 1900*, ed. R. Gray and D. Birmingham (London: Oxford University Press).

GRIERSON, P.

1959 "Commerce in the Dark Ages: A Critique of the Evidence," *Transactions of the Royal Historical Society*, Fifth Series, 9:123–40. (Reprinted in Dalton 1971c.)

HAGEN, E. E.

1962 *On the Theory of Social Change* (Homewood, Ill.: Dorsey Press).

HERSKOVITS, M. J.

1938 *Acculturation: The Study of Culture Contact* (New York: Alfred A. Knopf).

1940 *The Economic Life of Primitive Peoples* (New York: Alfred A. Knopf).

1952 *Economic Anthropology* (New York: Alfred A. Knopf).

HICKS, J.

1969 *A Theory of Economic History* (London: Oxford University Press).

HOBSBAWM, E.
1964   Introduction to K. Marx, *Pre-capitalist Economic Formations* (London: Lawrence & Wishart).

HUMPHREYS, S. C.
1969   "History, Economics, and Anthropology: The Work of Karl Polanyi," *History and Theory* 8:165–212.

HUNTER, G.
1967   *The Best of Both Worlds?* (London: Institute of Race Relations).
1969   *Modernizing Peasant Societies* (London: Institute of Race Relations).

KEYNES, J. M.
1936   *The General Theory of Employment, Interest, and Money* (New York: Harcourt, Brace).

KOSMINSKY, E. A.
1956   *Studies in the Agrarian History of England in the Thirteenth Century* (London: Oxford University Press).

KUHN, T. S.
1970   *The Structure of Scientific Revolutions* (Chicago: University of Chicago Press).

KUZNETS, S.
1966   *Modern Economic Growth: Rate, Structure, and Spread* (New Haven: Yale University Press).

LANDES, D. S.
1969   *The Unbound Prometheus: Technological Change and Industrial Development in Western Europe from 1750 to the Present* (Cambridge and New York: Cambridge University Press).

LECLAIR, EDWARD E.
1962   "Economic Theory and Economic Anthropology," *American Anthropologist* 64:1179–1203.

LECLAIR, E. E. AND H. K. SCHNEIDER (EDS.)
1968   *Economic Anthropology: Readings in Theory and Analysis* (New York: Holt, Rinehart and Winston).

LEEDS, A.
1961   "The Port-of-trade in pre-European India and as an Ecological and Evolutionary Type," in *Symposium: Patterns of Land Utilization and Other Papers*, ed. V. E. Garfield. Proceedings of the 1961 Annual Spring Meeting of the American Ethnological Society (Seattle).

LEWIS, C. S.
in press   "Nuer Cattle as Primitive Valuables," *American Anthropologist*.

LEWIS, W. A.
1954   "Economic Development with Unlimited Supplies of Labour," *The Manchester School*, May.

LITTLE, I. M. D.
1951   *A Critique of the New Welfare Economics* (Oxford: Oxford University Press).

LOASBY, B. J.
1971   "Hypothesis and Paradigm in the Theory of the Firm," *The Economic Journal* 81:863–85.

MAIR, L. P.
1957   *Studies in Applied Anthropology* (London: Athlone Press).

MALINOWSKI, B.
1922   *Argonauts of the Western Pacific* (London: Routledge & Kegan Paul).
1935   *Coral Gardens and Their Magic*, vol. 1 (New York: American Book Co.).

MARX, K.
1964   *Pre-capitalist Economic Formations* (London: Lawrence and Wishart).

MOORE, B., JR.
1966   *Social Origins of Dictatorship and Democracy* (Boston: Beacon Press).

MOORE, S. F.
1958   *Power and Property in Inca Peru* (New York: Columbia University Press).

MYRDAL, G.
1957   *Rich Lands and Poor* (New York: Harper & Row).
1960   *Beyond the Welfare State* (New Haven: Yale University Press).

NASH, M.
1966   *Primitive and Peasant Economic Systems* (San Francisco: Chandler Publishing Co.).
1967   "Reply to Reviews of *Primitive and Peasant Economic Systems*," *Current Anthropology* 8:249–50.

NEALE, W. C.
1957a   "Reciprocity and Redistribution in the Indian Village: Sequel to Some Notable Discussions," in *Trade and Market in the Early Empires*, ed. K. Polanyi, C. M. Arensberg, and H. W. Pearson (New York: Free Press).
1957b   "The Market in Theory and History," in *Trade and Market in the Early Empires*, ed. K. Polanyi, C. M. Arensberg, and H. W. Pearson (New York: Free Press).
1971   "Monetization, Commercialization, Market Orientation, and Market Dependence," in *Studies in Economic Anthropology*, ed. G. Dalton (Washington, D. C.: American Anthropological Association).

OBERG, K.
1940   "The Kingdom of Ankole in Uganda," in *African Political Systems*, ed. M. Fortes and E. E. Evans-Pritchard (London: International African Institute).

OPPENHEIM, LEO
1957   "A Bird's-eye View of Mesopotamian Economic History," in *Trade and Market in the Early Empires*, ed. K. Polanyi, C. M. Arensberg, and H. W. Pearson (New York: Free Press).

ORTIZ, S.
1967   "The Structure of Decision-making among Indians of Colombia," in *Themes in Economic Anthropology*, ed. R. Firth (London: Tavistock Publications).

PEARSON, H. W.
1957a   "The Secular Debate on Economic Primitivism," in *Trade and Market in the Early Empires*, ed. K. Polanyi, C. M. Arensberg, and H. W. Pearson (New York: Free Press).
1957b   "The Economy Has No Surplus: Critique of a Theory of Development," in *Trade and Market in the Early Empires*, ed. K. Polanyi, C. M. Arensberg, and H. W. Pearson (New York: Free Press).

PIRENNE, H.
1914 "The Stages in the Social History of Capitalism," *American Historical Review* (1914):494–515.
POLANYI, K.
1944 *The Great Transformation* (Boston: Beacon Press).
1947 "Our Obsolete Market Mentality," *Commentary* 3:109–17. (Reprinted in Polanyi 1968.)
1951 *The Livelihood of Man*, unpublished manuscript.
1957a "Marketless Trading in Hammurabi's Time," in *Trade and Market in the Early Empires*, ed. K. Polanyi, C. M. Arensberg, and H. W. Pearson (New York: Free Press).
1957b "The Economy as Instituted Process," in *Trade and Market in the Early Empires*, ed. K. Polanyi, C. M. Arensberg, and H. W. Pearson (New York, Free Press).
1960 "On the Comparative Treatment of Economic Institutions in Antiquity with Illustrations from Athens, Mycenae, and Alalakh," in *City Invincible: A Symposium on Urbanization and Cultural Development in the Ancient Near East*, ed. C. H. Kraeling and R. M. Adams (Chicago: University of Chicago Press). (Reprinted in Polanyi 1968.)
1963 "Ports of Trade in Early Societies," *The Journal of Economic History* 23: 30–45. (Reprinted in Polanyi 1968.)
1966 *Dahomey and the Slave Trade: An Analysis of an Archaic Economy* (Seattle: University of Washington Press).
1968 *Primitive, Archaic, and Modern Economies: Essays of Karl Polanyi* (New York; 2d ed. Boston: Beacon Press, 1971).
1971a "Primitive Feudalism and the Feudalism of Decay," in *Economic Development and Social Change*, ed. G. Dalton (New York: Doubleday & Co.).
1971b "Carl Menger's Two Meanings of 'Economic,'" in *Studies in Economic Anthropology*, ed. G. Dalton (Washington, D. C.: American Anthropological Association).
Mimeo
no. 1 Notes on the place occupied by economies in societies.
Mimeo
no. 2 University seminar on the institutionalizing of the economic process.
Mimeo
no. 3 Lecture notes for the course in General Economic History taught at Columbia University, 1947–53.
POSTAN, M.
1972 *The Medieval Economy and Society* (London: Weidenfeld & Nicholson).
QUIGGIN, A. H.
1949 *A Survey of Primitive Money* (London: Methuen & Co.).
RENFREW, C.
1972 *The Emergence of Civilisation* (London: Methuen & Co.).
REVERE, R.
1957 "Ports of Trade in the Eastern Mediterranean," in *Trade and Market in the Early Empires*, ed. K. Polanyi, C. M. Arensberg, and H. W. Pearson (New York: Free Press).

ROBBINS, L.

1935 *An Essay on the Nature and Significance of Economic Science* (London: Macmillan & Co.).

ROBINSON, J.

1970 *Freedom and Necessity* (London: George Allen & Unwin).

SAHLINS, M.

1965 "On the Sociology of Primitive Exchange," in *The Relevance of Models for Social Anthropology*, ed. M. Banton (London: Tavistock Publications).

1972 *Stone-age Economics* (Chicago: Aldine Atherton).

SAHLINS, M. D. AND E. R. SERVICE (EDS.)

1960 *Evolution and Culture* (Ann Arbor: University of Michigan Press).

SCHNEIDER, H. K.

1969 "Comment, on Dalton's 'Theoretical Issues in Economic Anthropology,'" *Current Anthropology* 10:89–91.

SINGER, H.

1960 "The Distribution of Gains between Investing and Borrowing Countries," *American Economic Review: Papers and Proceedings*, 11. (Reprinted in Dalton 1971a.)

SMELSER, N. J.

1963 "Mechanisms of Change and Adjustment to Change," in *Industrialization and Society*, ed. B. F. Hoselitz and W. E. Moore (Paris: Mouton). (Reprinted in Dalton 1971a.)

SMITH, A.

1776 *An Inquiry into the Wealth of Nations* (New York: Random House, Modern Library Edition).

SMITH, T. C.

1959 *The Agrarian Origins of Modern Japan* (Stanford: Stanford University Press).

SPICER, E. H. (ED.)

1952 *Human Problems in Technological Change* (New York: John Wiley & Sons).

STRATHERN, A.

1971 *The Rope of Moka* (London: Cambridge University Press).

THOMSON, D.

1949 *Economic Structure and the Ceremonial Exchange Cycle in Arnhem Land* (London: Routledge and Kegan Paul).

THURNWALD, R.

1932 *Economics in Primitive Communities* (London: International African Institute).

TITMUSS, R. M.

1970 *The Gift Relationship: From Human Blood to Social Policy* (London: George Allen & Unwin).

VENTRIS, M. AND J. CHADWICK

1956 *Documents in Mycenean Greek* (Cambridge, Eng.: Cambridge University Press).

VIDAL-NAQUET, P.

1972 "The Function of Money in Archaic Greece," in *European Economic His-*

tory, ed. W. I. Davisson and J. E. Harper (New York: Appleton-Century-Crofts).

WALLERSTEIN, I. (ED.)

1966 *The Colonial Situation: A Theoretical Approach* (New York: John Wiley & Sons).

WATSON, W.

1958 *Tribal Cohesion in a Money Economy: A Study of the Mambwe People of North Rhodesia* (Manchester, Eng.: Manchester University Press).

WHITE, L. A.

1949 *The Science of Culture* (New York: Random House).

WILCZYNSKI, J.

1972 *Socialist Economic Development and Reforms* (London: Macmillan & Co.).

WILSON, G. AND M. WILSON

1954 *An Analysis of Social Change Based on Observations in Central Africa* (Cambridge, Eng.: Cambridge University Press).

WOLF, E.

1959 *Sons of the Shaking Earth* (Chicago: University of Chicago Press).

1966 *Peasants* (Englewood Cliffs, N. J.: Prentice-Hall).

1972 "Comment, on Dalton's 'Peasantries in Anthropology and History,'" *Current Anthropology* 13:410–11.

YU, YING-SHIH

1967 *Trade and Expansion in Han China: A Study in the Structure of Sino-Barbarian Relations* (Berkeley: University of California Press).

3

Traders and Trade[1]

KARL POLANYI

Columbia University

DEFINITIONS OF TRADE

From the *institutional* point of view, trade is a method of acquiring goods that are not available on the spot. It is something external to the group, similar to activities which we are used to associating with quite different spheres of life, namely, hunts, expeditions, and piratic raids. The point of all these activities, including trade, is acquisition and carrying of goods from a distance. What distinguishes trade from the rest is a two-sidedness which also ensures its peaceful nature, absent in quests for booty and plunder.

Under the *market definition*, trade is the movement of goods on their way through the market, that is, an institution embodying a supply-demand-price mechanism. One commodity is moving in the one direction, the other in the opposite direction. The movement is controlled by prices. Trade and market are coterminous. All commodities—goods produced for sale—are potential objects of trade. The movement of trade is the function of prices, which, again, are the function of the market. Consequently, all trade is market trade.

The *institutional definition of trade* is independent of such a market. Under undisturbed primitive conditions it is—like a hunt, an expedition, or a raid—an organized group activity. It centers in the meeting of groups belonging to different communities. One of the purposes of such meetings is the exchange of goods. These meetings, as we know, do not produce rates of exchange, but, on the contrary, presuppose them. Neither individual traders nor individual motives of gain are involved; the chief or king may act for the community, after having collected the "export" goods, or numerous individuals may meet their counterparts on the beach. In either case ceremonial and ritual elements are interwoven with the proceedings, which never lack some social or political connotation.

Even under primitive conditions it may become apparent whether the community is engaged in active or in passive forms of trade, according to whether the site of the meeting is abroad or at home. Except when it happens to be in a neutral spot, one of the two parties is the visitor, the other the host. The first carries the goods and bears the brunt of the risk and initiative; the other merely responds to the occasion. Usually the parties alternate in this role. Later on, under archaic conditions, the distinction may develop into a sharp difference between active and passive trading which may involve the total organization of trade.

If it seems that we have unduly stressed "acquisition of goods from a distance" as the crucial factor in trade, we have done so, among other reasons, in order to work out more clearly the determinative role played by the *acquisitive* or *import interest* in the history of trade. Involved here, as we have seen, is the choice between peaceful and forcible methods of satisfying that interest, a matter which may affect, under given conditions, the total structure of the state as well as its modes of acting in history.

The different phases in the story of nomadic civilizations, such as the Mongol and the Arabic, illustrate the point. We should here distinguish between, on the one hand, the small-scale combination of raiding and trading, as found among some Homeric Greeks and Phoenicians or Old Testament Bedouins, and, on the other, the less obvious but much more consequential way in which the interest of great empires was served sometimes by military, sometimes by transactional methods of acquiring goods from a distance. The changing requirements of these alternatives decisively shaped domestic and foreign policy. The permanent background factor was the acquisitive or import interest in the products of their settled neighbors: the dependence on some "necessities" and, even more so, on some "luxuries" from these neighbors. Textiles and household articles belonged in the first group; gold, slaves, precious stones, silk and leather finery, cosmetics, and adornments in the latter. The distinction is, of course, more tenuous than is sometimes realized, for what we term "luxuries" were no more than the necessities of the rich and powerful, whose import interest determined foreign economic policy.

The acquisition of the goods on the part of the nomadic empire-builders could happen in several ways: (1) through mere predatory excursions, ranging from occasional raids to permanent conquest; (2) by the fostering of passive trade; (3) by the combination of predatory wars with passive trade; (4) by the development of active trade.

In each case, however, the character of the "empire" would tend to be different: (1) Mere marauding expeditions, on whatever scale, did not require more than the kind of pseudoempire of which Attila's Huns or the Avars could boast. (2) A full-fledged empire of nomadic clans (such as Genghis Khan's and his successors') which comprised far-flung trade routes would rely for its imports on passive trade, organized on an enormous scale. Military power served such empires as a mere auxiliary of trade by policing the caravan routes, securing the débouchés, and compelling the settled neighbors to grant access to their markets—that is, to their goods—to all those who traded in the service of the empire. A network of hostels for foreign merchants and a transcontinental postal service in the hands of the government were designed to further the wealth of the realm through an ever-increasing volume of imports. The result was a large volume of trade transacted by a host of traders and merchants of all nationalities along the endless trade routes of the empire, with no Mongol engaging actively in trade. (3) Upon the fall of the Yuan (Mongol) dynasty in China, the Mongol clan chiefs were forced to revert to their native haunts, and the flourishing passive trade of Genghis Khan's empire ceased forever. This situation offered a significant instance of the alternatives at issue. The fragments of Genghis

Khan's steppe empire had been engaged in a civil war which raged for a long time between the feudal squires of the West and the Genghis Khan–like princes of the East. The latter won the day and established their ascendancy over all the Khanates because they alone could act as a central power capable of alternately organizing predatory incursions into the territory of their neighbors and engaging in regular commercial relations with them. Vladimirtsov emphasized that success in either of these ventures—raid or trade—required not only central direction but also central "repartition"—of the booty in one case, of the imported goods in the other. (4) The Mongols never indulged in active trade, but Arabic empires, though starting from similar nomadic clan conditions, eventually evolved, thanks to their more democratic set-up, a broad commercial stratum, which provided for ample imports through its active trade without recourse to predatory methods. In this capacity for active trading, it may be surmised, lay the decisive historical superiority of the Islamic empires over the more transitory Mongol Khanate, with its passive trading system.

INSTITUTIONAL FEATURES OF TRADE

Since something must be carried by someone over a distance and this is to happen in two directions, trade must involve (1) personnel; (2) goods; (3) carrying; and (4) two-sidedness. All of these institutional features permit classification according to criteria which are either sociological or technological or both. On this depends the relevance of the following analysis for the enormous variety of forms and organizations of trade in history.

Personnel

Factor and Mercator: Status Motive and Profit Motive. Acquisition of goods from a distance may be practiced by a trader either from motives peculiar to his standing in society—and as a rule comprising elements of duty or public service (status motive)—or for the sake of the gain which may accrue to him from the buying and selling transaction in hand (profit motive). The typical (although by no means only) representative of the former kind of trader is the *factor*; the representative of the latter type is the *mercator*.

In spite of many combinations of the two, duty on the one hand and gain on the other stand out as sharply distinct primary motivations. If the status motive is reinforced by that of material benefit, the latter does not, as a rule, take the form of gain made on exchange, but rather that of gifts of treasure or landed revenue received by the trader from the master or lord by way of recompense. The transactional gains of the mercator usually add up to paltry sums that bear no comparison with the wealth showered by his lord upon the resourceful and successfully venturing trader. Thus he who trades for the sake of duty and honor grows rich, while he who trades for filthy lucre remains poor—an added reason why the profit motive is under a shadow in archaic society.

The distinction between status motive and profit motive might, to the historian, seem rather irrelevant, since most societies prior to our own were, broadly speaking, status societies and thus presumably would not have had room for the poor trader with his profit motive. To make this assumption, however, would be to confuse two different functions of status, a term which can refer to the *origin* of the rights and duties or to their *content*. In a status society the rights and duties of all groups are determined by birth, but the rights and duties themselves need not be of an honorific character. The higher-status groups are usually expected to act on honorific motives of duty, obligation, and self-respect, while the lower-status groups may well be encouraged to indulge in gainful occupations. These pursuits are looked down upon and are hardly profitable. In ancient Greece, for instance, the metic was in such a position. Obversely, our modern nonstatus societies have been for centuries familiar with the figure of the nonprofit trader, the agent or factor who trades for his company, not for himself, and to whom success means not profit but preferment.

But all this does not affect the basic distinction between factor and mercator. The latter is engaged in trade for the sake of the profit he hopes to make on the transaction, the former trades as a part of his general duties and obligations.

Upper, Lower, and "Middle" Class: Standards of Life. The place occupied by the trader on the ladder of standards of life has been very dif-

ferent in different societies and, indeed, even in one and the same
society at different times. The matter is in some cases complicated by
the simultaneous existence of more than one layer of trading population
in the society.

In archaic society the chief or king and his immediate entourage are
alone entitled to trade, that is, to initiate the more or less warlike and
diplomatic ventures which lead to the acquisition of goods from a distance. Piratic and treaty trade, whether separately or jointly practiced,
belong to the governmental sphere. The king may personally lead the
venture, like Mentes, the legendary ruler of the Taphians, or only super-
vise its execution, as Argesilaos, authentic king of the Cyrenaika, appears to have done. But chief's or king's trade by no means implies the
personal activity of the sovereign, who must in practice employ hundreds
or even thousands of traders as factors or "king's merchants" to carry on
trade for him. Some of them may belong to the royal family itself;
others rank as princes and rulers, owning fortresses and castles, vast manorial estates; still others may only count as court personages, enjoying
a revenue from royal donations or, much more frequently, from the
privilege of participating in the trading profits of the royal syndicate. In
all cases the "king's merchants" rank with army generals, civil governors,
and other high officials among the great men of the country.

In peasant-type societies, such as ancient Greece after the seventh
century B.C. or Rome after the end of the monarchy, king's and prince's
trade ceases. Foreign trade is either discontinued, as in Rome, or it is
reduced to passive trade. In the sixth century B.C. Solon is mentioned as
a merchant, and the Peisistratids as well as the Alkmeonids should certainly be inferred to have engaged at least incidentally in large-scale
foreign trading ventures. But these were exceptions. Solon himself assumed that Athens was dependent for her food supplies on foreign corn
merchants. The inland region of Israel developed king's trade under
David and on a considerable level under Solomon, but after the
breakup of the united empire it became entirely dependent on passive
trade. Of the Hebrews, the Greeks, and the Romans, the Greeks alone
produced lower-class traders in the *kapeloi*—the local retailers of food—
and the metic class of *naukleroi*, the trading skippers. Neither of them
ever developed into a middle class. The class much idealized by Aristotle under that name was a landed class, not a commercial class at all.

138

The commercial middle class of the nineteenth century was a late product of Western development. Typical medieval urban society consisted of a privileged merchant upper class of burghers and a broad stratum of artisans and traders—the "people." Together they were the urban community, above which ranked the landed aristocracy of the manorial countryside. Even in eighteenth-century England, the most advanced western commercial society of the time, the successful merchant rose into the landed class, leaving the "tradesman" behind him in the lower ranks of society. Not until the Reform Act of 1832 did a commercial middle class gain a standing in England.

In antiquity traders belonged either to the upper or to the lower class. Upper-class traders were connected with rulership and government; lower-class traders depended for their livelihood on manual labor. This fact is of the greatest importance in understanding the forms and organization of trade in ancient times.

We may outline the classes of trade as follows:

I. Upper range: king's trade
   A. Chieftain's and king's trade
      1. Tribal society
      2. Acropolitan state (*Burgenkoenigtum*)
      3. Pharaonic and temple trade
   B. Prince's and warrior's trade: archaic upper class
      1. Khorassan (pre-Arabic *muluk*, seventh century A.D.)
      2. Kievan boyars (tenth to thirteenth centuries)
      3. Mexico (the royal family and the other merchants, sixteenth century)
      4. Syrian emirs (Eldred and Tavernier, sixteenth and seventeenth centuries)
      5. Dahoman caboceers (eighteenth century)
   C. Burgher merchant
      1. Patriciate of Western Europe
      2. Guild merchant of Novgorod

II. Lower range: proletarian trade and carrying
   A. Castes and guilds of carriers and bazaar craftsmen in irrigational empires
   B. Metic in the Eastern Mediterranean polis

    C. Local retailer of food and household articles on the agora
       (*kapeloi*)

III. "Middle" range: commercial classes
    A. Byzantine empire (post-Roman nonfeudal area)
    B. Ptolemaic and Roman Alexandria, and early Islam from West
       Africa to India
    C. Nineteenth-century Western European "commercial classes"

*Tamkar, Metic, and Foreigner: Types of Traders in the Archaic
World.* The typical traders of antiquity were the tamkar, the metic, and
the foreigner. The *tamkar* dominated the Mesopotamian scene from the
Sumerian beginnings to the rise of Islam, a period of over 3,000 years.
The Nile Valley, too, knew only this type of trader. The *metic* trader
first became historically conspicuous in Athens and rose during the
Hellenistic era to be the prototype of the lower-class merchant from the
Indus to the Pillars of Hercules. (In effect, a similar floating population
of lowly merchants—not, this time, of the sea but of the land—produced
the burgher merchant class of Western Europe.) The third type of
trader, the *foreigner,* is, of course, ubiquitous. He is the stranger, the
bearer of passive trade, who neither belongs to the community nor even
enjoys the semistatus of resident alien, but is a member of an altogether
different community. Accordingly, in the great civilizations of the East
and of Africa the leading figure of commercial life was the tamkar; in
Hellenic civilization, the metic; both types of civilizations included a
sprinkling of foreigners.

It is on this deliberately oversimplified background, which must be
greatly qualified to show the enormous variety of configurations, that the
true picture of trade in antiquity can be sketched.

The tamkar belonged to the factor category; he became a tamkar
either in a hereditary way or by appointment of the king, priest or great
one. As a tamkar he possessed a status involving privileges and duties.
His livelihood was not dependent on the commercial transaction in
hand; it was secured by status revenue, mostly through landed property,
or at least through the claim to maintenance according to his rank
from the royal or temple store. If, as in Dahomey, his revenue was derived from some special commercial privilege, the transactions through
which he turned that privilege to cash were institutionally separated

140

from his transactions in his capacity of tamkar. Where guilds existed, to which the merchants or traders would by status belong, all this would largely be institutionalized through the guild system.

The Athenian metics, primarily a population of the ports, were sometimes artisans or craftsmen, but most of them were engaged in trade and tried to earn a living from the profits to be made by buying and selling goods. Apart from being a skipper and trader, the metic tried his hand at "banking," the menial occupation of testing and changing coins behind a bench in the marketplace. His money changer's commission fee was regulated by public authority; as a grain dealer he stood under strict supervision; and as a merchant skipper he had to comply with numerous trading restrictions, which would limit profits. But in general he was free to follow the urge of gain, a motive which was thought appropriate to his lowly status. His life was drudgery: physical exertion aggravated by exposure to the hated hardships of the sea. Yet he was to expect no riches in recompense. The metic was barred from owning land or a house; he could not hold a mortgage; consequently he could possess no property which would be reckoned as wealth. An occasional metic might accumulate a considerable amount of money, but that made little difference to his standards of life. A man who was debarred from owning land and houses could not, for instance, raise horses, give feasts, or erect a mansion. Even the few rich metics led unglamorous lives.

We may categorize the traders of the archaic world as follows:

I. Tamkar: trader by status, acts as a factor. Combines to a varying degree two different activities: carrying and negotiating.
   A. *Carrying* ranges from the task of a porter to that of operating caravans or fleets.
   B. *Negotiating* includes all kinds of jobbery, transmission of information, diplomacy, making arrangements, haggling, conclusion of deals.
   C. Related functions:
      1. Brokerage
      2. Auctioneering
      3. Trusteeship
         a. Keeper of safe deposits
         b. Agent of payments

   c. Maker of official loans and advances

   d. Public attorney

  1 and 2 are often combined functions.

 II. Metic: resident alien

  A. Social composition

   1. Native proselyte (Israel)

   2. Floating alien population of displaced persons (DPs); fragments of dismembered peoples; political refugees; exiles; fugitive criminals; escaped slaves; discharged mercenaries (DPs).

    So great is the wear and tear of archaic history that the very existence of an organized community becomes somewhat of a privilege on account of the enormous number of DPs (Thucydides).

  B. Occupation

   1. Small trader

   2. Skipper

   3. Money changer

   4. Money lender, with a stall in the market (in "liberal" times)

  C. Social groups partly assimilated to metics:

   1. Freedmen (Rome)

   2. Slaves (paying *apophora*)

 III. Foreigner: alien trader under king's protection

  A. Sources

   1. Trading peoples proper

   2. Periodically trading peoples

  B. Types

   1. Traveler: transient

   2. Settled colonist

   3. King's factor

    toward the foreigner's home community generally

Trading Peoples. Not all communities which practice trade have professional traders. A community may trade collectively. Or it may possess professional traders and regard them as belonging to a specific social class. In a few societies, active trade is the chief occupation of the bulk of the population. Groups like these latter we will designate as trading peoples.

The existence of trade, then, does not require traders, and even where professional traders are found, their relation to the community as a whole may be very different in different types of societies.

In *primitive society* trade is, as a rule, a collective undertaking, carried on either by the chief or through the general participation of the members. In the latter case, their purpose may be served by crowded meetings with their trading partners on the beach or by carrying some local foodstuffs or manufactured articles, sometimes by boat, to a neighboring island. Consequently, we will find here, as a rule, no one specializing in the profession of trader or merchant.

In *archaic society* the trader makes his appearance. Let us distinguish between peasant-type societies and empires, and, in regard to the latter, between nomadic and irrigational empires. In *peasant-type societies*, the royal household may employ a staff of traders, which usually disappears with the fall of the monarchy. This was probably the case in early Rome, as well as after the passing of the tyrannies in ancient Greece. In the *irrigational empire* the tamkar gains right of status. In the *nomadic empire* of the Mongols, trade was exclusively passive; no trader or merchant class made its appearance. This was also the case in the early African nomadic empires of the Berbers and early Arabs.

Trading peoples differ sharply from all of these societies; with them trade is a source of collective livelihood. Among themselves trading peoples differ again in an important respect: The trading peoples proper, as we may call them, are exclusively dependent for their subsistence on trade in which, directly or indirectly, the whole of the population is engaged. In the case of others—a much more numerous group—trade is only one of the occupations in which a considerable part of the population engages from time to time, traveling abroad with foods over shorter or longer periods.

We may categorize trading peoples as follows:

I. Trading people proper (everyone directly or indirectly engaged in trade)
   A. Sea
      1. Phoenicians

    2. Rhodians
    3. Western Vikings
  B. Desert
    1. Bedouins
    2. Tuareg
  C. River
    1. Eastern Vikings
    2. Kede (of the Niger)
II. Periodically trading peoples
  A. West African peoples
    1. Hausa
    2. Duala
    3. Mandingo
    4. Others
  B. Malayan peoples
III. Dislocated peoples
  A. Armenians
  B. Jews
  C. "Greeks"

Goods

The decision to acquire and carry goods from a distance obviously depends on the urgency of the need for the objects and on the difficulty of acquiring and transporting them. Moreover, the need must be felt by those who possess the political and technical means of executing the trade expedition. The decision to acquire some kind of goods from a definite distance and region is necessarily made under concrete circumstances different from those under which some other kind of goods would have to be acquired from somewhere else. *Archaic trade is, for this reason, a discontinuous business, restricted to definite undertakings which do not develop into a continuous enterprise.* Secondly, trading ventures differ according to the type of goods to be acquired and transported, thus forming separate branches of trade, each with its distinctive operational methods and organization.

All this may appear too obvious to mention. Yet it is useful to recall these facts in order to interpret correctly the incisive feature of nonmarket trade: There is here no such thing as "trading in general." All trade is originally specific according to the goods involved. It is easier to transport slaves and cattle who, so to speak, travel under their own steam, than to move huge rocks, say, or enormous tree trunks over hundreds of miles of roadless country. This specificity of archaic trade is enhanced in the usual course of things by the necessity of acquiring the imported goods by means of exported ones. For under nonmarket conditions, imports and exports tend to fall under different administrative regimes. The process of collecting the goods to be exported is often quite separate from that by which the imported goods have to be repartitioned. The first is a matter of tribute, taxation, feudal gifts, or some other means of making the goods flow to the center, while the repartition may descend in a hierarchic cascade on very different lines. Kievan Russia exported furs, flax, and honey collected by the prince and the boyars as tribute from their subjects; their "imports" were the precious silks, cloths, jewelry, and finery of Byzantium. In the Roman Empire, the food and other necessary articles which flowed from the provinces to the capital as *annona* represented an unrequited "import" of a purely political character. In this case the imports had to be first locally collected in the provinces themselves before they could be shipped to Rome. Fifteen-hundred years later, the African, East Indian, and West Indian trade of the chartered companies of Europe ran mainly in channels determined by the methods by which tribute goods were collected from the natives, either by their princes or by the Europeans themselves, for export to Europe.

We may outline as follows the kinds of goods involved in trade:

I. Treasure:
   A. Moventia—slaves and cattle—predestined as objects of piratic trade
   B. Moventia *plus* precious stones and metals: booty
   C. Booty *plus* land conquest: treasure (eventually: ivory and clothes)

II. Public requirements
   A. Staple foods: corn, oil, wine, dried fish, wool
   B. Military requirements:
      1. Navy: timber, tar, hemp
      2. Army: copper, tin, lead, iron

III. Luxuries:
   A. Spices
   B. Cosmetics
   C. Incense
   D. Rare woods
   E. Elaborate artifacts
IV. Bulky objects (hauling expeditions)
   A. Stones
   B. Timber
These goods are traded according to the following motives:

Four main types of trade:	Characteristic of trade interest:
I. Piratic: moventia and treasure	Booty
II. Staples: collective necessities (food)	Public policy matter
III. Luxuries	Class interest
IV. Bulky objects: stone and timber	Expeditionary

Transportation

The market is a leveler with regard to transportation as well as with regard to goods. It obliterates all differences; what nature made distinct, the market makes homogeneous. Even the difference between goods and their transportation is done away with, since both can be bought and sold in the market—the one in the commodity market, the other in the freight market. In either case there is supply and demand, and prices are formed in one and the same fashion. The various kinds of transportation services share a common denominator with the various goods in terms of costs, the caput mortuum of the market alchemy.

Such homogeneity makes for good economic theory but bad economic history. For the very differences which vanish in the market are the stuff of history. Different goods, as we have seen, create in archaic times distinctive branches of trade. The traded goods may be needed by people of different status, whose interests are expressed through different channels, who have different means at their disposal to achieve their ends, and who, therefore, develop different types of trade whose organization has hardly anything in common. To ignore the difference between goods that can move, like slaves and cattle, and goods that cannot, like stones and timber, would make the early history of trade unintelligible.

The routes traveled and the means and modes of carrying are of no less incisive relevance than the types of the goods carried. In both cases the geographical and technological facts interpenetrate with the social structure.

Transportation, the carrying of goods over a distance, involves (I) *routes,* (II) *means* of transportation, and (III) a definite *organization.*

  I. Routes:
    A. Maritime
    B. Riverine
    C. Overland
 II. Means of transport:
    A. Human
    B. Animal
    C. Mechanical
      1. Ships
      2. Wagons
III. Organization:
    A. Technical organization of the expedition or caravan
    B. Political organization
      1. The carrying body, its leadership, defense, etc.
      2. Transit through territory of foreign tribes, peoples, nations.

The organization must be able to cope with the perils and obstructions caused both by nature and by man. In seafaring, for instance, one type of vessel was used both against the hazards of nature and against those of war. Only comparatively late did fighting craft branch off from the merchant vessels which had served both peaceful and warlike purposes. In this light, the personnel of the war boat's crew is only a variant of the merchantman's. Its recruitment is, therefore, not primarily a business proposition—another pointer for the history of trade.

As to the dangers from pirates and robbers, overland routes and coastal trade are almost equally exposed. Only on the high seas does attack from pirates become an exceptional hazard. (This is, of course, less true in later times, when sea lanes are more heavily traveled.)

Policing of overland routes was the *raison d'être* of all but the earliest empires, which sprang directly from the political requirements of irrigation. Neither Babylonia nor Egypt nor China spread along overland routes; their transportation was predominantly riverine (the Akkadian term for a trading place is *port*). But the nomadic empires of the Turk, Mongol, Arabic, and Berber peoples were spread out like nets alongside transcontinental caravan routes. The purpose was to "own" the routes, which would provide a flow of imports, partly in the form of tolls and taxes, payment for safe-conduct, and the like, and partly in exchange for raw materials collected as tribute from the conquered peoples by the empire builders.

Caravans thus antedate empires. Their organization was dictated by the requirements of transit through nonpoliced areas. The early caravans, whether in the framework of king's trade or warrior trade, were doubtless set up and armed by the public powers for their tasks. In either case the trader was of the tamkar type. But even the later, independent caravan, often consisting of burgher merchants frequenting the traditional overland routes, remained a kind of small wandering state, threading its way between numberless smaller or larger settlements of peoples of a more or less predatory kind. This extraterritorial caravan was expected to keep strictly to the beaten track and look neither right nor left in traversing the countryside. Its participants often learned as little about the regions through which they were passing as the modern globe-trotter on his conducted tour, hopping by plane from hotel to hotel. Most of the ancient slave trade was carried on by this sort of caravan. Only rarely did individual traders, without the armed accompaniment of a caravan, lead whole slave transports across political frontiers, paying their dues at each boundary to the local sovereign. Probably this last type of travel by stages was the method by which hosts of slaves were sold "down the river" over hundreds of miles on the western coast of Equatorial Africa. Especially after the arrival of the Portuguese on the Congo Delta in the sixteenth century, such noncaravan, riverine trade passed its freighted canoes along the river's winding length very much as the boa constrictor digests its prey.

The caravan was also, in some respects, the source of an important military development. Rostovtzeff has pointed out that the Hellenistic army was one of the most original creations of the age, the economic importance of which cannot be overrated. He referred, of course, to the enormous concourse of men and beasts, numbering tens of thousands of sutlers and craftsmen, which formed the wandering capital of the empire. It was a maze of markets, enmeshed in the tissues of a monstrously enlarged military headquarters. In effect, this army was a glorified caravan, the first armed formation to attempt the task of making large wandering bodies of persons self-supporting. And yet it was a far cry from the modest Seleucid *skeue*, which impressed Rostovtzeff, to the Grand Mogul's summer journey, some two thousand years later, as described by Tavernier, from his dusty Indian capital to the high mountains. Nearly half a million camp followers, including the entire bazaar population of deserted Delhi, marched cross country like some sprawling monster, camping each night at a new site, an improvised city of fantastic proportions.

Two-sidedness

The acquiring of objects which are not available to the community on the spot necessarily engages the group in external activities. Its *pretrade* forms are the *hunt*, the *expedition*, and the *raid*. The movement of goods is one-sided in these activities. The catching, the quarrying, the felling, the robbing, or any other way of getting hold of the goods forms one part of the action; the carrying, hauling, or other way of transporting the acquisition, the other.

We meet with three main types of trade: *gift trade*, *administered* or *treaty trade*, and *market trade*.

Gift trade links the partners in relationships of *reciprocity*, such as those of guest friends, kula partners, and visiting traders. The *organization* of trading is usually ceremonial, involving mutual presentations, embassies, or political dealings between the chiefs or kings. The *goods* are treasure, objects of elite circulation; in the borderline case of visiting parties the goods may be of a more "democratic" character.

Administered or treaty trade has a firm foundation in treaty relationships of a more or less formal nature. On both sides the import interest is determinative, and for that reason the trade is organized through governmental or government-controlled channels. In a secondary way, this involves a similar organization of the export goods. Accordingly, the whole organization of trade is carried on by administrative methods.

These are, as a rule, also responsible for the manner in which business is transacted: arrangements concerning "rates" of units; port facilities; weighing; checking of quality; the physical exchange of the goods; storage; safekeeping; the control of the trading personnel; regulation of "payments"; credits; price differentials. Some of these are naturally linked with the details of the actual collection of export goods and the repartition of the imported ones; both of these activities fall into the redistributive sphere of the domestic economy. The mutually imported goods are standardized according to quality and package, weight, or other easily ascertainable criteria. Only "trade goods" of this sort can be traded. Equivalents are set out in simple relations; in principle, trade is 1:1. Haggling is not part of the proceedings; since in actual fact it often cannot be completely avoided, to meet the changing circumstances it is practiced only *on items other than price*, such as measures, quality, means of payment, and profits.

Market trade is the third typical form of trading. Exchange is here the form of integration that relates the partners to each other. The range of tradable goods—the commodities—is practically unlimited; the organization follows the lines traced by the supply-demand-price mechanism. The market mechanism is adaptable to the handling not only of the goods, but of every element of trade separately—storage, transportation, risk, credit, payments, and the like—by forming special markets for freight, loan, capital, warehouse space, short and long term credit, insurance, and so on.

The "origin" of trade is, of course, a different matter. The acquisition of goods from a distance, though a vital criterion of trade, in this regard holds no precedence over two-sidedness. Two-sided relationships that overcome distance are not limited to the acquisition of goods. Sexual organization, which centers on marriage and reproduction, is predominantly exogamic and very frequently, therefore, relates to groups that are surprisingly distant geographically. If, as usual, bride-price and, sometimes, dowry accompany the moving of the bride, the resulting two-sided movement of goods becomes an important source of the satisfaction of the "import interest" for at least one of the parties. Yet the reciprocity between them centers not on the exchange of goods but on the bride.

In a minor key, the noncommercial reciprocity of the kula ring precedes the two-sidedness of the trading transactions which, in a small way, accompany the fabulous traject of the heroes of the ring. And yet, here again, regular trade between kula partners may well originate in (and even outlive) the arabesques of the kula.

This does not, however, diminish the important implications of expeditionary and especially of raiding "trade" for the origins of trade proper. Even head-hunting and the trading of food are sometimes combined. According to Thurnwald, some New Guinea tribes return from their macabre expeditions laden not only with skulls but with corn bartered from their victims. In archaic society piratic trade is one of the starting points of both gift trade and treaty trade.

Institutional analysis, however, is not primarily concerned with origins, but with the structure and mechanism of institutions and their constituent parts. We may analyze external and internal trade as follows:

I. External trade
   A. Gift trade: widespread in some types of tribal society. Guest gifts; pomp; alliances. Political purpose of *à fonds perdu* gifts, such as those to Menelaus in Syria and Egypt or to Odysseus on the last stretch of his return: empires using gifts to secure advantages in relation to "barbarians."
      1. Rationale of gift trade
         a. Absence of any sanctions other than retaliatory measures.
         b. Geographical "division of labor" (ecological differential) ensuring utility of exchange.
         c. Automatic hostility in absence of countergifts.
         d. The weaker party may excel in gifts to gain favor (but may refuse tribute).
         e. The stronger may give gifts in order to win over the weaker and put him under obligations. (See Thucydides; also evidence from archaeology)
      2. Forms: embassy or special mission.
      3. Goods: *treasure:* slaves, gold, horses, ivory, clothes, incense, etc.
   B. Administered or treaty trade: presupposes relatively stable organized political or semipolitical bodies such as chartered com-

panies. The understanding may be tacit, as in the case of traditional or customary relationships. Between sovereign bodies, however, trade on a larger scale assumes the existence of explicit treaties even in relatively early times (e.g., between Etruscan Rome and Carthage in the sixth century B.C.).

But forms of administered trade, once established, generally come into use whether there is any treaty or not. Its main institution is the *port of trade*, the site of all administered foreign trade. Its function is to offer:

1. Military security
2. Civil protection to the foreign trader
3. Facilities of anchorage, debarcation, storage, etc.
4. Judicial authorities
5. Agreement on what goods are traded
6. Organizational arrangements concerning the "proportions" of the traded goods.

C. Market trade. This presupposes, of course, both trade and markets. As to the trade, its independent origin has been shown above. The markets, on the other hand, do not necessarily spring from trade, and we will see below that local markets certainly possess independent origins of their own. The catallactic notion that markets and trade are somehow the static and dynamic forms, respectively, of one economic energy is therefore erroneous.

For the economic historian the interesting question is: *When and how does trade get linked with markets?* Under what circumstances do markets become a vehicle of trade movements? And at what times and places do we first meet the result, market trade?

The question will be dealt with separately in regard to external and to internal markets. The *external market* problem is only another aspect of the problem of the origin of the *port of trade* and the circumstances which led to its development into regular international markets. The *internal market* problem, again, refers to the process by which the strictly controlled and limited agora of the polis and the very different bazaar of the oriental world were transformed into free meeting places of foreign traders.

The characteristics of a market are, in both cases: free accessibility and an organization of trade which favors the emergence of one price, and that a fluctuating one. With *ports of trade*, only one price obtains; but if the price is to fluctuate while there is free access to the market, the local population must be independent of the supplies which are traded there—a state of affairs which is hardly likely under primitive or even archaic conditions. The classic Greek *agora* by its very nature hardly ever developed into a regular place of market trade, as long as the polis was active and flourishing; its very separation from the emporium—i.e., the port of trade—would have obstructed such a development. The *bazaar*, which produces no single price and is therefore unsuitable as an organ of price enforcement, is limited to local supplies. If foreign traders are permitted to participate in it, they automatically gain the status of settled colonists or of resident aliens. If the bazaar happens to be an adjunct of the port of trade (as for instance with the Maydan in the Ispahan of the sixteenth and seventeenth centuries), the foreign trader is strictly enjoined to make use of the services of a broker in order to prevent the fusing of bazaar trade and foreign trade into anything in the nature of general marketing.

II. "Internal" trade
  A. Usually external to some smaller social unit, as in village-to-village trade.
  B. "Internalized" through incorporation into a neighboring group or federation into a larger unit.
  C. Ecological differences, such as those between regions, may lead to interprovincial trade.
  D. Internal trading is sometimes the result of the fragmentation of empires or at least the incipient paralysis of their central redistributive system.
  E. The latter fact may also lead to trade over sections of the border of formerly unified empires.

153

F. Another source of internal trade is the long traject of foreign trade before it can reach the centers from the boundary.

Proposition: Throughout, the external origin of trade is conspicuous; internal trade is largely a derivation of earlier external trade. As we will see later on, trade only presents in a striking way a feature general to the development of economic institutions, namely the polarity between the external and the internal lines of development. With trade the priority of the external line is evident.

NOTES

1. This posthumous paper is chapter 12 of an unpublished draft manuscript, dated March 1951, of a book entitled *The Livelihood of Man*. Published by permission of Ilona Polanyi. Harry Pearson of Bennington College is preparing the manuscript for publication in book form.

4

The Flag Follows Trade: An Essay on the Necessary Interaction of Military and Commercial Factors in State Formation

MALCOLM C. WEBB

University of New Orleans

The problem of the origins and nature of state systems is one of those key questions which appear to have dominated anthropological thought —at least intermittently—since the beginnings of the discipline. The mere mention of such names as Spencer, Maine, and Morgan reminds us that the search for more completely naturalistic explanations of the manner in which "civilization" might have first emerged from underlying stages of "savagery" and "barbarism" was in fact one of the key intellectual factors that led to the separation of anthropological thinking from the wider tradition of nineteenth-century European social philosophy. Indeed, the most cursory review of previous inquiries into the origin of the state indicates that a fascination with the state comes down to us from the very roots of the Western intellectual tradition. Passing back beyond the nineteenth-century intellectual milieu of Marx and Engels, Hegel, and Comte, beyond their early modern precursors such as the Edinburgh school, the Encyclopedists, Locke and Hobbes, and even beyond the Renaissance philosophers, medieval Christian and Moslem theologians, and the philosophers of Classical Greece and Rome, we may note that the earliest surviving example of connected, causally oriented, historical (or pseudohistorical) narrative in the Western world—the so-called Succession Narrative and associated accounts of I Samuel, II Samuel, and I Kings—deals extensively with the role of kingship in society (Whybray 1968). Significantly, that early attempt at analysis appears to date from a period in which the author's own society had recently experienced either the introduction or a considerable strengthening of state controls, as do the beginnings of the tradition of Hebrew ethical prophecy, which manifests similar concerns, although more completely blended with primarily theological interests (Anderson 1966; Berger 1969; North 1953; Heaton 1958). In the same way, recent analyses of the myths characteristic of the Near Eastern monarchies of the early Bronze Age confirm the view that these accounts deal at least as much with questions of the origins and stability of state social controls as they do with natural phenomena; such evidence would extend concern with the state back to the very time in which the phenomenon in question first appeared (Anthes 1961; Kramer 1961; Jameson 1961; Hooke 1963:79–88; Wilson 1946; Jacobson 1946).

A review of such precocious attempts at explanation reminds one forcefully how unfortunate it is that, as Fried (1960) has noted, by the middle of the nineteenth century the expansion of state systems, essentially throughout the world, had removed the possibility of firsthand observation of the emergence of such systems. At that very time, our knowledge of the operations of social processes had begun to reach the point of truly scientific understanding. I have, nevertheless, been much impressed by the strong strain of realism which can be seen running through so many of the ancient myths, sacred histories, and etiological accounts which are present in the earliest stages of archaic state societies in many parts of the world—a realism which is often surprisingly lacking among much more modern theorists of state origins. This realism consists of a deep appreciation of the full potentiality—if not actuality—of factionalism, force, conflict, and domination in the process of state formation and maintenance. It accords very well indeed with what —following the well-known discussion of Fortes and Evans-Pritchard (1940)—I believe to be the central problem of state origins. The problem is the specification of mechanisms whose operation would in time generate a monopoly of coercive force in the hands of the tribal leadership, in a situation where the previous lack of such a monopoly would of itself seem to preclude the possibility of ever securing just such a monopoly. In other words, the full emergence of the state would appear to require eventually the final overthrow of a previously existing traditional system of authority, social controls, and resource allocation whose inelasticity and whose decentralized and localized organization would indeed have very largely inhibited even the initial concentration of power and resources required for further significant steps in this direction. Despite the areas of continuity, or seeming continuity, between advanced tribal and incipient state systems of governance, the shift from the former to the latter entails a basic and total alteration in the manner in which the authority of the leadership is ultimately enforced and upheld. Both a radical, perhaps painful, shift from the older to the newly emergent system and a tendency to instability on the part of the new system during its early stages are, therefore, implied.

CHIEFDOMS AS THE NATURAL END
OF SOCIAL EVOLUTION

That this should be so follows from the contrasting natures of tribal and state systems. A state society is characterized by a central government—a body which functions permanently (in the sense that its status positions operate whenever needed; the actual persons who fill these offices may vary as determined by "democratic" or other selection procedures), which stands apart from and above every other organization or interest group in the society, and which has attached to it enough supporters to provide at least a skeleton bureaucracy, to form the nucleus of the national military forces, and to overawe and keep in check all other groups in the society. Such a war band, which must necessarily

157

be free of any other traditional tribal and kin loyalties, would be indispensable for the levying of taxes beyond the level of customary tribal gifts which a chieftain might expect. Once established on a self-supporting basis by means of this taxing power, such a group of retainers enables the emerging rulers to enforce jural decisions, undertake public works, conduct a cohesive foreign policy, mobilize the society for war, and otherwise provide for the common good in circumstances involving really large populations, extensive territories, or markedly heterogeneous social groupings. The primacy of coercive force in this description is not intended to imply that other developmental variables are unimportant; many, such as, for example, a continual growth of subsistence capacity, are obvious preconditions for state development. Similarly, although the development of institutions of leadership with superior organizational and information-processing capacities might provide sufficient advantages to attract relatively freely a following large enough to carry out some rather complex and even statelike activities (Wilmsen 1972; Flannery 1972; Johnson 1973), this might better be considered a terminal tribal-level precondition which does not really diminish the ultimate importance of a monopoly of coercive power in state evolution. It is difficult to conceive of any such system expanding to any significant size or enduring for a long period unless the leaders have secured an effective and reliable prop for their authority. Lacking this, they simply would not be able to enforce with assurance the many hard decisions required for the maintenance of state societies. This defect would be especially likely to be fatal if—as seems commonly to have been the case—states emerged in clusters under conditions of mutual competition.

It is for this very reason that the condition of "civilization," with all that it implies in regard to massive and complex public works, the support of large and dense populations, the incorporation of extensive territories into one sovereign polity, the organization of occupational specialization, and the extension of comprehensive social integration (all of which in turn both demand and make possible complex record keeping and symbolic systems), has in fact been essentially coterminous with that of state society (Childe 1951a; 1954; Redfield 1953). Nonstate societies, on the other hand, which lack such effective mechanisms for social control, have proven to be severely restricted both in size and in level of organizational complexity. Furthermore, the historical record suggests very strongly indeed that force and violence have been basic characteristics of the operation of state systems for as far back as their existence can be traced. Therefore, even though the precise point (the acquisition of a monopoly control of legitimate force or some earlier achievement of cultural elaboration at a more voluntary, tribal stage) at which one cuts the developmental continuum will (since such a break must always be arbitrary to some extent) determine which variables one will regard as most critical, this does not greatly matter in the end. While it is perhaps debatable whether or not coercion was absolutely inherent in the earliest origins of states—and so of civilization—there can be no question that it was utterly essential for their continued survival and further development.

It is, of course, quite true that chiefdoms, the most advanced sorts of tribal societies, appear in some cases to overlap with states in size and level of complexity. It can therefore be extremely difficult to distinguish chiefdoms from the smaller examples of states on the basis of the kinds of data typically available to anthropologists. On a day-to-day basis the two social types do much the same sort of thing and, in the short run, can produce the same kinds of results in terms of the establishment of public order, dispute resolution, defense against external enemies, monument erection, public works, record keeping, the provision of luxury goods, and the support of marked distinctions of rank; therefore it is often hard to decide whether a particular case is a highly developed chiefdom or a very incipient state. Such a decision requires long, continued examination of duration, of quantity, and of general style of life, which are not obvious from the sporadic accounts of early explorers or from ethnographic studies of short duration, and which are particularly difficult to decide on the basis of archaeological data (Service 1962:148–52, 170–77; Renfrew 1973:155–90). Even in cases for which sufficient evidence is available, equally competent scholars have arrived at contradictory conclusions as to the existence of state controls. In still other instances, studies of a series of societies of increasing complexity within the same broad geographical area seem to find no point at which the shift from nonstate to state can be said clearly to have taken place.

Thus, for example, Polynesian chiefdoms in the larger or more productive (in terms of the native technology) island groups, such as

Hawaii, Tonga, the Society Islands, and Samoa, came very close indeed to matching the achievements expected of states (Goldman 1955; Sahlins 1958; Suggs 1960), especially on those occasions when one leader was able to unite an entire island or even—at times—a considerable portion of an island group. While such unions apparently depended upon the timely concatenation of favorable circumstances and tended, therefore, to be of short duration, they were, as Sahlins (1958; 1963) and also Davenport (1964; 1969) have noted, of frequent occurrence and a basic part of the aboriginal pattern. Interestingly, Linton (1956:180–86) and Oliver (1961:73–75, 180–81, 256–58), although fully aware of the "primitive" or "tribal" nature of these cultures, found it quite natural to refer to their rulers as "kings," and Kroeber (1948:760–61), in discussing the same peoples, suggested that they represented a devolved remnant of something more complex. Readers of Steward and Faron's *The Native Peoples of South America* (1959) will recall that considerable development took place among the circum-Caribbean and Central American chiefdoms, although neither archaeological nor historical accounts are as full as might be wished. Sanders and Price (1968: 53–56, 118–34, 142–45) assign the cultures of Middle and Late Formative Mesoamerica to this stage, which they consider to have lasted through the Early Classic Period in lowland Mesoamerica. (I find the latter conclusion especially gratifying since I had independently concluded that the Mesoamerican Classic Period in a very real sense represented an unusually enduring transition stage between chiefdoms and fully developed states [Webb 1968; 1973]). This is the opinion of Steward (1955) as well. One may note too that Adams (1966:35–36, 86–95) has characterized the fifteenth-century Mexica in the same fashion, although I feel that he seriously underestimated the extent to which large-scale and stable state controls had been achieved in early Postclassic Mesoamerica as a whole (if not, perhaps, among that people in particular). Turning to sub-Saharan Africa, the general studies of Gluckman (1968), Mair (1962), and Schapera (1967) indicate a high degree of institutional continuity between such groups as the Anuak, Alur, and Shilluk, in which state controls are absent or nearly so, and relatively populous kingdoms such as the Lozi, Swazi, or Baganda, with quite small increments in complexity at each step of the developmental sequence. Mair and Gluckman in fact differ on the point at which one can properly begin to speak of states, although everyone would probably agree that the Alur (Southall 1953) or the Shilluk (Evans-Pritchard 1964) lie close to the borderline. I suspect too that the most advanced of the Mississippian cultures of the southeastern United States might be included among our examples, although in fact they appear to have been on a smaller scale than most we have mentioned—except of course for Cahokia (Sanders and Marino 1970; Willey 1966:288–308); many of the Bronze and Early Iron Age societies of Europe and western Asia also appear to belong on this level (Piggott 1965; Clark and Piggott 1965; Renfrew 1973). Such chiefdoms were probably the basic social type in the "formative" stages of all archaic civilizations (Service 1962: 144). Moreover, in regard to the Pacific and the circum-Caribbean regions in particular, one receives the impression that a condition of stability had been reached on the chiefdom level so that if the European conquest had not taken place the type would be with us yet.

It is clear, nevertheless, on the basis of the range of size and complexity characteristic of each system, that the chiefdom, lacking the expansive capacity of the state, peaks at the point where the latter begins its career. This would appear to be due to the fact that even the largest, richest, and most successful chiefdoms lack that ability to enforce absolutely the wishes of their rulers which is characteristic of states. Although the growth and consolidation of this power may occur in slow increments, until a point is reached at which governmental commands will be unfailingly obeyed no matter what, the difference would seem to be one of kind and not of degree. As we will see, it does in fact appear that chiefdoms typically emerge under circumstances in which factors that give rise to states are only partially present, but if these factors were insufficient to generate "extra" wealth and power (that is, disposable resources beyond those which might be generated in the course of normal social interaction), further progress would be impossible. Even though such chiefdoms might indeed be capable of rather spectacular things and even if the roots of a bureaucracy and an army were present in the subchiefs, retainers, and, perhaps, part-time specialists (who form, as it were, the material cause which stretches back from the state into the chiefdom and even to the simple tribe [Lowie 1960; 1962; Adams 1966:110]), they would still be dependent upon free obedience and so lack a truly effective locus of sovereignty (Service 1962:159–60,

170–72). The very inability of the leadership to enforce unpleasant orders would prevent the collection of taxes or provision of services which would gather and maintain a group of retainers sufficiently large to give the leaders that ability to enforce their wishes. It would then be extremely difficult—ultimately impossible—to carry out plans and policies whose benefits were at all remote in time or space or which did not completely satisfy all parties concerned (hence the weak development of public law and the reliance upon compromise in jural proceedings among societies of this type). Kept relatively small and absolutely simple in organization, these societies could develop neither social heterogeneity nor those economic or social interdependencies that might suggest the need for truly governmental controls, as Gluckman (1968: 190–98) has noted. This means that the level of integration actually maintained at any time would constantly fluctuate because of local circumstances—inheritance of office, rivalries among chiefs, the extent to which various chiefs were "operators." Indeed, Sahlins (1963) and also Epstein (1968) point out that the very gathering of the goods needed to act as a chief puts enormous strains on the larger chiefdoms since the accumulation process tends to divert too much of the chief's resources toward the support of the chiefly apparatus and away from immediate general redistribution—the only means of securing the goodwill needed to accumulate the goods. As I have noted elsewhere (Webb 1965), the power of the chief to innovate would also be severely limited since his position would ultimately rest on kin and customary ties. The ability of local magnates, if not common tribesmen, to stand up to even the mightiest chieftain ensures, therefore, the continued existence of a widely diffused tribal veto on governmental activity.

These considerations explain the two most characteristic features of chiefdoms. The first of these is cyclical instability, the tendency of a large chiefdom to break apart into its component segments, then to reunite, only to fall apart again (Service 1962:151–53; Gluckman 1968: 160, 168–70). It appears that any expansion of the system to the point of linking disparate groups, of undertaking novel tasks, or of requiring innovative policy making, causes it to snap. The second characteristic feature of chiefdoms, especially those whose size and complexity approach the maximum for the type, is that they are almost invariably theocracies (see Service 1962:171; Schapera 1967:125; Fried 1967:137–

41; Gluckman 1968:298–99; Turner 1966; Davenport 1964; Park 1966). I would suggset that this is the case not only because of the strength of religious sanctions. Perhaps just as importantly, it reflects the fact that religious ceremonies, in contrast to the "selfish" needs of the rulers or even to public works (which may be located in someone else's local territory), can be seen as beneficial to participants gathered from throughout the chiefdom. Feelings of tribal localism and equalitarianism (at least in respect to the interrelations of individuals on the chiefly level) are, therefore, not affronted by these goals and practices. In addition, cult activities are likely to be strongly patterned and to reflect the established ways. From the beginning, gods have not been bound by space or time. Granting this, we would expect the most advanced of chiefdoms— those most like states in their ability to support "civilized" traits—to be at the same time the most theocratic of societies and the most unstable and subject to total collapse. I have previously suggested that the Classic Period Maya of the Petén were an outstanding example of this situation and that this circumstance explains their collapse (Webb 1973). According to the argument, the maintenance of the Maya centers depended upon the believability of their cult and priest chiefs, and this in turn depended on the prestige which the leadership acquired by dealing in basically exotic cult practices and in luxury and symbolic goods— goods, as it happens, of foreign origin (a view supported by Tourtellot and Sabloff's recent study [1972] of the origin points of various Maya trade goods). At the end of the Classic Period, shifts in the trading patterns which had linked the Maya with other parts of Mesoamerica led—in conjunction with other stresses—to the collapse of the central Maya high chiefly system. Of course, for reasons which will become clear below, transformation of at least some chiefdoms in a given geographic area into states (perhaps followed by their conquest of the remaining chiefdoms) is more common than total decline. And, in fact, the Maya societies to the north and south of the Petén did continue to evolve throughout the Postclassic Period.

To describe such highly developed, sometimes fairly durable chiefdoms, which at least superficially appear to be transitional to the state (although in fact the transformation may never take place), I have used the term *conditional states*. Although I would suggest that the Mesoamerican Classic Period peoples—especially the Petén Maya—are the most striking expression of the type, the final "formative" or "proto-literate" stage in many of the great ancient civilizations would represent at least closely analogous situations. (The fact that some of these—for example, early Mesopotamia—may have been governed by corporations of priests as opposed to unitary priest chiefs does not, perhaps, represent a major complication.) The phenomenon has been noted in the ethnographic record as well. Thus Fenton (1951) refers to the developed Iroquois League as a "kinship state," Gearing (1961) classifies the colonial Cherokee as a "voluntary state," Mair (1962) includes the Anuak and the Alur in her class of "primitive states," and Southall (1953) calls the Alur a "segmentary state." Krader's study (1968:30, 48, 73–75) of various Old World states provides such terms as "state-like," "emergent state," "proto-state," and "nascent-state." Service (1962:171–74) also discusses this feature of chiefdoms, although he does not coin a special term. Unfortunately, some of these terms—namely "kinship" or "segmentary" states—emphasize characteristics which are as prominent among equalitarian tribes as among chiefdoms. Others—"primitive," "voluntary," "emergent," "nascent," and "proto-states"—seem to stress the view that an essential continuity exists between advanced chiefdoms and states, the latter merely representing a more advanced form of characteristics which actually are characteristic of the former only. I use the term *conditional* precisely to stress what I believe to be their essential nature, namely that, although they may be almost exactly like small states in all ways except that they lack a reliable source of force which may be applied in a crisis, this very deficit means that the obedience of the separate segments of society to the leadership is *conditional*. The leadership must constantly prove itself, must earn obedience. This in turn means that the success of the society would depend upon the exact balance of favorable circumstances beyond its control to a much greater extent than is true for states, with their greater capacity for unified and innovative policy making.

More important than questions of terminology, however, is the consideration that, despite the superficial similarity in day-to-day functioning, a state does not represent just more of the same. It is not simply a chiefdom whose internal evolution has passed some point in sheer size; the two systems actually depend on the operation of forces which ultimately are radically different (in scope, if not in basic nature). The

transition from chiefdom to state therefore represents a complete transformation in the bases of social control, a transformation which would
seem to be unique in the social evolution of mankind. For this reason,
the point in the archaeological record at which one begins to refer to
evolving polities as "states" (without qualification) is not, perhaps,
solely a semantic issue. Although, for example, states have been seen as
already present in Preclassic Mesoamerica (Coe 1968; Grove 1973) and
in Uruk Mesopotamia (H. Wright 1972; Johnson, this volume, chap. 7),
it would seem most appropriate to regard this kind of social control as
having indeed been only conditional in nature until reliance on force
attained a prominence unmistakably equal to that typical of essentially
all known states. It is this successive grade which represents the most
decisive rift in institutional continuity. The problem of state origins lies
precisely in explaining how—granting the above-mentioned factors
which would tend to inhibit development through the conditional stage
—this particular rift could have taken place.

It might appear that an equally radical break is required for the shift
from the level of equalitarian tribes to that of chiefdoms, supposing for
argument's sake that the former generally exist as a separate stage between the band and chiefdom levels in the absence of influences external to local development (Fried 1967:154–74). At first glance, the
diffuse, mutually balanced, nonhierarchical, and often intermittent or
impermanent systems of decision making and authority characteristic of
tribes appear as different from the centralized cajolery of the chiefdom
as the chiefdom is from the centralized and monopolistic coercion of
the state. In tribes, of course, organization beyond the local community
(and within larger communities) is based on kinship units or other
tribal sodalities in which membership is essentially automatic. Such
connecting links are basically similar to one another in character and
rank, and individual tribesmen commonly belong to two or more such
units with interlocking and crosscutting memberships, so that tribal
unity is strengthened at the cost of unified direction and control (Mair
1962:61–106; Service 1962:110–22, 140–43; Service 1963:xxiv; Schapera
1967:20–30). These characteristics are reflected in the limited powers
of individual community headmen, in the great reliance on public opinion as a community sanction, in the vesting of such wider authority as
may exist in a council of either kin elders or community leaders

("chiefs") whose decisions must be essentially unanimous, and in heavy reliance upon automatic social control mechanisms such as divination or institutionalized feud (Schapera 1967:38–66; Sahlins 1968:1–20).

Nevertheless, the distinction between tribes and chiefdoms is not comparable to that between chiefdoms and states. The feature in which chiefdoms most resemble states, namely the possession of a centralized apparatus of decision making, is of far less consequence than the characteristic which they continue to share with the tribal, nonstate, "primitive" pattern, namely the lack of effective and reliable coercive force. Lacking this coercive power, chieftains cannot command, they must persuade, nag, beg, or obligate their following by making the latter's obedience quite clearly worth their while. This necessity of total reliance upon the carrot as opposed to the stick does not prevent the emergence of a chiefdom because real benefits are much more efficiently provided for by having some central organizer—allocation of resources, organization of labor, protection, social occasions, bestowal (recognition) of desired status, access to desired goods, and dispute resolution. These all obtain and maintain a following (up to a point). As a result, chiefdoms appear whenever (1) the basic techniques of subsistence are productive enough easily to produce a surplus while maintaining a moderately dense population and (2) the environment is characterized by a wide distribution of varying resources that makes it advantageous to have a central redistributive node, which will be the chief (Sahlins 1958; 1963; Coe 1961; Service 1962; Sanders 1957; Sanders and Price 1968; Gluckman 1968:174–76). As the society expands, the population will be drawn toward this node and the man on the scene will rise in importance, because it is at the node that those goods and services most desired by the most persons will most likely be found. This sequence of events permits and even demands that a system be organized around the redistributive node. While chiefdoms apparently do arise in locations in which it is physically possible for one family to reach all subsistence resources (Finney 1966), and while the amount actually retained—or even redistributed—by the chief may be rather small (Lambert 1966), the chiefdom would still offer a gain in efficiency as well as in the noneconomic advantages provided by friendly meetings under unified direction—the chance to plan projects, consult for defense, ar-

166

range marriages, settle disputes, and so on. These latter benefits would be especially important in situations—probably quite common—in which a number of mutually competitive chiefly systems were emerging simultaneously in the same region. At this stage of development, as Sahlins (1972) has noted, not only are economic and political institutions essentially undifferentiated, but mechanisms which we might consider primarily economic often serve essentially political ends.

On the basis of the above, we would expect that a steady evolution of primitive societies up to the chiefdom level would occur wherever appropriate primary subsistence techniques and resources distributions existed. The chiefdom represents a distinct social type with its own history, quite independent of the state. We have failed in the past to be sufficiently aware of this for several reasons: first, the development of some chiefdoms has indeed been greatly influenced by contact with previously existing states; furthermore, certain mechanisms generally present in the emergence of chiefdoms, such as intertribal warfare, contribute under special conditions to the rise of states; and finally, it is quite possible that chiefdoms represent a necessary precondition of state evolution. Nevertheless, a full understanding of both social types and of the factors operative in the formation of each requires an awareness of their distinct natures.

For this reason, Renfrew's use of recalibrated carbon dates to demonstrate that the evolution of stratified societies in Western Eurasia down to the end of the later Bronze Age was independent of state development in the Near East (Renfrew 1970; 1971a; 1972), although initially shocking, has performed a most useful service. Even if evidence of rather early penetration of Europe by forces from the Near East may yet turn up, there is no reason to question the independence of chiefdom development in, for example, Polynesia. Yet if chiefdoms can emerge independently among stone-tool users in the Pacific, why not in the far richer environment and technology of late Neolithic and Bronze Age Europe? (There were of course indications of problems with the old European chronology even before the recent recalibration [Daniel 1963: 143–46].) The picture that appears to be emerging now indicates that chiefdoms appear more or less independently over a broad zone of favorable environments, while full states develop somewhat later and do so first in a portion of the larger zone which seems to have been relatively less favorable and developmentally a bit backward, namely the great river valleys of the arid Near East. Our knowledge of the evolution of advanced societies in Mesoamerica has indicated just such a scheme for many years. Thus, although Olmec, or perhaps "Olmecoid," traits are widespread in Mesoamerica in Middle Formatve times, with maximum development in certain lowland tropical forest areas, by the Protoclassic Period a different, much more restricted zone, the semiarid highland basins, has taken the lead. These basins continue as the centers of evolution throughout the Classic Period. (Even though the Petén Maya achieved a remarkably elaborate culture within the tropical forest zone during the Classic Period, they represent basically a late florescence of the old Olmec tradition; their formation appears to have been dependent on forces or even populations emanating from the nearby highlands, and their ultimate collapse was the result of competition from more advanced, fully evolved state societies [Willey, Culbert, and Adams 1967; Gifford 1968; Willey and Shimkin 1971; Willey and Gifford 1961; Coe 1963; Parsons 1967; Sharer and Gifford 1970].) A similar contraction and shift of primary focus seems to have taken place in Peru during the last millennium B.C. (Lanning 1967:82–106; Patterson 1971; Izumi 1971; Lathrap 1971). I suspect the same to have been true in early China (Treistman 1972; Chang 1968:80–94, 121–30, 150, 192–240) and India (Allchin and Allchin 1968:105–22, 321–24) as well.

This, then is the heart of our problem: Chiefdoms apparently represent the natural, inevitable end product, the natural culmination of the agricultural revolution.[1] As the highest achievement of primitive society they seem to be quite capable of providing at least as satisfactory a life for all their members as any other system and have in fact provided an image of the heroic "golden age" which has remained attractive from the early Iron Age to the present day. In the absence of any more advanced system, they would seem to have adequate survival potential. Moreover, evolution beyond the stage would appear to be precluded (Fried 1960; 1967). Nevertheless, despite inherent improbabilities, the chiefdom did give birth to a more advanced social form, the state, which not only burst the bonds of the older high tribal form of society but also eventually caused it to become totally extinct. We must now examine some at least of the preconditions for this emergence.

168

GEOGRAPHICAL, TEMPORAL, AND DEVELOPMENTAL PARAMETERS OF STATE FORMATION

A considerable variety of explanations have been suggested in recent years for the rise of state society. It is obvious, however, from the perspective of world culture history, that any such explanations must above all deal with the origins of pristine or *primary states,* that is, those whose beginnings seem to have been independent of any stimulation by contact with already existing states, in contrast to the much more common *secondary states,* those which ultimately owe their origin to forces radiating out from previously existing states—forces such as political incorporation, military pressure, or trade contact. It is certainly true that in the great majority of cases the birth even of secondary states represents an independent response by local populations to particular circumstances rather than the mere acceptance by ignorant natives of the benefits and techniques of "civilization" under the "influence"—often unspecified—of superior persons from state societies, a view to which Renfrew (1969; 1970; 1971a; 1973) has, quite properly, vigorously objected and one whose total explanatory inadequacy I noted a decade ago (Webb 1964; cf. Childe 1958:150–73; Finley 1970:13–21). Even though such states were secondary in point of time, the process of growth was—as will be seen—essentially an internal one. The local tribal leaders themselves took advantage of the various opportunities (generally newly available resources) and responded to the various problems (often the direct threat of conquest) presented by the contact with existing states in such a fashion as to achieve new levels of power consolidation. (For this reason some such terms as "intrasystemic states"—those formed by processes operative within one nuclear interaction sphere— and "intersystemic states"—those formed by processes involving long-distance contact between two such spheres—might be preferable to "primary" and "secondary"; I will continue to follow the accepted usage for the most part, but these qualifications must be borne in mind.) Nevertheless, insofar as already-existing states formed part of the environmental situation in response to which later states emerged, they represent at least a complicating factor, so that, as Fried (1960) has noted, a complete explanation must deal with those cases in which the very first states emerged from a completely tribal setting. As we shall see, the mechanisms operative in the formation of both primary and secondary states would appear to be differently developed but systematically related aspects of the same general processes. It is helpful to bear this point in mind, since the most recent of the few possible primary states seems to have taken form nearly a thousand years ago, whereas some secondary states are of quite recent origin.

It is clear that any explanation or combination of explanations must meet certain criteria if it is to be considered valid. The first of these, obviously, is that any proposed mechanisms must be consistent with both the archaeological and the historical evidence and also with the manner in which similar societies have been observed actually to operate. This is necessary even though the archaeological data are still sufficiently incomplete and our powers of theoretical generalization from the ethnographic present still so inadequate as perhaps to permit several alternate explanations. A second criterion—which can eliminate some otherwise apparently reasonable conjectures—is that the hypothesis must explain fully the distribution in time and space of both primary and secondary states, taking into account basic features of the environment, locational aspects, and the temporal succession of the expanding social type. Finally, and perhaps most importantly, any mechanism proposed would have to explain how the apparently inherently self-defeating limitations on sovereign power characteristic of tribal society were overcome—and overcome by mechanisms which at the beginning of their operation were normal for tribal society but which would in special circumstances evolve into something different. In other words, what is required is a process which is generally present with no significant consequences in tribal society but which became formed into a positive feedback loop at those times and places in which states arose and which in those cases where state formation was atypical was likely to have been effective precisely to the extent that state formation was complete.

A rapid survey suggests that we have between six and eight reasonably probable primary state areas. The most certain of these, along with the approximate times of their origins are: Egypt (about 3100 B.C.); lower Mesopotamia and Elam (at the same time or a little earlier); the Indus Valley (before 2000 B.C.); the Yellow River Basin of northern

China (shortly after 2000 B.C.); highland Mesoamerica (between 100 B.C. and 800 A.D.—it would appear that the region is marked by an unusually long transition stage); and coastal Peru (about the time of Christ). Although it has been suggested that the Egyptian state represents a response to Mesopotamian influence (for example, Frankfort 1956), the distinctiveness of the two areas' cultural patterns, Egypt's achievement of union over its entire river valley prior to Mesopotamia despite the fact that Mesopotamia developed various features of civilization, such as writing, at an earlier date, and the consideration that Mesopotamia was never so much more developed in this period as to penetrate Egypt directly (although diffusion of specific ideas or motifs may have occurred) indicate an independent process in each area (Childe 1957; 1959). In fact, a recent reexamination of the Egyptian Predynastic sequence indicates that there is no artifactual evidence of cultural intrusion into this area great enough to warrant our regarding developments there as anything other than native (Arkell and Ucko 1965). I believe that the same points can be made in regard to the Indus Valley and North China, despite the relatively undeveloped state of our knowledge in the former case and the relatively retarded date of developments in the latter (Piggott 1950; Clark and Piggott 1965:196–201; Wheeler 1966; Creel 1937a; 1937b; Cheng 1959; 1960; cf. Webb 1964). In the same way, although perhaps a case can still be made for the existence of a Nuclear American diffusion sphere in the period between the birth of agriculture and the end of the Olmec or Chavín periods (Willey 1955; Weaver 1972:288–90; Patterson 1971; Lathrap 1973), I know of no major authority on either Mesoamerica or Peru who believes that any strong or continuous contact between the two areas occurred during their Protoclassic or Early Classic periods (e.g., Wolf 1959; Willey 1962; Bennett and Bird 1960; Collier 1962; Lanning 1967; Weaver 1972). While it is possible to argue about the degree of independence of development in each of these six cases, I believe that one would be on safe ground in regarding them as the most likely to have been primary—to have been formed by essentially intrasystemic processes—of the various early state areas of which we have knowledge.

There are two additional possibilities whose interpretation is rather more difficult. The first of these is the Aegean region during the Bronze Age. In Crete the time of the emergence of civilization—the later Early

Bronze Age—would allow trading links with Old and Middle Kingdom Egypt and with the Levant; a fair number of stylistic ties, as well as some trade goods, do appear to indicate some contact of this sort (Renfrew 1970; Finley 1970; Childe 1951b:21–28; Hutchinson 1962:102–12, 147–49, 164–69; Pendlebury 1965:89, 120–22, 172–75, 222–26, 269–81). The rise of Mycenae would in similar fashion reflect a successful tapping of a Cretan-based trade network (Finley 1970:47–53; Childe 1951b:74–79; Vermeule 1964:32–38, 55, 59, 76, 88–99, 113–14). Nevertheless, as Renfrew notes (1973:194–212), the stylistic links with the older Near Eastern civilizations are rather diffuse, and the trade goods (which actually suggest that the Aegean was an exporter of *manufactured* goods) are in fact rather scanty, while many continuities exist with earlier periods in the Aegean. Therefore, despite a temporal and geographic distribution of emerging states in the eastern Mediterranean which remains highly suggestive of some causal mechanism linking this region with the older centers of civilization, it would perhaps be best to see the Minoan-Mycenaean development as a mixed case in which the possibility of securing really large amounts of trade wealth enabled rulers of the emerging states to pull themselves across the line separating barbarism from civilization more expeditiously than would otherwise have been the case. The second possibility is the area of the great Iron Age kingdoms of the Lake region of East Africa (Buganda, Bunyoro, etc.), whose legendary histories suggest that states existed early in the second millennium A.D. The extensive medieval trade contacts along the coast, the well-known role of trade in stimulating state formation in West Africa, and the rather generalized resemblance of many sub-Saharan African states to ancient Egypt make primary state status seem unlikely (Davidson 1959; 1966; 1969; Murdock 1959:36–39, 178–79; Oliver and Fage 1962:37–38, 100; Cole 1965:317–24). Nevertheless, since foreign trade contact with the interior seems to have been rather indirect, it may be better simply to reserve a final judgment in this case.

All of these regions tend to be characterized by two particularly outstanding environmental features. The first is that they are areas of extremely productive land surrounded by markedly less fertile zones. Except for the Aegean, they are, indeed, river valleys or lake systems surrounded by desert or at least very dry zones. The aridity of Egypt, Mesopotamia, and Pakistan at the present time is well known. Although

Egypt was rather less arid during the Neolithic Period than at present, by the time the evolution of the state in the Nile Valley was well advanced conditions there had apparently begun to approach those of recent times, so that areas away from the river were not able to support settled, high-level agriculture (Butzer 1964:438–60; Desmond Clark 1962; Arkell and Ucko 1965). It also appears reasonably certain that at the relevant times both lower Mesopotamia and Pakistan were as dry as they are today, or nearly so (Butzer 1964:461–71; Raikes and Dyson 1961). Turning to China, it may not be so well known that conditions of climate, soil, and topography combine to make intensive agriculture very difficult beyond the river margins in the Yellow River Basin (Stamp 1938:500–518; Cressey 1955). In early Shang times, natural conditions were no better, and the great irrigation systems had not yet been constructed (Von Wissmann et al. 1966; Chi 1936). Central highland Mexico south to Tehuantepec is also rather dry and in addition suffers from severe rain shadow effects in the highland basins and stream valleys that were the aboriginal population centers (Walker n.d.; West and Augelli 1966). The Peruvian coast has been extremely arid for the last 4,000 years (Lanning 1967:7–12, 41–65). Although the Lake region of Africa may not have been as dry as the other areas mentioned, it was at least semiarid; today it is marked by such irregularity of rainfall as to make permanent water sources highly desirable in many locations (Stamp 1953:369–72, 387–90, 403–7, figs. 4.6, 6.1). Finally, the situation in the Aegean was perhaps rather similar, since this is an area of rainfall stress and was characterized during the Bronze Age by the development of the Mediterranean system of wheat-olive-grape polyculture. The commitment to arboriculture and the need for a particular zoning of land types would serve to nucleate populations in a fashion similar to the effect produced by water sources in the other regions mentioned (Renfrew 1973:208–10).

These same conditions of general climatic stress, in combination on the one hand with the alluvial nature of the great river valleys, and on the other with the strongly developed zoning of resources characteristic of highland or island areas, give rise to the other characteristic environmental factor—a tendency for the sources of many useful raw materials either to be lacking entirely in the central zone or to be widely scattered. In both Mesopotamia and Egypt the early historical sources indicate considerable concern with securing products found altogether outside the river valleys, such as large timbers, ores, and building stone. Although sufficient data are not really available for the Indus region or for China, the former evidently had strong trade ties both to outlying regions and to the civilized states to the west, while the very nature of the raw materials used in northern China strongly suggests that the typical motivations existed there as well (Wheeler 1966:64–70; Allchin and Allchin 1968:266–72; Treistman 1972). Although the limitations characteristic of alluvial and arid zones were less severe in highland Mesoamerica owing to the smaller size of the river systems, a marked altitudinal zoning made it necessary to search for resources outside of metropolitan regions, while the division of the area into microenvironments apparently led to a major emphasis on smaller, intraregional exchange networks (Sanders and Price 1968:101–5, 128–34). In eastern Africa the earliest historical records also suggest a well-developed system of trading contacts with the coast, although in this instance the trade appears largely to have involved a late concern to secure the manufactured goods of a superior technology (Davidson 1959:306–10; Oliver and Fage 1962:100 ff; Cole 1965:300–310, 327–29; Murdock 1959). The Aegean too was marked by an extensive development of both local and long-distance trade because of its mosaic resource distribution and the possibilities of sea transport (Renfrew 1969). It would seem, then, that the only real exception was coastal Peru, where the river valley systems were so small that the local inhabitants could easily secure products from beyond these regions themselves; even in this case a coast-mountain trade remains a possibility (Lanning 1967:14–18, 88–90, 120; cf. Lathrap 1973).

If we examine current explanations for state origins, it is quickly evident that many fail to meet fully the tests suggested above. One hypothesis that comes immediately to mind is familiar to those who have used Braidwood's *Prehistoric Men* (1967) as a text. Braidwood's thesis is that, since the dryland river valley areas were immensely productive even on an essentially Neolithic level of technology once they had been drained and irrigated, they would be the sites of mutually reinforcing population and economic explosions. As a result they would quickly come to contain large, dense populations characterized by great social diversity, occupational specialization, and the breakdown of kin and

174

traditional controls. These factors would, in turn, both suggest the advantages of state controls and make possible their introduction (Braidwood 1967). Although I cannot myself see this process as an independent variable, it is perhaps true that in the past we have tended to underrate the transforming effects of sheer population growth (cf. Boserup 1965). As I have previously noted (Webb 1968), this proposition also strongly appeals to our Anglo-American bias toward cooperation, compromise, and constitutionalism.

Nevertheless, it accords neither with observed behavior nor with the actual distribution of early states. I believe that one can search the entire literature relating to the emergence of state institutions among tribal peoples without finding a single case of successful free unions of this sort; and indeed advanced, industrialized states seem to be every bit as reluctant to surrender local sovereignty, as advocates of U.N. reform, European union, or world federalism have discovered. Since the inability to concentrate power adequately is in fact the characteristic failing of chiefdoms, there would seem to be a need for some mechanism which would lead to such a free surrender of local autonomy. Moreover, as Carneiro (1961), among others, has pointed out, many regions that remained on a tribal level seem to have been as capable of producing a surplus as are preindustrial states. I would agree that it is to the primarily technological interface of culture and environment that we must look for the causes of social change, but such progress is not inevitable. Although it is possible to restate the voluntarist hypothesis in terms of specific adaptive advantages relating to such characteristic needs of complex societies as task management or information processing (Wilmsen 1972; Flannery 1972; Johnson 1973; Kottak 1974:197–219), this does not explain the source of the leadership group's ability to enforce their decisions—a rather critical point. Without adequate mechanisms to provide public order, dispute resolution, and resource allocation, there would be no possibility of complex economic specialization, and so technological advance would itself cease (Pearson 1957; Olive N. and Barba A. 1957; Harris 1959). Since on the advanced tribal and archaic state level social integrating mechanisms are more familial and political than economic ("market") in nature, we again arrive at the need for previously existing state mechanisms to ensure the operation of supposedly state-inducing forces (Polanyi, Arensberg, and Pearson 1957; Sahlins 1958; 1972). The advantages provided by union into a state for competition (including military conflict) with other groups at the same general developmental level provides no satisfactory answer either, since such competitive situations occur in areas where states did not emerge independently. As noted, some areas, such as Polynesia (Suggs 1960; Davenport 1969) and the northern Andes (Rouse 1962; Reichel-Dolmatoff 1961), do indeed appear to have stabilized on a high chiefly level despite a very high agricultural potential. It is also difficult to see Bronze Age Europe as very much less capable of surplus production than the great Near Eastern river valleys, yet it was in the latter that full civilization first emerged, despite the lack of any overwhelming developmental priority there during the preceding periods (Renfrew 1971b; Gimbutas 1972; 1973).

One method of avoiding these problems is by the use of the hypothesis usually associated with Karl Wittfogel: that quarreling tribes or tribal segments inhabiting a dryland river valley could be controlled by those in charge of pan-valley irrigation systems (Wittfogel 1957; Childe 1951a:88–90). This would introduce the necessary element of coercion, and recent research has confirmed the existence of irrigation or water storage in the formative stages of Mesopotamian, Indian, highland Mesoamerican, Peruvian, and, possibly, Chinese civilization (Adams 1956; 1965:35–46; Adams and Nissen 1972:11–18, 91–92; Allchin and Allchin 1968:258–62; Fowler 1969; Flannery 1968; Flannery et al. 1967; Willey 1953:109–11, 132–36, 157–77, 362–69; Chang 1968:180, 249). Nevertheless, it appears clear that no great pan-valley irrigation systems were constructed until *after* the establishment of state controls (Chi 1936; Lanning 1967:109–20). Tribal societies are, in fact, perfectly capable of constructing moderately large irrigation systems and of allocating the resulting water supply as well (Woodbury 1961); although differential access to irrigated land may help to create differences in wealth and may enlarge the social control powers of community leaders, it apparently does not lead to consolidation of political power on the tribal level (Gray 1963:161–71). In Mesoamerica, East Africa, and the Aegean, moreover, even relatively large areas were irrigated by means of many rather small water-control units; it is rather difficult to see how one can meaningfully speak of "control" of irrigation networks in these

176

cases (in contrast, for example, to control of populations or of total environmental zones).

Another theory finds the source of the elusive state controls in psychological and religious factors. According to this hypothesis, priests (perhaps functioning in situations of water stress) would gradually acquire state powers from their access to accumulated temple wealth, from the awe they inspired (perhaps backed up by not-so-veiled threats to withhold the rains or the annual flooding of the rivers), and from their continuity in policy making. Lowie (1960) felt that cult controls played a critical role in the rise of the Mesoamerican and Peruvian states. Essentially the same view was elaborately developed by Rushton Coulborn (1969) and also received considerable emphasis (in combination with other factors) from both Childe (1954: chaps. 4–6) and McNeill (1965:45–56). Netting (1972) has suggested that in sub-Saharan Africa increasing population density could cause ecological stresses which would give increasing prominence to and place greatly enlarged powers in the hands of tribal religious leaders. Water supply is, however, by no means the only severe and recurring problem which may face primitive peoples, so the correlation of early states with arid lands is left unexplained. There is also no reason to suppose that all the priest-chiefs in a community would stand together against kin and the community as a whole. More typically, priests can only play a secular role by seizing already existing state controls or by gaining power when secular rulers are seriously divided. The well-known theocratic cast of early states is more likely to reflect a rapidly vanishing condition in which, in the absence of state controls, only religious public works could be carried out, than to indicate the great force of specifically theocratic sanctions; the later history of states is one of a decreasing role of cultus in governmental affairs (Webb 1965; 1973). Therefore, even though it does appear that many archaic states were ruled by theocrats, who may have been truly devout men, the source of their power and the ends to which they applied it must have been ultimately secular. Their assumption of power in the emerging states was due simply to their being so placed in the older system that they could benefit the most from the changed conditions (see Adams 1966:133–50; Wilson 1968).

Perhaps the most straightforward explanation of the source of the required controls is among the very oldest: namely, that states arose when one community or ethnic group imposed themselves as rulers over another through military conquest. This state-forming mechanism has had an especially prominent place in the thought of anthropologists in the cultural evolutionary tradition, such as Spencer (Carneiro 1967:33–35, 73–81, 117–215), Tylor (1946 2:152–56), Morgan 1963:48–154, 253–66, 326ff.), and White (1959:297–98), but it has also commended itself to such nonanthropological students of early urbanism as Mumford (1961:21–46) and McNeill (1965:56–64). Conquest would certainly produce a dominating group with coercive powers over those being ruled. Moreover, the discipline of war, in conjunction with the loot derived from the defeated, could lead to the concentration of political authority even among the victors. For these reasons I myself feel that warfare has played a critical role at certain points in the process of state formation. Nevertheless, it is necessary to specify rather closely the key stages in the process, since large-scale fighting has been observed among many tribal peoples who seem not to have been developing states (see Dumond 1972a). Even though many of these societies may in fact have lacked advanced technologies, this was not true for post-Neolithic Europe, yet although warfare was endemic in that region from at least the Early Bronze Age (which Gimbutas [1973] now dates to the latter part of the fourth millennium), the initiation of stable states was delayed in most areas by several thousand years. Apparently intertribal war even among complex and densely settled tribal societies leads to greater elaboration of chiefdoms but—by itself—no further (Fried 1967:113–20, 178–82, 213–26), a view supported by recent studies of tribal warfare in Polynesia (Vayda 1956; 1961) and in lowland South America (Carneiro 1961; Meggers 1971:109–13, 144–49). The problem appears to be that normally the lack among the victors of the organization necessary to provide an army of occupation enables the defeated to expel them or at least simply to move away. Since the victors are unable to derive any benefit (beyond land for expansion) from the situation, no group within that society has access to the large concentration of extra resources that might give rise to the state controls required to maintain a standing army. As we shall see, Robert Carneiro's circumscription hypothesis—the theory that, in areas characterized by limited amounts of good farm land, population pressure must in time give rise

178

to conditions of increasingly severe war from which the defeated cannot escape (Carneiro 1961; 1970)—largely specifies the geographical parameters within which militarism is indeed of further developmental significance; part of my purpose here is to specify the boundaries of operation of this process in terms of developmental levels.

In order to do this we must now examine another theory of state origins which, like the conquest hypothesis, has proven to be very durable. It does indeed involve mechanisms which both begin on the prestate level and also have proven capable of transcending the limitations of tribal society—although (again like the conquest hypothesis) only at certain stages in the developmental process or under specific circumstances. This is the theory that, in technologically and economically expanding societies, the large-scale practice of intratribal and intertribal trade would lead to the steady concentration of economic and so of police powers in the hands of a small number of favorably situated chiefs and kin elders, who would then become a ruling merchant class. Both long-distance trade (required to secure scarce raw materials) and internal exchange (necessitated by economic specialization) can be seen as creating the social heterogeneity and the breakdown of kin controls which would be needed for continued advancement. Commercial wealth is a logical source of power which would be both socially novel and subject to increase by small increments, with the result that new loci of authority might emerge free of existing, traditional controls. Moreover, as noted, the special ecological setting of many pristine state areas would tend to necessitate trade. Since no one who observes the commanding role of wealth in modern societies can fail to be impressed, it is not surprising that this theory, first stated in its classic form by Engels ninety years ago (Engels 1942, chaps. 5–7), has particularly commended itself to such contemporary students as Sahlins (1958; 1963), Wolf (1959:134–44), Service (1962:143–76), Coe (1961), Grove (1968), and Renfrew (1969).

It has, moreover, the advantage of actually having been seen in operation. As noted, secondary states have continued to emerge on the fringes of civilized zones until recent times. The ethnographic and historical literature relating to the European penetration of North America, southern Africa, Guinea, and Polynesia contains perhaps two dozen fairly good examples of such state formation, while medieval sources

179

relating to the frontiers of Arabic, European, or Chinese civilization provide others. But these cases are precisely those in which foreign trade has introduced surplus wealth in large amounts. As I pointed out a number of years ago in a detailed study of state formation in aboriginal Hawaii (Webb 1965), this kind of wealth, which must pass through the hands of the most senior tribal chieftains because they are the center of the local redistributive network, provides the excess beyond what is needed by this leadership for customary redistributive activity. The redistributive channels clog up and overflow, as it were. The surplus in such cases has actually been observed in use to hire war bands—individuals from defeated tribes, exiles, and other rootless men—that are not bound by traditional ties to the society and can therefore be used in enforcing the will of the chief as opposed to that of the tribe as a whole. This surplus may also be used to offer the common tribesmen rewards greater than those available in the traditional system, so that force is supplemented by positive inducements to obedience. It is the surplus of trade wealth which in this case first enables the emerging king to support the army and bureaucracy necessary to collect the taxes necessary to support the army and bureaucracy internally—in other words to carry on the vital activity of the state. The importance of this wealth is surely the reason that tribal chieftains have so frequently tended to keep a monopoly control over trade with more advanced groups (Gluckman 1940; 1960; Webb 1965). The same concern is seen in the large role played by the government in commerce among archaic states generally (Polanyi 1966; Polanyi, Arensberg, and Pearson 1957; Kottak 1972).

There are, nevertheless, serious problems with this view as usually stated. The ethnographic record clearly indicates that tribal and peasant peoples have a great development of such devices as cargo systems, ceremonial inhibitions to resource allocation, and the division of power between secular and religious chiefs. These devices serve to prevent unusual concentrations of wealth and, more particularly, its application by the leadership to personal or nontraditional ends (Sahlins 1965; Webb 1965; Davenport 1964; 1969; G. A. Wright 1970; Fagan 1972). As Sahlins in particular has long maintained (Sahlins 1960; 1968; 1972), not only is economic power among primitive peoples a function of the generalized leadership role rather than the reverse, but economic decision making often reflects essentially political needs. The fact that in early Egypt (Hallo and Simpson 1971:221–35; Childe 1957:88–101), Mesoamerica (Brundage 1972:26–32, 43–47, 210–17; Chapman 1957; Acosta Saignes 1945), Peru (Mason 1968:144, 168–72; Moseley, Mackey, and Brill 1973), and—insofar as one can tell—China (Creel 1937a:89–94; Chang 1968:240–55) large-scale, long-distance trade was conducted or dominated by the state is at least as likely to indicate that trade was always under governmental domination as that merchants had great powers. In addition, there are real difficulties in conceiving how trade could become a monopoly or in demonstrating that trade was more vital in emerging primary states than in many other regions which never developed states independently.

From this I would conclude that trade is effective as a state-forming mechanism primarily in the case of secondary states, that only trade in relatively massive amounts or which involved a higher order of luxury and craft production—in other words, trade that would have to originate in an existing state—would be sufficient finally to override tribal mechanisms inhibiting stratification (Fried 1967:182–84, 203–4; Epstein 1968). However, even though both intrasocietal and intersocietal trade and exchange on the tribal level are significant primarily in the growth and consolidation of chiefdoms, they are nevertheless important for ultimate state formation since, as we will see, the existence of large and prosperous chiefdoms is apparently a necessary precondition for the successful operation of more specifically state-forming factors.

In any event, there appears to have been no lack of trade extending far into the background of many state areas. Long-distance trade in obsidian as well as other items appears with the establishment of stable Neolithic economies (if not before) in the Near East, Europe, and Mesoamerica (Dixon, Cann, and Renfrew 1968; Renfrew 1969; G. A. Wright 1969; Cobean et al. 1971; Clark 1966:76, 94–95, 180–94, 241–52). Indeed, the well-known Hopewell cultures of central North America display a positively fantastic ability to secure exotic goods in an area where statehood was never achieved under aboriginal conditions (R. Morgan 1952; Maxwell 1952; Prufer 1964a; 1964b; Struever and Houart 1972). Even though evidence for trade during later stages tends to consist of stylistic resemblances, ethnographic analogy from Melanesia,

Micronesia, the southwestern United States, and the simpler African societies suggests that emerging chiefdoms—and even nonranked societies—are quite capable of maintaining extensive, complicated trading networks and that the strengthening of such networks will frequently coincide, at least, with the strengthening of the chiefly office. Although the Early Bronze Age cultures of Europe are too early to reflect any "intersystemic" trade from the Near East, the late fourth millennium interconnections in southeastern Europe and the somewhat later Unetice-German-Brittany-Wessex ties do appear to reflect precisely the sort of trading practices one would expect for large, prosperous, coevally evolving chiefdoms (Renfrew 1969; 1971b; Gimbutas 1973; Coles and Taylor 1971; Clark 1966:256–61; Piggott 1965:120–30). The long history of theocratic public works, the emphasis on sumptuary goods, and the intense development of warfare (which, predictably, never led anywhere) characteristic of these societies confirm their status as chiefdoms (Daniel 1963:132–41; Gimbutas 1973; Piggott 1965; Coles and Taylor 1971).

A complication has recently been introduced by Pires-Ferreira who, on the basis of her finding that long-distance trade in obsidian in Mesoamerica broke down at the beginning of the Middle Formative Period— that is, at the point when the "Olmec" chiefdoms became consolidated —argues that once chieftains have emerged they will turn from intersocietal trade to intrasocietal redistribution as a means of consolidating their power (Pires-Ferreira in press; Pires-Ferreira and Evans in press). This view is eminently reasonable; yet, as noted, it is contradicted by the bulk of the historical and ethnographic evidence, which indicates a strong interest in foreign trade on the part of tribal chieftains. The conflict disappears, however, when it is recalled that such documentary evidence always reflects a situation in which contacts with existing states— always themselves interested in trade (Webb in press)—have been established. Even though their interest might center on internal redistribution, chieftains could be expected always to be interested in foreign trade to the extent necessary to secure essential raw materials or whatever exotic or useful manufactured goods were entering their region. The scattered distribution of faïence in western Eurasia and the "Amber Route"—assuming that the latter did in fact exist—may reflect such situations, in which the leaders took an interest in long-distance trade even though their primary concerns were more local (Piggott 1965:120–38; Clark 1966:260–70; Beck 1970; Deshayes 1969).

An emphasis on exchange systems appears to be a common characteristic of the "formative" stages of many emerging civilizations. Increasing evidence for the establishment of both long-distance and local, intercity exchange networks now exists for the one Old World primary state area for which data exist—Mesopotamia, including Elam; in particular, the tendency toward a clustering of sites around regional capitals becomes especially strong immediately prior to the emergence of the state (Lamberg-Karlovsky and Lamberg-Karlovsky 1971; Adams and Nissen 1972:17–19, 25–28; Adams 1965: fig. 2; Johnson, this volume, chap. 7). A similar pattern of site integration has been discerned among the Classic Petén Maya, whose cultural development peaked at this level (Marcus 1973; Hammond 1972a; 1972b). The strong orientation of the Maya leadership to both internal and external exchange involving both practical (Rathje 1971) and sumptuary (Tourtellot and Sabloff 1972) goods is well known (Tozzer 1941:94–98, 107; Roys 1957; Webb 1973) and apparently represents a special elaboration of a concern which developed throughout Mesoamerica during the Classic Period (Sanders 1967; Sanders and Price 1968:32–34, 142, 161–62, 168–69, 206–8; Coe 1962:115–16, 124–26; Spence 1967; Webb in press). A roughly similar pattern of site clustering and subregional differentiation seems to be emerging for the immediately pre-Harappan stages in the Indus Valley also (Allchin and Allchin 1968:112–25, 130; Wheeler 1966: fig. 2, pp. 54–60), while both Peru (Lanning 1967:116–19; Willey 1953:371–84, 395–96) and China (Chang 1968:92–112, 130–60, 194–228, 245; Treistman 1972:53–62, 73–84, 108–9) show site clustering, although the relation in these cases to exchange patterns is problematic. As noted, local, interregional exchange appears to have been very strongly developed in the Aegean from Neolithic times on (Renfrew 1969; 1973:205–12); moreover, the regular distribution of major sites in both mainland Greece and Crete presents clear analogies with the cases just given (Renfrew, this volume, chap. 1). Since comparable data are not available for Egypt or East Africa, our investigation has at last come to the critical point of state origins. It now remains for us to examine those circumstances in which the state finally broke through the last restraints of tribalism.

THE IRRUPTION AND EXPANSION
OF STATE SYSTEMS

As indicated, I believe that it is the so-called circumscription hypothesis of state formation which, with certain modifications, best fits the precise circumstances of primary state formation. This hypothesis has been maintained for a number of years by Carneiro (1961; 1970; 1972), although Dumond (1965) and Harner (1970) have suggested in similar fashion that a strong relationship exists between population size and density, and the centralization and concentration of social controls. The great merit of the circumscription hypothesis is that it demonstrates a way in which the widespread process of intertribal warfare, ineffective as a mechanism of state formation for most tribal peoples owing to their lack of an army of occupation, could, in the special circumstances of limited agricultural land, generate more advanced social systems. Carneiro (1961) noted that a great many portions of tropical Latin America which never developed states or even chiefdoms were theoretically able to support such systems under native conditions of subsistence, that chiefdoms in fact appeared only in areas where good farm land was limited in extent and sharply bounded by markedly poorer land, and that such areas were also characterized by especially severe warfare. From this he concluded that in these areas, as population inevitably grew to the point at which unused good land began to become scarce, the necessary struggle for agricultural resources among neighboring, confined groups generated more complex and centralized tribal organization. Because no group would be able to retreat without abandoning all hope of gaining the highly desirable territory, there would be a premium on staying put and fighting it out. This in turn would greatly enhance the power of tribal rulers both by creating an obvious need for firm leadership and by enabling leaders to reward their followers with the loot from raided groups (who could not easily move out of range). It would perhaps be more likely that such intensified warfare would be touched off by incursions into lightly settled buffer zones used for hunting or pasture than by invasions of the tribal heartland, but this would not basically alter the situation. Carneiro then considered what could be expected to happen if very populous chiefdoms in very rich areas with very sharply constricted agricultural zones, such as river valleys or lake basins in arid regions, were to fight in this way.

Applying this hypothesis to the primary state areas, with their highly limited land, we see that in fact it would now be possible for chieftains to escape controls on the alienation of group property and the individual accumulation of tribal wealth. The war chief, who would have the right to divide spoils, would be able to take the surplus of defeated groups, who could not resist and would be absolutely tied down by the environment. Because the land, while limited, was so very highly productive, this loot would provide the chief with a source of wealth unparalleled in quantity and in freedom from internal tribal controls. Even after the customary ceremonial and redistributive obligations had been met, enough would be left over to enable him to overcome local and kin loyalties and to gather about him a group of retainers or a war band large enough to keep in check all other groups in the society. This wealth plays the same role as do the profits from trade with existing states in the case of secondary state formation. In the absence of such large-scale trade, plunder and tribute from defeated competitors provide the most likely source of free wealth in really significant amounts—provided that the vanquished cannot escape.

With his new following, the chief now could enforce decisions, collect taxes, undertake public works, and mobilize the society for external defense—in a word, subvert the tribal constitution and establish the state (Carneiro 1970). Moreover, the task would be made easier by the fact that at the beginning of the lengthy process no one could foresee the end result. Tribal equalitarianism would gradually vanish even as it was being offended, without any awareness of the nature of the change, and the final achievement of absolute control would at that point probably seem merely a minor alternation of established custom. The consolidation of governmental power would have taken place as a series of natural, beneficial, and only slightly (if at all) extralegal responses to current conditions, with each new acquisition of state power representing only a small departure from contemporary practice. Thus by the time the remnants of the old council of tribal priests and kin elders finally sank into impotence before the rising power of the king (the situation seen in early historic Mesopotamia or among the Aztecs, for example [Adams 1966:139–42]), no one would remember the time—possibly several generations earlier—when the king had been only a war leader, holding his office temporarily at the pleasure of the council. Over the same time span, the emerging leadership group would have become so powerful and wealthy as to seem to be quite different kinds of creatures from the common tribesmen, who could not move out because of the environment, even if their own condition had come to equal that of defeated groups (cf. Adams 1966:109–10; Fried 1967:153–54; Sanders and Price 1968:215–17). The mechanism in question could fully operate only in the large dryland river valleys and lake basins, which explains the otherwise puzzling fact that primary states for the most part arose in precisely such areas. It is interesting to note that both the Aegean and the Lake region of East Africa represent cases in which these environmental factors were less applicable and in which there is also reason to suspect some impact of "intersystemic" wealth on the process of state consolidation. Perhaps we may regard these instances as cases of a hybrid or transitional form of state development.

In any case, it seems certain that all of the regions discussed were characterized by large and expanding populations and by a considerable increase in warfare in the stages immediately preceding the emergence of the state. Recent settlement pattern surveys appear to demonstrate such population growth clearly for Mesopotamia (Adams 1965:36–38; Adams and Nissen 1972:29–33, 86–91), all relevant portions of Mesoamerica (Sanders 1972; but see also Dumond 1972b), and Peru (Willey 1953:377–78, 390–94, 420; Lanning 1967:115–16), and to indicate it strongly for India (Allchin and Allchin 1968:121–30) and China (Chang 1968:128–58). The older and rather more tenuous data from Egypt appear to support the same conclusion (Arkell and Ucko 1965). In East Africa the Iron Age was marked by population growth and increasing reliance on cattle keeping, which combined to make suitable land a more and more critical factor (Davidson 1969:40–56). In the Bronze Age Aegean, as noted above, the introduction of Mediterranean polyculture provided the basis for population expansion even as it introduced a nucleating influence (Renfrew 1973:207–9). For all areas one receives the impression of an increase not only in the total number of sites but also in the density of distribution, size, and elaboration of sites.

186

The same increase applies to warfare as well, although this seems to have occurred slightly later in the evolutionary sequence. Egypt's legendary history begins with a tale of conquest, and the archaeological record shows the process of territorial consolidation and associated social stratification to have been matched by a shift in artistic productions from representations of quarrels between nomes to celebrations of victory by high chiefs already wearing the regalia associated with the historic pharaohs; weapons and (apparently) fortifications appear at the appropriate points (Childe 1957: chaps. 4 and 5). The same process took place in Mesopotamia, with destruction levels, population displacements, weaponry, and representations of slaves and battles all appearing by the Uruk period and culminating late in Early Dynastic times (Childe 1954:71–73, 88, 99–100; Childe 1957; Adams 1965:38–39; Adams and Nissen 1972:19–23, 88, 91). The latter stages of this development were characterized by an increasing abandonment of smaller sites and an emphasis on military frontiers (Adams and Nissen 1972:21, 28; Johnson, this volume, chap. 7). Predictably, the historical record shows a process of replacement of theocratic and kin leaders by increasingly conquest-minded secular rulers (Adams 1966:139–41, 156–59). In the same fashion the documentary evidence from Shang China also indicates a possibly even greater emphasis on militarism than was the case in Egypt and Mesopotamia, while fortifications are a prominent feature not only of the Shang but also of the immediately preceding Lungshan culture, one site of which shows evidence of having withstood a siege (Creel 1937a:57–60, 141–57; Creel 1937b:179–82; Chang 1968:128, 203–7, 243). Recent research has revealed that the Indus Valley, which until recently appeared to be something of an exception owing to the lack of evidence from the early stages of the Harappa culture, was also characterized by warfare in its formative stages. At the site of Kot Diji near Khairpur in the Harappan heartland, the excavators uncovered a Harappan town immediately above a strongly fortified Neolithic pre-Harappan village which was either evolving into the Harappan civilization or was under strong influence from it, and whose occupation was terminated by conquest (Wheeler 1966:30–33, 57–60). Apparently this situation was by no means unique (Allchin and Allchin 1968:118–23). The prominence of fortifications and weaponry (Samuel 1966:28, 41, 66, 101, 139; Finley 1970:24–27, 41–42, 47–55) suggests that warfare came to be strongly developed in Bronze Age Greece (although evidently not—on the basis of present evidence—in Crete); as is well known, a similar situation existed in East Africa in the period prior to European penetration (Davidson 1969).

In the New World, both coastal Peru and Mesoamerica show a long history of warfare; indications of fighting are present in both regions early in their formative or theocratic stages, no later than the start of the first millennium B.C. (Lanning 1967:92–93; Covarrubias 1957: figs. 27, 28, 31; Coe 1968:92). In Peru, developments appear to have been essentially continuous thereafter, since forts and defensive walls became quite common in the later preclassic periods (Willey 1953:92–101, 354–63, 374–77, 395–96). The great importance of warfare among the classic (Florescent Period in local terms) Moche is indicated by the frequent representations of fighting, captivity, and torture in their art, while the south coastal Nazca placed a high value on trophy heads (Mason 1968:66–68, 74–82; Kidder, Lumbreras, and Smith 1963; Lanning 1967:92–94, 106–15, 120–22). In contrast, similar developments appear to have been somewhat delayed in Mesoamerica, since during the Protoclassic and Early Classic periods warfare does seem to have been rather less prominent than one might expect (although by no means so uncommon as was once supposed [cf. Sanders 1967]), a feature which I would suggest was probably due to an unusually rich environment associated with a less severe degree of land limitation (Webb 1973). Interestingly enough, Dumond (1972b) has recently presented evidence suggesting that population growth during the Classic Period in highland Mesoamerica may have been very slow; therefore competition for agricultural resources might have become really severe relatively later than was the case in the other nuclear areas of state formation. This would perhaps have enabled tribal priest-chiefs to achieve rather more features of civilization and to maintain their power against military leaders longer than usual. Thus the Mesoamerican Classic Period does come closer to the concept of statehood achieved by priestly controls than do the other primary state areas; its strongly theocratic nature has long been recognized (Wolf 1959; Webb 1968). In the perspective of world history, however, this means that Mesoamerica experienced an unusually rich and extended period of transition from chiefdom to state. Steward (1955: chap. 11), in fact, classified the Mesoamerican

Classic with the periods which marked the transition to civilization in the Old World. In the long run, the difference was only a matter of delayed development, since the transition to the Postclassic Period was characterized by the emergence of an extreme emphasis on militarism, political boundaries, and commercial wars (Webb in press).

Since the coincidence of warfare within areas of limited agricultural land and the rise of primary states is so very striking, it is tempting to regard this process as the cause of primary state emergence without further qualification. However, as Dumond (1972a) has noted, population expansion in circumscribed areas could conceivably result in nothing more than increasingly overcrowded, labor-intensive, squabbling local equalitarian communities. The situation existing or apparently developing among such warring equalitarian groups as the River Yumans (Driver 1961:338–39, 368–72, 397–403) and the New Guinea highlanders (Brookfield and Brown 1967; Rappaport 1968; Gardner and Heider 1968; Heider 1970; Waddell 1972; Netting 1971), as well as Earle's recent examination of the Lurín Valley of Peru (Earle 1972), suggest that, in societies lacking already-existing chiefly hierarchies, intensified struggle over land may occur without giving rise to centralization, even under conditions of considerable crowding. Thus, although these exceptions must be viewed with some care, since they may represent cases in which the local development was interrupted, it would appear that the process of primary state formation requires not only that warfare in circumscribed regions which is necessary (in the absence of trade with existing states) for the generation of wealth additional to the traditional system, but also the prior existence of a chiefly hierarchy, which is essential (at least in most cases) for the effective consolidation and deployment of that wealth.

Various students have attempted to combine the circumscription and the trade hypotheses in the past. Coe (1968:105–15) and Flannery (Flannery 1968; Flannery et al. 1967; Flannery and Coe 1968) have suggested that control both of limited areas of good land and of trade wealth were the bases of chiefly—and even state—authority early in the "Olmec" horizon, while Sanders and Price (Sanders 1957; Sanders and Price 1968) have discerned the same processes working throughout Mesoamerican history. Gluckman (1968:174–76) has made a similar suggestion for the rise of state societies south of the Sahara. I wish to stress three points here: First, the precise order in which the two major factors operate is also critical. *Only* a period of tribal, chiefly trade, succeeded just prior to its expected peak by an epoch of military struggle for limited resources, would produce the expected feedback. A second point follows from this: When the stage of large-scale warfare was reached, the societies engaged would almost certainly be so developed that the competition might well not be *directly* over land but over the stored surplus produced by that land and even over trade goods and routes. The chief effect of agricultural circumscription at this point would be to keep all parties to the contest in place until it was decided. Precisely because these societies had become prosperous and complex, the parties would have to maintain access to many resources which were restricted in distribution, and they would have to control the loci of a number of different kinds of large-scale capital investment. A third point is that the successively shifting emphasis from trading chiefs (who might well form a corporation of tribal priests and who might perhaps direct or participate in the direction of raiding) to a warring king (who might well be divine and who might well patronize merchants) explains very nicely the characteristic difference in cultural style or "tone" between the various formative, heroic, protoliterate, early dynastic, classic (in Mesoamerica) periods and the periods which succeeded them in the course of state evolution.

One may consider the limitation of agricultural (and other) resources as the more critical factor, although it only operates with sufficient force in cases where the previous development of extensive exchange has already produced large and prosperous chiefdoms. Or one may consider the necessity of securing trade on favorable terms the more crucial factor, but only in cases where a marked limitation of resources generates a situation of intense rivalry and competition. The choice probably does not matter greatly in the end. In any case, when fully effective states were at last on the scene, both trade and war would continue to operate, becoming ever more blended into one process as they did so. The ability of states finally to develop higher levels of economic specialization and to undertake innovative policies often produces an almost explosive surge of economic, demographic, social, and political expansion. Yet the still relatively undeveloped technologies and the reinvestment-inhibiting class systems of such societies com-

monly give rise to a typical pattern of resource overuse, with the conse-
quent necessity for continuous access to pioneer areas. States, therefore,
have a vastly increased appetite for trade goods (often more pragmatically valuable than the status goods of chiefdoms) to match their much
greater ability to secure such goods over a wide area. An expansion and
rationalization of foreign trade with a characteristic direction of diplomacy and war to this end is the result, if efforts are not directed
simply toward securing the needed resources by conquest or plunder in
the first place. The history of state expansion beyond the nuclear areas
therefore shows a radiation out along routes of communication and
transportation.

In Europe the final spread of true states beyond the eastern Mediterranean basin seems largely to have occurred not in the Bronze but
rather in the Iron Age. This does not seem to have been due to any
aberrant features of Aegean civilization. Whatever the precise mix of
"intrasystemic" and "intersystemic" factors in their growth, and whatever their precise institutional structure, the Mycenaean centers seem
to have emerged as typical states with a marked orientation to commerce and commercial wars (Chadwick 1972). Nevertheless, despite
some early penetration of the western Mediterranean by the Mycenaeans (Hutchinson 1962:113–15), the political and economic crisis of
the Late Bronze Age delayed further operation of secondary state formation in that area until the Iron Age Greek and Phoenician penetration
stimulated the rise of the Etruscan-Latin states, whose trade in turn
initiated the rise of marcher kingdoms among the Celtic and Germanic
peoples. The full effects of this process in fact extended into the early
Middle Ages (Piggott 1965: chaps. 5 and 6; Pallottino 1954; Wheeler
1955).

Further east in Eurasia very similar developments appear to have
taken place. By the start of the second millennium B.C. Assyrian trading colonies were well established in Anatolia, where they had extensive
dealings with the "princes" (chieftains) of the area in which the Hittite Empire was soon to emerge (Ozgue 1963; Lloyd 1956:112–26;
Hallo and Simpson 1971:89–97). In India the spread of the Indus
civilization along the western coast and into the upper Ganges established centers (some of which may have survived the collapse of Indus
civilization) in regions which in any case move fully into the light of

history under the full influence of military and commercial penetration from the Persian empire (Wheeler 1966:85–114; Thapar 1966:50–64; Allchin and Allchin 1968:208–22). The north Indian civilization in turn moved rather suddenly south into peninsular India, which was also subject to commercial contact from the west (Wheeler 1966:128–31; Thapar 1966:92–115); the further growth of this western commerce seems to have played a large role in the spread of Indian civilization through Southeast Asia in the early part of the Christian era (Thapar 1966:118–23). The spread of Chinese civilization both to the south and into Central Asia, from later Shang times on, seems to reflect a similar development of marcher states, some of which later became major centers of influence in their turn (Chang 1968:351–62, 376–430; Treistman 1972:130–43; Lattimore 1940). The basic pattern seems to have been established by the period when Chou replaced Shang at the end of the second millennium B.C. (Chang 1968:256–87).

As we move out from the Old World nuclear centers of state formation, the evidence of both history and archaeology, predictably, becomes more and more incomplete and difficult to interpret. The question of the extent to which "Sudanic monarchies" reflect old Egyptian influence as opposed to independent, functional parallel developments and the still more convoluted problem of Bantu origins are cases in point (Oliver and Fage 1962:44–52; Collins [ed.] 1968). Nevertheless, it would appear from the very geographical and temporal distributions of early states in sub-Saharan Africa that these arose either in response to long-distance trade from existing states outside the region or as marcher states responding to the commerce and commercial wars of nearby, previously established African states. Meroe and early Ethiopia certainly fit (Arkell 1961; Oliver and Fage 1962:40–42), as do the pre-fifteenth-century states of West Africa, since the latter first emerged in areas rich in resources prominent in the trans-Saharan trade and expanded to the east and south as necessary for the opening up of new areas of raw materials. (Despite some possible minor borrowing of symbols, this development seems clearly to have been a local response of indigenous populations and societies to expanding contacts with outside traders [Fage 1964:6–21; Oliver and Fage 1962:44–52, 58–64, 80–90; Davidson 1959:59–70, 81–98; Davidson 1966:33–87; Shaw 1969].) By this interpretation the same processes would have been operative which can be seen at work in the later expansion in response to European traders of the coastal kingdoms, whose orientation to and dependence upon commerce—and commercial wars—is well known (Oliver and Fage 1962:102–22; Fage 1964:50–74, 87–98; detailed analyses of individual kingdoms can be found in Forde and Kaberry 1967 and Polanyi 1966). In fact, since even the coastal kingdoms seem generally to owe their first beginnings to penetration from states situated further north in the savanna zone, what appears to have been taking place was a shift in trading orientation from Saharan to Atlantic coastal commerce. The distribution of early states along the coast of East Africa also coincides exactly with the areas environmentally suitable for medieval coastal trade (Oliver and Fage 1962:95–100; Marsh and Kingsnorth 1965:3–21; Kirkman 1966), while areas of governmental elaboration back in the interior generally show an orientation to presumed early interior-coast contact (Davidson 1959:216–82; Mathew 1963; Oliver 1963). The possibility that, as suggested above, the region north and west of Lake Victoria served as a largely "intrasystemic" center from which influences also radiated cannot be ignored, however (Davidson 1969:40–56; Cole 1965:319–23; Oberg 1940). Since the process of state formation in eastern and southern Africa continued into the period of nineteenth-century European trade, we possess excellent accounts of the care with which chieftains and kings controlled trade and of the effects of trade upon their power; in this period tribal dislocations with resulting land shortages were common, and trade was often concerned precisely with access to European weapons, leaving no question of the mutually reinforcing nature of the processes (Gluckman 1940; 1960; Schapera 1940; Richards 1940; Barnes 1951).

Since state evolution in the New World was still at an essentially Bronze Age level at the time of the European conquest, and since state expansion had not by then proceeded into secondary state areas at any distance from the nuclear regions, our historical accounts deal either with inherently archaic primary states or with the ultimately unsuccessful attempts of tribal peoples to respond to the incursions of trade and war from regions with far more advanced technologies. But, as noted, it is clear that Mesoamerica was characterized in the sixteenth century by a predictable development of commerce and of commercial wars and that this emphasis can be traced back archaeologically to the time when states emerged (Webb in press). In Peru the beginnings of the Huari-Tiahuanaco expansion can be interpreted as a mixed case of trade and partial circumscription; at a lower developmental level some such set of forces may explain the otherwise puzzling rise of chiefdoms in the Mojos area of Bolivia (Browman in press). In colonial North America we see among both the southeastern "civilized" tribes (Gearing 1962: 5-7, 99–105) and among the Iroquois (Hunt 1960:16-22, 32–37) not only a keen appreciation of the value of trade but also a great increase in the power of military leaders. Exactly the same developments form the main thread of political evolution in nineteenth-century Polynesia (Webb 1965) and, apparently, Fiji (Dodge 1963), although in Polynesia the process is blended with conversion to Christianity both because the missionaries were so great a source of support and also because of the need for a new cult for purposes of state consolidation. Another area that provides a number of interesting illustrations is Madagascar (Kottak 1972).

Although the above examples could no doubt be greatly elaborated or expanded upon, enough has probably been said. Fighting and trade, both of which are apparently quite common among the larger tribal societies, inevitably became inseparably linked during the emergence of civilization, and they have expanded in scope and intensity ever since that time. We should not, then, be surprised that coercion and conflict have been the main theme of state evolution down to the present.

NOTES

1. There are a few reports of exceptional cases in which chiefdoms were supported by nonagricultural peoples living in unusually rich environments (Goggin and Sturtevant 1964); these, however, simply serve to make more clear the basic continuity of this social and political type with other, simpler tribal societies. Because of the social and political limitations which restrict their size, complexity, and extent of occupational specialization, chiefdoms do not—as a type—require subsistence beyond levels which may, very occasionally, be provided by especially productive hunting, collecting, fishing, and shellfish gathering. In most cases, of course, agriculture would be required, particularly as one approached the upper ranges of the type. My point is simply that chiefdoms, unlike states, do not represent a basic break with major patterns of social control which had evolved early in the agricultural stage or even before.

References

ACOSTA SAIGNES, M.

1945 *Los Pochteca, Acta Antropológica*, epoca 1, vol. 1, no. 1 (Mexico City: Sociedad de Alumnos, Escuela Nacional de Antropología e Historia).

ADAMS, R. MCC.

1956 "Some Hypotheses on the Development of Early Civilizations," *American Antiquity* 21:227–32.

1965 *Land behind Baghdad* (Chicago: University of Chicago Press).

1966 *The Evolution of Urban Society* (Chicago: Aldine Publishing Co.).

ADAMS, R. MCC. AND H. J. NISSEN

1972 *The Uruk Countryside* (Chicago: University of Chicago Press).

ALLCHIN, B. AND R. ALLCHIN

1968 *The Birth of Indian Civilization* (Harmondsworth, Eng.: Penguin Books).

ANDERSON, G. W.

1966 *The History and Religion of Israel* (London: Oxford University Press).

ANTHES, R.

1961 "Mythology in Ancient Egypt," in *Mythologies of the Ancient World*, ed. S. N. Kramer (Garden City, N. Y.: Doubleday & Co., Anchor Books).

ARKELL, A. J.

1961 *A History of the Sudan from the Earliest Times to 1821*, 2d ed. (London: University of London, Athlone Press).

ARKELL, A. J. AND P. J. UCKO

1965 "Review of Predynastic Development in the Nile Valley," *Current Anthropology* 6:145–66.

BARNES, J. A.

1951 "The Fort Jameson Ngoni," in *Seven Tribes of British Central Africa*, ed. E. Colson and M. Gluckman (Manchester: Manchester University Press for the Rhodes-Livingston Institute, Northern Rhodesia).

BECK, C. W.

1970 "Amber in Archaeology," *Archaeology* 23:7–11.

BENNETT, W. C. AND J. BIRD

1960 *Andean Culture History* (New York: American Museum of Natural History).

BERGER, P. L.

1969 *The Sacred Canopy: Elements of a Sociological Theory of Religion* (Garden City, N. Y.: Doubleday & Co., Anchor Books).

BOSERUP, E.

1965 *The Conditions of Agricultural Growth* (Chicago: Aldine Publishing Co.).

BRAIDWOOD, R. J.

1967 *Prehistoric Man*, 7th ed. (Glenview, Ill.: Scott, Foresman and Co.).

BROWMAN, D. L.

in press "Toward the Development of the Tiahuanaco State," paper to be published in the Proceedings of the IXth International Congress of Anthropological and Ethnological Sciences.

BROOKFIELD, H. C. AND P. BROWN
1967   *Struggle for Land* (Melbourne: Oxford University Press in association with the Australian National University).

BRUNDAGE, B. C.
1972   *A Rain of Darts: The Mexica Aztecs* (Austin: University of Texas Press).

BUTZER, K. W.
1964   *Environment and Archaeology* (Chicago: Aldine Publishing Co.).

CARNEIRO, R. L.
1961   "Slash and Burn Cultivation among the Kuikuru and Its Implications for Cultural Development in the Amazon Basin," in *The Evolution of Horticultural Systems in Native South America: Causes and Consequences*, ed. J. Wilbert (Caracas: Sociedad de Ciencias Naturales La Salle).
1967   *The Evolution of Society: Selections from Herbert Spencer's Principles of*
(ed.)   *Sociology* (Chicago: University of Chicago Press).
1970   "A Theory of the Origin of the State," *Science* 169:733–38.
1972   "From Autonomous Villages to the State, A Numerical Estimation," in *Population Growth: Anthropological Implications*, ed. B. Spooner (Cambridge, Mass.: M.I.T. Press).

CHADWICK, J.
1972   "Life in Mycenaean Greece," *Scientific American* 227(4):36–44.

CHANG, KWANG-CHIH
1968   *The Archaeology of Ancient China*, rev. and enlarged ed. (New Haven: Yale University Press).

CHAPMAN, A. C.
1957   "Port of Trade Enclaves in Aztec and Maya Civilization," in *Trade and Market in the Early Empires*, ed. K. Polanyi, C. M. Arensberg, and H. W. Pearson (New York: Free Press).

CHENG TE-K'UN
1959   *Archaeology in China*, vol. 1: *Prehistoric China* (Cambridge, Eng.: W. Heffer and Sons).
1960   *Archaeology in China*, vol. 2: *Shang China* (Cambridge, Eng.: University of Toronto Press).

CHI CH'AO-TING
1936   *Key Economic Areas in Chinese History* (London: George Allen and Unwin).

CHILDE, V. G.
1951a   *Man Makes Himself* (New York: New American Library, Mentor Books).
1951b   *The Dawn of European Civilization*, 5th ed. (New York: Alfred A. Knopf).
1954   *What Happened in History* (Harmondsworth, Eng.: Penguin Books).
1957   *New Light on the Most Ancient East* (New York: Grove Press).
1958   *The Prehistory of European Society* (Harmondsworth, Eng.: Penguin Books).

CLARK, J. G. D.
1966   *Prehistoric Europe, The Economic Basis* (Stanford: Stanford University Press).

196

CLARK, J. AND S. PIGGOTT
1965 *Prehistoric Societies* (New York: Alfred A. Knopf).

COBEAN, R. H., M. D. COE, E. A. PERRY, JR.,
K. K. TUREKIAN, AND D. P. KHARKAR
1971 "Obsidian Trade at San Lorenzo Tenochtitlan, Mexico," *Science* 174:666–71.

COE, M. D.
1961 "Social Typology and the Tropical Forest Civilizations," *Studies in Society and History* 4(1):65–85.
1962 *Mexico* (New York: Frederick A. Praeger).
1968 *America's First Civilization* (New York: American Heritage Publishing Co. and the Smithsonian Institution).

COLE, S.
1965 *The Prehistory of East Africa* (New York: New American Library, Mentor Books).

COLES, J. AND J. TAYLOR
1971 "The Wessex Culture: A Minimal View," *Antiquity* 45:6–14.

COLLIER, D.
1962 "The Central Andes," in *Courses Toward Urban Life*, ed. R. J. Braidwood and G. R. Willey (Chicago: Aldine Publishing Co.).

COLLINS, R. O.
1968
(ed.) *Problems in African History* (Englewood Cliffs, N. J.: Prentice-Hall).

COULBORN, R.
1969 *The Origin of Civilized Societies* (Princeton: Princeton University Press).

COVARRUBIAS, M.
1957 *Indian Art of Mexico and Central America* (New York: Alfred A. Knopf).

CREEL, H. G.
1937a *The Birth of China* (New York: Reynal and Hitchcock).
1937b *Studies in Early Chinese Culture, First Series* (Baltimore: Waverly Press).

CRESSEY, G. B.
1955 *Land of the 500 Million: A Geography of China* (New York: McGraw-Hill).

DANIEL, G.
1963 *The Megalith Builders of Western Europe* (Harmondsworth, Eng.: Penguin Books).

DAVENPORT, W.
1964 "Hawaiian Feudalism," *Expedition* 6(2):14–27.
1969 "The 'Hawaiian Cultural Revolution': Some Political and Economic Considerations," *American Anthropologist* 71:1–20.

DAVIDSON, B.
1959 *The Lost Cities of Africa* (Boston: Little, Brown and Co.).
1966 *A History of West Africa to the Nineteenth Century* (Garden City, N. Y.: Doubleday & Co., Anchor Books).
1969 *A History of East and Central Africa to the Late Nineteenth Century* (Garden City, N. Y.: Doubleday & Co., Anchor Books).

DESHAYES, J.
1969 "New Evidence for the Indo-Europeans from Tureng Tepe, Iran," *Archaeology* 22:10–17.

DESMOND CLARK, J.
1962 "Africa South of the Sahara," in *Courses Toward Urban Life*, ed. R. J. Braidwood and G. R. Willey (Chicago: Aldine Publishing Co.).

DIXON, J. E., J. R. CANN, AND C. RENFREW
1968 "Obsidian and the Origins of Trade," *Scientific American* 218(3):38–46.

DODGE, E. S.
1963 "Early American Contacts in Polynesia and Fiji," *Proceedings of the American Philosophical Society* 107:102–6.

DRIVER, H. E.
1961 *Indians of North America* (Chicago: University of Chicago Press).

DUMOND, D. E.
1965 "Population Growth and Cultural Change," *Southwestern Journal of Anthropology* 21:302–21.
1972a "Population Growth and Political Centralization," in *Population Growth: Anthropological Implications*, ed. B. Spooner (Cambridge, Mass.: M.I.T. Press).
1972b "Demographic Aspects of the Classic Period in Puebla-Tlaxcala," *Southwestern Journal of Anthropology* 28:101–30.

EARLE, T. K.
1972 "Lurin Valley, Peru: Early Intermediate Period Settlement Development," *American Antiquity* 37:467–77.

ENGELS, F.
1942 *The Origin of the Family, Private Property and the State* (New York: International Publishers).

EPSTEIN, A. L.
1968 "Power, Politics and Leadership: Some Central African and Melanesian Contrasts," in *Local-Level Politics*, ed. M. J. Swartz (Chicago: Aldine Publishing Co.).

EVANS-PRITCHARD, E. E.
1964 "The Divine Kingship of the Shilluk of the Nilotic Sudan (The Frazer Lecture, 1948)," in *Social Anthropology and Other Essays*, by E. E. Evans-Pritchard (New York: Free Press).

FAGAN, B. H.
1972 "Ingombe Ilede: Early Trade in South Central Africa" (Reading, Mass.: Addison-Wesley Modular Publications).

FAGE, J. D.
1964 *An Introduction to the History of West Africa*, 3d ed. (Cambridge: Cambridge University Press).

FENTON, W. N.
1951 "Introduction: The Concept of Locality and the Program of Iroquois Research," in *Symposium on Local Diversity in Iroquois Culture*, ed. W. N. Fenton. Bulletin of the Bureau of American Ethnology 149 (Washington, D. C.: Smithsonian Institution).

FINLEY, M. I.
1968 *Aspects of Antiquity* (New York: Viking Press).
1970 *Early Greece: The Bronze and Archaic Ages* (London: Chatto and Windus).
FINNEY, B.
1966 "Resource Distribution and Social Structure in Tahiti," *Ethnology* 5:80–86.
FLANNERY, K. V.
1968 "The Olmec and the Valley of Oaxaca: A Model of Inter-regional Interaction in Formative Times," in *Dumbarton Oaks Conference on the Olmec*, ed. E. P. Benson (Washington, D. C.: Dumbarton Oaks Research Library and Collection and Trustees for Harvard University).
1972 "Summary Comments: Evolutionary Trends in Social Exchange and Interaction," in *Social Exchange and Interaction*, ed. E. N. Wilmsen. University of Michigan Museum of Anthropology, Anthropological Papers no. 46.
FLANNERY K. V. AND M. D. COE
1968 "Social and Economic Systems in Formative Mesoamerica," in *New Perspectives in Archaeology*, ed. S. R. Binford and L. R. Binford (Chicago: Aldine Publishing Co.).
FLANNERY, K. V., A. V. T. KIRKBY, M. J. KIRKBY, AND
A. W. WILLIAMS, JR.
1967 "Farming Systems and Political Growth in Ancient Oaxaca," *Science* 158:445–54.
FORDE, C. D. AND P. M. KABERRY
1967 *West African Kingdoms in the Nineteenth Century* (London: Oxford Univer-
(eds.) sity Press for the International African Institute).
FORTES, M. AND E. E. EVANS-PRITCHARD
1940 "Introduction," in *African Political Systems*, ed. M. Fortes and E. E. Evans-Pritchard (London: Oxford University Press for the International African Institute).
FOWLER, M. L.
1969 "A Preclassic Water Distribution System in Amalucan, Mexico," *Archaeology* 22:208–15.
FRANKFORT, H.
1956 *The Birth of Civilization in the Near East* (Garden City, N.Y.: Doubleday & Co., Anchor Books).
FRIED, M. H.
1960 "On the Evolution of Social Stratification and the State," in *Culture in History, Essays in Honor of Paul Radin*, ed. S. Diamond (New York: Columbia University Press for Brandeis University).
1967 *The Evolution of Political Society* (New York: Random House).
GARDNER, R. AND K. G. HEIDER
1968 *Gardens of War* (New York: Random House).
GEARING, F.
1961 "The Rise of the Cherokee State as an Instance in the Class: The 'Mesopotamian' Career to Statehood," in *Symposium on Cherokee and Iroquois Culture*, ed. W. N. Fenton and J. Gulick. Bulletin of the Bureau of American Ethnology no. 180 (Washington, D. C.: Smithsonian Institution).

1962 *Priests and Warriors: Social Structure for Cherokee Politics in the 18 Century.* Memoirs of the American Anthropological Association, no. 93 (Washington, D. C.: American Anthropological Association).

GIFFORD, J. C.

1968 "The Earliest and Other Intrusive Population Elements at Barton Ramie May Have Come from Central America," paper read at the Sixty-seventh Annual Meeting of the American Anthropological Association, Seattle.

GIMBUTAS, M.

1972 "The Culture of Old Europe c. 7000–3500 B.C., The Earliest European Peoples," *Journal of Indo-European Studies* 1:1–20.

1973 "The Beginning of the Bronze Age in Europe and the Indo-Europeans: 3500–2500 B.C.," *Journal of Indo-European Studies* 1:163–214.

GLUCKMAN, M.

1940 "The Kingdom of the Zulu in South Africa," in *African Political Systems*, ed. M. Fortes and E. E. Evans-Pritchard (London: Oxford University Press for the International African Institute).

1960 "The Rise of a Zulu Empire," *Scientific American* 202(4):157–68.

1968 *Politics, Law and Ritual in Tribal Society* (New York: New American Library, Mentor Books).

GOGGIN, J. H. AND W. C. STURTEVANT

1964 "The Calusa: A Stratified Nonagricultural Society (With Notes on Sibling Marriage)," in *Explorations in Cultural Anthropology, Essays in Honor of George Peter Murdock*, ed. W. H. Goodenough (New York: McGraw-Hill).

GOLDMAN, I.

1955 "Status Rivalry and Cultural Evolution in Polynesia," *American Anthropologist* 57:680–97.

GRAY, R. F.

1963 *The Sonjo of Tanganyika: An Anthropological Study of an Irrigation-Based Society* (London: Oxford University Press for the International African Institute).

GROVE, D. C.

1968 "The Pre-Classic Olmec in Central Mexico: Site Distribution and Inferences," in *Dumbarton Oaks Conference on the Olmec*, ed. E. P. Benson (Washington, D. C.: Dumbarton Oaks Research Library and Collection and Trustees for Harvard University).

1973 "Olmec Altars and Myths," *Archaeology* 26:128–35.

HALLO, W. W. AND W. K. SIMPSON

1971 *The Ancient Near East: A History* (New York: Harcourt, Brace, Jovanovich).

HAMMOND, N.

1972a "The Planning of a Maya Ceremonial Center," *Scientific American* 226(5):82–91.

1972b "Obsidian Trade Routes in the Mayan Area," *Science* 178:1092–93.

HARNER, M. J.

1970 "Population Pressure and the Social Evolution of Agriculturalists," *Southwestern Journal of Anthropology* 26:67–85.

HARRIS, M. H.
1959 "The Economy Has No Surplus?" *American Anthropologist* 61:185–99.

HAURY, E. W.
1962 "The Greater American Southwest," in *Courses Toward Urban Life*, ed. R. J. Braidwood and G. R. Willey (Chicago: Aldine Publishing Co.).

HEATON, E. W.
1958 *The Old Testament Prophets* (Harmondsworth, Eng.: Penguin Books).

HEIDER, K. G.
1970 *The Dugum Dani*. Viking Fund Publication in Anthropology, no. 49 (New York: Wenner-Gren Foundation for Anthropological Research).

HOOKE, S. H.
1963 *Middle Eastern Mythology* (Harmondsworth, Eng.: Penguin Books).

HUNT, G. T.
1960 *The Wars of the Iroquois, A Study in Intertribal Trade Relations* (Madison: University of Wisconsin Press).

HUTCHINSON, R. W.
1962 *Prehistoric Crete* (Baltimore: Penguin Books).

IZUMI, S.
1971 "The Development of the Formative Culture in the Ceja de Montana of the Central Andes," in *Dumbarton Oaks Conference on Chavin*, ed. E. P. Benson (Washington, D. C.: Dumbarton Oaks Research Library and Collection and Trustees for Harvard University).

JACOBSON, T.
1946 "Mesopotamia," in *Before Philosophy: The Intellectual Adventure of Ancient Man*, by H. Frankfort et. al. (Harmondsworth, Eng.: Penguin Books).

JAMESON, M. H.
1961 "Mythology of Ancient Greece," in *Mythologies of the Ancient World*, ed. S. N. Kramer (Garden City, N.Y.: Doubleday & Co., Anchor Books).

JOHNSON, G. A.
1973 *Local Exchange and Early State Development in Southwestern Iran*. University of Michigan Museum of Anthropology, Anthropological Papers no. 51.

KIDDER, A. V., II, L. G. LUMBRERAS S., AND D. B. SMITH
1963 "Cultural Development in the Central Andes—Peru and Bolivia," in *Aboriginal Cultural Development in Latin America: An Interpretive Review*, ed. B. J. Meggers and C. Evans. Smithsonian Miscellaneous Collections, vol. 146, no. 1 (Washington, D.C.: Smithsonian Institution).

KIRKMAN, J.
1966 "The History of the Coast of East Africa up to 1700," in *Prelude to East African History*, ed. M. Posnansky (London: Oxford University Press).

KOTTAK, C. P.
1972 "A Cultural Adaptive Approach to Malagasy Political Organization," in *Social Exchange and Interaction*, ed. E. N. Wilmsen. University of Michigan Museum of Anthropology, Anthropological Papers no. 46.
1974 *Anthropology, The Exploration of Human Diversity* (New York: Random House).

KRADER, L.
1968 *Formation of the State* (Englewood Cliffs, N.J.: Prentice-Hall).

KRAMER, S. N.
1961 "Mythology of Sumer and Akkad," in *Mythologies of the Ancient World*, ed. S. N. Kramer (Garden City, N.Y.: Doubleday & Co., Anchor Books).

KROEBER, A. L.
1948 *Anthropology* (New York: Harcourt, Brace and Co.).

LAMBERG-KARLOVSKY, C. C. AND M. LAMBERG-KARLOVSKY
1971 "An Early City in Iran," *Scientific American* 224(6):102–11.

LAMBERT, B.
1966 "The Economic Activities of a Gilbertese Chief," in *Political Anthropology*, ed. M. J. Swartz, V. W. Turner, and A. Tuden (Chicago: Aldine Publishing Co.).

LANNING, E. P.
1967 *Peru before the Incas* (Englewood Cliffs, N.J.: Prentice-Hall).

LATHRAP, D. W.
1971 "The Tropical Forest and the Cultural Context of Chavin," in *Dumbarton Oaks Conference on Chavin*, ed. E. P. Benson (Washington, D.C.: Dumbarton Oaks Research Library and Collection and Trustees for Harvard University).
1973 "The Antiquity and Importance of Long Distance Trade Relationships in the Moist Tropics of Pre-Columbian South America," *World Archaeology* 5:170–86.

LATTIMORE, O.
1940 *Inner Asian Frontiers of China.* American Geographical Society Research Series, no. 21 (New York: American Geographical Society).

LINTON, R.
1956 *The Tree of Culture* (New York: Alfred A. Knopf).

LLOYD, S.
1956 *Early Anatolia* (Harmondsworth, Eng: Penguin Books).

LOWIE, R. H.
1960 "Some Aspects of Political Organization among the American Aboriginees," in *Lowie's Selected Papers in Anthropology*, ed. C. DuBois (Berkeley and Los Angeles: University of California Press).
1962 *The Origins of the State* (New York: Russell and Russell).

MCNEILL, W. H.
1965 *The Rise of the West: A History of the Human Community* (New York: New American Library, Mentor Books).

MAIR, L.
1962 *Primitive Government* (Harmondsworth, Eng.: Penguin Books).

MARCUS, J.
1973 "Territorial Organization of the Lowland Classic Maya," *Science* 180:911–16.

MARSH, Z. A. AND G. W. KINGSNORTH
1965 *An Introduction to the History of East Africa*, 3d ed. (Cambridge: Cambridge University Press).

MASON, J. A.
1968 *The Ancient Civilizations of Peru* (Harmondsworth, Eng.: Penguin Books).
MATHEW, G.
1963 "The East African Coast until the Coming of the Portuguese," in *History of East Africa*, vol. 1, ed. R. Oliver and G. Mathew (Oxford: Clarendon Press).
MAXWELL, M. S.
1952 "The Archaeology of the Lower Ohio Valley," in *Archaeology of the Eastern United States*, ed. J. B. Griffin (Chicago: University of Chicago Press).

MEGGERS, B. J.
1971 *Amazonia: Man and Culture in a Counterfeit Paradise* (Chicago: Aldine Publishing Co.).
MORGAN, L. H.
1963 *Ancient Society, or Researches into the Lines of Human Progress from Savagery through Barbarism to Civilization*, ed. E. B. Leacock (Cleveland: World Publishing Co., Meridian Books).
MORGAN, R. G.
1952 "Outline of Cultures in the Ohio Region," in *Archaeology of the Eastern United States*, ed. J. B. Griffin (Chicago: University of Chicago Press).
MOSELEY, M. E., C. J. MACKEY, AND D. BRILL
1973 "Chan Chan, Peru's Ancient City of Kings," *National Geographic* 143:318–45.
MUMFORD, L.
1961 *The City in History* (New York: Harcourt, Brace and World).
MURDOCK, G. P.
1959 *Africa: Its Peoples and Their Culture History* (New York: McGraw-Hill).
NETTING, R. MCC.
1971 *The Ecological Approach in Cultural Study* (Reading, Mass.: Addison-Wesley Modular Publications).
1972 "Sacred Power and Centralization: Aspects of Political Adaptation in Africa," in *Population Growth: Anthropological Implications*, ed. B. Spooner (Cambridge, Mass.: M.I.T. Press).
NORTH, C. R.
1953 *The Old Testament Interpretation of History* (London: Epworth Press).
OBERG, K.
1940 "The Kingdom of the Ankole in Uganda," in *African Political Systems*, ed. M. Fortes and E. E. Evans-Pritchard (London: Oxford University Press for the International African Institute).
OLIVE N., J. C. AND B. BARBA A.
1957 "Sobre la Desentegración de las Culturas Clásicas," *Anales del Instituto Nacional de Antropología e Historia* 9:57–72.
OLIVER, D.
1961 *The Pacific Islands* (Garden City, N. Y.: Doubleday & Co., Anchor Books).
OLIVER, R.
1963 "Discernible Developments in the Interior c. 1500–1840," in *History of East Africa*, vol. 1, ed. R. Oliver and G. Mathew (Oxford: Clarendon Press).

OZGUE, T.
1963 "An Assyrian Trading Outpost," *Scientific American* 208(2):96–106.

PALLOTTINO, M.
1954 *The Etruscans* (Harmondsworth, Eng.: Penguin Books).

PARK, G. K.
1966 "Kinga Priests: The Politics of Pestilence," in *Political Anthropology*, ed. M. J. Swartz, V. W. Turner, and A. Tuden (Chicago: Aldine Publishing Co.).

PARSONS, L. A.
1967 "An Early Maya Stela on the Pacific Coast of Guatemala," *Estudios de Cultura Maya* 6:171–98.

PATTERSON, T. C.
1971 "Chavin: An Interpretation of Its Spread and Influence," in *Dumbarton Oaks Conference on Chavin*, ed. E. P. Benson (Washington, D. C.: Dumbarton Oaks Research Library and Collection and Trustees for Harvard University).

PEARSON, H. W.
1957 "The Economy Has No Surplus: Critique of a Theory of Development," in *Trade and Market in the Early Empires*, ed. K. Polanyi, C. M. Arensberg, and H. W. Pearson (New York: Free Press).

PENDLEBURY, J. D. S.
1965 *The Archaeology of Crete* (New York: W. W. Norton and Co.).

PIGGOTT, S.
1950 *Prehistoric India* (Harmondsworth, Eng.: Penguin Books).
1965 *Ancient Europe* (Chicago: Aldine Publishing Co.).

PIRES-FERREIRA, J. W.
in press "Obsidian Exchange Systems in Formative Mesoamerica," paper to be published in the Proceedings of the IXth International Congress of Anthropological and Ethnological Sciences.

PIRES-FERREIRA, J. W. AND B. J. EVANS
in press "Mossbaur Spectral Analysis of Olmec Iron Ore Mirrors: New Evidence of Formative Period Exchange Systems in Mesoamerica," paper to be published in the Proceedings of the IXth International Congress of Anthropological and Ethnological Sciences.

POLANYI, K.
1966 *Dahomey and the Slave Trade* (Seattle: University of Washington Press).

POLANYI, K., C. M. ARENSBERG, AND H. W. PEARSON
1957
(eds.) *Trade and Market in the Early Empires* (New York: Free Press).

PRUFER, O. H.
1964a "The Hopewell Complex of Ohio," in *Hopewellian Studies*, ed. J. R. Caldwell and R. L. Hall. Illinois State Museum Scientific Paper no. 12 (Springfield, Ill.).
1964b "The Hopewell Cult," *Scientific American* 211(6):90–102.

RAIKES, R. L. AND R. H. DYSON
1961 "The Prehistoric Climate of Baluchistan and the Indus Valley," *American Anthropologist*, 61:265–81.

RAPPAPORT, R. A.
1968   *Pigs for the Ancestors: Ritual in the Ecology of a New Guinea People* (New Haven: Yale University Press).

RATHJE, W. L.
1971   "The Origin and Development of Lowland Classic Maya Civilization," *American Antiquity* 36:275–85.

REDFIELD, R.
1953   *The Primitive World and Its Transformations* (Ithaca: Cornell University Press).

REICHEL-DOLMATOFF, G.
1961   "The Agricultural Basis of the Sub-Andean Chiefdoms of Colombia," in *The Evolution of Horticultural Systems in Native South America: Causes and Consequences*, ed. J. Wilbert (Caracas: Sociedad de Ciencias Naturales La Salle).

RENFREW, C.
1969   "Trade and Culture Process in European Prehistory," *Current Anthropology* 10:151–60.
1970   "New Configurations in Old World Archaeology," *World Archaeology* 2:199–211.
1971a   "Carbon 14 and the Prehistory of Europe," *Scientific American* 225(4): 63–72.
1971b   "Sitagroi, Radiocarbon and the Prehistory of South-East Europe," *Antiquity* 45:275–82.
1972a   "Beyond a Subsistence Economy: The Evolution of Social Organization in Prehistoric Europe," paper presented at Cambridge (Massachusetts) Archaeological Seminar on Complex Societies.
1972b   "Malta and the Calibrated Radiocarbon Chronology," *Antiquity* 46:141–44.
1973   *Before Civilization: The Radiocarbon Revolution and Prehistoric Europe* (New York: Alfred A. Knopf).

RICHARDS, A. I.
1940   "The Political System of the Bemba Tribe—Northern Rhodesia," in *African Political Systems*, ed. M. Fortes and E. E. Evans-Pritchard (London: Oxford University Press for the International African Institute).

ROUSE, I.
1962   "The Intermediate Area, Amazonia and the Caribbean Area," in *Courses Toward Urban Life*, ed. R. J. Braidwood and G. R. Willey (Chicago: Aldine Publishing Co.).

ROYS, R. L.
1957   *The Political Geography of the Yucatan Maya* (Washington, D. C.: Carnegie Institution of Washington).
1966   "Native Empires in Yucatán," *Revista Mexicana de Estudios Antropológicos* 20:153–77.

SAHLINS, M. D.
1958   *Social Stratification in Polynesia* (Seattle: University of Washington Press).
1960   "Political Power and the Economy in Primitive Society," in *Essays in the Science of Culture in Honor of Leslie A. White*, ed. G. E. Dole and R. L. Carneiro (New York: Thomas Y. Crowell Co.).

1963 "Poor Man, Rich Man, Big Man, Chief: Political Types in Melanesia and Polynesia," *Comparative Studies in Society and History* 5(3):285–303.

1965 "On the Sociology of Primitive Exchange," in *The Relevance of Models for Social Anthropology*, ed. M. Banton. Association of Social Anthropologists Monographs, no. 1 (London: Tavistock).

1968 *Tribesmen* (Englewood Cliffs, N. J.: Prentice-Hall).

1972 *Stone Age Economics* (Chicago: Aldine-Atherton).

SAMUEL, A. E.

1966 *The Mycenaeans in History* (Englewood Cliffs, N. J.: Prentice-Hall).

SANDERS, W. T.

1957 "Tierra y Agua ("Soil and Water"): A Study of the Ecological Factors in the Development of Mesoamerican Civilization," Ph.D. diss., Harvard University.

1967 "Life in a Class Village," in *Teotihuacán*, ed. I. Bernal (Mexico City: Sociedad Mexicana de Antropología).

1972 "Population, Agricultural History and Societal Evolution in Mesoamerica," in *Population Growth: Anthropological Implications*, ed. B. Spooner (Cambridge, Mass.: M.I.T. Press).

SANDERS, W. T. AND J. MARINO

1970 *New World Prehistory* (Englewood Cliffs, N. J.: Prentice-Hall).

SANDERS, W. T. AND B. J. PRICE

1968 *Mesoamerica: The Evolution of a Civilization* (New York: Random House).

SCHAPERA, I.

1940 "The Political Organization of the Ngwato of Bechuanaland Protectorate," in *African Political Systems*, ed. M. Fortes and E. E. Evans-Pritchard (London: Oxford University Press for the International African Institute).

1967 *Government and Politics in Tribal Societies* (New York: Schocken Books).

SERVICE, E. R.

1962 *Primitive Social Organization: An Evolutionary Perspective* (New York: Random House).

1963 *Profiles in Ethnology* (New York: Harper and Row).

SHARER, R. J. AND J. C. GIFFORD

1970 "Preclassic Ceramics from Chalchuapa, El Salvador, and Their Relationships with the Maya Lowlands," *American Antiquity* 35:441–62.

SHAW, T.

1969 "Archaeology in Nigeria," *Antiquity* 43:187–99.

SOUTHALL, A. W.

1953 *Alur Society: A Study in Processes and Types of Domination* (Cambridge: W. Heffer and Sons).

SPENCE, M. W.

1967 "Los Talleres de Obsidiana de Teotihuacán," in *Teotihuacán*, ed. I. Bernal (Mexico City: Sociedad Mexicana de Antropología).

STAMP, L. D.

1938 *Asia: A Regional and Economic Geography*, 4th ed. (New York: E. P. Dutton and Co.).

1953 *Africa: A Study in Tropical Development* (New York: John Wiley and Sons).

206

STEWARD, J. H.
1955   *Theory of Culture Change* (Urbana: University of Illinois Press).

STEWARD, J. H. AND L. C. FARON
1959   *Native Peoples of South America* (New York: McGraw-Hill).

STRUEVER, S. AND G. L. HOUART
1972   "An Analysis of the Hopewell Interaction Sphere," in *Social Exchange and Interaction*, ed. E. N. Wilmsen. University of Michigan Museum of Anthropology, Anthropological Papers, no. 46.

SUGGS, R. C.
1960   *The Island Civilizations of Polynesia* (New York: New American Library, Mentor Books).

THAPAR, R.
1966   *A History of India*, vol. 1 (Harmondsworth, Eng.: Penguin Books).

TOURTELLOT, G. AND J. A. SABLOFF
1972   "Exchange Systems among the Ancient Maya," *American Antiquity* 37: 126–35.

TOZZER, ALFRED M. (ed.)
1941   "Landa's Relacion de las Cosas de Yucatan," a translation. *Papers of the Peabody Museum of American Archaeology and Ethnology, Harvard University*, vol. 18 (Cambridge, Mass.).

TREISTMAN, J. M.
1972   *The Prehistory of China* (Garden City, N. Y.: Doubleday & Co., Natural History Press).

TURNER, V. W.
1966   "Ritual Aspects of Conflict Control in African Micro-Politics," in *Political Anthropology*, ed. M. J. Swartz, V. W. Turner, and A. Tuden (Chicago: Aldine Publishing Co.).

TYLOR, E. B.
1946   *Anthropology: An Introduction to the Study of Man and Civilization*, 2 vols. (London: Watts and Co.).

VAYDA, A. P.
1956   "Maori Conquests in Relation to the New Zealand Environment," *Journal of the Polynesian Society* 65:204–11.
1961   "Expansion and Warfare among Swidden Agriculturalists," *American Anthropologist* 63:346–58.

VERMEULE, E.
1964   *Greece in the Bronze Age* (Chicago: University of Chicago Press).

VON WISSMAN, H., H. POECH, G. SMOLLA, AND F. KUSSMAUL
1956   "On the Role of Nature and Man in Changing the Face of the Dry Belt of Asia," in *Man's Role in Changing the Face of the Earth*, ed. W. L. Thomas (Chicago: University of Chicago Press).

WADDELL, E.
1972   *The Mound Builders: Agricultural Practices, Environment and Society in the Central Highlands of New Guinea* (Seattle: University of Washington Press).

WALKER, J.

n.d. "A Study of the Rainfall of Mexico," M.A. thesis, Department of Geography, Louisiana State University, Baton Rouge.

WEAVER, M. P.

1972 *The Aztecs, Maya and their Predecessors; Archaeology of Mesoamerica* (New York and London: Seminar Press).

WEBB, M. C.

1964 "The Post-Classic Decline of the Petén Maya: Examination in the Light of a General Theory of State Society," Ph.D. dissertation, University of Michigan.

1965 "The Abolition of the Taboo System in Hawaii," *Journal of the Polynesian Society* 74:21–39.

1968 "Carneiro's Hypothesis of Limited Land Resources and the Origins of the State: A Latin Americanist's Approach to an Old Problem," *South Eastern Latin Americanist* 12(3):1–8.

1973 "The Petén Maya Decline Viewed in the Perspective of State Formation," in *The Classic Maya Collapse*, ed. T. P. Culbert (Albuquerque: University of New Mexico Press, School of American Research Books).

in press "The Significance of the 'Epi-Classic' Period in Mesoamerican Culture History," paper to be published in the Proceedings of the IXth International Congress of Anthropological and Ethnological Sciences.

WEINBERG, S. S.

1965 "The Relative Chronology of the Aegean in the Stone and Early Bronze Ages," in *Chronologies in Old World Archaeology*, ed. R. W. Ehrich (Chicago: University of Chicago Press).

WEST, R. C. AND J. P. AUGELLI

1966 *Middle America: Its Lands and Peoples* (Englewood Cliffs, N. J.: Prentice-Hall).

WHEELER, M.

1955 *Rome beyond the Imperial Frontiers* (Harmondsworth, Eng.: Penguin Books).

1966 *Civilizations of the Indus Valley and Beyond* (New York: McGraw-Hill).

WHITE, L. A.

1959 *The Evolution of Culture* (New York: McGraw-Hill).

WHYBRAY, R. N.

1968 *The Succession Narrative*. Studies in Biblical Theology, 2d Series, no. 9 (London: SCM Press).

WILLEY, G. R.

1953 *Prehistoric Settlement Patterns in the Viru Valley, Peru*. Bulletin of the Bureau of American Ethnology, no. 155 (Washington, D. C.: Smithsonian Institution).

1955 "The Interrelated Rise of the Native Cultures of Middle and South America," in *New Interpretations of Aboriginal American History: 75th Anniversary of the Anthropological Society of Washington*, ed. B. J. Meggers (Washington, D. C.: Anthropological Society of Washington).

1962 "Mesoamerica," in *Courses toward Urban Life*, ed. R. J. Braidwood and G. R. Willey (Chicago: Aldine Publishing Co.).

1966 *An Introduction to American Archaeology*, vol. 1: *North and Middle America* (Englewood Cliffs, N. J.: Prentice-Hall).

WILLEY, G. R., T. P. CULBERT, AND R. E. W. ADAMS
1967 "Maya Lowland Ceramics: A Report from the 1965 Guatemala City Confer-
(eds.) ence," *American Antiquity* 32:289–315.
WILLEY, G. R. AND J. C. GIFFORD
1961 "Pottery of the Holmul I Style from Barton Ramie, British Honduras," in
Essays in Pre-Columbian Art and Archaeology, by S. K. Lothrop et al. (Cambridge, Mass.: Harvard University Press).
WILLEY, G. R. AND D. B. SHIMKIN
1971 "The Collapse of the Classic Maya Civilization in the Southern Lowlands: A
Symposium Summary Statement," *Southwestern Journal of Anthropology*
27:1–18.
WILMSEN, E. N.
1972 "Introduction: The Study of Exchange as Social Interaction," in *Social Exchange and Interaction*, ed. E. N. Wilmsen. University of Michigan Museum
of Anthropology, Anthropological Papers, no. 46.
WILSON, J. A.
1946 "Egypt," in *Before Philosophy, The Intellectual Adventure of Ancient Man*,
by H. Frankfort et al. (Harmondsworth, Eng.: Penguin Books).
WILSON, M.
1968 "Ritual in Local Politics," in *Local Level Politics*, ed. M. J. Swartz (Chicago:
Aldine Publishing Co.).
WITTFOGEL, K. A.
1957 *Oriental Despotism: A Comparative Study of Total Power* (New Haven: Yale
University Press).
WOLF, E. R.
1959 *Sons of the Shaking Earth* (Chicago: University of Chicago Press).
WOODBURY, R. B.
1961 "A Reappraisal of Hohokam Irrigation," *American Anthropologist* 63:550–60.
WRIGHT, G. A.
1969 *Obsidian Analyses and Prehistoric Near Eastern Trade: 7500–3500 B.C.* University of Michigan Museum of Anthropology, Anthropological Papers, no. 37.
1970 "Current Anthropology Comment 'On Trade and Culture Process in Prehistory,'" *Current Anthropology* 11:171–73.
WRIGHT, H. T.
1972 "A Consideration of Interregional Exchange in Greater Mesopotamia: 4000–
3000 B.C.," in *Social Exchange and Interaction*, ed. E. N. Wilmsen. University of Michigan Museum of Anthropology, Anthropological Papers, no. 46.

5

Ancient Trade as Economics
or as Ecology

K. C. CHANG

Yale University

In the archaeological study of trade, *space* and *natural resources* are obvious focal concepts. Trade may be characterized as an essential form of the movement through space of natural resources, raw and processed, and one method of archaeological recognition of trade is to retrace the movement through the identification of the loci either of exploitation of raw materials or of manufacture of goods or both. American archaeology has in recent years begun to emphasize the ecosystemic study of prehistoric cultures, and in such studies the importance of trade is inevitably brought to the forefront of new research designs. An ecosystemic perspective in archaeology must focus upon the spatial distribution of natural resources, and trade is an important mechanism for their spatial movement.

One can have no quarrel with the ecosystemists' purpose or with those who attempt to study trade ecosystemically. A scientific treatment of such perennial archaeological topics as trade is long overdue. But it cannot be emphasized enough that the human individual does not relate to the natural environment without significant social intervention. Archaeological ecosystemists often seem to assume that the population as a whole, or its procuring segments, act in concert, according to survival needs. The homogeneity of the population in terms of its survival interest as a whole is also implicitly assumed. Without these assumptions I cannot see how the archaeologist can make processual interpretations—as he often has—only on the basis of the archaeological data on environmental resources, exploitative technology, and spatial relationship.

In the long run, these assumptions are perhaps warranted, as long as natural selection as an evolutionary process still does its job. But in the short run, at the operational level, an ecosystemic interpretation must take due account of the way in which individuals are organized into populations, and it is more often than not these human organizations that determine what natural resources are to be exploited, processed, and distributed, and in what way. Man often interacts with his environment in peculiar ways that are sometimes detrimental to his own interests or to the interests of some members of his own group. This is particularly true at the stage of civilization, in which human organization becomes even more complex. Colin Renfrew (1972:11) sees

> the process of the growth of a civilisation as the gradual creation by man of a larger and more complex environment, not only in the natural field through increasing exploitation of a wider range of resources of the ecosystem, but also in the social and spiritual fields. And, whereas the savage hunter lives in an environment not so different in many ways from that of other animals, although enlarged already by the use of language and of a whole range of other artefacts in the culture, civilised man lives in an environment very much of his own creation. Civilisation, in this sense, is the self-made environment of man, which he has fashioned to insulate himself from the primeval environment of nature alone.

To the extent that this definition underlies the qualitatively increased importance of that "self-made environment of man," I subscribe to it. At the risk of seeming extreme, I further believe that prehistoric and ancient trade must be approached within the context of the social units involved in the transaction; that settlement archaeology, defined as the study of archaeological data within a framework of social relationships, can best provide that context; and, above all, that prehistoric and ancient culture ecology (or human paleoecology) must be accompanied by, or incorporate as a significant component, prehistoric and ancient economics. Particularly in the study of ancient civilizations, there can be no cultural ecology without economics.

Fredrik Barth was perhaps the first serious advocate of ecological archaeology when he wrote, in 1950:

> It can no longer be the archaeologist's ultimate ambition to make chronological charts of cultures. . . . The only way the archaeologist can contribute to the general field of anthropology is by asking questions of *why*, for which a general framework is needed. One simple and directly applicable approach is that of ecologic analysis of cultural adaptations, treating problems of relationship of the ecologic area, the structure of the human group, and its cultural characteristics (Barth 1950:339).

Have archaeological researchers aiming at ecological analysis adequately taken into account "the structure of the human group"? Too often it has been taken for granted. But it should not be, for without it there can be no contact between the "ecologic area" and the "cultural characteristics"—no understanding of the structure of the human groups, no useful ecological analysis.

If this view prevails, one must conclude that trade can be studied only in the total context of the distribution of raw and processed natural resources within a societal framework. The archaeological data pertaining to the identification and distribution of natural resources (in various forms) through space merely pose the problem. The solution may begin with archaeological clarification of the following points:

  (a) the various social units involved, and their stratified hierarchy;
  (b) the quality of reciprocity ("balanced" or "unbalanced") in the flow of resources between pertinent units;
  (c) the means by which the transaction was effected, i.e., whether the flow was bilateral, whether it was redistributive, whether the direction and quality of the flow were controlled by voluntarism or by coercion, and so forth.

All of the above, obviously, are not trade. What is trade and what it is not may be simply a semantic question, but my own feeling is that only balanced reciprocal flow of goods between groups, effected by forces other than military coercion, can be profitably studied as trade, because this kind and other kinds of flow are governed by widely divergent factors and produce very different results.

The problem with this definition of trade is the perhaps insurmountable difficulty of evaluating reciprocity in archaeology. I use the word *reciprocity* here in the common sense of a balanced, mutual exchange. Wheat grains may easily be found to have been moved from a place of origin (such as a farmhouse) to a place of consumption (such as a storage bin in town). How they got there may make a lot of difference in our attributing to this spatial fact any significance. They may have been moved there in one of several ways:

(a) as part of land tax from farmer to landlord or town hall;

(b) as part of a tribute;

(c) as part of a raid;

(d) by having been purchased at a local market by barter or with money;

(e) as part of a "gift" brought by country relatives to some townsmen; or

(f) in some other possible fashions.

Some of these (d, e) carry definite qualities of balanced reciprocity; others (c) do not; still others may or may not (a, b). Archaeologically, one can seldom if ever distinguish among these diverse situations, and consequently the quality of reciprocity is hard to characterize in terms of individual units of material goods.

Another difficulty lies in the fact that material goods increase in value in the course of processing because of energy input (the Marxian labor), and the amount of increase is relative to factors beyond precise calculation in archaeology. Value can also be measured in services as well as goods. Neither labor nor services in the empirical sense leave any archaeological imprint.

For these reasons I do not believe that in archaeological study trade should be treated as a separate subsystem of the culture system, parallel to the other subsystems such as subsistence, technological, social, and symbolic (Renfrew 1972:22–23). In fact, the other subsystems are so closely and multifariously intertwined that, although subsystemic formulation is necessary, none can be entirely devoid of serious flaws. But since we are dealing with trade only, it suffices to say that trade can only be studied archaeologically as a facet of the total economic behavior of ancient societies. After we have reconstructed the flow patterns of raw and processed natural resources, through space, among social units of various levels, we may use trade as a mechanism to interpret the pattern that we see. We may even speculate about the roles, if any, trade may have played in the formation of the civilization in question, or in the formation of civilization in general. We may even take another step forward and, on the basis of our speculation, formulate research designs and test implications to try out such ideas in the field. But I do not see how trade can be treated as a discrete archaeological phenomenon that can be isolated on the ground, and I do not see that the concept of trade can be applied directly to the spatial patterns of distribution of raw and processed natural resources in order to account for these patterns. In other words, I am skeptical of our ability to undertake any ecosystemic study of trade without undertaking it only as a facet of a larger ecosystemic study of ancient society.

Most of what I have said involves fundamental attitudes and epistemological positions with regard to archaeology generally. We have come to realize by now that in archaeology many such attitudes and positions are in conflict, perhaps irreconcilable. Those who agree with me will find what I have said commonplace; those who do not will think my ideas shocking or naïve. But to give some archaeological meaning to these generalizations, allow me to use an example from Shang China.

I tried to ask myself the question called for by this symposium: What was the place of trade in the structure and formation of the Shang civilization? I believe this is a necessary question. But I find that one is unable to proceed from the question directly to a study of Shang trade, for trade cannot be defined archaeologically a priori. One must go back to the larger Shang society and go through its many facets (including, of course, the whole matter of the spatial flow of raw and processed natural resources) before one can identify a few areas that can probably be related to or referred to as trade.

First, the phenomenon of spatial movement of natural resources is easy enough to identify when the distance involved is large. But resource flow is by no means limited to long distance. In fact, most of these flows are extremely short in distance. But distance is not all that is pertinent; it must be studied with reference to the social units involved. Goods were moved across social units within a larger or smaller area, or they were moved within social units occupying the same area. Within each unit they were moved across or within subunits, or across or within units of a different order. But what kinds of things were being moved around in space? Since we cannot possibly talk about retracing the footsteps of every single item that we find, we must operate at a higher significant level, with reference to a few focal categories. In looking through the material remains of the Shang civilization, I group them, for the present purpose, into the following categories:

(a) Agricultural produce. Remains of grains and containers for grains are found at all sites, those near which farming was done and those where farming was apparently not done or at least was not important. Unquestionably, there were major flows of grains and other agricultural produce between villages and between villages and towns.

(b) Animals for special purposes. The flow of fish, game meat, meat of domestic animals, and wild plant produce was evidently similar to that of agricultural produce. But a few animals for special purposes deserve special attention. Oracle bone inscriptions refer to the presentation to the royal court of cattle, sheep, and horses (Hu 1944a). These were all ritually significant animals, and the horses were also used for pulling chariots. Archaeologically recovered faunal remains include bones of animals (such as elephants, tapirs, and others) that are now native to areas far to the south of the Shang territory (Young and Teilhard de Chardin 1936). These could have been animals transported from the south for the royal zoo, as is sometimes speculated, but more likely they suggest a warmer native climate then than now. Whale bones have also been found, and there can be no question of their having been transported from the coast.

(c) Handicrafts. Pottery, stone objects, wooden objects, and bronzes are the major archaeologically significant items of handicraft. Many workshops have been found at Shang sites. At least two segments of natural resource flow were involved: the first from the quarries of raw materials (wood, stones, clays, copper, tin) to the workshops, and the second from the workshops to the places of consumption.

(d) Prestige and precious goods. These include cowrie shells, turtle shells, jade, turquoise, probably salt, and ochers of tin (the last was listed above but deserves additional mention). These items were probably not locally available, which alone may account for their high value.

Cowrie shells (*Cypraea moneta, C. annulus*) are found in the coastal waters of southern and southeastern China, and those used by the Shang were probably procured from the same area. According to Shang inscriptions, five cowrie shells were usually strung together, and two strings formed a standard unit (Kuo 1933:100–102). The royal giving of a handful of such units to a subject was considered an event worthy of being made the object of divination in order to ensure propriety on the part of the giver, and worthy of commemoration on the part of the receiver through the casting of a bronze vessel. Raids were also recorded in which cowrie shells were part of the spoil (Wang 1957: 11–19).

Turtle shells were polished and retouched to serve as the basic instrument for royal divinations (P. Chang 1967). Some of the turtles were of a species (*Ocadia sinensis*) that is now produced only in the southern coastal areas of China, and another species is said only to live in the Malay Peninsula. Some shells bear an inscription of their origin from a tribute state or town: "Submitted by So-and-so," or "[A batch] of fifty submitted by So-and-so" (Hu 1944a). Many of these towns or states were in North China and so have procured the shells in turn from points further south, relay fashion.

Jade is traditionally attributed to quarries in southern Sinkiang, although other centers of origin are also known (Laufer 1912). No scientific study that I know of has been made to determine the origins of specific Shang jade specimens, but it is unlikely that they came from local sources. The exact sources of tin are also unknown at this time. Tin deposits are known from Honan and other parts of North China (Shih 1955), but in early Chinese texts good tin ochers are said to have come from South China (Kuo 1965:252). Turquoise is said also to have come from the south (Tung 1965:17). Salt was known only on the east coast and in one place in Shansi.

In addition to these, one is strongly tempted to include slaves or war captives in this list of movable resources. Humans were one of the most important "natural resources" of the Shang society. Groups of men were given by the king to his lordly uncles and brothers to bring to

217

their newly enfeoffed towns, and some battles are recorded to have resulted in hundreds or even thousands of captives, presumably to be brought back to work and to be sacrificed in rituals (Ch'en 1956). Archaeologically, human "goods" take the form of skeletons in sacrificial burials. But perhaps these should be grouped together with labor and services, which will be important for the problem of reciprocity.

The spatial flow patterns of the materials listed above provide some basic empirical data for Shang archaeology. Once we have plotted sites onto maps, and the various goods onto the sites, we can then proceed with interpreting the spatial pattern. Should we at this point attempt to connect sites into exploitative and exchange systems through the nature of the sites' respective contents of goods? My belief is that this connecting must wait. There are many lines to connect, and the apparent lines, the shortest lines, or what to us are the best lines may not be the right lines. In order that locational analysis can be undertaken meaningfully in regard to the content, and before an ecosystemic network can be constructed, prerequisite work must be done: the social units must be worked out, the reciprocal quality of the flow of goods and services among them must be determined, and the means and manners of the flow must be ascertained. In fact, these lines of inquiry are necessary for any thorough ecosystemic study in archaeology which must, therefore, be undertaken on the basis of excavated data rather than mere reconnaissance. Before we relate populations to natural resources, or before we cut up populations in accordance with their procuring relations to natural resources, let us first find out how our populations are internally organized, because members and member units of our populations may be related to natural resources differentially in terms of artificial economic status, rather than in terms of natural symbiosis.

Relevant here are some large and rather unexplored topics in Shang studies. This is not the place to present detailed discussions about them, but a few important facts and speculations may be offered.

(1) The economically significant political units of Shang society may be described as follows: At the lowest level there were the settlement networks such as the An-yang complex. Here Hsiao-t'un served as the hub of administration and rituals, drawing on the support of a number of specialized villages all located within an area of some 24 km.² Some of these villages were workshops of various kinds, but others

were probably farming villages (K. Chang 1968:214). A settlement net-work of this sort, standing alone but not as a part of a larger unit, is prob-ably the political unit—"tribe"—just one step up the evolutionary ladder from the autonomous village, and I use Colin Renfrew's term Early State Module (ESM) to refer to it.

The Shang ESMs were, of course, further organized into larger units at a higher level. At the highest level there was the Shang state, extend-ing in a large area of North China, from southern Shansi and eastern-most Shensi in the west to Shantung in the east, from northern Hopei in the north to northern Kiangsu, northern Anhwei, and central Hupei in the south. Political entities beyond the state the Shang referred to as *fang* (e.g., Kung fang, T'u fang, and the like). At the royal capital (i.e., the An-yang ESM in late Shang period), the other Shang ESMs were referred to as *to po yü to t'ien*, meaning "the multitude of *po* and *t'ien*." (These terms later evolved into the Chou "feudal" ranks of Po and Nan [Hu 1944b].) Between individual ESMs and the overall Shang state there probably were economically significant intermediate levels of organization. Since all Shang writings come from the state capital, the regional organization of the ESMs is difficult to reconstruct. But there was at least a regional unit above the royal ESM itself. Late Shang inscriptions refer repeatedly to an area of royal hunt ("t'ien lieh ch'ü" in the parlance of modern Shang studies), probably in northern and western Honan near the modern town of Hsin-yang (Kuo 1933:iv). The ESMs within this area probably had a closer mutual relationship than any or all of them with other, more distant ESMs in Shangtung or central Hupei.

(2) When individual Shang sites are organized into ESMs, HSMs (Higher State Modules, my term—apologies to Colin Renfrew), and the state, we take another look at the natural resources flow with regard to both direction and quality. Issues here are highly complex, and not all of them are archaeologically apparent. According to oracle bone in-scriptions, one can reasonably speculate that agricultural produce flowed within the ESM from villages to the center, within the HSM from the subordinate ESM to the chief ESM, and within the state from all over to the royal capital (Su 1956:49). Handicraft items essentially follow the same centripedal pattern, although raw materials such as tin were transported from longer distances, from one HSM to another or from

outside the state. Handicraft products of high prestige value, such as ceremonial bronzes and "white pottery," were exclusive to the ESM, HSM, and state centers. Sometimes they flowed back from the center to an outlying unit as a royal or princely gift. As for high value and prestige items such as cowrie, turtle shells, and jade, they were mostly transported from outside the state.

Once the social units involved in the transaction are identified, we are in a better position to find out whether a flow was characterized by balanced reciprocity, and, in the case of an unbalanced flow, which side got the upper hand. In looking at Shang data in this area, one is struck by two facts. The first is the high proportion of human energy that was involved in the economic transaction between spatially distinct social units. I refer to the concentration of elaborate handicraft items at a small number of centers, and the resultant sharp contrast in the material wealth between different sites and between loci of sites; the huge constructions—*not* "public" works by any means—that served the royal house and the lords (town walls, large buildings, large graves); and the masses of sacrificial human victims that were used in the royal rituals.

The second remarkable fact is the evident unevenness of the flow of natural resources, especially but not necessarily when the energy flow (labor and services) is fed into the equation. To be sure, many parts of the exchange are not archaeologically recoverable or are not materialistic in the first place. But when one is faced, within the An-yang ESM, with the contrast between Hsiao-t'un and Hsi-pei-kang (where perhaps more than 90 percent of all major constructions, all elaborate handicraft objects, and all prestige items are located) and a workshop site or a village (with a few underground dwelling pits and a few stone implements and potsherds); or the contrast between the An-yang ESM and a provincial ESM (like Hsing-t'ai, for example, where large structures, elaborate handicraft items, and prestige objects are scarce and writings nonexistent)—one recognizes a situation of unmistakable and gross inequality. To be sure, An-yang gave its affiliated towns and states protection and prestige, but these were paid for dearly. We recognize the greatness of civilizations such as the Shang mainly through large structures, elaborate handicraft items, and prestige objects. One can easily arrive at the following proposition: Other things (natural endowment, location, population, and so on) being equal, the more uneven and unbalanced is the resource flow, the greater are the civilization's achievements that are traditionally recognized. Great civilizations in the ancient world were the ones that divided their people into those who provide energy and those who employ that energy to produce "great civilization" hallmarks. Mencius put it this way: "There are those who use their minds and there are those who use their muscles. The former rule; the latter are ruled. Those who rule are supported by those who are ruled" (Lau 1960:101). Perhaps there are other civilizations that we may come to regard, archaeologically, as dull, impoverished, and not so great, but perhaps these are the ones in which fewer people starved. We might do well to take a second look at what we mean by "great."

(3) The uneven flow pattern among the various villages within the ESM and among the various ESMs within the state could only have been maintained through coercion, as opposed to voluntarism, and the Shang's military machine must be regarded one of the largest and strongest of its time. Some half of all bronze objects are weapons, and horses and chariots are a prominent part of any archaeological find. Oracle bones record battles with northwestern and northern *fang*, which were traditional adversaries, but a major expedition is known to have taken place at the very end of Shang period against the Jen Fang in the Huai River Valley in the Southeast, traditional habitat of friendly and stateside HSMs (Tung 1945: chap. 9). Thus, force was employed within the state against Shang's own people as well.

If cowrie shell units were used as currency, as seems almost certain, there were presumably monetarily based exchanges at several levels: within the ESM, within the HSM, within the state, and outside the state. In bronze inscriptions there is a class of emblems consisting of a human figure carrying cowrie strings (Li 1955:54–55). It may designate a lineage or clan of traders or entrepreneurs, and trading appears to be a special kin-linked profession. As their emblems appear on prestige objects, we can be certain that members of the trading profession, or at least its leading members, enjoyed respectable social status.

What about the question of the role of trade in the structure and formation of the Shang civilization? Perhaps the first thing one must decide is which kinds of the resource flow described above *are* trade. The unilateral flow of grains and human energy, maintained by coercion,

221

certainly is not trade, but the state may have exchanged grains for precious and prestige goods (such as tin, jade, shells) or horses in reciprocal trade. Some handicraft artisans may be part of the upper class, and they may have traded off their products and skills for raw materials such as tin. Most if not all raw materials for prestige and precious objects were traded from outside the state, presumably through the efforts of professional traders. After they came in, the raw materials were processed to become prestige and precious objects, which were then concentrated in the hands of the upper class. Thus, consideration of the Shang trade must be confined to the spatial exchanges of resources between the state and the alien, and, within the state, between the local elites and between the professions, and to those exchanges that involved a qualitative balance between parties. All these exchanges had mainly to do with prestige and precious objects, whereas the flow of life's essentials (grains and labor) was mainly internal, vastly unbalanced, and coerced. Ancient trade became prominent when the internal economic imbalance enabled it to be so, and the traded items in turn played an important part within the Shang society in bringing about or at least helping along that internal economic imbalance.

References

BARTH, FREDRIK
1950 "Ecologic Adaptation and Culture Change in Archaeology," *American Antiquity* 15:338–39.

CHANG, KWANG-CHIH
1968 *The Archaeology of Ancient China* (New Haven and London: Yale University Press).

CHANG, PING-CH'ÜAN
1967 "Chia-ku wen ti fa-hsien yü ku po hsi-kuan ti k'ao-cheng" (The Discovery of Oracle Bone Inscriptions and the Study of Bone Divination), *Bulletin of the Institute of History and Philology, Academia Sinica* 37:827–79.

CH'EN, MENG-CHIA
1956 *Yin Hsü Po Tz'u Tsung Shu* (A Comprehensive Description of the Oracle Inscriptions at Yin Hsü) (Peking: Science Press).

HU, HOU-HSÜAN
1944a "Wu Ting shih-tai wu chung chi shih k'o tz'u k'ao" (A Study of Five Kinds of Inscriptions of Record of the Wu Ting Period), in *Chia Ku Hsueh Shang Shih Lun Ts'ung*, vol. 1 (Ch'engtu: Ch'i-lu University).
1944b "Yin tai feng chien chih-tu k'ao" (A Study of the Feudalism of the Yin Dynasty), in *Chia Ku Hsueh Shang Shih Lun Ts'ung*, vol. 1 (Ch'engtu: Ch'i-lu University).

KUO, MO-JO
1933 *Po Tz'u T'ung Ts'uan* (A General Study of Oracle Inscriptions) (Tokyo: Bunkyudo).
1965 *Ch'ing T'ung Shih-tai* (The Bronze Age), new ed. (Peking: Hsinhua Press).

LAU, D. C.
1970 Translation of *Mencius* (Harmondsworth, Eng.: Penguin Books).

LAUFER, B.
1912 *Jade* (Chicago: Field Museum of Natural History).

LI, YA-NUNG
1955 *Yin-tai She-hui Sheng-huo* (Social Life of Yin Dynasty) (Shanghai: Jenmin Press).

RENFREW, COLIN
1972 *The Emergence of Civilisation* (London: Methuen).

SHIH, CHANG-JU
1955 "Yin-tai ti chu t'ung kung yi" (Bronze Metallurgy of the Yin Period), *Bulletin of the Institute of History and Philology, Academia Sinica* 26:95–129.

SU, SHIH-CHENG
1956 "Hsia tai ho Shang tai ti nu-li chih" (The Institution of Slavery in Hsia and Shang Periods), *Li-shih Yen-chiu* 1956(1):31–61.

223

TUNG, TSO-PIN

1945 *Yin Li P'u* (Yin Calendrical Charts) (Li-chuang: Institute of History and Philology, Academia Sinica).

1965 *Chia Ku Hsüeh Liu-shih Nien* (Sixty Years of the Study of Oracle Inscriptions) (Taipei: Yi-wen Press).

WANG, YÜ-CH'ÜAN

1957 *Wo Kuo Ku-tai Huo-pi ti Ch'i-yüan ho Fa-chan* (Origin and History of Ancient Chinese Coinage) (Peking: Science Press).

YOUNG, CHUNG-CHIEN, AND P. TEILHARD DE CHARDIN

1936 *On the Mammalian Remains from the Archaeological Site at An-yang*, Palaeontologia Sinica, n.s. C, 12(1).

PART III

CASE STUDIES

6

Satyānṛta in Suvarṇadvīpa
From Reciprocity to Redistribution
in Ancient Southeast Asia[1]

PAUL WHEATLEY
University of Chicago

"All art is a dialogue. So is all interest in the past. And one of the parties lives and comprehends in a contemporary way, by his very existence. . . . In the end, it can be only a dialogue in the present."
—Moses I. Finley

INTRODUCTION

Every society makes use of four primary modes of exchange corresponding to its four functional subsystems, and each employs these modes in a combination of emphases and elaborations appropriate to its value system, the degree of differentiation of its social structure, and the imperatives of its general internal and external situations. The four modes of exchange are *reciprocity*, which obtains primarily among those social units—such as families, neighborhood communities, and religious groups—concerned with pattern maintenance and tension management; *redistribution*, which involves the allocation of rewards and facilities in conformity with the integrative requirements of society; *mobilization*, which provides mechanisms for the acquisition, control, and disposal of

227

resources in the pursuit of collective goals—that is, broadly speaking, in the political field; and *market exchange,* the main instrument for the production of those generalized facilities by which the adaptive subsystem of society is able to achieve a variety of aims in a variety of situational contexts, and which provides a framework for the autonomous operation of the supply-demand-price mechanism that to the modern mind endorses a process as being essentially "economic."[2] But in no society are the boundaries of the functional subsystems inexorably fixed, established for all time by divinely ordained structural necessity. Rather, as a society evolves, so the sphere of operation of each of its subsystems changes in extent and intensity, thereby inducing parallel mutations in the modes of exchange associated with the subsystems. It will be the purpose of this chapter to suggest one way in which such changes in modes of economic integration may have occurred in ancient Southeast Asia.

During the closing centuries of the pre-Christian era, as far as the meagerly documented archaeological record permits an opinion, Southeast Asia was occupied exclusively by societies whose most advanced level of political organization was the chiefdom and among whom the instrumental exchanges characteristic of a reciprocative mode of integration predominated (Sahlins 1968:9–10; 1972: especially chap. 5). During these centuries the region was penetrated by two alien groups. From the north the Chinese imposed their political dominion on the Lặc tribes of the Tong-king lowlands, and concomitantly extended the mobilizative sector of their economy into the Red River Valley in the form of an external tribute system. This abrupt imposition of a superordinate mobilizative mode of economic integration on a predominantly (though by no means exclusively) reciprocative system of exchanges contrasted markedly with the more gradual transformations that were taking place in western Southeast Asia at roughly the same time, and which it will be the purpose of this paper to elucidate. In these latter territories Indian entrepreneurial advances, both private and corporate, induced societal dysfunctions which set in operation a sequence of changes that resulted in the emergence of redistributively based political entities, several of which subsequently developed strong mobilizative sectors in their economies. The role of market exchange, however, is obscure until

228

comparatively recent periods, owing largely to the strong political, administrative, ceremonial, and religious biases common to both archaeological and early literary sources. Because redistributive and mobilizative institutions were closely associated with the practice of government and administration, they were not totally excluded from epigraphic and other chancellery records, but the voluble chaffering of the marketplace was not something to be recorded in noble Sanskrit periods. For that we must turn to popular literature, which in Southeast Asia only developed in periods long subsequent to those with which we are concerned here.

This chapter differs from the others in the volume in that its interpretation of systemic change in ancient Southeast Asia relies as much on literary records as on archaeological materials. In any case, a relatively high proportion of the latter are epigraphs which, in view of the nature of the skills required to elicit their information, should perhaps be more properly considered as part of the literary heritage. Because the functional societal change of which literacy is born normally cannot itself be recorded in script, the climacteric phase of pristine state formation and its associated process of urban generation (as opposed to the imposition of symbolic and organizational patterns developed elsewhere) are seldom even partially documented in written records. In Southeast Asia, however, a considerable and diverse corpus of writings from China, India, Southwest Asia, and even from the Classical cultures of the West, if used with discrimination, can provide some degree of control over reconstructions based solely on archaeological evidence. Careful evaluation is also mandatory in the use of epigraphic resources and indigenous chronicles (though these chronicles appear late in the historical sequence and are of only minor relevance to the present inquiry). Not only are both typically fragmentary, intractable, and equivocal, but they are also often less records of events than vehicles for the aspirations and values of later ages. In a word, their substance has usually been subjected to the process that ultimately produces myth, partly through an unconscious transmutation natural to the passage of time and partly as a result of consciously undertaken historiographical redaction and exegesis. One need not be as skeptical as Professor Berg is of Javanese sources[3] in order to realize that many, perhaps most, of the available texts and epigraphs were composed to validate and glorify a historical present, to establish a particular dynast or dynasty as the foundation of political, social, economic, moral, and cosmic order. This does not imply that the transmitted texts and epigraphs are worthless but that the meaning to be attached to them by the social scientist of the present day is often quite different from that which their authors intended them to convey. It also implies that the only body of material which can be regarded as primary for the study of trade in ancient Southeast Asia is scientifically acquired archaeological evidence.

Under these circumstances it is doubly regrettable that archaeologists have until very recently conceived their mission in Southeast Asia to be the recovery of remains, with the natural result that they have directed their investigations to sites judged likely to yield the most spectacular material finds, namely the great architectural monuments such as the Bàyon at Yaśodharapura, the temples of Mĭ-sỏn, or the shrines on the Dieng Plateau. Archaeological (as distinct from epigraphical) research designed specifically to elucidate aspects of the institutional basis of any of the functional subsystems of society has been virtually nonexistent in Southeast Asia. So far as ancient commerce is concerned, such studies as exist have been undertaken with the limited aims of identifying within a more or less static framework the commodities traded, and charting the routes over which they moved. Only nominal attention has been devoted to exchange values, and none at all to the fundamental and exigent question of the precise modes of exchange involved and the manner in which they articulated with political, administrative, social, religious, and other institutions. I have elsewhere referred to studies of this kind, many of high excellence in their way, as black-box models (Wheatley 1968:294), by which I mean that they have provided a good deal of information as to *what* happened, but have said little about *how* it happened. The difficulties inherent in eliciting the second type of information will be only too apparent in the following pages. In any case I can do no more on this occasion than provide a grossly simplified version of what were in fact highly diverse and extremely intricate, though still poorly understood, institutional nexuses spread through one of the world's major cultural realms.

THE DEVELOPMENT OF LONG-DISTANCE
TRADE TO AND THROUGH SOUTHEAST ASIA

At about the beginning of the Christian era, the sea-lanes of Southeast Asia were being incorporated into the great maritime trade route that ultimately came to extend from the Red Sea to South China. More accurately it should be described as a series of trade routes, for during this period no one group of merchants operated throughout its length and no one class of merchandise traveled from end to end. The only characteristic common to all its commodities was their status as luxury articles. The western sectors of this trade route are, generally speaking, better documented than the eastern. Until the end of the first century A.D. the trade of the Arabian Sea was virtually an Arab monopoly, but from about that time Greek and Egyptian mariners began to compete for shares of the Indian cargoes that brought rich rewards when sold in the cities of the Roman empire. However, there is no reason to believe that these Mediterranean and Egyptian merchants penetrated far beyond the cape that they knew as Komari or Komaria (Schoff 1912:46; Frisk 1927; Renou 1925:6, l. 8), present-day Comorin, the southernmost point of the Indian subcontinent. Even the author of the *Periplus Maris Erythraei*, a skipper of wide practical experience, had not voyaged much beyond Nelkynda on the Malabar coast.[4] Beyond that point the commerce of the Bay of Bengal was in the hands of Indian merchants. Many of these intruded deep into the waters of the Southeast Asian archipelago, but the bulk of the carrying trade in Malaysian waters (Malaysian in the ethnic sense, of course) and in the South China Sea seems to have been controlled by various seafaring peoples referred to collectively by the Chinese of the time as **Mwan-i* (Modern Standard Chinese *Man-i*), or *barbarians* (*Ch'ien-Han Shu* 28B:32 a–b: Wheatley 1957:115–16). No extant source specifies the precise identities of these Southeast Asian traders, but it may be plausibly inferred that they were the folk subsequently known to the Chinese as **K'uən-luən* (MSC K'un-lun), an ethnicon that apparently subsumed a succession of peoples ranging from Malays in the archipelago to Chams along the coasts of Indochina (Ferrand 1919; R. A. Stein 1947: 209–311; Christie

231

1957). In the Gulf of Tonkin and along the South China coast the carriers of both merchandise and merchants were *Jiwɐt (MSC Yüeh) sailors. The final, but very attenuated, sector of this trade route was defined by a trickle of commodities high in value but small in bulk that were transported from South China overland to the capital at Lo-yang (*int. al.*, *Huai-nan Tzŭ* 18:27; *Shih Chi* 129:8b–9b; *Ch'ien-Han Shu* 28B: 31b). It was presumably over the several stages of this trade-route that the relatively numerous Mediterranean artifacts unearthed in Southeast Asia had traveled eastward,[5] and it was doubtless along this route in the reverse direction that had passed the tales of the land of This, "below Ursa Minor," which the author of the *Periplus* had incorporated in his trade manual (Schoff 1912:48; Frisk 1927:126). It is surely significant, though, that the archaeological evidence for Chinese trade goods having been shipped westward along this route is extremely meager, even in excavations conducted in neighboring countries such as Indochina (Malleret 1959–63:3:395).

At this time we do not know when Indian merchants first explored the seaways of Southeast Asia, but it is certain that by the early centuries of the Christian era they were already engaging in trade with the tribal societies of both the mainland and the archipelago. And there is no reason to suppose that such exchanges were of particularly recent origin. Indeed, passages in the *Rāmāyaṇa*, the *Vāyu Purāṇa*, the *Jātaka*, the *Sīhaḷavatthuppakaraṇa*, and similar texts would seem to carry them back well into the prehistoric period.[6] In the earlier literature relevant to this theme, Southeast Asia figured in generalized form as an eldorado beneath the sunrise; in Sanskrit texts it was Suvarṇadvīpa, the Golden Island, and in Pali Buddhist writings it was Suvaṇṇabhūmi, or the Land of Gold.[7] With the passage of time, within the vaguely defined, and probably flexible, bounds of Suvarṇadvīpa, nebulous regional entities became discernible; they bore names such as Malayadvīpa (the Mountainous Land),[8] Yāvadvīpa (the Land of Java), Karpūradvīpa (Camphor Land), Narikeladvīpa (Coconut Land), and Takkola ([Land of] Cardamom), to which merchant venturers from India set sail in ever increasing numbers.

Among the various explanations that have been proposed to account for the intensification of Indian trading activity in Southeast Asia at about the beginning of the Christian era, perhaps the most credible is that formulated by George Coedès (1964: 44–49), who attributes the reorientation of Indian commercial interests to changing political conditions in the Mediterranean and Central Asia. Vespasian (A.D. 69–79) prohibited the export of precious metals from the Roman empire and thereby aggravated a scarcity of gold that had obtained in India since nomadic disturbances in Central Asia during the two centuries preceding the Christian era had closed the Bactrian trade routes over which Siberian gold had hitherto found its way to South Asia. In default of other readily accessible sources of this metal, it is suggested, Indian merchants turned eastward to the half-legendary regions beneath the sunrise where not only could gold allegedly be picked up from the surface of the ground, but where other profitable cargoes, notably spices and aromatics, could be obtained. Southeast Asia has never been one of the world's major gold-producing regions, but in ancient times this metal was a much rarer commodity than at present, so that primitive methods of working it were proportionately more profitable. In any case, and for whatever reason, the motive for an overwhelming proportion of the voyages described in the several genres of Indian literature relating to this period was commercial profit. "If literature," says Majumdar (1937–38: 61), "mirrors the interests of an age, then trade and commerce must have been a supreme passion in India in the centuries immediately preceding and following the Christian era."[9]

Two developments appear to have facilitated the undertaking of voyages to Southeast Asia at this time. The first was of a technological nature. The early centuries of the Christian era witnessed innovations in ship construction which originated in the Persian Gulf and spread rapidly round the shores of the Indian Ocean. Perhaps the most significant of these technical improvements was the use of a rig that allowed vessels to sail closer to the wind. Ships were also built on a larger scale. Among the larger ships were the κολανδια which the *Periplus* describes as sailing directly from South India to Khryse, and which were probably the **k'uən-luən tân* (MSC k'un-lun tan) of a sixth-century Chinese commentary.[10] Other vessels that sailed the Indian Ocean at least as early as the third century A.D., and probably a good deal earlier, were known as **k'uən-luən b'ek*, (MSC k'un-lun p'o). Allegedly they measured 200 feet from stem to stern, and were capable of transporting some 600 or 700 men and more than 300 tons of cargo from South China to

Southwest Asia[11] in about two months (*T'ai-p'ing Yü-lan* 769:6a, citing the third century *Nan-Chou I-wu Chih by* Wan Chen; Pelliot 1925:255–57; Hsiang To 1930:4:27–28; R. A. Stein 1947:65–66; Needham 1971:458–60). These dimensions and capacities may appear unrealistic, particularly in view of Pliny's regarding an Indian ship of 75 tons as large, but the consensual testimony of a considerable corpus of texts and traditions in East and South Asia is not to be rejected casually. It is known, for example, that in the third century A.D. the Yüeh-chih transported horses by ship even as far as Indochina, which implies vessels of substantial displacement (*T'ai-p'ing Yü-lan* 359:15a, citing *Wu-shih Wai-kuo Chuan*; *Liang Shu* 54:22b), while in A.D. 414 the monk Fa Hsien voyaged from Ceylon to China on two vessels each of which carried more than 200 souls (Wheatley 1961:39–39).[12]

The second development that tended to facilitate, perhaps even encourage, overseas travel by Indians was the expansion of Buddhism. The old Brahmanism had paid heed to the laws of Manu which totally prohibited such voyages (*Manusaṃhitā* III:158), while the *Baudhāyana Dharmasūtra* placed them at the head of *pataniyani* and prescribed a three-year penance. Although in practice the prohibition seems to have been frequently flouted, there is no doubt that such an authoritative command must have exerted considerable restraint on foreign voyages.[13] Buddhism, by contrast, by rejecting brahmanical ideas of racial purity and the ensuing fear of pollution through contact with mleccha, did much to dispel the Hindu repugnance to travel. The greater freedom of movement associated with Buddhist beliefs is reflected not only in the prominence accorded the merchant in the *Jātaka* tales but also in the fact that in several realms of Southeast Asia the earliest material evidence of Indian culture is a statue of the Buddha Dīpaṃkara, "Calmer of the Waters," a favorite talisman of Indian seamen (Lévi 1929; Foucher 1900–1905:1:77–84).[14]

There has been considerable debate as to the regional provenance of the Indian traders who voyaged to Southeast Asia in early times, with the historians of North and South India supporting their respective homelands. Both regions are, in fact, represented by scripts, plastic arts, architecture, literature, toponymy, and ethnological data, while the topographic texts at our disposal testify to sailing routes from virtually the whole length of the Indian littoral. Whereas the *Periplus Maris*

Erythraei (§ 60) mentioned Kamara (Ptolemaic Khabêris, i. e. Kāviri [paṭṭinam]), Podoukê (probably close to Pondicherry), and Sōpatma, all on the Coromandel coast, as the points from which *kolandia* set sail for Khryse, Ptolemy (VII, i, 15) located his port of departure (ἀφετήριον) farther north, either in the composite delta of the Kistna and Godavari rivers or possibly in the neighborhood of present-day Śrīkākulam. The Chinese pilgrim I Ching in the seventh century, as well as several of the monks whose biographies he recorded (*Ta-T'ang hsi-yü ch'iu-fa kao-seng chuan:* 98a–b and passim: Wheatley 1961:41–45), both arrived at and embarked from Tāmraliptī at the mouth of the Hooghly, but others passed through Nāgapaṭṭinam and the ports of Ceylon, as indeed had Fa Hsien nearly three centuries previously. Nor was this traffic restricted to east-coast ports, for the *Jātaka* tell of voyages to Suvaṇṇabhūmi from Bharukaccha (Ptolemaic Barygaza: modern Broach), Śūrpāraka (Ptolemaic Souppara), and Muchiri (Ptolemaic Mouzêris, usually located in the neighborhood of Kranganur), all on the western side of the peninsula.[15] However, during the past quarter of a century it has become increasingly evident that the preponderant cultural influence on Southeast Asia emanated from southern India (Vallée-Poussin 1935:293; Coedès 1964:58–69; Wheatley 1961: 189–93; Filliozat 1966:passim). Without doubt, though, the region whose contribution has been most underrated is Ceylon, one of the two islands that were particularly identified with the cult of the Buddha Dīpaṁkara (the other being Yāvadvīpa—possibly the Island of Java, but more probably the Malaysian world as a whole),[16] and the style center for at least three of the erroneously ascribed Amarāvatī Buddhas that constitute the earliest South Asian archaeological finds in Southeast Asia (Levi d'Ancona 1952; Dupont 1954).[17]

To summarize briefly: By the beginning of the Christian era, Indian merchants had worked their way through the sea-lanes of Southeast Asia and familiarized the tribesmen of certain strategically situated territories with a range of material products, and probably also with some of the less tangible benefits, of Indian civilization. Within a century or two, in the same territories there had emerged kingdoms whose governance was based on Indian (Hindu or Buddhist) conceptions of social order. It is to be presumed that there was some evolutional relationship between the tribal and the state levels of sociocultural integration in these regions, and it is our present task to elicit from exceedingly intractable evidence the mechanisms of that transformation; to explain why, when at the beginning of the Christian era the type representative of Indian civilization in Southeast Asia was the seasonally visiting merchant-mariner, a few centuries later it had become the divine monarch claiming to rule over the four varnas, to follow the Veda, observe the dharma, and generally behave according to the prescriptions of the Smṛti canon.

STATE FORMATION IN INDIANIZED SOUTHEAST ASIA

For the earlier European historians of precolonial Southeast Asia, carrying among their intellectual baggage the categories of nineteenth-century imperial politics, the causal relationship between trade and state was obvious and direct: the polities that emerged in the early centuries of the Christian era were empires of conquest strung along the eastern sectors of the great South Asian trade route and ruled by Indian dynasts *au sang pur*. Political power had reached out along the trade routes to the east as European flags had followed in the wake of commerce during the eighteenth and nineteenth centuries. At a slightly later phase in the intepretative process, the emphasis shifted from colonies of conquest to colonies of settlement that constituted communities of Indians planted amid aboriginal tribes to whom they brought the blessings and benefits of a superior civilization. This was the theme that permeated the numerous books by the Indian historian R.C. Majumdar (1937–38, 1944, 1955 [note the words "colonization" or "colonies" in the titles of these works]; 1954:chap. 24) and, with few exceptions, the works sponsored by the Greater India Society. It was also espoused from time to time by Indian public figures who were not primarily historians, notably by Rabindranath Tagore who once referred to "that age when she [India] realised her soul, and thus transcended her physical boundaries" (Tagore 1934); Ratzel would surely have approved of this way of looking at events. Subsequently one particular variant of this theme attributed the initiation of the process of state formation to the organizing skills of a relatively small number of Indians, primarily traders, who by precept and action, often aided by

236

intermarriage with indigenous women, established Indian cultural traditions on the soil of Southeast Asia. Perhaps this point of view received
it most imaginative expression in the writings of Gabriel Ferrand,[18] but
it was carried to its logical conclusion in the magistral expositions of
Krom (1923; 1931). Nor was it entirely absent in the works of George
Coedès, dean of historians of this period, and author of the most comprehensive theory of so-called Indianization to date (1953; 1954; 1964).
In a metaphor reminiscent of *Manu* IX:35–40, Coedès categorized
Indian culture in Southeast Asia as a transplant rather than a graft:
"L'Inde . . . a exporté partout la même plante qui, suivant la nature du
terrain où elle s'est développée, a produit des fruits de saveur différente"
(1953:377). The types of interpretations cited thus far have all attached
considerable importance to the activities of Indian traders in Southeast
Asia, either as precursors or agents of political control or as themselves
transmitters of Indian cultural traits. Almost unique in denying traders
any significant role in this momentous transformation was Jacob
Cornelis van Leur (1934), who constructed his theory of Indianization
around the ritualistic and consecratory roles of the brahmana priesthood.

It is apparent that none of these explanations is completely satisfying.
In fact, the conquest interpretation is no longer viable, while various
objections can be, and often have been, advanced against any particular
version of the alternative hypotheses: that traders would, generally
speaking, have been incapable of transmitting the subtler concepts of
Indian thought; that Hinduism was not a missionary religion; that it
would have been difficult to integrate non-Indians into the Hindu social
system except in the role of mleccha; that the culture which had defined
itself in Southeast Asia by the fifth century A.D. was one of *clercs*,
neither merchants nor warriors; and so forth. The truth of the matter is,
I suppose, that each hypothesis contains some truth, some elements that
should be included in any reinterpretation of what must have been
one of the most momentous instances of acculturation in the history of
the world. My own opinion is that the available evidence, both archaeological and literary, is so meager and obscure that several internally
consistent hypotheses can be devised to account for it. In these circumstances it would seem reasonable to proceed on broadly hypothetico-
deductive principles, to generate a testable hypothesis that can be proved
unequivocally erroneous rather than to attempt to apply inductive

methods to wholly inadequate evidence. What follows is one interpretation that seems, given the inchoate state of the investigation, to offer a reasonably coherent, though generalized and inevitably partial, explanation of events in Southeast Asia during the early centuries of the Christian era.

The Brahmanization of Western Southeast Asia[19]

It is our present thesis that the entrepreneurial activities of Indian traders induced the emergence of dysfunctional partial structures—here defined as roles, regulative norms, values, possibly even subgroups— which inhibited the fulfillment of some of the social needs of the relatively segmentary societies and chiefdoms characteristic of Southeast Asia in the late centuries B.C.[20] Let us envisage a tribal settlement of this type located at some sheltered bayhead or estuary readily accessible to Indian traders on their seasonal visits—and in this connection we would do well to remember that before the advent of steam all deepwater sailing in the Indian Ocean and the South China Sea was seasonal in response to the half-yearly reversal of the dominant wind systems that obtained throughout South and East Asia.[21] The chieftain of this settlement, as the mediator of commercial transactions between the tribe as a corporate entity and the visiting merchants—and probably as instigator and organizer of the collection of forest products such as aromatics, drugs, woods, minerals, and so forth—would have been subjected to a range of experiences beyond the ken of his fellows in remoter regions. He would have been led to develop new perceptions of the world, new life goals, and to acquire organizational skills foreign to tribal society. In the course of time he would have ceased to be, as the Malay proverb has it, a frog under a coconut shell (*Katak di-bawah tĕmpurong*), his ecumene bounded by the *kuala*, *hilir*, and *hulu* of a single river valley, and have become instead a cultural broker on the expanding frontier of a great civilization. And, as the principal beneficiary from the profits of this commerce, a disproportionate share of which probably took the form of ceremonial regalia, beads, textiles, and other chiefly perquisites, he would have acquired a vested interest in the continuation, and perhaps expansion, of the system. But the customary law of the tribe, forged through time to sustain the solidarity of the group, would have provided neither sanctions for some innovations that the chief might have deemed desirable nor authority for new types of decisions that he might have been called upon to make. In circumstances such as these a chieftain might well have come to feel greater empathy with the intrusive community, whose creature in a sense he was, than with his own folk. Possibly by association with the aliens he came to share in their prestige, and when that happened he was but a short step from validating his own status in terms that the foreigners established for him. The only political institution of adequate authority and flexibility likely to be within the cognizance of a Southeast Asian chieftain of the time would have been an Indian model structured around divine kingship.

It may be helpful at this point to outline the function of kingship in South Asia at this time. During the centuries preceding the Christian era Hindu social theorists, speculating in a cultural milieu that made no clear distinction between spiritual and temporal, had come to conceive of Aryan society as comprised of a clearly defined quadruple warp of predominantly endogamous classes (varnas) transected by an ideal, but often imperfectly realized, quadruple weft of life stages (asramas), all part of the framework of a set of rules (*varṇāśramadharma*) which, by establishing a code of behavior appropriate to an individual in any class at any time in his life, also implied a general norm of conduct for all society. It is not surprising that, in this context, government was a class function, to be exercised specifically by a leader of the *kṣatriyavarṇa*.[22] In fact, the prevailing instrument of government was a monarchy which, while basing its authority on a mystical assumption of divinity, did not explicitly reject the overtones of contractual validation that had permeated classical Indian literature.[23] In the parallel strand of political theory that evolved in Buddhist India the origin of kingship was indeed traced back to a primitive form of social contract (*Dīgha Nikāya* 3:92–93; *Mahāvastu* 1:347–48). From the time of the Mauryas there also developed in both Hindu and Buddhist thought the concept of the universal emperor (chakravartin), whose cosmic role admitted no doubt of his divinity.

It is interesting to note that an instrument for the validation of royal authority already existed in India. This was the *vrātyastoma*, the brahmanic rite by which indigenous chieftains could be inducted into the *kṣatriyavarṇa* (Vallée-Poussin 1924:168, 169, 174, 178; 1935:361; Lévi 1905–8:1, 220; Renou 1931:143, 334; Coedès 1964:53–54), and it is this stage in the acculturation process that seems to be reflected in Southeast Asian epigraphy by the Sanskritization of dynastic styles in successive generations. Early in the third century A.D., for example, a ruler who had established control over the lower Mekong Valley and neighboring territories assumed the style Maharaja of the Mountain, "the Mountain" presumably signifying Mount Mahendra, the seat of the god Śiva.[24] Even more significant assumptions of an Indian titulary are recorded from the archipelagic territories. According to a sacrificial inscription from Muara Kaman in eastern Kalimantan dated to about A.D. 400, the reigning king of a small principality bore the name Mūlavarman, and was the son of "the renowned Aśvavarman," founder of the dynasty (*vaṁśakartri*). Both these names are good Sanskrit, but an apparently predynastic ruler, father of Aśvavarman, was referred to as "the famous prince Kuṇḍuṅga," which seems to have been an Indonesian, or perhaps a Tamil name (Vogel 1918; Chatterjee 1933:8–19; Chhabra 1945, 1949; Casparis 1947: 77–82; Minattur 1964). Another and later inscription, this time from Javanese Matarām and dated to 732, records that Sanjaya, founder of his line and bearer of a Sanskrit name, was nephew and successor to Sannaha, who bore a Javanese name Sanskritized (Kern 1917b; Chatterjee 1933:29–34; Chhabra 1935:37). Here surely we see one of the devices of an emergent political elite seeking to legitimize its authority on an Indian pattern.

In this interpretation I have postulated the presence, at least seasonally, of Indian merchants—or what comes to the same thing, of merchants from some other Southeast Asian locality already subject to Indian cultural influence—in a tribal society. I am thinking here of the sort of small trading ventures that are mentioned so frequently in the *Jataka* and *kathā* literature,[25] but the outcome would have been much the same if the vehicle of cultural diffusion had been the settlement of a ksatriyan adventurer and his band of retainers or the trading factory of a mercantile corporation. The alleged role of ksatriyan settlers has been emphasized by Mukerji (1912:40), Berg (1929:12), and Moens (1937: 317), but although in the more popular literature of medieval India it is the high-caste entrepreneur who predominates as ship owner, investor, and speculator,[26] scientifically attested records of ksatriyan settlement

240

(by which I mean records acquired through controlled excavation) are almost totally lacking. Not a single *prasasti* recording a *digvijaya* that might have resulted in the establishment of a ksatriyan-led colony, not a single *vamsavali* ascribing high birth to ancestors has come to light on any archaeological site in Southeast Asia relating to the earlier centuries of the so-called Indianization process (Bosch 1961:8). Yet in the mythologized literature such ksatriyan enterprises are by no means unknown. According to the traditional chronicles of Burma, for instance, the earliest kingdom in the Irrawaddy Valley, centered on Tagaung, was founded by a prince who had been deprived of his lands in India (Phayre 1883:3–5), while in the Javanese Pañji narrative cycle the dispossessed prince from beyond the sea who founds a kingdom is a familiar figure. And, if Filliozat is correct in his interpretation of the Võ-cạnh stela, either the petty dynast MāRaN (Sanskritized in the inscription as Śrī Mara) or one of his descendants may have been a scion of the Pāṇḍyan royal house who, for reasons unknown, settled in southern Indochina (Filliozat 1969:115–16). It may possibly be a *digvijaya* of this type that appears, transmuted in the collective memory of the Kĕdah peasantry, in the *Hikayat Marong Mahawangsa*, late though that text be.[27] These events, and others like them, have only too patently been mythologized into heroic situations, and the participants transformed into culture heroes, so that the reality they mask is now probably lost irretrievably. Nevertheless, they may be capable of transmitting, if not echoes of actual events, then resonances of those echoes.

For Indian commercial settlements in Southeast Asia there is some archaeological evidence in the form of three inscriptions recording the presence of Tamil merchant corporations. The first, dated to the ninth century A.D., was discovered at Takuapa on the isthmus of the Siamo-Malay Peninsula (Coedès, 1924–29:1:50; Nilakanta Sastri 1932, 1949). It records the placing of a tank constructed in the locality under the protection of the Maṇigrāmam, a powerful mercantile corporation from South India.[28] The second inscription, from Labu Tuwa in western Sumatra, dated 1088, also refers to a so-called merchant corporation, the Aiññuṟṟuvar, well known in South India (Nilakanta Sastri 1932); the third inscription was found in Pagan, Burma (Hultzsch 1902). These references to corporate commercial activity in Southeast Asia are relatively late in time, but they illustrate a mode of cultural transference

241

that may possibly have operated in much earlier periods, and which has in fact been postulated by van Naerssen (1947; 1948a:414; 1948b). Both ksatriyan colonies and mercantile corporations were potentially able to expand and diversify the customary livelihoods and goals of neighboring tribesmen. Those individuals with the most compelling reasons to change the old order of society—presumably those members of the chiefly class who, by acting as spokesmen for their tribes, came to function as intermediaries between the tribe and the intrusive aliens— would have manipulated the new alternatives or inconsistencies thus created in the indigenous scheme of values in an effort to strengthen their own prestige and ultimately to achieve some degree of freedom from the restrictive bonds of tribal custom. For these chiefs too, as for chieftains dealing with seasonal traders (p. 238 above), wherever customary sanctions inhibited the extension of authority to validate the power required for supravillage rule, the concept of the god-king would have proved especially attractive. The assumption of divinity, by translating the ultimate source of authority from—in Weber's terminology (1925:133–34)—consensus to charisma, freed such chieftains from the traditional restraints of tribal custom and simultaneously afforded a basis for stratifying the tribe, henceforth to be divided into rulers and subjects.

We have seen that divine kingship[29] was a cultural borrowing that revolutionized the structure of authority relationships in certain strategically situated parts of Southeast Asia during the early centuries of the Christian era. It also involved a partnership between ksatriya and brahmana. A prerequisite for kingship on the Indian model was consecration, an elaborate ceremony which was a jealously guarded prerogative of the *brāhmaṇavarṇa*; and as early as the third century A.D. the presence of brahmanas was attested in Southeast Asia, specifically in a kingdom situated somewhere in the northern sector of the Siamo-Malay Peninsula. Chinese envoys to Southeast Asia in about 245 reported that more than a thousand brahmanas resident in the kingdom "devoted themselves solely to study of the sacred canon . . . and practiced piety ceaselessly by day and night" (*T'ai-p'ing Yü-lan* 788:1b, citing the third-century *Nan-chou I-wu Chih*; Wheatley 1956a:21).[30] It is interesting to observe that these brahmanas were reported in a state whose commercial relations with places as far distant as Parthia and India in the west

and with Tong-king in the east were strongly stressed by Chinese an-
nalists. Because of its advantageous location where the land "curves
round and projects into the sea for more than 1000 *li* [i.e., where the
Siamo-Malay Peninsula projects south-southeastward]," says the *Liang
Shu* (54:7a), "all the countries beyond the frontier [i.e., the Chinese
frontier, implying all the countries of Southeast Asia] come and go in
pursuit of trade. . . . At this mart East and West meet together so that
every day great crowds gather there. Precious goods and rare merchandise—they are all there." Nor was it fortuitous, I think, that there were
some 500 Persian and/or Sogdian (*γuo:* MSC hu) households in the
kingdom (*T'ai-p'ing Yü-lan* 788:1b).[31] Even though Pelliot's (1903:
279*n*4) suggestion that the Chinese distinction between brahmana
and *γuo* implied that the latter constituted a merchant class still
awaits verification, it is sufficiently evident that the brahmanas in this
isthmian state had voyaged along the seaways pioneered by the merchant
fraternity. Another state in which brahmanas were in evidence from a
comparatively early date, probably the fifth or sixth century, was that
known to these Chinese as *$B'u\hat{a}n$-$b'u\hat{a}n$* (MSC (P'an-p'an), and believed to have been located in what is today southern Thailand. Of this
kingdom it was recorded that "numerous brahmanas have come from
India to seek wealth by serving the king, with whom they are in high
favor" (*Wen-hsien T'ung-k'ao* 331; commentary in Wheatley 1961:47–
51).[32] At the beginning of the seventh century Chinese envoys to
Raktamṛttikā, another city-state on the Siamo-Malay isthmus, described
the important ceremonial and ritual functions of a corps of several
hundred brahmanas (*Ch'ih-t'u Kuo Chi,* preserved in *Sui Shu* 82:3a–
5b; trans. in Wheatley 1957a:122–26).[33] The earliest epigraphic references to brahmanas in Southeast Asia occur in three of the four
sacrificial inscriptions of King Mūlavarman that we have already mentioned as dating from the beginning of the fifth century A.D. There we
read of a munificent gift of cattle by the king to "the twice-born resembling fire" (brahmanas) associated with the shrine of Vaprakeśvara (cf.
p. 240 above). Half a century later the ruler of a principality in western
Java was performing brahmanic rites and bestowing gifts on brahmanas
at the inauguration of a waterway and probably also at the incorporation
into his realm of new territory (Vogel 1925; Chatterjee 1933:20–27;
Schnitger 1934:4; Stutterheim 1932; Sarkar 1959). From that time on-

243

ward epigraphy and literature both bear unequivocal witness to the role of brahmanas at the royal courts of Southeast Asia as purveyors and conservators of the *siddhānta* (esoteric knowledge) necessary for stable government. Some of the clearest evidence for this comes from classical Kambujadeśa, where numerous Sanskrit inscriptions testify that the *varṇāśramadharma* was established, albeit in somewhat attenuated form, with Khmer kings as ksatriyas consecrated by and receiving the advice of brahmana *purohitas* (court chaplains).[34]

There has been considerable debate among historians of Southeast Asia as to whether the brahmanas mentioned in Chinese texts and Southeast Asian epigraphy were actual immigrants from South Asia or merely signified the adoption by indigenous courts of an Indian institution. For some brahmanas of classical Cambodia the answer is not in doubt, for their careers were summarized in inscriptions. One named Divākarabhaṭṭa, for instance, was born in Kalindi, that is, in the country of Mathurā, Vṛndāvana, and the Yamunā. Others traced their birth to the Āryadeśa, perhaps here to be understood as the Āryāvarta, the territory that, extending from the western to the eastern ocean, lay between the Vindhya and Himalaya mountains (*Manu* II, 22, 23). And still another came to Cambodia from the Dakṣiṇāpatha (Filliozat 1966:98, citing relevant passages from *Inscriptions Sanskrites de Campā et du Cambodge*, 1893). These texts were all post–eighth century, but it is not unreasonable to suppose that if Indian brahmanas traveled to Southeast Asia during later centuries, then they may well have done so in earlier periods. But this raises the question of the Smṛti prohibition of foreign travel mentioned above (p. 234), which applied with especial force to brahmanas. According to the purists, a sea voyage in particular vitiated brahmanical status. In evaluating this argument we must remember that the Smṛti precepts tended to become more authoritative with the passing of time, a fact reflected in the lack of opprobrium attaching to brahmanas whose journeys to Suvarṇadvīpa were recorded in Sanskrit literature such as *Vetālapañcaviṁśatikā* (Filliozat 1966:97). Moreover, it is certain that these brahmanas carried with them to Southeast Asia several dharmasastras, authoritative works which could hardly have been at variance with their own teachings. Coedès (1964:68*n*2, citing Robert Lingat) has also drawn attention to a passage in the *Baudhāyana Dharmaśāstra* (I, i, ii, 4) in which sea voyaging (*samudrasaṁyānam*)

is cited as a custom peculiar to brahmanas of North India. There is, however, abundant evidence that South Indian brahmanas also played prominent roles in this cultural transference.[35]

It has also been objected from time to time that, since it is highly
improbable that Indian women ever traveled overseas in these early
days, the great brahmana ministerial families that are epigraphically
attested in some states could never have come into being, let alone have
prospered, had their founders been true Indian immigrants. To Indian
brahmanas, it is alleged, the very idea of miscegenation would have been
abhorrent. Yet at least one Chinese text reports that in a state on the
Siamo-Malay Peninsula, probably during the second half of the fifth
century A.D., the local folk espoused the Hindu faith and gave their
daughters to the brahmanas in marriage. It then adds significantly,
"Consequently numerous of the brahmanas remain there." (*T'ai-p'ing
Yü-lan* 788, citing *Fu-nan Chi* by Chu Chih; Wheatley 1956a:21).
Presumably these brahmanas, and numerous others like them employed
for their consecratory powers and magical skills at the courts of Southeast Asian rulers, would have invoked in justification of their marriages
and of the brahmanic status of their offspring the text of *Manu IX*:35–
40, according to which the *jāti* of a tree is determined by the seed rather
than the field. In other words, the offspring of a brahmana by any
mother retains the varna of the father.[36]

In the present context it is pertinent to note that the *brāhmaṇavarṇa*
was not solely and invariably a caste of *clercs* performing ritual services.
That brahmanas engaged professionally in commerce is evident from
numerous records from medieval India (Venkatarama Ayyar 1947:269–
70), while it is beyond dispute that the Dayśasta Marāthā brahmanas
of Maharashtra traditionally pursued careers in trade and intermarried
with merchant communities. If these things happened in medieval
times when the Smṛti rules had come to constitute an unimpeachable
authority, then it is not unlikely that they also happened in ancient
times. Possibly some of the brahmanas who figured in Chinese texts and
Southeast Asian epigraphy were also merchants. Those who were reported to be serving the king of **B'uǎn-b'uǎn* in the hope of material
rewards (p. 243 above) come to mind in this context. In India itself it
appears that Dravidian shamans were occasionally assimilated to the
brāhmaṇavarṇa, and there is no reason why, when the process of brah-

manization extended across the ocean, such inductions could not have occurred in Southeast Asia. In this connection we may recall Max Weber's remarks on the Kammalars, the skilled craftsmen in metal, wood, and stone who, claiming descent from the artisan god Viśva-karma, "gerufen von den Königen, weithin nach Birma, Ceylon, Java verbreitetin und den Rang vor den Priestern, auch den zugewanderten Brahmanen, beanspruchten. Sie wurden, offenbar als Träger magischer Kunst, auch von andern Kasten als guru's, geistliche Seelenleiter, in Anspruch genommen: »der Kammalar ist der Guru aller Welte«" (Weber 1923:64$n1$). The possibilities of brahmana interaction with Southeast Asian societies in transition were numerous. What is certain is that the Smṛti texts are an inadequate guide to the intricacies of the so-called brahmanization process in South India, let alone to events on the farthest frontiers of Āryadeśa.

The Formation of the Nāgara

After this digression let us resume the thread of our argument. Political power in Southeast Asia traditionally derived from control over labor, and those chieftains subject to the pressures for change that have been described doubtless sought to extend their authority so as to be able to draw on labor rights in as many neighboring settlements as possible. No doubt opposition to this policy developed at an early stage, from both less successful and more remote chiefs, who, political status being evaluated in terms of labor rights, regarded any diminution in their own labor forces as a subversion of their power; at a later stage opposition would have come from competing supravillage chiefs and nascent kings. At the same time, the maintenance of a state appropriate to a god-king and his priesthood demanded the ministrations of increasing numbers of craftsmen and artisans, the more skilled of whom were often accommodated within the royal enceinte. Also required were the labor, on the land surrounding the royal residence, of a peasantry who contributed the surplus produce of its fields as a tax in kind for the support of the court, and the services of a band of armed retainers who acted as household guards, organized the peasantry in times of military emergency, and generally enforced the will of the god-king. Concomitantly there developed material defenses such as walls and palisades encircling the royal demesne. In short, there had evolved the city-state, the *nāgara*, focused on a new architectural feature, the temple. The whole complex represented the outcome of a series of social and political transformations that replaced the tribal chief by a divine king, the shaman by a brahmana, the tribesman as warrior by a ksatriya, and the tribesman as cultivator by a peasant, that is a farmer bound to the ceremonial center in an asymmetrical structural relationship that required him to produce in one form or another a fund of rent (Redfield 1953:31, 53; 1956: passim; Wolf 1966:9–10). At the same time gerontocracy or patriarchalism yielded to patrimonialism (and eventually, in times with which we are not here concerned, to sultanism), occupational specialization assumed the character of *jāti*, age-sets were transmuted into *āśrama*, the tribal meeting was formalized as an assembly on the model of the *sabhā*, and custom broadened into law within the framework of the Dharmasastra. Concurrently the gift was transposed into tribute or tax, and the old reciprocative mode of exchange was overlaid by a superordinate redistributive system of integration. These institutional transformations, in turn, were manifested morphologically in the conversion of the chief's hut into a palace, the spirit house into a temple, the spirit stone into the *linga* that was to become the palladium of the state, the boundary marker into the city wall (and, incidentally, the boundary spirits into the Lokapālas presiding over the cardinal directions). In other words, the kampong had become the *nāgara* through a series of social, political, and economic transmutations that signified the transition from culture to civilization.

Thus far we have been discussing the extension from India to Southeast Asia of an administrative technique superior in efficacy to any political instrument previously devised in the latter realm, and central to which was the transformation from consensual to hereditary charismatic authority. But the transformation was not confined to the differentiation of bureaucratic roles and modes. In Indian civilization the spiritual and the temporal were so closely interwoven that the adoption of specific political and social institutions was impossible without some measure of adherence to Indian religious norms. This was particularly true of Hinduism, which constituted a total way of life, with the result that the assumption of authority relationships on the Hindu pattern could not but induce the adoption of an Indian cultural configuration involving religious symbols, prescribed social relationships, laws, and codes of behavior, all subsumed within the compass of the *varṇāśra-madharma*. The relative rapidity with which this process of cultural diffusion was accomplished owed a good deal to two factors. In the first place the predominantly syncretic nature of Indian thought and culture facilitated the absorption of alien elements while yet allowing them to retain their original character with only slight modifications. In the second place, the autochthonous groups within Southeast Asia recognized in Indian cultural patterns certain customs and beliefs which were common to the whole of tropical Asia but which had received more sophisticated formulation at the hands of Indian exegetes as Dravidian and pre-Dravidian culture had fused with that of the Aryans.[37]

It has sometimes been argued that this process of acculturation affected only the upper classes of the Southeast Asian society that it had itself created, while the mass of the population maintained its former customs and beliefs. This was the thesis of Krom in his magistral *Hindoe-Javaansche Geschiedenis* (1931), and subsequently of Stutterheim and Bosch in their numerous publications on precolonial Indonesia,[38] but possibly this point of view received its most extreme expression in the works of J. C. van Leur, distilled in the famous phrases, "The sheen of the world religions and foreign cultural forms is a thin and flaking glaze; underneath it the whole of the old indigenous forms has continued to exist . . ." (1934:95). It is true that epigraphy and literature both tend to emphasize cultural components of a religious and scholastic character, "elements," as Bosch (1961:11) puts it, "which remind us of the manuscript, the code of law, the recluse's cell, the monastery," in short, of those whom, in the terminology of the Middle Ages, we call *clercs*. The inscriptions make much of the *caturvarṇa* but say little or nothing of *jāti* and are virtually silent on the rules of commensality, marriage, and the like. It is also true that the Great and Little traditions in Southeast Asia have often appeared to be unusually divergent, particularly in the early phases of "Indianization." But with the development of permanent institutional structures through the process that Weber (1925:770–71) termed "routinization of charisma,"[39] we observe a continuum of degrees of imperceptible change linking the traditions rather than a gulf separating them. It is difficult to believe that a bureaucracy such as that of Kambujadeśa, which was capable of mobilizing the whole state in one gigantic corvée, could have failed to influence to a considerable degree the habits of thought and ways of life of its peasant communities. The fact that these people were peasants at all instead of folk collectors or cultivators is impressive testimony to Indian cultural influence. Surely the peasants called to labor on national temples or the shrines of aristocratic families could not have returned home totally ignorant of Indian iconography. And there is no doubt that, although they possessed little understanding of the religious values underpinning the Great Tradition of India, they often adopted the gods of that tradition in modified form into the pantheon of the village. Nor could the peasant who paid his taxes in kind to a temple official, or marched in the army of the god-king, have been wholly immune to the influence of the bureaucracy. The very large numbers of villagers adscripted to the service of Khmer temples will be discussed in the next section, and the same circumstances prevailed, though less fully attested in epigraphy, in the complexes of shrines at Pagan, in Campā, in Javanese Matarām, and elsewhere. It is implicit in the interpretation of "Indianization" presented here that the royal temple-city was a center of diffusion for Indian customs and beliefs, with the less prestigious foundations of royal scions and aristocratic commoner families functioning as secondary centers of diffusion.

THE ERA OF REDISTRIBUTIVE INTEGRATION

It has been shown that during the early centuries of the Christian era there emerged in western Southeast Asia centralized states based on Indian conceptions of polity. Kings with Indian titularies and bound by the rules of the *kṣatriyavarṇa* reigned by the principles of kingship expounded in Indian treatises from capitals laid out as reduced images of the Indian cosmos (Heine-Geldern 1930). Below the king, princes and dignitaries constituted an ethnically mixed oligarchy, a substantial proportion of whom claimed brahmanical status. In Raktamṛttikā at the beginning of the seventh century the most important state officials, according to the report of a Chinese envoy, were a chief minister with the title of *sārdhakāra* (literally "colleague"), two *dhanadas* ("bestowers of benefits"), three *karmikas* ("agents"), and one *kulapati* ("head of the family") charged with the administration of criminal law (*Sui Shu* 82:3a–5b; Wheatley 1961:26–36; Coedès 1964: 150). At about the same time the ruler of the kingdom known to the Chinese as *Tân-tân* (MSC Tan-tan) was assisted by eight high officers of state, all brahmanas, representing the Lokapālas guarding the eight directions of the Hindu universe (*T'ung Tien* 188; *Hsin T'ang-Shu* 222c: 5b; Wheatley 1961:51–52; Wolters 1967:201–6). Below the largely brahmanic oligarchy, inscriptions bear witness to a hierarchy of functionaries serving both the metropolitan territory and the provinces. Sanskrit was the language of the chancelleries and of the higher echelons of the bureaucracies. The people at large in, say, Kambujadeśa were apportioned among a number of corporations according to their occupations (Nath Puri 1956). They lived in villages under the nominal authority of elders and notables much as in pre-Indian times, except that now decisions of the village assembly were subject to the control of inspectors in the royal service. In Java the population was similarly divided among divers administrative "circles" (*maṇḍala*), semiautonomous communities, religious fiefs, and occupational groups. What distinguished both Khmer and Javanese cultivators—and indeed Cham, Mōn, Pyū, Burmese, and Malay cultivators—from their tribal neighbors was the fact that the former were peasants owing duties to a state and subject ultimately, however imperfectly they might understand their position, to an authority founded on the dharmasastras. But it cannot be emphasized too strongly that the rules embodied in these codes were less prescriptions than norms, not so much institutions as frameworks for institutional development. "Le droit hindou," wrote Lingat (1952: 112), "au lieu d'imposer ses injonctions et de se superposer à des règles coutumières qu'il aurait prétendu évincer, n'a cherché qu'à offrir des principes et des méthodes, des classements et des distinctions, grâce auxquels un véritable droit local a pu s'organiser."

The earliest states to be formed in the manner described were already in existence by the middle of the third century A.D. in the valley of the lower Mekong, on the plains of what is today central Vietnam, and on the isthmian tracts of the Siamo-Malay Peninsula (Coedès 1964:chap. 3; Briggs 1951:chap. 1; Wheatley 1961:282–89 and passim). By the beginning of the sixth century other polities had emerged in west Java and Sumatra and, seemingly, in eastern Kalimantan (Wolters 1967). Apart from the last mentioned, all these nuclear regions of statehood lay along the main maritime trade route between India and China. In subsequent centuries states predicated on similar principles came to occupy the Pyū country of central and upper Burma, the coastal plains of Arakan, the Mōn lands around the lower courses of the Irrawaddy and Chao Phraya rivers, and other parts of Java and Sumatra. All, with the significant exception of some of the Javanese kingdoms, were based in, and in most respects restricted to, the lowlands. If I may adapt a phrase of—I believe—D. G. Hogarth, the Sanskrit tongue was chilled to silence at 500 meters.

What is of interest in the present context are the modes of economic integration that prevailed in these states. At the core of all of them was a cosmomagically delimited capital, the heart of which was a national temple, axis of the universe, the earth, the kingdom, and the royal city, and seat of the palladium of the state. In its sophisticated Cambodian form this latter often assumed the shape of a sacred *linga* in which was embodied the eternal "subtle-self" or personality of the king.[40] In later times the national temple also housed a statue of the king, invested with the attributes of a god, which had been animated by Indian religious rites so that it prefigured the final apotheosis that the monarch would undergo on the dissolution of his mortal body in death. Nor were these cult practices restricted to the king. Other members of the royal house and of the nobility, high officers of state, dignitaries of the priesthood, and successful commanders in war also sought to augment their karma by dedicating shrines to patron deities, and they, too, often took care to ensure the perpetual existence of their "subtle-selves" through the animation of their portrait statues (Coedès 1947:chap. 3, and 1960; Groslier 1956:22–27). On their descendants devolved the duty of maintaining these shrines, which were apparently regarded as new architectural bodies for the *sūkṣmātman* of the cosmicized man, much as the flesh had been during the man's lifetime. Many such shrines were, in fact, maintained for several generations. It followed that over the centuries, as a result of the popularity of these personal cults which were also ancestor cults, the face of ancient Kambujadeśa became diversified by innumerable temples and shrines. It is scarcely an exaggeration to regard the

251

economy of the country in its entirety as one great oblation organized for the appeasement of the gods of the Indian pantheon, and thus designed to maintain that harmony between the macrocosmos and microcosmos without which there could be no prosperity in the world of men.

In all the other main political units of Southeast Asia similar centripetalizing exchange systems came into being during the first half of the first millennium A.D. or shortly thereafter, but the most fully documented is certainly that of ancient Kambujadeśa. A good example is afforded by the foundation stela of the great shrine of the Rājavihara (now called Ta Prohm), dedicated by Jayavarman VII in 1186 to his mother in her apotheosis as Prajñāpāramitā, the Perfection of Wisdom. As many as 3,140 settlements with a total population of 79,365 persons were enfeoffed to this shrine, among them 18 high priests 2,740 officiants of one sort or another, 2,202 assistants, and 615 female dancers. The recorded property of the same shrine included a set of golden dishes weighing more than 500 kilograms, a silver service almost as large, 35 diamonds, 40,620 pearls, 4,540 gems, 876 Chinese veils, 512 sets of silk bedding, and 523 parasols. The schedule of daily and seasonal offerings listed huge quantities of rice, *ghṛta* for lustration purposes, molasses, oil, various seeds and cereals, wax, sandalwood, and camphor, and it is interesting to note that no less than 2,387 changes of clothing were supplied by the royal treasury for the adornment of the temple statues. And all, so the inscription ends, so that, "because of the virtue of the good deeds I have accomplished, my mother, once delivered from the ocean of transmigration, may enjoy the state of Buddhahood" (Coedès 1960: stanza CXLI, 69 and 81). The provisioning of the Jayaśrī shrine (now known as the Prāḥ Khǎn) was on an even more ample scale, requiring contributions in kind from no less than 97,840 persons, both male and female, in 5,324 settlements (Coedès 1941a). Equally impressive were the quantities of drugs and provisions consumed annually by the 102 asylums for the sick established by Jayavarman VII throughout his kingdom and dedicated to the Buddha Bhaishajyaguru Vaidūryaprabhā, "the master of remedies with the shining beryl," namely 11,192 tons of rice produced by 838 villages with an aggregate population of 81,640 persons, 2,124 kilograms of sesame, 105 kilograms of cardamom, 3,402 nutmegs, 48,000 febrifuges, and 1,960 boxes of salves (Coedès 1941b).

From these and other similar records it is evident that in classical

Cambodia there was a continuous and massive movement of products from the villages toward nodes in a network of ceremonial centers. In the context of the individual temple, this movement appears to have exhibited superficial similarities with the *Tempelwirtschaft* postulated for Sumeria by an earlier generation of scholars, notably Deimel (1931). These pioneer interpretations have proved to be certainly overgeneralized, and possibly misconstrued even at the level of the individual temple, and it may be that similar interpretative errors are being repeated in contemporary investigations of the ancient Cambodian economy. Nevertheless, allowing for the likelihood of conceptual reevaluations of the records, it seems established beyond reasonable doubt that the old reciprocity, marching with segmentary distance (Sahlins 1968:84), had been overlain by an institutionalized superordinate system that today would be categorized as redistribution par excellence. The allocative pressures of numerous temple-cities were generating appropriational movements primarily toward themselves, though subsequently and secondarily centrifugally outward. In the case of some commodities this doubtless involved a physical relocation of goods, followed perhaps by storage and ultimately a partial return to the countryside; in other instances it was probably merely appropriational, involving only rights of disposal over the goods. In either case, the quantities of commodities involved in the transfers recorded in the two stelae cited above—and there were literally hundreds of such temples in ancient Cambodia, though admittedly most were smaller than the Ta Prohm and the Práh Khǎn—imply that the centripetally induced flow of goods and services amounted to a sizable proportion of the total available supply of such commodities and services. Redistribution, in this technical sense, has little to do with economic calculation and price payments as those terms are usually understood. Such calculations as are undertaken seem to be based on the principle that, in the interests of societal integration, each class should be assigned what is conceived to be its proper allocation of resources and facilities. In short, the redistributive mode of economic integration is concerned primarily with the stratification of rewards in terms of wealth, power, and prestige. Appropriately enough, it was a Buddhist ruler who diverted a significant proportion of these rewards away from the upper echelons of the social order and into the hands of the poor and afflicted.

253

The Mobilizative Sector of the Economy

One mode of economic integration which is not always in practice easily distinguishable from redistribution is that generally termed *mobilization*. Conceptually it differs from redistribution in that it does not sustain social stratification but rather channels goods and services into the hands of those responsible for the achievement of broadly political goals. In other words, it subordinates economic arrangements to the pursuit of collective aims, usually the maintenance of the political integrity of the society in question (Smelser 1959:179). An unusually clear instance of such a mobilizative system is afforded by Cambodia under the rule of Jayavarman VII, the Khmer monarch whose redistributive policies have just been discussed. In order to render his kingdom a worthy offering to the gods of Mahayana Buddhism, this king, during a reign of less than four decades (1181–1218), carried out a building program that involved the hewing, transportation, and shaping of a greater quantity of stone than had been employed by all his predecessors since the beginning of Khmer history. Perhaps the earliest of the shrine-cities that he built was the Pūrvatatathāgata or "Buddha of the East," now known as the Banteay Kdei. In 1186 the great shrine of the Rājavihara was dedicated to the king's mother. Five years later the temple Jayaśrī, housing a pantheon of 430 images, was dedicated to his father in the likeness of the Bodhisattva Lokeśvara. Attached to it were ancillary temples such as those of the Krol Ko and Ta Som, and the tower sanctuary of Rajyaśrī (now the Neak Peân), described in its foundation stela as "a famous island, glorying in its lakes which cleanse the mud of transgressions from those who visit it" (Finot and Goloubew 1923:402). A hundred miles to the northwest, at the foot of the Danrêk Mountains, Jayavarman established the city whose immense ruins, spread over an area of approximately 2000 by 2500 meters, are today known as Banteay Chhmar to fulfill the dual role of frontier fortress and funerary temple dedicated to one of the king's sons. On the bank of the Mekong River just above Phnom Penh the king raised the temple presently called Văt Nokor, and in the province of Bati he built another shrine which has subsequently been dubbed the Ta Prohm.[41] While all this monumental building was taking place, Jayavarman was also erecting 121 "houses with fire," rest houses for pilgrims journeying along the main routes of his kingdom toward the great shrines at Angkor (Coedès 1940), together with the 102 hospitals for the sick that we have already had occasion to mention. But the most impressive of all this monarch's architectural undertakings was the remodeling of the capital at Yaśodharapura on such an extensive scale that it became virtually a new city; its remains are known to the modern Cambodian as Angkor Thom. The previous capital, laid out by King Udayādityavarman II so as to pivot on the temple-mountain of the Bàphûon, was almost completely overlaid by a new foundation focusing on the Bàyon, an *axis mundi* whose symbolism rendered it a veritable reduced image of the Khmer kingdom (Mus 1936). Round the perimeter of the whole ceremonial enclave, a distance of more than 10 miles, Jayavarman raised a wall flanked on its outer side by a moat more than 100 yards in width. Immediately north of the geometrically central Bàyon he erected his palace, which he connected with other parts of the central precinct by a series of carved terraces. The terrace known today as the Terrace of the Elephants, which served as a royal reviewing stand for festivals and parades, was over 300 yards long. Finally Jayavarman excavated several artificial lakes and added the final adaptations to the hydraulic system of the Angkor region so that it came to serve both agronomic and symbolic functions. At its maximum development it combined ingenious solutions to engineering problems with a scheme of transcendent cosmic symbolism, thereby ensuring the prosperity of the sacred city in a manner that neither undertaking could achieve independently. All this constructional activity—surely one of the most remarkable implementations of a mobilizative policy in the whole of the traditional world—was the more significant in that it did not end with the erection of the buildings. Indeed, that was only a prelude to the work of an army of craftsmen who carved gallery after gallery of reliefs depicting the worlds of gods and men. According to the foundation stela of the Prâḥ Khǎn, by 1191—some three decades before the program was terminated by the death of Jayavarman—there were already more than 20,000 statues in gold, silver, bronze, and stone distributed throughout the realm, and no less than 306,372 persons, living in 13,500 villages and consuming 38,000 tons of rice annually, were employed in their service (Coedès 1941a:stanzas 44–165). It should be noted, though, that the preceding account does not take into consideration the already existing foundations which Jayavarman added to or restored.

And all this was done barely fifty years after a period of only slightly less frenzied construction by Suryavarman II which had witnessed the building of, among other shrines, Angkor Wat, the Banteay Samrè, Beng Mealea, and a large part of the Práḥ Vihar. Not altogether surprisingly, some modern authors have seen this intensification of the mobilizative sector of the economy to a degree probably unparallelled in the premodern world as a factor contributing powerfully to the decline of the Khmer state (Finot 1908:223–24; Coedès 1947:208; Briggs 1951: 236, 260–61).

Market Exchange

The mode of exchange that figured least prominently in archaeological, epigraphic, and literary records was that which was conducted in the marketplace. The biases of all three bodies of evidence militated against the preservation of information concerning those economic mechanisms that operated outside the institutional nexuses supportive of social stratification, political authority, and kinship. Indeed, the Sanskrit language, in which the epigraphs were mainly inscribed, was an inadequate instrument for expressing the institutionalized subtleties of economic rationality that governed the rules of behavior in such markets. Isolated allusions to bazaars do occur from time to time, and the presumption is that the bazaars were price-fixing, but the references carry no implications as to whether they were truly self-regulating markets, much less as to whether they were integrated into self-regulating market systems. The Chinese emphasis on the number of traders and volume and variety of merchandise in the capital of the Kingdom of the Five Cities in the third century A.D., where "all the countries beyond the [Chinese] frontier come and go in pursuit of trade" (*Liang Shu* 54:7a; Wheatley 1956a:17–18), surely implies something in the nature of bazaar exchange. The same can be said of the mart at Sĕluyut in the eighth century, where "traders passing back and forth meet together" (*Hsin T'ang-Shu* 222C:5b; Wheatley 1961:58),[42] and of Kalāh in the tenth century as described by Abū Zayd (Bibliothèque Nationale *MS* 2281; Ferrand 1913–14:I:96; Tibbetts 1956:24–25; Wheatley 1961: 217). Chou Ta-kuan's account of Yaśodharapura in 1296–97 (Pelliot

1951:27) is a little more explicit, referring to a daily market held from 6:00 A.M. to noon and operated almost exclusively by women, but it relates to a period too late to be of much relevance to our present investigation.

CONCLUSION

I hold it to be self-evident that trade can be profitably discussed only in terms of functional subsystems of society. It is these subsystems individually rather than society as a whole that generate exchange, each within the framework of its own particular mode of economic integration, and it is upon these subsystems that externally induced trade acts to effect structural changes. It is true that these structural changes in a particular subsystem may ultimately engender far-reaching transformations in an entire society, but initially it is the subsystem that absorbs and adapts to the impact. The modulative effects of trade on the predominantly reciprocative economies of tribal groups have been described by, among others, Lewis (1942) and Jablow (1951), while Alpers (1969), Goody (1971), Kottak (1972), and Meillassoux (1971) have recently explored the ramifications of trade-induced change in somewhat more complex societies. In this chapter I have attempted to pursue this line of thought by adumbrating the total transformation of economies and societies that was engendered by the extension of South Asian commercial entrepreneurship into the southeastern angle of the continent. The argument, in brief, is that the forging of this cross-cultural link between India and western Southeast Asia evoked partial structures inimical to the functioning of certain societies in the region, which in turn led to the adoption of new sets of authority relationships, new models of leadership and motivation. Ultimately the societies concerned were transformed from congeries of tribal groups into polities so thoroughly permeated and imbued with Indian values that the earliest Western travelers, regarding them as an extension of South Asian culture, referred to them as Further India or the East Indies. The fact that from the vantage—or perhaps in this instance disadvantage—point of the twentieth century the sequence of changes outlined above appears to have developed with an inherent inevitability deriving from some principle of internal logic should not blind us to the frictions, disjunctions, failures, and obliterations that a fuller study would certainly reveal.

The preceding interpretation is intended as no more than a sketch of a process that was in reality infinitely more complex than it is depicted here. The limitations of the chapter reflect exigencies of space and, much more important, exigencies of knowledge—knowledge irreparably distorted by prevailing biases in the records, whether archaeological, epigraphic, literary, mythological, or folk. Because, generally speaking, these records preserve the deeds and values of elites, they emphasize those institutions that were devised for ritual, administrative, governmental, and, to some extent educative, purposes. Consequently their information is more relevant to the study of the redistributive and mobilizative modes of exchange than to reciprocity and marketing systems. Even for the former two sectors the model proposed in the preceding pages is still very much of the black-box type. The most important questions have not yet been broached. We know what Indian traders did, we possess a glimmering of understanding of a few aspects of their corporate commercial institutions as they functioned in the subcontinent, but we know nothing of the manner in which they operated in Southeast Asia, the ratio of peddlers to high-class entrepreneurs, the proportion of commenda agents to independent traders, or precisely where and how the business of exchange was carried on. Only occasionally does the investigator stumble upon a reference—such as that specifying the existence of a marketplace where the *Miuən-lâng (MSC Wen-lang) savages exchanged aromatics for other unspecified commodities (Li Tao-yüan, Shui-Ching Chu: 23a, citing Lin-i Chi), or that mentioning silent barter between the *Zįwo-lâng (MSC Hsü-lang) and their neighbors (ibid.: 29a)—which affords a fleeting glimpse of a reality that is invariably ignored by epigraph, lontar leaf, and scroll alike, and which archaeology so far has made no attempt to recover. Nor, for the same reasons, are we even tolerably well informed as to the administrative instruments employed for surplus extraction and concentration in the redistributive and mobilizative systems that were such a prominent feature of medieval Southeast Asian polities. In particular we would like to achieve a more precise understanding of the extent to which these two systems were institutionally distinct in the several political units into which the area was divided. Nor do we know the extent to which a market-exchange network persisted or developed beneath the superordinate redistributive and mobilizative systems characteristic of those states. It is unlikely that many new texts relating to the formative period of these kingdoms will become available in the future, or that reevaluation and reinterpretation of the existing corpus will do more than raise, rather than answer, novel sets of questions. The burden of advancing our understanding of economic exchange in ancient Southeast Asia must therefore be shouldered by archaeologists, specifically by archaeologists capable not only of recovering artifacts but also of imaginatively reconstructing the institutional bases of past societies. In my opinion this implies the use of research designs radically different from those employed thus far in the protohistoric archaeology of Southeast Asia.

NOTES

1. In this paper the term Southeast Asia will be used in the strict sense to denote the territories both continental and archipelagic situated to the east of the Indian subcontinent and to the south of China.

Satyānṛta, "a mixture of truth and falsehood," was the epithet with which Manu (IV, 6) characterized trade; the regional designation *Suvarṇadvīpa* is explained on p. 232.

2. The four functional subsystems referred to are those specified by Talcott Parsons and his associates. This paradigm for a society or other type of social system conceived as an integrative subsystem of a general system of action was first presented fully in Parsons et al. (1961:1:30–79), and since then it has informed the works of both the master and his disciples. The dominant modes of economic integration are defined, illustrated, and elaborated in Polanyi, Arensberg, and Pearson (1957), Dalton (1968), Parsons and Smelser (1956), and Smelser (1959; 1963).

3. Berg rejects the Javanese chronicles almost totally as records of events but acknowledges their potential value as sources for reconstructions of the nature of the societies that produced them, and particularly of the values that informed court life. Berg also believes that, provided the investigator is cognizant of the magical function of the records, it is possible to make informed guesses as to actual happenings. The evolution of Berg's thought on Javanese historiography is scattered through a series of articles in *Indonesië* and other journals. There is a brief summary of his point of view in Berg (1961). See also Berg (1962; 1965:86–117), Bosch (1956), Damais (1962:416), and Wolters (1970).

4. Compare also Procopius's remark that, even as late as the sixth century A.D., Persian merchants "always locate themselves at the very harbors where the Indian ships make their landfall" (*History of the Wars* I, xx, 12: Loeb Classical Library 1914). Beyond Cape Comorin the character of the information in the *Periplus*

changed, losing its customary precision and becoming increasingly speculative, as if picked up casually from Eastern traders encountered in the ports of Malabar. The *Periplus* is usually ascribed to about the middle of the first century A.D., though Jacqueline Pirenne (1961) has argued persuasively for a date early in the third century.

5. Cf. Malleret 1959–63:4:chap. 23. The artifacts of Mediterranean provenance that have been excavated at the port city of Oc-èo in southern Indochina include medallions, intaglios, beads, coins, and even a bronze bust of the Roman emperor Maximinus (A.D. 235–38). Techniques and ideas from the Mediterranean and the Roman Orient are manifested most clearly in Hellenistic and Roman influences on the representational art of Indochina, notably in a Lysippan-style figurine excavated at Trà-vĩnh (Picard 1956), in the Dionysian motifs discernible in a statuette recovered from a Han-dynasty tomb in Thanh-hoá (Janse 1957–58), and a bronze Alexandrine lamp probably of the second century A.D. from the lower Mae Klong Valley (Picard 1955).

6. *The Rāmāyaṇa*, the *Vāyu Purāṇa*, the *Jātaka*, and the *Sīhaḷavatthuppakaraṇa*, in the form in which we now know them, are cumulative texts. The *Rāmāyaṇa* is essentially a work of the third or fourth century B.C., to which were added numerous interpolations from as late as the second century A.D. Parts of the *Vāyu Purāṇa* derive from as early as the fifth century B.C., but additions were being incorporated as late as the sixth century A.D. Many of the *Jātaka*, a collection of folktales adapted to Buddhist purposes, were in existence in the immediately pre-Christian period, but the corpus continued to grow for several more centuries. The *Sīhaḷavatthuppakaraṇa* is a translation from Old Sinhalese into Pali of a collection of tales that were apparently current in South Asia at the beginning of the Christian era. For expositions and evaluations of these and other sources pertaining to Indian trade with Southeast Asia in ancient times see van Leur (1955:1–144), Majumdar (1937–38), Wheatley (1961:Part III; 1964:chap. 3), and Wolters (1967:chap. 2).

7. Dvīpāntara (Skt., Pali Dīpāntara), which a Sanskrit-Chinese lexicon of the seventh or eighth century A.D. cites as a synonym for *K'uən-luən, is another such generalized name denoting at least the Malaysian world in its entirety, but its antiquity is obscure: cf. Lévi (1931a), Nilakanta Sastri (1942), Paranavitana (1966:148, 159, 168–69).

8. Sanskrit *dvīpa* (Pali *dīpa*) strictly denotes land with water on two or more sides, but in medieval Indian literature the term seems to have been used with the general connotation of land in or beyond the ocean.

9. Cf. Lévi (1930) in the more restricted context of the *Jātaka*: "Un grand nombre de récits du Jàtaka ont trait à des aventures de mer; la mer et la navigation tenaient manifestement une grande place dans la vie de l'Inde à l'époque où ces récits furent imaginés." Cf. also Lévi (1931b:173 and 1931c:371). Also Mohan Singh (1961).

10. *Shui-Ching Chu*:23b. This work, an extended commentary on the *Classic of the Waterways*, was prepared by Li Tao-yüan (biography in *Wei Shu* 89:9b–10b) at the beginning of the sixth century A.D., but seems often to have incorporated information from earlier periods. Coedès (1910:XVII, note 1; 1964:63) has related the term *kolandia* to the *kola* mentioned in certain Sanskrit Buddhist texts and the *kalam* of Tamil Śaṅgam literature: cf. also Meile (1940) and Christie (1957).

11. Lit. "to the kingdom of Ta Ch'in [= the Roman Orient]." K'ang T'ai, *Wu-shih Wai-kuo Chuan, apud T'ai-p'ing Yü-lan* 771.

12. It is probably vessels of the *k'uən-luən b'vk* type that constitute the majority of those sculptured in bas-relief on the galleries of the great stupa of Borobudur in Java, which dates from about A.D. 800: Krom and van Erp (1927–31:Ser. 1b, pl. XXVII, fig. 53, pl. XLIII, fig. 86, pl. XLIV, fig. 88, pl. LIV, fig. 108; and Ser. II, pl. XXI, fig. 41). Also Mukerji (1912: frontispiece, pp. 48 no. 3,46 no. 1, 47 nos. 5 and 6); Hornell (1946:pl. XXXIIIB; 1941:fig. 5; Kempers (1959:pl. 78), Needham (1971:fig. 973), and elsewhere. From these representations, and from Hui Lin's eighth-century commentary on the Vinaya Canon (*I-ch'ieh Ching Yin-i*: Japanese Tripiṭaka, Wei sectn. IX, 155a), which incorporates a paragraph or two on Southeast Asian shipping in a textual gloss, it appears that *k'uən-luən b'vk* hulls were sewn rather than nailed, the reason offered by Hui Lin being that "the heating of the iron would cause fires." In any case, the mode of construction produced a resilient ship well adapted to withstanding the stress of monsoon storms and the jarring shocks of rock and reef. The vessels depicted on the Borobudur also displayed large outriggers, and the elongated, canted square-sails characteristic of certain classes of Indonesian boats in more recent times, the latter being especially significant because, as Needham has demonstrated (1971:458), canting was in all probability the first stage in the development of fore-and-aft sailing. The *p'vk* of Hui Lin and the Borobudur were some four centuries later than those of Wan Chen, so the comparison between them must not be pushed too far. But sailing technology in South Asia seems not to have changed all that rapidly, and the vessels described by Wan Chen were clearly of substantial size.

13. A passage in the *Mṛgendrāgama* actually considers sea voyages for conquest or profit to be permissible (Bhatt 1962:76).

14. Standing Buddhas of this type have come to light on sites in Thailand (Coedès 1927:16–20; 1928), Vietnam (Rougier 1912:212–13; Coomaraswamy 1927:197), Sumatra (Schnitger 1937:pl. I), eastern Java (Cohn 1925:28), and Sulawesi (Bosch 1933a; 1933b:35). Originally these statues were ascribed to the Amarāvatī school of Buddhist art, but subsequent examination has shown that most, if not all, of them were of Gupta date (Levi d'Ancona 1952; Dupont 1954; Paranavitana 1966:191–95). Dīpaṁkara has been interpreted as signifying "Island-Maker" because "it is a support to people in the sea which is devoid of all support": Paranavitana (1966:176), citing verbatim King Kassapa V in his *Dampiyā-aṭuvā gäṭapada*, D.B. Jayatilaka's edition: 6. Paranavitana (ibid.) also mentions the existence in Anurādhapura in the sixth century A.D. of a corporation of bankers who had taken the Buddha Dīpaṁkara as their patron, indicating thereby that they were financing overseas trade, almost certainly with Southeast Asia partly if not wholly.

15. E.g., Jataka 3:124 and 4:86 (here and subsequently cited in E. B. Cowell's translation: Cambridge, 1895–1913); *Jātakamāla* 14.

16. Foucher (1900–1905:1:189–209) reproduces two miniature paintings of the Buddha Dīpaṁkara from Ceylon (Siṁhaladvīpa) and two from Yavadvīpa that are included in an illuminated palm-leaf manuscript of *Prajñāpāramitā* from Nepal, now preserved in the University Library at Cambridge. Cf. also Paranavitana (1966:176–77, 191–98).

17. For further details of the relations between Ceylon and Southeast Asia in early times see Casparis (1961) and, with caution, Paranavitana (1966).

18. For example, see Ferrand (1919:15–16):
La réalité a du être à peu près ceci: deux ou trois navires de l'Inde naviguant de conserve arrivent de proche en proche jusqu'à Java. Les nouveaux venus entrent

en relation avec les chefs du pays, se les rendent favorables par des présents, par des soins donnés aux malades et par des amulettes. Dans tous les pays de civilisation primitive où j'ai vécu, du golfe d'Aden et de la côte orientale d'Afrique à la Chine, les seuls moyens efficaces de pénétration pacifique restent partout les mêmes: cadeaux de bienvenue, distribution de médicaments curatifs et de charmes préventifs contre tous les maux et dangers, réels et imaginaires. L'étranger doit être et passer pour riche, guérisseur et magicien. Personne n'est à même d'employer de tels procédés aussi adroitement qu'un Hindou. Celui-ci se prétendra sans doute d'extraction royale ou princière, ce dont son hôte ne peut qu'être favorablement impressionné.

Immigrés en cette *terra incognita*, les Hindous ne disposent pas d'interprète. Il leur faut donc apprendre la langue indigène qui est si différente de la leur et surmonter ce premier obstacle pour acquérir droit de cité chez les *Mleccha*. L'union avec des filles de chef vient ensuite, et c'est alors seulement que l'influence civilisatrice et religieuse des étrangers peut s'exercer avec quelque chance de succès. Leurs femmes indigènes, instruites à cet effet, deviennent les meilleurs agents de propagande des idées et de la foi nouvelles: princesses ou filles nobles, si elles en affirment la supériorité sur les moeurs, coutumes et religions héritées des ancêtres, leurs compatriotes ne pourront guère y contredire.

19. I use this term merely as a convenienient way of referring to the interaction between representatives of the Great Tradition of India on the one hand and of Dravidian (including subcultural variants) and Southeast Asian elements on the other. I am aware that, like its virtual synonyms, *sanskritization* and *aryanization*, *brahmanization* is a problematical term of limited applicability. Cf. Srinivas (1956); Barnabas (1961).

20. Prior to the 1960s the poorly defined transition phase between the late Neolithic and the formation of the so-called Indianized states was known as the Ðông-sỏn period, after a type site in the Democratic Republic of Vietnam excavated during the 1920s and 1930s (Goloubew 1929; Janse 1951; summarized in van Heekeren 1958:92–98; cf. also Heine-Geldern 1934; 1937; 1945:142–45; Goloubew 1932; Karlgren 1942). Recent excavations in Thailand by Solheim (summarized in 1967, 1969) and others, e.g., Bronson and Dales 1973; Gorman 1971; Watson and Loofs 1967), together with the results of excavations in the Chinese province of Yün-nan, have necessitated a thorough, but still uncompleted, reevaluation of the cultural development sequence in Southeast Asia. As I understand it, Solheim's (1969:137) proposed term *Extensionistic* subsumes both Heine-Geldern's Ðông-sỏn and the preceding Middle and Late Neolithic of earlier writers such as van Heekeren (1957) and Tweedie (1953). A generalized but convenient summary of the ethnological characteristics of Southeast Asia at the beginning of the Christian era as reconstructed by an earlier generation of scholars is available in Coedès (1964:26–27).

21. Cf. Dale (1956); Wheatley (1961:xviii–xx and passim).

22. There were numerous exceptions to this ideal: the Suṅga and Kāṇva dynasties, for example, were brahmanic, Harṣavardhana was a member of the Vaiśya varna, the Nandas were certainly, and the Mauryas possibly, of Śudra origin. It does appear, however, that royal families from the lower varnas were often eventually assimilated to the ksatriyan class, whence derived the adage that he who rules is a ksatriya.

23. The earliest myth validating the origin of kingship, that which occurs in the *Aitareya Brāhmaṇa* (I, 14), a later Vedic text dating possibly from the seventh or

eighth century B.C., adopts a specifically contractual explanation. In any case, as the principles of dharma both limited the exercise of the king's power and constrained his subjects to obey his edicts, the idea of a social covenant was implicit in the theory of divine kingship. On this topic see Rangaswami Aiyanger (1916:104–7) and Drekmeier (1962: chap. 14).

24. For the South Indian conception of Śiva (rather than Indra) as the king of the gods residing on the Mahendraparvata see Māṇikkavācakar, *Tiruvācakam* 2:8, 10, 100, 28:9, 43:2,9; Filliozat (1966:101–3).

25. Representative tales of such voyages are related in *Jātaka* 3:124, 4:86, 6:22; *Kathāsaritsāgara, taranga* 54: *śloka* 86, 97; 56:56–64; 57:72; 60:2–6; 86:33, 62 (Penzer 1924).

26. This conclusion drawn from Indian literary records is not necessarily in conflict with Van Leur's (1955:133, 135–37, 197–200) assertion (actually a projection into earlier times of conditions in the sixteenth century) that the vast majority of the traders were what he termed *pupulo minuto*, peddlers, each with a few dozen pieces of silk cloth in his single chest, a few *corges* of porcelain, a few dozen bags of pepper, a few *bahar* of cloves or nutmeg, a few hundredweight of mace. Until very recently even popular literature drew its heroes from the elite classes. The humble peripatetic trader, unless he demonstrated picaresque proclivities, was not likely to figure even in the *kathā* literature.

27. English translation by Low 1849; summary in Winstedt 1958:133–34; Rumi transliteration by Sturrock 1916. In this potpourri of myths, Marong Mahawangsa is said to have come with a band of followers from beyond the Sea of Hindustan to impose himself as ruler over the aboriginal inhabitants in the vicinity of Gunong Jĕrai in Kĕdah. Although this text in its present form dates from early in the nineteenth century, and incorporates events that occurred as late as the eighteenth century (Winstedt 1958:134), it also includes material from much earlier periods.

28. In the conventional view the Maṇigrāmam was a corporation of "men of different *jāti* doing business like men of the same *jāti*" (Venkatarama Ayyar 1947:272), but recently Indrapala (1970:29) has suggested that South Indian medieval mercantile associations should be regarded less as guilds and corporations than as dispersed communities bound by a common code of conduct. Indrapala (1970:30) notes pertinently that "even in modern times, the business community of Cettis have their own fiscal year, stick to their own system of book-keeping and follow their own type of business practices and customs. But they could hardly be called a corporation on these grounds." In any case, whatever their precise nature may have been, Maṇigrāmams were widespread in peninsular India. Tālakkāḍ and Kollam on the Kerala coast, and Tittāṇḍattānapuram and Kāvēripaṭṭanam on the east coast were well-known Maṇigrāmam cities, as were, for instance, Kuttālam in the far south and Baligāmi in the Deccan.

29. In those territories for which evidence is most abundant and explicit, namely Kambujadeśa, Campā, and ancient Java, it is apparent that the king was not Śiva or Vishnu or the Buddha, but rather shared in the divinity of the deity who manifested himself at the point of ontological transition between the modes of existence, namely the sacred *axis mundi regnique* where was constructed the capital of the kingdom. (For the role of the *axis mundi*, or, as Geertz has felicitously designated it, the exemplary center, in Southeast Asia see Heine-Geldern [1930], and more generally Eliade [1949:chap. 1].) During his lifetime the king secured his apotheosis by animating a

statue of himself or a *liṅga* that bore his own regnal style combined with that of the god. On his death, when the *sūkṣmātman* of the king had remerged with that of the god, the continued existence of that aspect which had been embodied in the statue was ensured by enclosing the image in a funerary temple. For further details of the nature of divine kingship in early Southeast Asia see Foucher (1910); Coedès (1947:chap. 3; 1960); Filliozat (1966).

30. The Chinese referred to this kingdom as *Tuən-suən*, apparently a transcription of a proto-Mōn * *udᵱsun*, meaning "five cities" (Shorto 1963:583).

31. The term *ɣuo* (MSC *hu*) seems to have denoted for the Chinese of the time mainly Iranians of one sort or another, with Persians and Sogdians perhaps the most prominent. The matter is summarized in Wheatley (1964:47–48). Cf. also Ishida (1961).

32. Compilation of the *Wen-hsien T'ung-k'ao* was completed by Ma Tuan-lin in about 1254, but it was not published until 1319. Although it is a relatively late encyclopedia, it does incorporate numerous quotations from earlier works.

33. I am here assuming that the *Tśʻiäk-t'uo* (MSC Ch'ih-t'u = Red-Earth) Kingdom of the Chinese is to be equated with the *Raktamṛttikā* mentioned in an inscription excavated near Guak Kěpah in Kědah by Colonel James Low 125 years ago (Low 1848:62–66; Laidlay 1848:66–72; Wheatley 1957b:101–2; 1961:273–74).

34. It was probably at about this stage in the so-called process of Indianization that a new instrument of culture transference appeared in the form of proselytizing activities by Southeast Asian neophytes and traders who returned to their own kingdoms after visiting, and perhaps sojourning in, India (Bosch 1952:passim; Coedès 1962:55; 1964: 56–57). The nature of the records on which we depend makes it difficult to specify unequivocal instances of the diffusion of Indian concepts by this means in the earlier phases of state formation, but it may have been an event of this sort that inspired an account of the rise to power in Langkasuka, toward the end of the fifth century A.D., of a revolutionary allegedly trained in India (*Liang Shu* 54:14a; transl. in Wheatley 1956b:390–91).

It is also true that dysfunctional partial structures could have been induced in Southeast Asian societies by factors other than trade, in particular by technological innovation. Possibly the transition from swidden to wet-paddy cultivation or the introduction of the plow (both chronologically appropriate in the Southeast Asian context) may have stimulated a sequence of changes something after the manner of that documented by Linton and Kardiner (1952) for the Tañala of Madagascar. When any technological innovation selectively converts land into a potential capital investment, it is an ever-present possibility that a small caucus of families will emerge as hereditary landholders and that competition for a scarce resource will nourish the rise of militarism. Such a transformative process probably did occur in Southeast Asia, especially in the subcontinental interiors where elaborate political structures were based on wet-paddy production, but it was still Indian traders who first forged the link between India and Southeast Asia and who, in my opinion, were the primary generators of dysfunctional structures.

35. Filliozat (1966:97) has pointed out that even Manu himself (III:158) merely excluded the sea-voyager (*samudrayāyin*) from the *śrāddhas*, but did not expel him from his varna. This is confirmed indirectly by a passage in the Ādityapurāṇa (preserved in the *Dharmasindhu*) which takes it to be the part of wisdom to abstain from communication with the *dvija* who crosses the ocean, as a precaution against loss of

dharma (*dharmalopabhayāt*), but which makes no reference to an automatic loss of caste by such a traveler (cf. Kane 1930–46: vol. 3, corresponding to note 1803).

36. For a discussion of the brahmanas, tracing their spiritual lineage to the *kailāyaparamparai* (Skt. *kailāsaparamparā*) and professing the doctrine of the Śaivasiddhānta, who are still active in Bangkok and Phnom Penh see Filliozat (1966:98–100). According to the Śaivasiddhānta and the Āgamas, which are believed to have been revealed by Śiva himself, the rites are not reserved solely to brahmanas. Consecration is, in fact, available to all varnas by *dikṣā*, though the rites do differ from varna to varna. *Dikṣā* is bestowed according to the *anuloma* system. It follows, therefore, that the priests are not necessarily, or even customarily, brahmanas. It is not suggested that these modern Thai and Cambodian "brahmanas" are the descendants of those of ancient times—indeed it is known that they came from different parts of India probably as recently as the Ayutthaya period (1350–1767) or perhaps even later. All have intermarried with the local community (Wales 1931:chap. 5).

37. Cf. Mus (1933:393): ". . . Lorsque l'hindouisme, avec sa littérature sanskrite, a eu gagné l'Extrême-Orient, c'est avec lui surtout à une expansion des vieilles idées asiatiques que l'on assiste: idées aussitôt reconnues, comprises et endossées par des peuples qui n'ont peut-être pas eu toujours conscience de changer tout à fait de religion en adoptant celle de l'Inde." And again on p. 394: "L'hindouisme, dans ses marches lointaines, se résorbe en ce dont, dans l'Inde même, nous l'avions vu sortir."

38. Cf. also Christie (1964: passim).

39. This is the process that Geertz (1956:83–84) more recently, and in the Javanese context, has termed "retraditionalization."

40. The *liṅga* was the symbol of Siva (Iśvara), and in Cambodia, as throughout India, was named after the king who established it. Indreśvara, for instance was the *liṅga* set up by King Indravarman.

41. Not to be confused with the Rājavihara mentioned above, which today is also known as the Ta Prohm. For descriptions of these temple-cities built to the command of Jayavarman VII see Aymonier (1903), Lajonquière (1911), Commaille (1912),· Marchal (1928), Glaize (1948), Stern (1948), Parmentier (1960).

42. I am accepting, though with no great enthusiasm for the drastic aphesis involved, Moens's (1937:337) identification of *Lâ-jïwvt* (MSC Lo-yüeh) with Sĕluyut, now a river, hill, and district at the head of the Johore estuary.

APPENDIX

References to Merchants and Markets
In Early Indonesian Epigraphy

Compiled by Jan Wisseman

Abbreviations

Casparis, *Prasasti Indonesia* II	J. G. de Casparis, *Prasasti Indonesia*, vol. 2 (Bandung: Masa Baru, 1956).
Goris, *Prasasti Bali*	R. Goris, *Prasasti Bali: inscripties vóór Anak Wungçu*, 2 vols. (Bandung, 1954).
OJO	*Oud-Javaansche oorkonden. Nagelaten transscripties van wijlen Dr. J. L. A. Brandes*. Uitgegeven door Dr. N. J. Krom, *Verhandelingen van het Bataviaasch Genootschap van Kunsten en Wetenschappen*, vol. 60 (1913).
Sarkar, *Corpus*	H. B. Sarkar, *Corpus of the inscriptions of Java (Corpus inscriptionum Javanicarum) (up to 928 A.D.)*, 2 vols. (Calcutta: Firma K. L. Mukhopadhyay, 1971).

MERCHANTS AND TRADERS

Several terms referring to traders appear in Indonesian inscriptions. They range from *banyāga* (a long-distance or seafaring merchant) to *dwal* and *apikul* (local peddlers).

I. *Banyāga*. This term is presumably derived from the Sanskrit *vaṇij/ vaṇik* (=merchant). As used in Indonesian inscriptions, it appears to refer to long-distance and seafaring merchants. The term appears relatively early in inscriptions of Sumatra, Java, and Bali.

A. *Sumatra*. The earliest mention of *banyāga* in Indonesia is in a

266

Śrī Vijayan inscription, Tĕlaga Batu, from Palembang. Date c.
686 A.D. It appears in a list of classes of people:
line 4: . . . sthāpaka puhāwaṃ vaṇiyāga pratisāra . . . [sculptors,
naval captains, merchants, commanders] (Casparis, *Prasasti Indonesia* II, pp. 32, 37).

B. *Java*. The earliest mention is in the Hariñjing A inscription
from E. Java. Dated 804 A.D. It also appears in several other
inscriptions:

Garung, C. Java. 819 A.D. (Sarkar, *Corpus* I, pp. 53–55).

Śīwagĕrha, provenance uncertain. 856 A.D. (Casparis, *Prasasti
Indonesia* II, pp. 315, 316, 326, 329).

Jurungan, C. Java. 876 A.D.

Mulak I, C. Java. 878 A.D. (Sarkar, *Corpus* I, pp. 208–14).

Taji, E. Java. 901 A.D. (Sarkar, *Corpus* II, pp. 4–14).

Three later mentions, all from East Java, are of particular interest:

1. Kaladi. 909 A.D. Here the *banyāga* appears in a list of foreigners who have connections with the court:

7b2: . . . tan tumamā irikang sima muang surā ni kilalan
kling ārya singhala drawila banyaga 4 paṇḍikir campa ram-
mān kismmira . . . [and also not allowed to enter the free-
hold (*sima*) are those of the group of collectors (of the
king's property, i.e. some sort of dues or taxes): Kalingas,
Aryyas, Singhalese, Dravidians, 4 merchants (*banyāga*),
Paṇḍikiras, Chams, Ramanyadeśis (?), Khmers (?).] (A.
Barrett, M. A. thesis, University of Sydney, 1968, p. 129.)

2. Palĕbuhan (Goreng Gareng). 927 A.D.

1a8: . . . kunang sa kweh ning drĕbya haji kilalān (..) . . .
singhala paṇḍikira mamvang ramman huñjamān kutak
banyāga bantal tan (..) . . . [moreover, all the collectors
of the king's property. . . . Singhalese, Paṇḍikiras, *mambang*
(?), Ramanyadeśis (?), *huñjamān* (?), *kutak* (?), merchants (*banyāga bantal*) may not.] (Sarkar, *Corpus* II, pp.
215–19).

3. Kamalagyan. 1037 A.D. (*OJO* LXI)

12–13: . . . kapwa ta sukhmanaḥ nikāng maparahu samanghulu mangalap bhāṇḍa ri hujung galuh tka rikāng parapuhawang prabaṇyāga sangkāring dwīpāntara . . . [all are contented (in agreement?) among the perahu-handlers, pilots (commanders?), gatherers of cargo at Hujung Galuh, including the ship-captains and merchants from the other islands.]

An associated term is *kabanyagan*. From the contexts in which it is found, it would seem to imply a locality, such as a merchants' settlement or quarter.

Tulang Air I, C. Java. 850 A.D.   (Sarkar, *Corpus* I, pp. 114–24).

Lintakan, C. Java. 929 A.D.   (Sarkar, *Corpus* II, pp. 162–82).

Padlĕgan, E. Java. 1116 A.D.   (*OJO* LXVII).

C. *Bali*

Bebetin AI. 896 A.D. (Goris, *Prasasti Bali*, no. 002, vol. I, p. 120).

IIb3–4: . . . tua banyaga turun ditu panikĕn di hyangapi parunggaḥña ana mati ya tua banyaga parduan dṛbyaña prakāra ana cakcak lañcangña kajadyan papagĕrangĕn kuta . . . [Should a (seafaring) merchant (*banyaga*), after landing at that place, die, a portion of his possessions is to be yielded to the Fire-temple. If his vessel has been wrecked, its planks must be used for the palisading of the fortified village (*kuta*).]

Pengotan AI. 924 A.D. (Goris, *Prasasti Bali*, no. 105)

II. *Banigrama* (Sanskrit *vaṇiggrāma* = merchant group or community). This term appears in inscriptions in Java and Bali, and does not seem to imply a locality as does the term *kabanyagan*.

A. *Java*

Kaladi, E. Java. 909 A.D. (A. Barrett, M.A. thesis)

Kambang Śrī, E. Java. 964 A.D. (*OJO* LXIII)

B. *Bali*

Sembiran B. 955 A.D. (Goris, *Prasasti Bali*, no. 201)

Sembiran AII. 975 A.D. (Goris, *Prasasti Bali*, no. 209)

Unfortunately, little information can be gathered from these inscriptions about the nature or function of the *banigrama* in early Indonesia.

III. *Dagang.* This appears to refer to a smaller-scale, local merchant. Mentions occur rather frequently in Java and less so in Bali.

   A. *Java.* A *tuha dagang* (chief of *dagang*-s) or *juru dagang* (minor official in charge of *dagang*-s) appears in lists of minor officials in several inscriptions:

      Garung, C. Java. 819 A.D.

      Kuṭi, E. Java. 840 A.D.

      Kañcana, E. Java. 860 A.D.

      Waharu I, E. Java. 873 A.D.

      Sugih Manek, E. Java. 915 A.D.

   padagang (= small-scale merchant) appears in several inscriptions, mostly late:

      Kubu Kubu Bhadrī, E. Java. 905 A.D.

      Turun Hyang, E. Java. 11th cent.

      Et al.

   B. *Bali*

   adagang (= merchant) appears in Batur Pura Abang A (Goris, *Prasasti Bali*, no. 305). Dated 1011 A.D.

IV. *Dwal* and *Apikul.* (peddlers: *pikul* means to carry on the shoulder).

   A. *Java*

      dwal appears in Balingawan, E. Java. 891 A.D.

   B. *Bali*

      apikul appears in Batur Pura Abang A. 1011 A.D.

      Et al.

MARKETS

I. JAVA

   A. Pĕkan (= market: Old Javanese)

     1. Hariñjing A, East Java. 7(2)6 Ś : 8(o)4 A.D.

        a9–10: apkan ḍa pu indun . . . [the *apkan* (= market official, market master?) Ḍa Pu Indun.] (appears in a list of officials).

        a13–14: // rama i bagu winkas ḍa pu tahani . . . awatas ḍa man banyaga apĕkan ḍa man bahang . . . [the *rama* at Bagu Winkas, Ḍa Pu Tahani . . . the *awatas* Ḍa Man Banyaga, the *apĕkan* (market official) Ḍa Man Bahang.] (It is curious that *banyaga*, which means "merchant," should here be used as a personal name).

2. Garung, Central Java. 741 Ś : 819 A.D.

1a4: sang mangilala drabya haji . . . rumwān banyāgā bantal huñjamman manghuri senamukha tuha dagang mapakkan ityemādi . . . [the mangilala drabya haji (collectors of the king's property, i.e. taxes. Note this is the earliest dated occurrence of the term) . . . the *rumwān* (?), the *banyāgā bantal* (some sort of merchant), *huñjamman* (?), the *manghuri* (?), the *senamukha* (a military leader), the *tuha dagang* (chief of traders, probably implying small-scale, local merchants), the *mapakkan* (market official, same as *apĕkan*), etc.]

3. Tulung Air I, Central Java. 772 Ś : 850 A.D.

a23–24: mapakan si mulyang . . . [the *mapakan* (market official) Si Mulyang]

a33–34: rama si napal mapakan ing munggu antan si laya (. . .) marhyang ing prasada ing kabanyagan si kaṇḍi . . . [the *rama* Si Napal, the *mapakan* at Munggu Antan, Si Laya (. . .), the priest at the *prasada* of the *kabanyagan* (merchant settlement or quarter), Si Kaṇḍi.]

4. Tunahan, Central Java (Polengan I). 794Ś:872 A.D.

1b7: mapkan si kahuripan . . . [the *mapkan* (market official) Si Kahuripan.]

Mapkan (market official, market master) also appears in lists of officials in the following inscriptions:

Humaṇḍing (Polengan II), C. Java. 797 Ś : 875 A.D.

Haliwangbang (Polengan IV), C. Java. 799 Ś : 877 A.D.

Mamali, C. Java. 800 Ś : 878 A.D.

Salimar III, C. Java. 802 Ś : 880 A.D.

Taragal, C. Java. 802 Ś : 880 A.D.

Wukajana, C. Java ?. 830 Ś : 908 A.D.

Sugih Manek (Singosari), East Java. 837 Ś : 915 A.D.

Er Kuwing, C. Java. 837 Ś : 915 A.D.

etc.

5. Palĕpangan (Barabudur), C. Java. 828 Ś : 906 A.D.

1a8–9: . . . sawah rāma nta lamwit 1 blah 1 katuhalasan

tampah 4 kapkanan tampah 1 nāhan pratyeka ning sawah rāma nta sampun yan inukur i tampah haji . . . [The sawah fields of the *rāmantas* shall be lamwit 1 blah 1 of the *katuhalasan* (the united body of *tuhalas*), also 4 tampahs of the *kapkanan* (united body of market officials?) 1 tampah. Such are the specifications of the sawah fields of the *rāmantas*: henceforth they are measured by tampah haji.]

B. Pasar (=market)

1. Talaga Tañjung, C. Java. 783 Ś : 861 A.D.

b3–4: . . . sang wahuta alih tatapa pu diwū pasaranak pu iṇḍu . . . [the two *wahutas*: (*wahuta*) *tatapa* Pu Diwu, (*wahuta*) *pasaranak* Pu Iṇḍu (a market official ??).]

2. Er Kuwing, C. Java. c.837 Ś : 915 A.D.

1b18: . . . wahuta pasaraṇak si lucira . . . [the *wahuta pasaraṇak* Si Lucira.]

1b20: . . . wahuta pasaraṇak si śiwā . . . [the *wahuta pasaraṇak* Si Śiwā.]

(*wahuta pasaranak* appears here twice in a list of officials which also includes a *mapkan*).

3. Gilikan I, C. Java. c.845 Ś : 923 A.D.

a5: . . . (sa)mgat pamasaran pu bandhyā . . . [the (*sa*)*mgat pamasaran* (possibly an official having some connection with the *pasar*).]

4. Gilikan II, C. Java. c. 845 Ś : 923 A.D.

b1–2: . . . samgat pamasaran . . . [the *samgat pamasaran*.]

5. Plumbangan (Blitar), E. Java. (*OJO* LXIX). 1062 Ś : 1140 A.D.

b11: . . . kidul ning pasar . . . [south of the *pasar*.]

b12: . . . kidul ning pasar mangaran anurida . . . [south of the pasar mangaran anurida (?).]

II. BALI

A. Pasar

1. Sukawana AI (Goris .001). 804 Ś : 882 A.D.

IIIa1–2: rggas pasar wijapura . . . [*pasar* day *wijayapura*] (This appears as part of the date in most of the earlier Old Balinese language inscriptions: the other 2 *pasar* days appearing in these inscriptions are *wijayamanggala* and *wija-*

yakranta. Later, in some of the Old Javanese language inscriptions, *pkan* is substituted for *pasar*).

IIa2: . . . lagad pasar . . . [*pasar* table (made of bamboo).]

2. Dausa, Pura Bukit Indrakila AI (Goris .107). 857 Ś : 935 A.D.

IIb5–6: . . . thāpi kasiddhan ya bangunan pasar lamātan simaña ditu tani saladyan ulih sair pasar hulu sambaḥ mai saladyan ya panaikan di sattra ditu kajadyan atithi ana manghalu ya ka pasar di tanah winait . . . [However, they may establish a *lamatan pasar* (*lamatan* perhaps refers to cockfighting); they will not be charged the *salad*-tax by the *ser pasar* (market master) or the inspector of the holy place. Should they be charged the *salad*-tax the proceeds must go to the rest house that is set up for guests. If they take their goods for sale to the *pasar* at Tanah Winait, they will not be charged the *salad*-tax there either.]

3. Manik Liu AI (Goris .202). 877 Ś : 955 A.D.

IIa2: . . . me tani kawakatĕn tikasan di pasar di pandhar dikḍi di tapahaji salaran tambangan ḷbḷb . . . [they will not be charged the *tikasan*-tax at the market, at the *pandhar*, at the *kdi*, etc.]

Ser pasar (market master) appears in several Balinese inscriptions other than Dausa:

Bebetin AI (Goris .002). 818 Ś : 896 A.D.

Sembiran AI (Goris 104). 844 Ś : 922 A.D.

Sembiran AII (Goris 209). 897 Ś : 975 A.D.

Batuan (Goris 352). 944 Ś : 1022 A.D.

References

ALPERS, EDWARD A.
1969   "Trade, State, and Society among the Yao in the Nineteenth Century," *Journal of African History* 10:405–20.
in press "Malawi and Yao Responses to External Economic Forces, 1505–1798," in *East Africa and the Orient: Problems of Cultural Synthesis in Pre-colonial Times*, ed. H. N. Chittick and R. I. Rotberg (New York: Africana Publishing Co.).
AYMONIER, ETIENNE
1903   *Le Camboge*, 3 vols. (Paris).
BARNABAS, A. P.
1961   "Sanskritization," *Economic Weekly* 13(no.15):613–18.
BERG, C. C.
1929   *Hoofdlijnen der Javaansche Litteratuurgeschiedenis*. Inaugural lecture, University of Leiden. (Groningen, Netherlands).
1950   "Kertanagara, de miskende empirebuilder," *Orientatie*: 1–32.
1950   "De geschiedenis van pril Majapahit," *Indonesië* 4:481–520, and 5:193–233.
–51
1951   "De saḍeng-oorlog en de mythe van Groot-Majapahit," *Indonesië* 5:385–422.
1961   "Javanese Historiography—a Synopsis of Its Evolution," in *Historians of South East Asia*, ed. D. G. E. Hall (London: Oxford University Press).
1962   *Het rijk van de Vijfvoudige Buddha*. Verhandlingen der Koninklijke Nederlandsche Akademie van Wetenschappen, Afdeeling Letterkunde 59(1) (Amsterdam).
1965   "The Javanese Picture of the Past," in *An introduction to Indonesian historiography*, ed. Soedjatmoko, Mohammad Ali, G. J. Resink, and G. McT. Kahin (Ithaca, N.Y.: Cornell University Press).
BHATT, N. R.
1962   *Mṛgendrāgama*. Publications de l'Institut Français d'Indologie 23 (Pondicherry).
BOSCH, FREDERIK D. K.
1933a   "Het bronzen Buddha-beeld van Celebes westkust," *Tijdschrift voor Indische Taal-, Land-, en Volkenkunde uitgegeven door het Bataviaasch Genootschap van Kunsten en Wetenschappen* 73:495–514.
1933b   "Summary of Archaeological Work in Netherlands India in 1933," *Annual Bibliography of Indian Archaeology* 8.
1952   " 'Local Genius' en Oud-Javaanse kunst," *Mededeelingen der Koninklijke Nederlandsche Akademie van Wetenschappen* 15(1):1–25.
1956   "C. C. Berg and Ancient Javanese History," *Bijdragen tot de Taal-, Land- en Volkenkunde van Nederlandsch-Indië* 112:1–24.
1961   *Selected Studies in Indonesian Archaeology* (The Hague: Martinus Nijhoff).
BRIGGS, LAWRENCE PALMER
1951   *The Ancient Khmer Empire*. Transactions of the American Philosophical Society, n.s. 41 (Philadelphia).

BRONSON, BENNET AND GEORGE F. DALES

1973   "Excavations at Chansen, Thailand, 1968 and 1969: a Preliminary Report," *Asian Perspectives* 15:15–46.

CASPARIS, J. G. DE

1947   "Yupa Inscriptions," *India Antiqua* (Leiden, Netherlands).

1961   "New Evidence on Cultural Relations between Java and Ceylon in Ancient Times," *Artibus Asiae* 24:241–48.

CHATTERJEE, BIJAN RAJ

1933   *India and Java*, part 2 (Calcutta: Greater India Society).

CHHABRA, B. CH.

1935   "Expansion of Indo-Aryan Culture during Pallava Rule, as Evidenced by Inscriptions," *Journal of the Asiatic Society of Bengal, Letters* 1:1–64.

1945   "Three More Yūpa Inscriptions of King Mūlavarman from Koetei (E. Borneo)," *Journal of the Greater India Society* 12:14–17.

1949   "Three More Yūpa Inscriptions of King Mūlavarman from Koetei (E. Borneo)," *Tijdschrift voor Indische Taal-, Land- en Volkenkunde* 83:370–74.

CHRISTIE, A.

1957   "An Obscure Passage from the Periplus: κολανδιοφωντα τὰ μέγιστα," *Bulletin of the School of Oriental and African Studies* 19:345–53.

1964   "The Political Use of Imported Religion: An Historical Example from Java," *Archives de Sociologie des Religions* 9:53–62.

COEDÈS, GEORGE

1906   "La stèle de Ta Prohm," *Bulletin de l'Ecole Française d'Extrême-Orient* 6:44–81.

1910   *Textes d'auteurs grecs et latins relatifs à l'Extrême-Orient, depuis le IVe siècle av. J. C. jusqu'au XIVe siècle* (Paris).

1924   *Recueil des inscriptions du Siam*, 2 vols. (Bangkok: National Library of Siam
–29   [vol. 1]; Royal Institute [vol. 2]).

1927   "Excavations at P'ong Tük in Siam," in *Annual Bibliography of Indian Archaeology* (Leiden, Netherlands).

1928   "The Excavations at P'ong Tük and Their Importance for the Ancient History of Siam," *Journal of the Siam Society* 21:204–7.

1940   "Les gîtes d'étape à la fin du XIIe siècle," *Bulletin de l'Ecole Française d'Extrême-Orient* 40:347–49.

1941a "La stèle du Pràḥ Khằn d'Aṅkor," *Bulletin de l'Ecole Française d'Extrême-Orient* 41:256–301.

1941b "L'assistance médicale au Cambodge à la fin du XXIIe siècle," *Revue Médicale Française d'Extrême-Orient*.

1947   *Pour mieux comprendre Angkor* (Paris: Adrien Maisonneuve).

1953   "Le substrat autochthone et la superstructure indienne au Cambodge et à Java," *Cahiers d'Histoire Mondiale* 1(2):368–77. (N.B.: The author was not responsible for the title of this paper, which is not consonant with the views of the Indianization process that he expresses in the text.)

1954   "L'osmose indienne en Indochine et en Indonésie," *Cahiers d'Histoire Mondiale* 1(4):827–38.

1960   "Le portrait dans l'art khmer," *Arts Asiatiques* 7(3):179–98.

1962 *Les peuples de la Péninsule Indochinoise.* (Paris: Dunod).

1964 *Les états hindouisés d'Indochine et d'Indonésie,* 3rd ed. (Paris: E. de Bocard).

COHN, WILLIAM

1925 *Buddha in der Kunst des Ostens* (Leipzig, Germany: Klinkhardt & Biermann).

COMMAILLE, J.

1912 *Guide aux ruines d'Angkor* (Paris).

COOMARASWAMY, ANANDA

1927 *History of Indian and Indonesian Art* (New York: E. Goldston).

DALE, W. L.

1956 "Wind and Drift Currents in the South China Sea," *The Malayan Journal of Tropical Geography* 8:1–31.

DALTON, GEORGE (Ed.)

1968 *Primitive, Archaic and Modern Economies. Essays of Karl Polanyi* (New York; 2d ed. Boston: Beacon Press).

DAMAIS, LOUIS-CHARLES

1962 "Etudes javanaises, II: Le nom de la déité tantrique de 1214 Śaka," *Bulletin de l'Ecole Française d'Extrême-Orient* 50:407–16.

DEIMEL, ANTON

1931 "Sumerische Tempelwirtschaft zur Zeit Urukaginas und seiner Vorgänger," *Analecta Orientalia* 2. (Rome).

DREKMEIER, CHARLES

1962 *Kingship and Community in Early India.* (Stanford, Calif.: Stanford University Press).

DUPONT, PIERRE

1954. "Les Buddhas dits d'Amarāvatī en Asie du Sud-Est," *Bulletin de l'Ecole Française d'Extrême-Orient* 49:631–36.

ELIADE, MIRCEA

1949 *Le mythe de l'éternel retour: archétypes et répétition* (Paris: Librairie Gallimard).

FERRAND, GABRIEL

1913 *Relations de voyages et textes géographiques arabes, persans et turks relatifs*
–14 *à l'Extrême-Orient du VIIIe au XVIIe siècles,* 2 vols. (Paris).

1919 "Le K'ouen-louen et les anciennes navigations interocéaniques dans les mers du sud," *Journal Asiatique,* IIe série 13:239–333, 431–92, and 14:6–68, 201–41.

FILLIOZAT, JEAN

1966 "New Researches on the Relations between India and Cambodia," *Indica* 3:95–106.

1969 "L'inscription dite de Vỏ-caṇh," *Bulletin de l'Ecole Française d'Extrême-Orient* 55:107–16.

FINOT, LOUIS

1908 "Les études indochinoises," *Bulletin de l'Ecole Française d'Extrême-Orient* 8:221–33.

FINOT, LOUIS AND VICTOR GOLOUBEW

1923 "Le symbolisme de Năk Păn," *Bulletin de l'Ecole Française D'Extrême-Orient* 23:401–5.

FOUCHER, ALFRED

1900 *Etude sur l'iconographie bouddhique de l'Inde, d'après des documents nou-*
–05 *veaux,* 2 vols. (Paris).

1910 "Séance du 10 mars 1910," *Bulletin de la Commission Archéologique de l'Indochine, Année* 1910: 133–35.

FRISK, J. I. H.

1927 "Le Périple de la Mer Erythrée,"*Högskolas Årsskrift* 33.

GEERTZ, CLIFFORD

1956 *The Development of the Javanese Economy: a Socio-cultural Approach* (Cambridge, Mass.: Center for International Studies, Massachusetts Institute of Technology).

GLAIZE, MAURICE

1948 *Les monuments du groupe d'Angkor. Guide* (Saigon: Albert Portail).

GOLOUBEW, VICTOR

1929 "L'âge du bronze au Tonkin et dans le Nord-Annam," *Bulletin de l'Ecole Française d'Extrême-Orient* 29:1–46.

1932 "Sur l'origine et la diffusion des tambours métalliques," *Praehistorica Asiae Orientalis* 1:137–50.

1940 "L'hydraulique urbaine et agricole à l'époque des rois d'Angkor," *Cahiers de l'Ecole Française d'Extrême-Orient* 24:16ff.

GOODY, JACK

1971 *Technology, Tradition, and the State in Africa* (London: Oxford University Press).

GORMAN, CHESTER

1971 "The Hoabinhian and After: Subsistence Patterns in Southeast Asia during the Late Pleistocene and Early Recent Periods," *World Archaeology* 2:300–320.

GROSLIER, BERNARD-PHILIPPE

1956 *Angkor. Hommes et pierres* (Paris: Arthaud).

HEEKEREN, H. R. VAN

1957 *The Stone Age of Indonesia.* Verhandelingen van het Koninklijk Instituut voor Taal-, Land- en Volkenkunde XXI (The Hague).

1958 *The Bronze-Iron age of Indonesia.* Verhandelingen van het Koninklijk Instituut voor Taal-, Land- en Volkenkunde XXII (The Hague).

HEINE-GELDERN, ROBERT VON

1930 "Weltbild und Bauform in Südostasien," *Wiener Beiträge zur Kunst- und Kulturgeschichte Asiens* 4:28–78.

1934 "Vorgeschichtliche Grundlagen der kolonialindischen Kunst," *Wiener Beiträge zur Kunst- und Kulturgeschichte Asiens* 8:5–40.

1937 "L'art prébouddique [sic] de la Chine et de l'Asie du Sud-Est et son influence en Océanie," *Revue des Arts Asiatiques* 11:177–206.

1945 "Prehistoric Research in the Netherlands Indies," in *Science and Scientists in the Netherlands Indies,* ed. P. Honig and F. Verdoorn (New York: Board for the Netherlands Indies).

1951 "Das Tocharerproblem und die pontische Wanderung," *Saeculum* 2:225–55.

HORNELL, J.

1941 "Sea Trade in Early Times," *Antiquity* 15:233–56.

1946   *Water Transport: Origins and Early Evolution* (Cambridge; reprint Newton Abbot, Eng.: David & Charles).

HSIANG TA
1930   "Han-T'ang-chien Hsi-yü chi Hai-nan chu-kuo ku ti-li-shu hsü-lu." *Kuo-li Pei-p'ing T'u-shu-kuan K'an* 4.

HULTZSCH, E.
1902   "A Vaishnava Inscription at Pagan," *Epigraphia Indica* 7:197–98.

INDRAPALA, K.
1970   "Some Medieval Mercantile Communities of South India and Ceylon," *Journal of Tamil Studies* 2(2):26–39.

ISHIDA, MIKINOSUKE
1961   "The Hu-chi, Mainly Iranian Girls Found in China during the T'ang Period," *Memoirs of the Research Department of the Toyo Bunko* 20:35–40.

JABLOW, JOSEPH
1951   *The Cheyenne in Plains Indian Trade Relations 1785–1840.* American Ethnological Society Monograph 19 (New York).

JANSE, OLOV R. T.
1947   *Archaelogical Reseach in Indo-China,* 3 vols. Harvard Yenching Institute
–58   Monograph Series VII (Cambridge, Mass. and Bruges, Belgium).
1957   "Dionysos au Vietnam," *Viking*:36–50.
–58

KANE, P. V.
1930   *History of Dharmaśāstra,* 3 vols. (Poona: Bhandarkar Oriental Research In-
–46   stitute).

KARLGREN, BERNHARD
1942   "The Date of the Early Dong-son Culture," *Bulletin of the Museum of Far Eastern Antiquities* 14:1–28.

KEMPERS, A. J. BERNET
1959   *Ancient Indonesian art* (Cambridge, Mass.: Harvard University Press).

KERN, HENDRIK
1917a   "Over de Sanskrit-opschriften van (Muara Kaman, in) Kutei (Borneo). (± 400 A.D.)," *Verspreide Geschriften onder zijn Toesicht Verzameld* 7:55–76.
1917b   "De Sanskrit-inscriptie van Canggal (Keḍu), uit 654 Cāka," *Verspreide Geschriften onder zijn Toesicht Verzameld* 7:115–28.

KOTTAK, CONRAD P.
1972   "A Cultural Adaptive Approach to Malagasy Political Organization," in *Social exchange and interaction,* ed. Edwin N. Wilmsen, University of Michigan Museum of Anthropology, Anthropological Papers 46 (Ann Arbor).

KROM, NICHOLAAS J.
1923   *Inleiding tot de hindoue-javaansche kunst* (The Hague: Martinus Nijhoff).
1931   *Hindoe-javaansche geschiedenis.* 2d ed. (The Hague: Martinus Nijhoff).

KROM, NICHOLAAS J. AND T. VAN ERP
1927   *Barabudur; Archaeological and Architectural Description.* 3 portfolios and 3
–31   vols. (The Hague: Martinus Nijhoff).

LAIDLAY, J. W.
1848   "Notes on the inscriptions from Singapore and Province Wellesley," *Journal of the Asiatic Society of Bengal* 17(2):66–72.

LAJONQUIÈRE, LUNET DE
1911   *Inventaire descriptif des monuments du Cambodge*, 3 (Paris).
LÉVI, SYLVAIN
1905   *Le Népal. Etude historique d'un royaume hindou*, 3 vols. (Paris).
–08
1929   "Les 'marchands de mer' et leur rôle dans le bouddhisme primitif," *Bulletin de l'Association Française des Amis de l'Orient*: 19–39.
1930   "Maṇimekhala, divinité de la mer," *Bulletin des Lettres de l'Académie Belgique*: 282.
1931a "Kouen-louen et Dvīpāntara," *Bijdragen tot de Taal-, Land- en Volkenkunde van Nederlandsch-Indië* 88:621–27.
1931b "On Manimekhala 'The Guardian Deity of the Sea," *The Indian Historical Quarterly* 7:173–75.
1931c "More on Manimekhala," *The Indian Historical Quarterly* 7:371–76.
LEVI D'ANCONA, MIRELLA
1952   "Amarāvatī, Ceylon and the Three 'Imported bronzes,'" *The Art Bulletin* 34:1–17.
LEWIS, OSCAR
1942   *The Effects of White Contact upon Blackfoot Culture, with Special Reference to the Role of the Fur Trade*. American Ethnological Society Monograph 6 (New York).
LINGAT, ROBERT
1952   "Les régimes matrimoniaux du Sud-Est de l'Asie," Publications d'Ecole Française d'Extrême-Orient 34.
LINTON, RALPH AND ABRAHAM KARDINER
1952   "The Change from Dry to Wet Rice Cultivation in Tanala-Betsileo," in *Readings in Social Psychology*, ed. T. M. Newcomb and E. L. Hartley (New York: Henry Holt & Co).
LOW, JAMES
1848   "An Account of Several Inscriptions found in Province Wellesley, on the Peninsula of Malacca," *Journal of the Asiatic Society of Bengal* 17(2):62–66.
1849   "A Translation of the Keddah Annals," *Journal of the Indian Archipelago and Eastern Asia* 3:1–23, 162–81, 253–70, 314–36, 467–88.
MAJUMDAR, RAMESCH C.
1927   *Ancient Indian Colonies in the Far East*: vol. 1, *Champā* (Lahore: Punjab Sanskrit Book Depot).
1937   *Ancient Indian Colonies in the Far East*: vol. 2 *Suvarnadvipa. Part I, Political*
–38   *History; Part II, Cultural History* (Dacca and Calcutta: Asutosh Press).
1944   *Hindu Colonies in the Far East* (Calcutta: Firma K. L. Mukopadhyay).
1954   "Colonial and Cultural Expansion in South-East Asia," In *The History and Culture of the Indian People, III: the Classical Age*, ed. Majumdar (Bombay: Bharatiya Vidya Bhavan).
1955   *Ancient Indian Colonisation in South-East Asia*. The Maharaja Sayajirao Gaekwad Honorarium Lectures 1953–54 (Baroda, India: University of Baroda Press).
MALLERET, LOUIS
1959   *L'archéologie du delta du Mékong*: 1, *L'exploration archéologique et les fouilles*

-63   d'Oc-èo; 2, *La civilisation matérielle d' Oc-èo*; 3, *La culture du Fou-nan*; 4,
       Le Cisbassac (Paris: Ecole Française d'Extreme-Orient).

MARCHAL, HENRI
1928   *Guide archéologique aux temples d'Angkor* (Paris: Editions G. Van Œst).

MEILE, PIERRE
1940   "Les Yavana dans l'Inde tamoule," *Journal Asiatique* 232:90–92.

MEILLASSOUX, CLAUDE (ed.)
1971   *The Development of Indigenous Trade and Markets in West Africa*. (London:
        Oxford University Press).

MINATTUR, JOSEPH
1964   "A Note on the King Kundungga of the East Borneo Inscriptions," *Journal
        of Southeast Asian History* 5(2):181–83.

MOENS, J. L.
1937   "Srīvajaya, Yāva en Katāha," *Tijdschrift voor Indische Taal-, Land- en
        Volkenkunde* 77:317–486.

MOHAN SINGH, MADAN
1961   "India's Oversea Trade as Known from the Buddhist Canons," *The Indian
        Historical Quarterly* 1961 (2 & 3):177–82.

MUKERJI, RADHAKAMUD
1912   *Indian Shipping; a History of the Sea-borne Trade and Maritime Activity of
        the Indians from the Earliest Times* (Bombay and Calcutta).

MUS, PAUL
1933   "Cultes indiens et indigènes au Champa," *Bulletin de l'Ecole Française
        d'Extrême-Orient* 33:367–410.
1936   "Le symbolisme à Angkor Thom. Le 'grand miracle' du Bayon." *Académie
        des Inscriptions et Belles-Lettres: Comptes-rendus des Séances*: 57–68.

NAERSSEN, F. H. VAN
1947   *Culture Contacts and Social Conflicts in Indonesia*. Occasional Papers of the
        Southeast Asia Institute, no. 1 (New York).
1948a   "De aanvang van het Hindu-Indonesische acculturatie-proces," in *Orientalia
        Neerlandica* (Leiden).
1948b   "Het sociaal aspect van acculturatie in Indonesia," *Zaïre* 2:625–38.

NATH PURI, BAIJ
1956   "Administrative System of the Kambuja Rulers," *Journal of the Greater India
        Society* 15:60–70.

NEEDHAM, JOSEPH
1971   *Science and Civilisation in China: IV, 3, Civil engineering and nautics* (Cam-
        bridge: Cambridge University Press).

NILAKANTA SASTRI, K. A.
1932a   "Mahīpāla of the Caṇḍakauśikam," *Journal of Oriental Research* 6:191–98.
1932b   "A Tamil Merchant Guild in Sumatra," *Tijdschrift voor Indische Taal-, Land-
        en Volkenkunde* 72:314–27.
1942   "Dvīpāntara," *Journal of the Greater India Society* 9:1–4.
1949   "Takuapa and its Tamil Inscription," *Journal of the Malayan Branch of the
        Royal Asiatic Society* 22:25–30.

PARANAVITANA, SENARAT
1966   *Ceylon and Malaysia* (Colombo, Ceylon: Lake House Investments).

PARMENTIER, HENRI
1960 Angkor. Guide Henri Parmentier. 3d ed. (Phnom-Penh: Enterprise Khmère de Librairie, d'Imprimerie, et de Papeterie).

PARSONS, TALCOTT, AND NEIL J. SMELSER
1956 Economy and Society. A Study in the Integration of Economic and Social Theory (London: Routledge and Kegan Paul).

PARSONS, TALCOTT, EDWARD SHILS, KASPAR D. NAEGELE, AND JESSE R. PITTS (eds.)
1961 Theories of society. Foundations of modern sociological theory. 2 vols. (New York: Free Press).

PELLIOT, PAUL
1903 "Le Fou-nan," Bulletin de l'Ecole Française d'Extrême-Orient 3:248-303.
1925 "Quelques textes chinois concernant l'Indochine hindouisée," in Etudes Asiatiques publiées à l'occasion du vingt-cinquième anniversaire de l'Ecole Française d'Extrême-Orient, 2 vols., ed. G. Van Œst (Paris: Ecole Française d'Extrême-Orient).
1951 Mémoires sur les coutumes du Cambodge de Tcheou Ta-kouan. Oeuvres posthumes de Paul Pelliot, III (Paris: Adrien-Maisonneuve).

PENZER, N. M.
1924 The Ocean of Story: Being C. H. Tawney's Translation of Somadeva's Kathā Sarit Sāgara (London: C. J. Sawyer).

PHAYRE, SIR ARTHUR P.
1883 History of Burma including Burma Proper, Pegu, Taungu, Tenasserim, and Arakan, from the Earliest Times to the End of the First War with British India (London).

PICARD, CHARLES
1955 "La lampe alexandrine de P'ong Tuk [Siam]." Artibus Asiae 18:137-49.
1956 "A Figure of Lysippan Type from the Far East: the Tra Vinh Bronze 'Dancer,'" Artibus Asiae 19:342-52.

POLANYI, KARL, CONRAD M. ARENSBERG, AND HARRY W. PEARSON (eds.)
1957 Trade and Market in the Early Empires. Economies in History and Theory (New York: Free Press).

PIRENNE, JACQUELINE
1961 "La date du 'Périple de la Mer Erythrée,'" Journal Asiatique 249:441-59.

RANGASWAMI AIYANGAR, K. V.
1916 Considerations on Some Aspects of Ancient Indian Polity (Madras: University of Madras).

REDFIELD, ROBERT
1953 The Primitive World and Its Transformations (Ithaca, N. Y.: Cornell University Press).
1956 Peasant Society and Culture. (Chicago: University of Chicago Press.)

RENOU, LOUIS
1925 La Géographie de Ptolémée, l'Inde (VII, 1-4) (Paris: Librairie Ancienne Édouard Champion).
1931 Bibliographie védique (Paris: Adrien-Maisonneuve).

ROUGIER, VIRGILE
1912   "Nouvelles découvertes chames au Quang-nam," in *Bulletin de la Commission Archéologique de l'Indochine* (Paris).

SAHLINS, MARSHALL D.
1965   "On the Sociology of Primitive Exchange," in *The Relevance of Models for Social Anthropology*, ed. Michael Banton. Association of Social Anthropologists Monograph 1 (London and New York).
1968   *Tribesmen* (Englewood Cliffs, N. J.: Prentice-Hall).
1972   *Stone Age Economics* (Chicago: Aldine-Atherton).

SARKAR, HIMANSU BHUSAN
1959   "Four Rock Inscriptions of Batavia," *Journal of the Asiatic Society* 1(2):135–41.

SCHNITGER, F. M.
1934   Tārumānāgara," *Tijdschrift voor Indische Taal-, Land- en Volkenkunde* 74:
1937   *The Archaeology of Hindoo Sumatra*. Supplement to vol. 35 of *Internationales Archiv für Ethnographie* (Leiden).

SCHOFF, WILFRED H.
1912   *The Periplus of the Erythraean Sea. Travel and Trade in the Indian Ocean by a Merchant of the First Century* (London, Bombay, and Calcutta).

SHORTO, H. L.
1963   "The 32 *Myos* in the Medieval Mon Kingdom," *Bulletin of the School of Oriental and African Studies* 26:572–91.

SMELSER, NEIL J.
1959   "A comparative view of exchange systems," *Economic Development and Cultural Change* 7:173–82.
1963   *The Sociology of Economic Life* (Englewood Cliffs, N. J.: Prentice-Hall).

SOLHEIM, WILHELM G., II
1967   "Southeast Asia and the West," *Science* 157:896–902.
1969.   "Reworking Southeast Asian Prehistory," *Paideuma* 15:125–39.

SRINIVAS, M. N.
1956   "A Note on Sanskritization and Westernization," *The Journal of Asian Studies* 15:481–96.

STEIN, BURTON
1967   "Brahman and Peasant in Early South Indian History," *The Adyar Library
–68   Bulletin* 31–32:229–69.

STEIN, R. A.
1947   "Le Lin-yi, sa localisation, sa contribution à la formation du Champa et ses liens avec la Chine," *Han-Hiue* 2:i–xvi, 1–336.

STERN, PHILIPPE
1948   "Le problème des monuments khmèrs du style du Bayon et Jayavarman VII," in *Actes du XXIe Congrès des Orientalistes* (Paris).

STUTTERHEIM, W. F.
1932   "De voetafdrukken van Pūrṇawarman," *Bijdragen tot de Taal-, Land- en Volkenkunde van Nederlandsch-Indie* 89.

STURROCK, A. J.
1916   "Hikayat Marong Maha Wangsa or Kedah Annals," *Journal of the Straits Branch of the Royal Asiatic Society* 72:37–123.

TAGORE, RABINDRANATH
1934 "Foreword," *Journal of the Greater India Society* 1:n.p.
TIBBETTS, G. R.
1956 "The Malay Peninsula as Known to the Arab Geographers," *The Malayan Journal of Tropical Geography* 8:21–60.
TWEEDIE, M. W. F.
1953 "The Stone Age in Malaya," *Journal of the Malayan Branch of the Royal Asiatic Society* 26(2):1–90.
VALLÉE-POUSSIN, L. DE LA
1924 *Indo-Européens et Indo-Iraniens jusque vers 300 av. J. C.* (Paris: E. de Boccard).
1935 *Dynasties et histoire de l'Inde depuis Kanishka jusqu'aux invasions musulmanes* (Paris: E. de Boccard).
VAN LEUR, JACOB CORNELIS
1934 *Eenige beschouwingen betreffende den ouden Aziatischen handel* (Middelburg), Netherlands: G. W. den Boer).
1955 *Indonesian trade and society. Essays in Asian social and economic history* (includes translation of Van Leur 1934) (The Hague: W. van Hoeve, Ltd.).
VENKATARAMA AYYAR, K. R.
1947 "Medieval Trade, Craft, and Merchant Guilds in South India," *Journal of Indian History* 25:269–80.
VOGEL, JEAN PHILIPPE
1918 "The Yupa Inscriptions of King Mulavarman from Koetei (East Borneo)," *Bijdragen tot de Taal-, Land- en Volkenkunde van Nederlandsch-Indie* 74: 167–232.
1925 "The Earliest Sanskrit Inscriptions of Java," *Publicaties van den Oudheidkundigen dienst in Nederlandsch-Indië* 1:15–35.
WALES, H. G. QUARITCH
1931 *Siamese State Ceremonies: Their History and Function* (London: Quaritch).
WATSON, WILLIAM AND HELMUT H. E. LOOFS
1967 "The Thai-British Archaeological Expedition, a Preliminary Report on the Work of the First Season 1965–66," *The Journal of the Siam Society* 55:237–72.
WEBER, MAX
1923 *Gesammelte Aufsätze zur Religionssoziologie II: Hinduismus und Buddhismus* (Tübingen, Germany: J. C. B. Mohr).
1925 *Grundriss der Sozialökonomik, III Abteilung: Wirtschaft und Gesellschaft II.* (Tübingen, Germany: J. C. B. Mohr).
WHEATLEY, PAUL
1956a "Tun-sun," *Journal of the Royal Asiatic Society*:17–30.
1956b "Langkasuka," *T'oung Pao* 44:387–412.
1957a "Ch'ih-t'u," *Journal of the Malayan Branch of the Royal Asiatic Society* 30(1):122–33.
1957b "The Seat of All Felicities," *The Historical Annual*:99–106.
1957c "Possible References to the Malay Peninsula in the Annals of the Former Han," *Journal of the Malayan Branch of the Royal Asiatic Society* 30(1):115–21.
1961 *The Golden Khersonese. Studies in the Historical Geography of the Malay Peninsula before* A.D. 1500 (Kuala Lumpur: University of Malaya Press).

1964 "Desultory Remarks on the Ancient History of the Malay Peninsula," in *Malayan and Indonesian studies. Essays Presented to Sir Richard Winstedt on his Eighty-fifth Birthday*, ed. John Bastin and R. Roolvink (London: Clarendon Press).

1964b *Impressions of the Malay Peninsula in Ancient Times* (Singapore: Eastern Universities Press).

1968 "Review of O. W. Wolters, *Early Indonesian commerce: a study of the origins of Srivijaya*," *Bijdragen tot de Taal-, Land- en Volkenkunde* 124:291–94.

WINSTEDT, SIR RICHARD

1958 "A history of classical Malay literature," *Journal of the Malayan Branch of the Royal Asiatic Society* 31(3):1–261.

WOLF, ERIC R.

1966 *Peasants* (Englewood Cliffs, N. J.: Prentice-Hall).

WOLTERS, O. W.

1967 *Early Indonesian Commerce. A Study of the Origins of Śrīvijaya* (Ithaca, N. Y.: Cornell University Press).

1970 *The Fall of Śrīvijaya in Malay History* (London: Lund Humphries).

7

Locational Analysis and the Investigation of Uruk Local Exchange Systems[1]

GREGORY A. JOHNSON

Hunter College (CUNY)

INTRODUCTION

A chapter on local exchange may seem somewhat out of place in a volume on trade. The term *trade* usually evokes a picture of the movement of goods over long distances, while local exchange obviously refers to a purely local phenomenon. They are, however, complementary processes. While long-range trade provides economic links between more or less independent settlement systems, local exchange provides similar linkage within individual systems.

Here the term *local exchange* is used in a very general sense denoting reciprocal movement of goods or services or both within a single settlement system. The exact form, extent, and intensity of this movement is not specified and may vary from case to case.

This chapter has two goals: first, a general discussion of the theoretical and practical problems involved in the investigation of local exchange systems through locational analysis of archaeological settlement pattern data; second, a presentation of two related examples of such studies. It is hoped that these examples will contribute to our understanding of one ancient civilization, that of the fourth millennium Uruk Period in Mesopotamia. Let us deal first with the confusion of theory, leaving the confusion of data for later consideration.

LOCATIONAL THEORY, ASSUMPTIONS, AND "REALITY": PROBLEMS OF GOODNESS OF FIT

Locational Theory

It is not possible to speak of a unified locational theory. We have, rather, a number of more or less related models or sets of models dealing with different locational problems. Central Place theory is a subset of locational theory. As in the case of general locational theory, Central Place theory is not a unified construct, but a series of related models proposed by Christaller (1966), Lösch (1954), Isard (1956), and others. These models are of particular interest here, as they deal specifically with the spatial organization of local exchange systems.

For present purposes, we will consider the relatively simple construct of Christaller as the point of departure for a partial central place model appropriate to archaeological data on complex societies. The outline of Christaller's construct is well known and need not be repeated in detail here.

Briefly, Christaller (1966) proposed a series of models of the spatial organization of a settlement system associated with a modern market economy. The models were designed to allow most efficient performance of certain types of work. This work involved the production and distribution of goods and services.

In a settlement system organized according to Christaller's "Marketing Principle," central places, or service centers, of the same functional size are equidistant from one another and when most efficiently located have a hexagonal distribution. Each center serves a surrounding, hexagonally shaped, complementary region. Smaller central places and associated complementary regions may be hierarchically nested within this system to form an intricate settlement lattice. The hexagonal distribution of central places allows immediately adjacent placement or packing of complementary regions such that no settlement remains unserviced and the average distance between a given central place and the edge of its complementary region is minimized (Haggett 1966:49).

Christaller proposed two related models; in each the form of this lattice is altered depending upon whether efficiency of transportation or administration is the primary factor in determination of settlement location. He emphasized that the structure of actual settlement systems should not be expected to conform exactly to one or another of his models. Deviations could result from the operation of a combination of his ordering principles or from the influence of variables not included in his theory.

Since Christaller's initial work, a considerable body of literature has appeared on both the theoretical and practical aspects of his models. While one effort has been directed at on-the-ground identification of settlement systems conforming to Christaller's predictions, another has been directed at refinement and elaboration of his models to bring them more in line with actual field conditions. Olsson (1965:7) concludes on the basis of available studies that settlement systems analogous to those proposed by Christaller ". . . exist in many parts of the world, in spite of divergent levels of economic development and marked differences in culture."

The vast majority of these studies have dealt with settlement systems associated with modern market economies of the sort for which the theory was designed. Application of a central place model to analysis of most archaeological settlement patterns raises a number of questions involving basic assumptions. These questions must be considered before analysis can be undertaken.

Assumptions and "Reality"

Christaller's central-place model requires an elaborate set of initial conditions and assumptions to generate hexagonally distributed settlement hierarchies. The model specifies as the initial condition an isotropic surface with uniform distributions of resources, population, and purchasing power (Garner 1967:307). The model's most important assumption is economic maximization: that decisions affecting the economic position of an individual or group are always made in order to maximize that position.

Sahlins has stressed that economic maximization theories are seldom if ever applicable to non-money-market economies (Sahlins 1972). Acceptance of this position would seem to cast considerable doubt on the validity of the application of Christaller's theory to the analysis of most archaeologically interesting settlement pattern data. Can Christaller's conditions and assumptions be relaxed so that the resulting modified central place model will be applicable to nonmodern economic systems? I believe that they can.

An initial series of assumptions is basic to most locational models (see Garner 1967:304–5). We will assume that:

(1) There is a tendency for human activities to agglomerate because gains in efficiency are obtainable by concentration of related activities at the same spatial locus.
(2) Locational decisions are made in general to minimize energy expended in movement.
(3) All locations are accessible, though some are more accessible than others.

The following definitions will be used in conjunction with these assumptions:

(1) *Central Place:* The spatial locus of an activity agglomeration involving production and distribution of goods or services or both, primarily for use within a surrounding complementary region. Such loci are usually, but not necessarily, associated with permanent settlements.
(2) *Central Place Function:* An activity or activity set, involving production or distribution or both of goods or services or both, which is localized in a central place and is qualitatively or quantitatively differentiated from activities or activity sets localized in lower-order places.
(3) *Central Place Hierarchy:* A discontinuous distribution of the size of central place function agglomerations and associated complementary regions. Spatially, lower order central places and associated complementary regions may be nested within

288

the complementary regions of higher order central places. Higher order central places are characterized by the presence of central place functions unavailable in lower order central places.

In the present model, structural hierarchies (definition 3) of central places (definition 1) and associated complementary regions may, but do not necessarily, develop as a function of the interaction of activity agglomeration (assumption 1), movement minimization (assumption 2), and differential accessibility (assumption 3). While we have assumed a tendency for activity agglomeration, we must distinguish between simple agglomeration and the *differential* agglomeration (centralization) among a series of spatial loci, which is characteristic of a central-place system as defined above. Conditions favoring initial centralization are probably highly variable. One such condition has been proposed by Kochen and Deutsch (1970:171) who suggest that "in general, uneven spatial distribution of demand moderately favors centralization...."

Once centralization has begun, subsequent development of a central-place hierarchy should proceed (1) to the extent that least-effort considerations influence the spatial organization of production and distribution of goods and services, and (2) to the extent that the operation of other variables does not intervene in this process.

Note that the model still requires an element of effort minimization related to economic maximization. The critical phrase is "to the extent that". Effort minimization may appear to a greater or lesser extent in the context of market, redistributional, or mixed economies. Application of this model is thus not restricted to the modern market situation.

When present in a region, central places will *tend* to have a regular hexagonal distribution defined by simple linear distance under the following conditions:

(1) The region contains more than one central place.
(2) Either no portion, or only a very small portion, of the settlement region is external to the complementary region of at least one central place.
(3) Effort expended in movement to and from each central place is minimized.
(4) The topography of the region approaches a uniform plain.

Presence of a single central place (deviation from condition 1) should produce a roughly circular associated complementary region. Less efficient, nonhexagonal distributions may be expected as the result of deviation from conditions 2, 3, and 4.

Although the partial model proposed here is applicable to a wider range of cases than Christaller's original central place construct, relaxation of the economic maximization assumption renders prediction of the configuration of settlement distributions impossible, even if the other conditions of the model are met. This will have a major effect on the conclusions that can be drawn from observed settlement distributions. This point will be elaborated below.

Problems of Goodness of Fit

Locational theory consists of a number of models of the behavior of a series of interrelated variables. As with all models, these are useful not because they describe real world phenomena, but because they are simplified and understandable abstractions which seem to have real world analogs. They furnish a frame of reference for analysis and interpretation of field data. The nature and utility of these models is often misunderstood. Such misunderstanding can have unfortunate consequences, two extreme examples of which follow.

Consider our central place model. At one extreme, identification of on-the-ground settlement distributions of the type described by the model may be taken as proof of the operation of particular economic and/or political processes. The model, especially as modified above, makes no claim to account for the only process through which such distributions might occur. Completely unrelated processes might well result in similar or identical distributions. As David Clarke recently noted, "Aspects of central place theory appear to work where they ought not to work, in contexts where optimalization, rationalized planning, even towns and villages are not found . . ." (Clarke 1972:51). Hexagonal or at least polygonal distributions are common. In most cases a settlement distribution can only be taken as an indicator variable suggesting, in a theoretical context, the operation of particular political and/or economic processes. Identification of the operation of such processes is then subject to independent testing and verification.

At the other extreme, the possible implications of a regular settlement distribution may be ignored for equally "theoretical" reasons. Perhaps a particular field situation does not conform to the assumptions of Central Place theory as classically defined. It was suggested above that the assumptions of the theory may be modified so that a revised model may be applied to a wider range of economic systems.

Failure of a field situation to conform to the initial conditions of a central place model is an additional problem. This is particularly the case for the initial topographic condition, a uniform plain (see Adams 1972:745 ff.). Although no one expects to find an isotropic surface in the field, little work has been done on the theoretical implications of deviation from this ideal condition. We will encounter this problem in a later section of this chapter, where it will become clear that access to differentially distributed water was an important determinant of settlement location.

In practice, the decision to use a central place model in analysis of settlement data depends not on conformation of the field situation to specific topographic, demographic, or other conditions, but on the degree to which the field situation departs from ideal conditions. This raises the difficult issue of the amount of deviation that may be tolerated for valid application of the model. There is no easy answer to the question, and as far as I know, the problem has never been systematically considered. In the absence of greater theoretical sophistication, we are thrown back onto the application of common sense and an occasional distance transformation. For the present, I suggest that the model may be used whenever its application results in important and testable hypotheses relevant to problems of interest. I admit that utility of result is not the best test of validity of application, but it will have to do for the moment.

Locational theory has considerable potential for analysis of archaeological settlement pattern data if both excessive zeal and excessive skepticism can be avoided. At present, locational approaches answer few questions in archaeology, but ask many. Application of a central place model or other locational construct serves as a hypothesis-generating mechanism. It directs attention to possible regularities in settlement pattern data which might otherwise be ignored. Two examples of hypothesis generation through locational analysis will be presented below.

First, however, additional problems involved in the application of our central place model to archaeological settlement pattern data require attention.

CENTRAL PLACE MODELS AND ARCHAEOLOGICAL SETTLEMENT PATTERN DATA

As we have seen, our central place model deals with the spatial organization of settlement hierarchies. These hierarchies are based on the relative functional sizes of their component settlements. By functional size, we mean the number of types of economically related activity carried out in a settlement. The number of types of goods and services produced by a settlement would be a satisfactory measure of its functional size. As this type of information is unavailable from settlement survey, a substitute measure must be found.

A number of field studies by geographers have indicated a close relationship between the population of a settlement and various measures of its functional size. Haggett (1965:115–16) quotes significant linear correlation coefficients obtained from such studies which range from 0.75 to 0.91. Again, all of these studies have dealt with modern, market-oriented societies. For the present then, we will proceed with the archaeologically untested assumption that there is a close positive relationship between population and functional size. Indeed, we will assume that these variables vary in direct proportion to one another.

Reliance on population as an index of functional size is not as happy a solution as it might seem. We are left with the difficult problem of population estimation. Population estimation is difficult enough in dealing with an excavated site, where estimates of the size and density of residential architecture or other features can be made. These problems are severely compounded when only survey data are available. The conventional solution to this problem has been to assume a direct proportional relationship between the population of a settlement and its areal size.

For Near Eastern material, this assumption is primarily founded on modern demographic data from 53 traditional villages in Khuzistan, Iran (Gremliza 1962). These data reveal a significant linear correlation coefficient of 0.85 between village population and areal size, with an average population density of about 200 persons per hectare of village area. It is possible that the relationship between settlement areal and population size is allometric rather than linear. Unfortunately few demographic data are available to test this possibility (Schacht 1973:30 ff). For most periods, moreover, we have virtually no data with which to test this relationship archaeologically. Even though the supporting evidence is very tenuous, we will assume that the areal size of a settlement is directly proportional to its population and thereby to its functional size.

Our use of survey data for the investigation of local exchange systems is now dependent on accurate determination of settlement areal sizes. This is a difficult, if familiar, field problem, which will only be mentioned here. Further application of recent advances in survey methodology should help alleviate these difficulties (see Whallon 1969 and Redman and Watson 1970).

Though we now have at least an operational index of settlement functional size, we are faced with yet another problem. Our central place model deals not merely with settlement hierarchies, but with discontinuous hierarchies. There has been considerable discussion in the geographical literature as to whether functional hierarchies are really discrete or are actually continuous (Berry and Garrison 1958; Berry 1961; Olsson 1965:243–48). We have already assumed a direct proportional relationship between areal and functional size. Any discontinuities in a distribution of settlement areal sizes will therefore be assumed to indicate discontinuities in a distribution of functional sizes.

At least two rather disparate difficulties remain. The first is chronology. Geographers work with distributions of settlements which are known to be contemporaneous. The same can rarely be said of archaeologists. Let us only note that the better the available relative chronology, the greater the potential for analysis.

The second problem concerns definition of a study area. If we are interested in local exchange within a settlement system, how do we define that system? This is something of a nonproblem, in that definition of settlement system boundaries is a goal, rather than a precondition, of analysis. Acknowledging that boundary phenomena present notoriously difficult problems, it is best to take a relatively large area as the unit for analysis. There is no magic figure to solve this problem. Appropriate areas undoubtedly vary from one geographical region to another and from one level of cultural complexity to another. Here we will consider state-level societies; both areas to be discussed exceed 3,000 square kilometers.

It has taken several pages to consider a few theoretical and methodological problems in the application a central place model to the investigation of archaeological local exchange systems. I have asserted that locational models can be a valuable analytical tool in this pursuit. The time has come to support this contention with examples.

EXAMPLES STUDIED

Introduction

In this section we will consider two related examples of the use of settlement pattern data in the investigation of local exchange systems. The data are derived from my own survey of Uruk sites on the Susiana Plain of Khuzistan, Iran and from the Warka survey conducted by Adams and Nissen in southern Iraq. The apparent Middle and Late Uruk local exchange systems of the Susiana area will be compared to that suggested by the Late Uruk settlement pattern in the vicinity of Warka.

The 1970–71 Susiana Survey

The Susiana survey was conducted during the fall and winter of 1970–71 as part of the Southwest Iran Project of The University of Michigan Museum of Anthropology and the Muzeh-e Irān-e Bāstān, Teheran. The survey data and results of analysis have been published in full elsewhere (Johnson 1973). Presentation of data and statistical manipulations will thus be very cursory here. Readers should refer to the original publication for this detailed material.

The Susiana survey area is bounded on the west and east by the Karkeh and Karun rivers, on the south by the Haft Tepe anticline, and on the north by the first range of the Zagros Mountains (see figure 16).

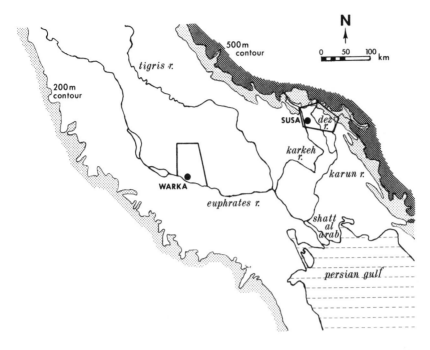

FIGURE 16. LOWER MESOPOTAMIA: LOCATION OF THE 1970–71 SUSI-
ANA AND WARKA SURVEY AREAS

Fifty-two Middle Uruk and fourteen Late Uruk settlements of perhaps
3500–3150 B.C. were located in this area.

The Settlement Hierarchy

The first step in analysis of these settlement data was to evaluate the
presence of a settlement size hierarchy. Virtually all sites were mapped
in the field with an alidade and plane table. Surface collections were
made with an "area pickup" technique. In this technique, a site was
normally divided into two or more topographically distinct areas, and
diagnostic Uruk ceramics, if present, were collected from each area.
While this technique provided data on changes in site size over time,
in the future it will be necessary to apply more sophisticated randomized
sampling techniques in the investigation of intrasite variability.

Figure 17 presents site-size histograms for Middle and Late Uruk

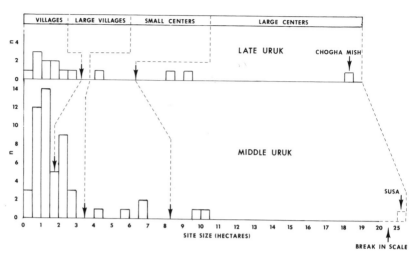

FIGURE 17. 1970–71 SUSIANA SURVEY URUK SITE AREAS—HISTO-GRAMS. Definition of site areal size classes.

occupations of the survey area. Modal divisions are indicated within each histogram. The number of sites involved in the analysis is too small to permit statistical definition of multimodality. Division is thus made at "natural breaks" in each site-size distribution. Such division constitutes a working hypothesis rather than a conclusion of analysis. The hypothesis might be tested in two ways. First, utility of the resulting hierarchy in subsequent analysis would provide support for the initial division. Second, there should be a higher degree of nonareal similarity among settlements within a given level of the hierarchy than between levels of the hierarchy. Obviously, this second test prediction will be much more difficult to evaluate than the first. Limited data relevant to this problem are, however, available and will be presented below.

Returning to the immediate topic, three modal breaks are suggested for the Middle Uruk settlement size distribution, resulting in a four-level settlement hierarchy. Breaks are made at 1.75, 3.50, and 8.25 hectares. The settlements distinguished by these divisions have been termed: Villages (.01–1.74 hectares), Large Villages (1.75–3.44 hectares), Small Centers (3.45–8.24 hectares), and Large Centers (8.25–25.00 hectares). The term *center* is used both for its specific theoretical connotations and to avoid such designations as "town," "city," or "urban center."

Indirect Evidence of Local Exchange

Figure 18 presents the suggested Middle Uruk settlement system on the Susiana, incorporating the four-level settlement hierarchy defined above. Indirect evidence indicates the presence of a local exchange system at this period. At least by Middle Uruk, some traditional craft production had been concentrated in workshops and centralized in the major settlements on the plain. The evidence is primarily from ceramic production. Uruk ceramic kilns and concentrations of kiln wasters are known only from the three largest sites in the area. These sites include Susa, Chogha Mish (KS-1), and Abu Fanduweh (KS-59). These are the three sites classified as Large Centers on the basis of the Middle Uruk site-size histogram.

Although the evidence is not available, it is probable that other crafts were similarly concentrated in these large settlements. Centralization of ceramic production indicates the presence of some method of distri-

FIGURE 18. THE MIDDLE URUK SETTLEMENT SYSTEM ON THE SUSIANA PLAIN

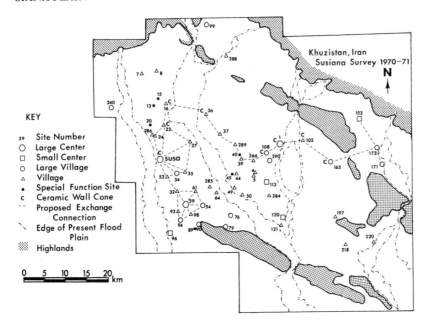

bution and implies reciprocal movement of other goods or services or both, in other words local exchange.

Locational Evidence of the Organization of Local Exchange

Delineation of the organization of this exchange is another problem. Two aspects of the distribution of Middle Uruk settlements on the Susiana are of particular importance here (see figure 18). Note the particularly regular distribution of settlements on the western portion of the plain. Both the size and location of settlements in the vicinity of Susa and Abu Fanduweh (KS-59) roughly conform to our central place model. Such patterning is not evident on the eastern side of the plain in the area of Chogha Mish (KS-1). Our Early Uruk data indicate developmental primacy for the western portion of the plain. Chogha Mish seems to have been founded as a major center early in Middle Uruk in response to administrative requirements in its area. Its marginal location relative to other settlements in the area would appear to have been at least partially a factor of immediate sustaining-area requirements for a large center (Johnson 1973:109–11).

The second important feature of the settlement pattern concerns the distribution of settlements associated with a particular artifact type, the ceramic wall cone. These cones were used as an element in architectural decoration and have been associated with temples or other major public buildings in large centers. Such cones were unexpectedly found on the surface of a number of small sites in the Susiana area.

Presence of cones is indicated by the letter c next to the appropriate sites indicated on figure 18. Since cone mosaics have never been found in association with simple residential architecture, it is assumed that their location on these small settlements is indicative of the presence of some kind of public building(s), necessarily much smaller than those known from large centers. The presence of public (official) buildings markedly distinguishes these settlements from other sites in the Village–Large Village size range, and suggests that they were of some particular significance.

Given the apparent economic importance of the sacred and/or secular institutions represented by public buildings in major settlements, the possible public buildings on these particular small settlements may reflect the presence of similar specialized economic activity. Furthermore, note that the distribution of these sites forms a rough line across the plain, possibly *connecting* the two largest centers of the area, Susa and Chogha Mish.

These diverse considerations lead to the hypothesis that these small cone sites may have played a specialized role in the local exchange system of the area. Specifically, the hypothesis states that small cone sites functioned at least in part as specialized administrative centers in the mediation of local exchange. If this hypothesis is correct, these administrative outposts probably provided links between Large Centers or between centers and lesser settlements. One would predict the presence of evidence on these sites for such activities as transshipment of goods, and collection and/or redistribution of goods and/or services. This hypothesis will be at least partially tested below.

The settlement pattern data thus suggest a rather elaborate local exchange system. This system apparently involved centralized production of at least certain craft items in Large Centers. These goods were then distributed to outlying settlements, presumably in return for other goods and/or services. This probable redistributional system was apparently highly administered, as suggested by the distribution of small cone sites.

Hypothesis Testing

The above description of the Middle Uruk local exchange system consists, of course, of a number of hypotheses generated from primarily locational considerations. Independent test procedures are required to evaluate these hypotheses.

Ceramics are the primary materials available with which to test these hypotheses. It should be possible, for example, to distinguish ceramics produced in different workshops and trace their distribution through a local exchange system. Such a procedure involves a number of difficult problems.

The most important of these problems involves our ability to detect workshop variability: to distinguish vessels of the same general type produced in different workshops. (At present there is no evidence that different centers produced differing ranges of vessel types.) Unfortunately we know little about Uruk ceramic workshops on the Susiana beyond the mere fact of their existence.

This problem has been approached through use of a specialized attribute analysis of ceramics from our surface collections. This approach uses the location of a collection as well as various metric attributes in the analysis of individual ceramic types. The method has been most successful in the case of incised crosshatch bands (Johnson 1973:113 ff.).

Incised crosshatch bands are a common form of decoration on Uruk jar shoulders. It has been possible to isolate both temporal and spatial variability within this type. Sixty-four examples were available from our survey collections. An additional series of twenty-six specimens from Chogha Mish (KS-1) were measured with the kind permission of Dr. Helene Kantor of the Oriental Institute of the University of Chicago. Ninety examples were thus available for study. Of a series of six attributes considered, two showed bimodal distributions.

The first of these is an angular measurement of the intersection of individual diagonal incisions forming the crosshatch design. The second bimodally distributed attribute is a measure of the width of a horizontal incised line bounding the crosshatch pattern. Figure 19 presents histograms and figure 20 shows a cross plot of these attributes.

The division of the sample on the modal break in diagonal intersection angle appears to be chronologically significant. Fifty-six specimens fall into a narrow angle group. Of these, eight examples are associated with crosshatch triangles, a characteristic Late Uruk motif (see figure 20). None of the thirty-four examples in the wide angle group are associated with this motif. The division would thus appear to be chronologically significant. The earlier group is primarily Middle Uruk, while the later group is apparently restricted to late Middle and Late Uruk.

The division of the sample on the modal break in horizontal line thickness would appear to be spatially significant, defining workshop groups. If the sample is stratified according to location of collection east or west of the Dez River, Student's t tests reveal a significant difference in mean horizontal line width for all examples ($p=0.000$), early examples ($p=0.013$), and late examples ($p=0.004$). A Chi Square analysis reveals a significant ($p =$ less than 0.001) association of early and late wide line examples with settlements east of the Dez, and of early and late narrow line examples with settlements west of the Dez.

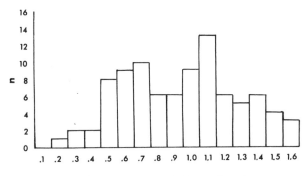

Horizontal Line Thickness (mm)

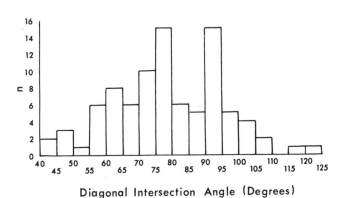

Diagonal Intersection Angle (Degrees)

FIGURE 19. URUK CROSSHATCH BANDS—HISTOGRAMS

This analysis indicates the presence of at least two workshops, one west of the Dez and one east of the Dez. Only one settlement in the eastern area, Chogha Mish, is known to have contained a ceramic workshop. Workshops are known at two sites in the western area, Susa and Abu Fanduweh. Sufficient material is not yet available to differentiate the products of these two centers.

The areal association described above is not perfect. This is to be expected in a local exchange situation. Figure 21 presents a plot of the presence of each of the two early crosshatch band types. Figure 21 also

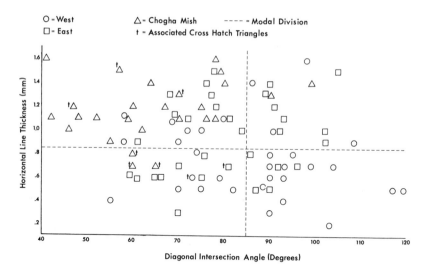

FIGURE 20. URUK CROSSHATCH BANDS—SCATTER PLOT

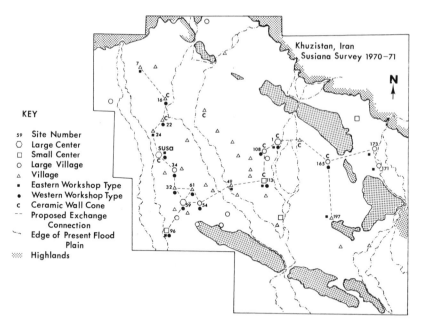

FIGURE 21. THE MIDDLE URUK LOCAL EXCHANGE SYSTEM ON THE
SUSIANA PLAIN: DISTRIBUTION OF EARLY CROSSHATCH BANDS

presents a partial outline of local exchange connections based on this evidence.

Given the small sample of material available, and sampling problems in general, additional supporting evidence is required. Such evidence is available from analysis of a second ceramic type, strap handles (Johnson 1973:118 ff.).

Strap handles are characteristic of, though not restricted to, Middle Uruk. Two handle types were defined on the basis of a bimodal distribution of handle width. The wide type will concern us here. When the sample is stratified on the basis of location of collection as above, handles from the area of Chogha Mish (KS-1) are significantly thicker than handles from the area of Abu Fanduweh (KS-59) and Susa (Student's t, $p = 0.013$). A Chi Square analysis reveals that thin handles are significantly associated with the western area of the plain, while thick handles are associated with the eastern area of the plain (p = less than 0.02).

This analysis reveals the same pattern as that demonstrated in the case of crosshatched bands. Again, the associations are not spatially exclusive, as is illustrated in figure 22. In addition to a significant differential spatial distribution, wide strap handles as a group are significantly associated with small cone sites (Chi Square, p = less than .05). Such association would be expected if these particular sites functioned as specialized administrative centers in the mediation of local exchange.

The results of these two analyses may be combined to produce a composite picture of ceramic evidence for Middle Uruk local exchange connections (see figure 23). Most of the connections proposed from locational considerations were supported, while others are added.

One additional source of data is available from the excavations at Tepe Sharafabad carried out in 1971 by Henry T. Wright. Tepe Sharafabad (KS-36) is one example of what has been referred to as a small cone site. If such sites were minor administrative centers, they should contain at least a higher density of administrative artifacts than do other small sites. A series of administrative artifacts, primarily sealed jar stoppers and bale sealings, were found at Sharafabad in a clear Middle Uruk context. (Wright 1971: personal communication). Although no excavation samples are available from other small Uruk sites in the area, the evidence from Sharafabad does not contradict our hypothesis. Exca-

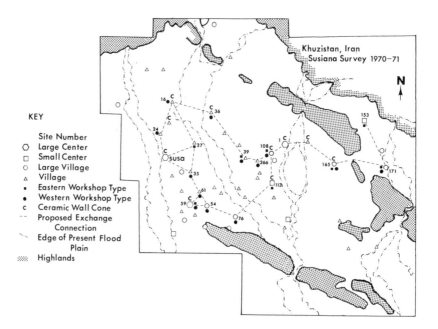

FIGURE 22. THE MIDDLE URUK LOCAL EXCHANGE SYSTEM ON THE SUSIANA PLAIN: DISTRIBUTION OF WIDE STRAP HANDLES

vation of small Uruk sites having no surface evidence of administrative specialization is an important future research requirement.

We have, then, at least preliminary evidence of administered movement of centrally produced craft items from the upper to the lower levels of the Middle Uruk settlement hierarchy. Exchange, however, includes reciprocal movement of goods or services or both from small settlements through the hierarchy to centers. Preliminary evidence indicates that labor and agricultural produce were two components of this reciprocity.

Analysis of a restricted sample of Uruk bevel-rim bowls suggests that this vessel type was produced in relatively standardized volumes of .90, .65, and .45 liters or 1.00, .72, and .50 volume units. This preliminary evidence of vessel volume standardization, in addition to the very high frequency of bevel-rim bowls in Uruk contexts, supports the hypothesis proposed by Nissen (1970:137) that this vessel type functioned primarily in an administered redistribution or ration system. Corvée laborers

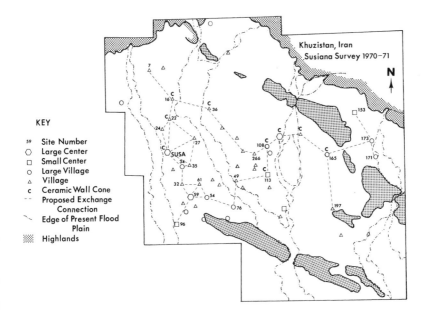

FIGURE 23. THE MIDDLE URUK LOCAL EXCHANGE SYSTEM ON THE SUSIANA PLAIN: COMBINED CERAMIC EVIDENCE

recruited from centers and outlying settlements would have been the most likely recipients of such rations (Johnson 1973:129 ff.).

Estimation of Large Center agricultural sustaining areas during Early Uruk provides a clue to the second factor involved in small-settlement exchange reciprocity. During Early Uruk, Susa had an estimated sustaining area of 2.12 (2.0) hectares per individual of its resident population. The figure for Abu Fanduweh was 2.19 (2.0) hectares per person. Near-capacity traditional agricultural production on the plain today involves sustaining areas of an average of 1.92 hectares per person (Gremliza 1962:38). It would appear that the resident agricultural population of Early Uruk Large Centers was involved in near capacity production. Increase in center population without expansion of available sustaining areas would thus require agricultural inputs in excess of the capacity of a resident agricultural population. This assumes, of course, no significant change in agricultural intensity or technology, an assumption that seems reasonable.

305

With no apparent increase in sustaining area, the population of Susa increased an estimated 100 percent from Early to Middle Uruk. The population of Abu Fanduweh (KS-59) increased an estimated 38 percent. These increases would seem to indicate the initial necessity, if not marked increase, of movement of agricultural produce and possibly labor from smaller settlements to the larger Middle Uruk centers (Johnson 1973:94 ff.).

In summary, the Middle Uruk local exchange system on the Susiana Plain seems to have involved a rather elaborate administered redistribution system. Minimally, certain mass-produced craft items and administrative services were exchanged for labor and agricultural produce. Considerable additional work will be required to further elucidate the operation of this system.

We suspect that the system was, in fact, much more complex than is suggested here. For example, while production of certain craft items was concentrated in Large Centers, specialized production of at least one item (lithic blade cores) was undertaken at a non–Large Center location. Our survey data indicate the presence of a lithic workshop on KS-284. This site is located on the eastern side of the plain, below Chogha Mish (see figure 18). This is the only such workshop known outside of a Large Center, and it probably represents a case of village specialization. As such the organization of exchange involving blade cores must have been quite different from that for materials produced in centers.

It seems that we are dealing not with a single exchange network, but more probably with a complicated set of exchange subsystems. We will encounter a similar situation when we consider the Late Uruk settlement system of the Warka area.

Late Uruk

Let us now look briefly at developments on the Susiana in the Late Uruk period. Recall that the incised crosshatch band motif discussed above could be divided into two temporally distinct groups. Whereas the first pertained to Middle Uruk, the second was restricted to late Middle and Late Uruk. The type thus allows investigation of possible changes in the local exchange system in the Middle–Late Uruk transition. Eastern versus western workshop varieties of this temporally transitional type are plotted in figure 24. Comparison of this plot with that illustrated in figure 21 seems to indicate a marked restriction in the local exchange system, particularly in the areas north of Susa and between Susa and Chogha Mish (KS-1).

This observation is confirmed by the distribution of Late Uruk settlements (see figure 25). The settled population reduction evidenced here probably amounted to some 40 percent (see the Late Uruk settlement-size histogram, figure 17). Changes in settlement pattern are equally striking. The pattern seems to have been resolved into two highly independent components or enclaves. The remarkably uniform distance separating these settlement units suggests formation of a boundary area between at least potentially hostile political units (Rowlands 1972:445).

Although the available ceramic data are not sufficient to test this hypothesis in terms of highly differential local exchange patterns, it is

FIGURE 24. THE TRANSITIONAL MIDDLE-LATE URUK LOCAL EXCHANGE SYSTEM ON THE SUSIANA PLAIN: DISTRIBUTION OF LATE CROSSHATCH BANDS

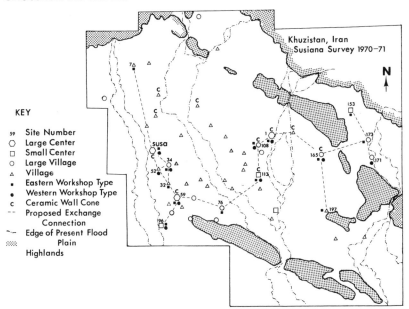

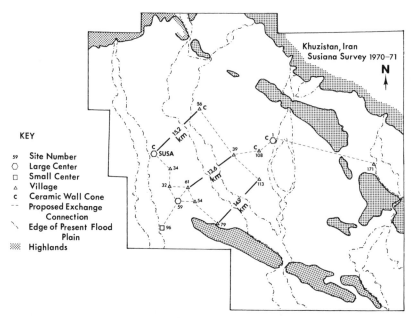

FIGURE 25. THE LATE URUK SETTLEMENT SYSTEM ON THE SUSI-
ANA PLAIN

clear that the minimal two-workshop pattern of the Middle Uruk system was maintained (Johnson 1973:147 ff.). Highly restricted artifactual evidence is at least consistent with the hypothesis of the
emergence of major hostilities on the Susiana Plain during Late Uruk.

I include this Late Uruk pattern primarily for contrast with the extensive and intricate settlement system present during Late Uruk in the
area of Warka. Analysis of this system will constitute the second example study to be presented here.

THE WARKA SURVEY

Uruk settlement data from the area of Warka in Southern Iraq have
been reported in *The Uruk Countryside,* a recent volume by Adams and
Nissen (1972). Only Late Uruk sites reported from the Warka Survey
will be considered. This limitation is imposed for several reasons.

Most important of these is the present uncertainty about Uruk relative chronology. While I have developed a three-phase system for the

Susiana area, Adams and Nissen have defined a two-phase system for the Warka area. We agree, however, on the basic ceramic types to be used in identification of the Late Uruk phase. Late Uruk will be considered here not only because there is basic agreement on its definition, but because it is the best-represented Uruk phase in the Warka area. As such it presents the best opportunity for analysis.

Furthermore, comparison of analyses from two different areas but of generally the same temporal range should be very instructive. As independent cases of similar developments, they can function reciprocally as test cases for hypothesis evaluation. An attempt will be made to point out the similarities and differences between the Uruk settlement systems in the Susiana and Warka areas, and to suggest their implications relative to the possible differential organization of local exchange in these areas.

Critical conclusions reached by Adams and Nissen about the Late Uruk occupation of the Warka area may be summarized as follows. The Late Uruk settlement hierarchy consisted of two levels with a single site, Warka, occupying the upper level, and a unimodal distribution of smaller settlements occupying the lower level. The conclusion is drawn that "a hierarchy of settlement sizes, presumably linked to the emergence of specialized economic, religious, military, or administrative functions that required some centers with larger residential populations, thus had only just begun to make its appearance in the Late Uruk period (Adams and Nissen 1972:18). The authors go on to say that "whereas Uruk itself was already a flouring theocratic center, the small average size and absence of a well developed hierarchy among outlying settlements implies only a minimal development of the economic or administrative structures that are concomitants of centralized control" (Adams and Nissen 1972:18).

Instead of a uniformly dispersed, hexagonal settlement distribution of the sort predicted by Central Place theory, Late Uruk settlements exhibit a clustered or contagious distribution. "This 'contagious' distribution reflects the presence of multiple prevailing small, closely spaced, presumably interrelated settlements as a significant component of the settlement pattern as a whole" (Adams and Nissen 1972:22).

The authors also note a large number of binary or reflexive nearest-neighbor settlement pairs which, on the basis of ethnographic analogy with the Marsh Arabs, may indicate alternating seasonal occupation of such a settlement pair by a single social group (Adams and Nissen 1972:23). Finally, there appears to be a marked shift in settlement pattern between the area immediately adjacent to Warka and the area 15 kilometers and farther from this site. Settlements in the former area tend to be smaller and more clustered than do settlements in the latter area. This difference may be indicative of a shift in social organization beyond the range of immediate influence of the major Late Uruk center at Warka (Adams and Nissen 1972:27).

Bearing these conclusions in mind, let us proceed with a reanalysis of the Late Uruk settlement data from the Warka area. It is important to remember that the type of analysis undertaken by an investigator will be highly determined by his research interests. Adams and Nissen are primarily concerned with the origins and development of urbanism. Here the emphasis will be on the organization of local exchange. Different approaches to analysis often produce different results and different interpretations. When focused on different problems, one set of analysis and interpretation is not necessarily better or more useful than another, but merely different.

The Settlement Hierarchy

Adams and Nissen report 118 Late Uruk sites from the Warka area. Not all of these sites, however, had definite Late Uruk occupations. With one exception, to be discussed below, only sites definitely identified as having Late Uruk occupations are used in this study. This reduces the sample by 17 percent, from 118 to 98 sites.

The areas of all sites were determined from information contained in the survey volume. Maximum length-width measurements were given for most sites. These areas were calculated as .8 length times width. Multiplication by .8 provides an estimate of elliptical site area. In some cases sites were roughly circular, and a diameter was given. In such cases, site areas were calculated with the standard formula for the area of a circle. Occasionally, dimensions of a site were not given in the text, but a sketch map was provided. In these cases a millimeter grid was superimposed over the sketch map and the site area determined by counting the grid squares occupied by the site and applying a scale correction factor to the result. Finally, the Late Uruk occupation of a site could occasionally be localized to a particular portion of the site. All such information was considered in the final site area estimates.

The areal size estimates for the 98 Late Uruk sites under consideration are presented in table 3. This table contains additional information that will be of importance later.

Certain site area estimates require additional comment.

1. Warka: By Early Dynastic times, Warka had reached an areal size of some 400 hectares (Adams and Nissen 1972:18). Its Late Uruk size is, however, unknown. Given the major architectural features of the Late Uruk Level IV at Warka (Lenzen 1968), the site is here assumed to have been quite large, certainly in excess of 30 hectares.

2. WS-198: This is a site of some 114 hectares. Its primary occupation was late Early Dynastic with probable Uruk through Early Dynastic I components. Ceramic wall cones were, however, recovered from its surface. As seen in the earlier discussion of the Susiana area, this is an important artifact type, and for this reason WS-198 was included in the present study. The absence of clear Uruk ceramics from the surface of this site suggests that if it was occupied at all during the Late Uruk phase, the occupation was probably quite small. The site was arbitrarily considered to have been about 5 hectares during Late Uruk.

3. WS-129 and 286: Although both these sites contain definite Late Uruk material, they consist of only surface-level sherd scatters. Both were included in the study and considered to have been small, perhaps on the order of 1 hectare.

Figure 26 presents a histogram of Late Uruk site sizes, WS-129, 198, and 286 have been omitted. Inspection of this histogram suggests that the distribution of site sizes below that of Warka may not be unimodal. I suggest three modal breaks resulting in a four-level site hierarchy. These breaks occur at 2.75, 7.25, and 17.00 hectares. The settlements distinguished by these divisions have been termed: Villages (.01–2.74 hectares), Large Villages (2.75–7.24 hectares), Small Centers (7.25–16.99 hectares), and Large Centers (17.00 hectares and larger). Figure 27 illustrates the Late Uruk settlement pattern incorporating the four-level hierarchy suggested here.

If the actual sizes of the larger Late Uruk sites were known, a case might be made for a five-level hierarchy. Warka was most probably the

TABLE 3
WARKA SURVEY: LATE URUK SITE SIZE, SIZE CLASS,
AND DISTANCE TO NEAREST NEIGHBOR
WITHIN SIZE CLASS

Site	Site Size (ha.)	Size Class	Nearest Neighbor	Distance (km.)
Warka	?	1	242	18.51
125	20.00	1	242	16.99
168	50.27	1	125	20.79
230	42.24	1	125	17.53
242	19.63	1	125	16.99
020	9.60	2	110	18.90
110	8.40	2	201	11.36
163	14.40	2	201	8.75
190	12.00	2	201	3.62
201	8.80	2	190	3.62
282	8.23	2	387	12.64
387	8.74	2	163	11.37
460	8.64	2	387	21.90
009	3.74	3	012	2.87
012	6.16	3	012	2.87
018	4.52	3	166	6.14
042	4.48	3	009	9.98
051	2.84	3	082	6.09
071	3.19	3	109	5.51
082	4.90	3	087	1.95
086	3.33	3	181	2.87
087	6.16	3	082	1.95
109	4.81	3	112	4.02
112	3.80	3	109	4.02
126	3.14	3	051	1.17
127	3.14	3	126	1.17
152	5.28	3	126	2.30
162	4.30	3	218	2.99
166	3.14	3	051	6.14
181	4.52	3	086	2.87
185	3.46	3	191	1.57
191	3.20	3	185	1.57
198	?	3 (assumed)	236	10.54
218	5.15	3	162	2.99
236	3.80	3	198	10.54
245	4.80	3	282	9.86

Site	Site Size (ha.)	Size Class	Nearest Neighbor	Distance (km.)
260	5.76	3	264	2.64
262	2.81	3	264	1.59
376	3.80	3	236	8.94
407	4.44	3	264	11.40
453	2.93	3	376	23.82
028	2.28	4	044	7.87
044	.62	4	060	7.30
048	1.13	4	083	5.45
060	1.44	4	095	5.07
076	1.54	4	083	3.76
083	.88	4	076	3.76
095	.50	4	060	5.07
105	.50	4	133	4.16
106	1.33	4	108	2.21
108	.79	4	106	2.21
114	2.29	4	119	3.03
115	1.33	4	124	2.64
119	1.01	4	124	1.84
120	1.54	4	124	.94
123	1.21	4	129	2.46
124	2.01	4	120	.94
128	1.29	4	153	1.59
129	?	4 (assumed)	123	2.46
133	.19	4	137	2.09
137	1.22	4	144	1.76
139	2.16	4	137	1.57
144	1.60	4	137	1.76
153	1.54	4	128	1.59
160	.64	4	153	4.90
173	2.01	4	178	3.17
178	.58	4	173	3.17
187	.44	4	193	2.30
193	2.40	4	187	2.30
203	.50	4	129	2.60
209	1.13	4	193	7.21
219	1.12	4	160	7.30
237	.73	4	209	8.05
267	.51	4	272	2.63
272	2.20	4	274	1.49
274	.72	4	276	.83
276	1.56	4	274	.83
285	.64	4	286	.70
286	?	4 (assumed)	285	.70

Site	Site Size (ha.)	Size Class	Nearest Neighbor	Distance (km.)
292	.80	4	293	.99
293	1.36	4	292	.99
297	1.30	4	386	1.09
309	.49	4	310	.37
310	.71	4	309	.37
314	.49	4	334	1.62
317	.10	4	318	.41
318	.90	4	317	.41
325	1.67	4	331	1.95
331	.84	4	314	1.62
334	.29	4	314	1.62
338	2.01	4	350	4.76
350	1.57	4	338	4.76
367	2.40	4	237	8.48
386	1.38	4	297	1.09
407	.62	4	318	3.17
417	.22	4	418	2.32
418	.28	4	417	2.32

largest Late Uruk site in the area, and it would occupy the uppermost level of the hierarchy. The second level would then be occupied by WS-125, 168, 230, and 242. For present purposes, however, the proposed four-level division will be maintained. It is assumed that the site areas used in construction of the histogram are at least proportional to the sizes of the actual Late Uruk occupations.

Maximum deviation from this assumption probably occurs in the larger sites, particularly those in the Large Center range. It is unlikely that WS-168 and 230 even approached their indicated sizes during Late Uruk. More probably their areas were on the order of 25 hectares (cf. Adams and Nissen 1972:17, fig. 7).

There are, then, a number of problems involved in accepting the proposed Late Uruk settlement-size hierarchy. As we will see below, however, use of this hierarchy in conjunction with an independently measured variable, site-to-site distance, produces a number of important and testable hypotheses about the locational structure of Late Uruk settlement in the Warka area. This internal consistency of patterning

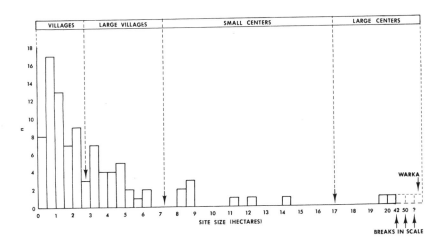

FIGURE 26. WARKA SURVEY LATE URUK SITE AREAS—HISTOGRAM.
Definition of site areal size classes.

in independently measured variables suggests that the proposed settlement hierarchy reflects the actual Late Uruk settlement-size distribution.
In the next section, this relationship between hierarchy and distance
will be considered in detail.

Hierarchy and Distance

The basic principles of a central place model were presented earlier.
One of the implications of this model is that in a settlement system
where efficiency of local exchange or redistribution is a major determinant of settlement location, there should be an inverse relationship
between the number of settlements at each level of the settlement hierarchy and the average nearest-neighbor distance between settlements at
each level of the hierarchy. The Warka area appears to have a four-level
settlement hierarchy in Late Uruk. Large Centers should be spaced
farther apart than Small Centers. Small Centers should be spaced farther apart than Large Villages. Large Villages should be spaced farther
apart than Villages. If the centralized organization of local exchange
were an important factor determining settlement location in the Warka
area, this relationship would be predicted to occur there.

315

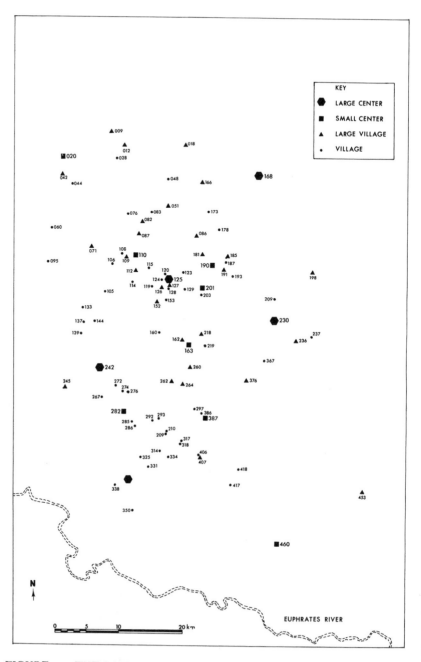

FIGURE 27. THE LATE URUK SETTLEMENT PATTERN IN THE WARKA AREA

This prediction was evaluated as follows. First order nearest-neighbor distances were determined for each settlement within each size class. The linear distance between each Large Center and its closest Large Center neighbor was measured. Similarly, the linear distance between each Small Center and its nearest Small Center neighbor was considered. These measurements were made for each level of the settlement hierarchy. All measurements were made with a vernier caliper from the general survey map presented by Adams and Nissen (1972:2–3). Measurements were made from site center to site center and recorded to .001 cm. These measurements were then converted to kilometers, using the conversion figure of 1.000 cm = .435 km. The resulting data set is presented in table 3 (pages 312–13). Greater accuracy is implied by the distance measurements in this table than can probably be justified. Measurement error should, however, be consistent throughout.

Nearest-neighbor distances were then averaged for each size class. All distance measurements were used for each class, with one exception. The nearest-neighbor distance for a single Large Village (WS-453) was excluded from this portion of the analysis due to the very isolated location of this site in the extreme southeastern corner of the survey area. Table 4 presents the resulting average nearest-neighbor distances for each size class.

TABLE 4
THE LATE URUK SETTLEMENT HIERARCHY
AND ASSOCIATED FIRST ORDER NEAREST-
NEIGHBOR DISTANCES

	n	*Average Distance (km.)*
Large Centers	5	18.16
Small Centers	8	11.52
Large Villages	29	4.58
Villages	56	2.83

Inspection of this table reveals the presence of the predicted inverse relationship. A Spearman's rank correlation coefficient of −1.000 significant at the .05 level was obtained from these four observations. I would conclude that the null hypothesis of no significant inverse relationship between the number of settlements at each level of the settlement hierarchy and the average nearest-neighbor distance between settlements within each level of the hierarchy may be rejected. The presence of the predicted relationship is thus supported.

These hierarchy-distance data have additional interesting implications. The proportional relationships between the number of settlements at each level of the settlement hierarchy will be examined below. Similar relationships between average nearest neighbor distances will also be considered.

The proportion between the number of settlements at a given level of a settlement hierarchy and the number of settlements at the next lower level will be called a bifurcation ratio. For example, if a system had ten Small Centers and thirty Large Villages, the bifurcation ratio between these two settlement levels would be equal to 3.0. These ratios were calculated between each level of the Late Uruk settlement hierarchy. A similar ratio was calculated between the average nearest neighbor distances associated with each settlement level. These ratios are presented in table 5.

TABLE 5
BIFURCATION AND DISTANCE RATIOS

	n	Bifurcation Ratio	Average Distance	Distance Ratio
Large Centers	5		18.16	
		1.60		1.58
Small Centers	8		11.52	
		3.63		2.52
Large Villages	29		4.58	
		1.93		1.62
Villages	56		2.83	

Average Bifurcation Ratio = 2.39
Average Distance Ratio   = 1.91

Both average bifurcation and distance ratios closely approximate a value of 2.00, the closest integer value to each average ratio. It is necessary to recognize that both ratios may incorporate boundary effects which are not controlled in this study.

It is possible, however, to evaluate the significance of the difference between our observed settlement-size distribution and that which would be predicted in a settlement system with a four-level settlement hierarchy, five Large Centers, and a bifurcation ratio of 2.00. The significance of this difference was evaluated with the Kolmogorov-Smirnov two-sample test (Siegel 1956:127 ff.). This nonparametric test focuses on the maximum deviation between two cumulative frequency distributions.

It appears, then, that the Late Uruk settlement hierarchy in the Warka area has a bifurcation ratio essentially equal to 2.00. We will proceed with the assumption that the distance ratio of the system is, as indicated above, also 2.00. These ratios have considerable significance for interpretation of the Late Uruk settlement pattern.

As Adams and Nissen have pointed out (1972:19), the Warka area is hardly a uniform plain. Settlement location must have been highly conditioned by access to irrigation water. Most settlements were on or near natural or artificial watercourses (see Adams and Nissen 1972:13, fig. 3). The results of the analysis described above are consistent with these observations.

Figure 28 illustrates a settlement system having a four-level settlement hierarchy with bifurcation and nearest-neighbor distance ratios of 2.00. The illustrated pattern would seem to be the most efficient solution to these conditions.

This model settlement system and the foregoing analysis suggest that Late Uruk settlement in the Warka area closely followed a highly structured, linear pattern. This linear patterning was apparently most pronounced at the level of a single Large Center and its associated settlements. In the next section a model of the overall locational structure of the Late Uruk settlement in the Warka area will be developed.

The Expected Late Uruk Primary Settlement Lattice

Small sites containing ceramic wall cones among their surface materials were of considerable importance in the analysis and interpretation of the 1970–71 Susiana survey. These sites were interpreted as specialized administrative centers functioning in the mediation of local exchange.

Similar sites having a similar function would be expected in the Warka area if local exchange were also an important factor there. Eleven small

TABLE 6

OBSERVED AND PREDICTED SETTLEMENT-SIZE
DISTRIBUTIONS

	Observed	Predicted
Large Centers	5	5
Small Centers	8	10
Large Villages	29	20
Villages	56	40

TABLE 7

KOLMOGOROV-SMIRNOV TWO-SAMPLE TEST:
OBSERVED VS. PREDICTED SETTLEMENT-
SIZE DISTRIBUTIONS

Formula: $D = \text{maximum } Sn_1(X) - Sn_2(X)$
where: D = the test statistic
$Sn_1(X)$ = the cumulative step function of sample 1
$Sn_2(X)$ = the cumulative step function of sample 2

	Large Centers	Small Centers	Large Villages	Villages
Observed	$\frac{5}{98}$	$\frac{13}{98}$	$\frac{42}{98}$	$\frac{98}{98}$
Predicted	$\frac{5}{75}$	$\frac{15}{75}$	$\frac{35}{75}$	$\frac{75}{75}$
Observed	.051	.133	.429	1.000
Predicted	.067	.200	.467	1.000
Deviation	.016	.067	.038	0.000

$D = .067$, $n_1 = 98$, $n_2 = 75$, p = greater than .10

The null hypothesis of significance difference
between the two distributions is rejected.
The hypothesis of no significant difference
between the two distributions is supported.

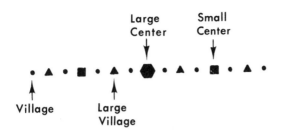

FIGURE 28. SETTLEMENT SYSTEM WITH A FOUR-LEVEL SETTLE-
MENT HIERARCHY. Bifurcation and distance ratios equal 2.00.

sites with ceramic wall cones were noted by Adams and Nissen on the
Warka survey (1972:211). If their function was similar to that suggested
on the Susiana, they should have been located at nodal points on local
exchange routes between Large Centers.

As shown above, the settlement pattern for single Large Centers and
associated settlements was basically linear. How then did small cone
sites fit into this linear patterning? Table 8 presents data on distances
between small cone sites and nearest neighboring Large Centers.

TABLE 8
DISTANCE FROM SMALL CONE SITES TO NEAREST
NEIGHBORING LARGE CENTERS

Site	Large Center	Distance (km.)
082	125	9.62
133	242	9.30
181	125	6.23
198	230	9.17
218	125	9.62
219	230	11.33
245	242	6.10
260	125	13.48
293	Warka	10.39
406	Warka	11.61
407	Warka	11.61

n = 11, Average Distance = 9.86 kilometers

The average nearest-neighbor distance between small cone sites and Large Centers was 9.86 kilometers. The expected distance between Small Centers was 9.08 kilometers. Given our linear model, the expected distance between Small Centers and Large Centers was 4.54 kilometers. This is very close to one-half (.47) of the average observed distance between cone sites and Large Centers. There were 5 Large Centers and 11 small cone sites, or 2.2 (2.0) small cone sites for each Large Center. These observations allow incorporation of small cone sites into our linear model as illustrated in figure 29.

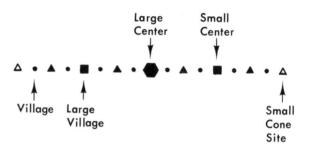

FIGURE 29. THE LOCATION OF SMALL CONE SITES IN THE MODEL LATE URUK SETTLEMENT SYSTEM OF A SINGLE LARGE CENTER AND ASSOCIATED SETTLEMENTS

Note that small cone sites are entered into the model at the Large Village size range, the only size possible if the specified pattern of alternating settlement sizes is to be maintained. Table 9 presents the actual sizes and size classifications of these 11 sites. Of the 11 sites considered, 7 are of the predicted size class. The significance of this association may be tested with the Chi-Square statistic (see table 10).

In figure 29 small cone sites were incorporated into the linear settlement pattern model for a single Large Center. The size of these settlements was predicted by the model. Their addition does, however, alter the bifurcation and distance ratios of the linear pattern. This change would seem to reflect the special function of small cone sites rather than indicate a significant deviation from the settlement pattern model employed.

We are now in a position to consider the basic locational structure of the Warka area as a whole. This analysis will focus on the relative

TABLE 9

SMALL CONE SITES: SIZES AND SIZE CLASSES

Site	Size (ha.)	Size Class
082	4.90	Large Village
133	.19	Village
181	4.52	Large Village
198	?	Large Village (assumed)
218	5.15	Large Village
219	1.12	Village
245	4.80	Large Village
260	5.76	Large Village
293	1.36	Village
406	.62	Village
407	4.44	Large Village

TABLE 10

CHI-SQUARE TEST: CERAMIC WALL CONES VS. SITE SIZE

	Large Villages	Villages	Marginal Totals
Cones	7	4	11
No Cones	22	52	74
Marginal Totals	29	56	85

Formula: $X^2 = \sum_{n}^{1} \dfrac{(Ob\text{-}Ex)^2}{Ex}$ where: X^2 = the test statistic

Ob = observed frequencies

Ex = expected frequencies under conditions of random association

Result: $X^2 = 4.91$

df = 1

p = less than .05

Conclusion: The null hypothesis of no significant association between ceramic wall cones and Large Villages is rejected. The hypothesis of significant association between ceramic wall cones and Large Villages is supported.

distributions of Large Centers and small cone sites as the nodal points of a proposed settlement lattice.

Recall that Large Centers were spaced an average of 18.16 kilometers apart; that small cone sites were located at an average of 9.86 (9.08 km.; see p. 322) kilometers from Large Centers; and that there were about 2 (2.2) small cone sites for each Large Center in the area. Figure 30 presents a model primary settlement lattice based on these considerations, and the actual primary settlement lattice proposed for the Warka area.

It is important to remember that the spatial relationships in the model (expected) lattice are completely derived from the spatial relationships observed in the Warka area. Site numbers are indicated on both the expected and observed lattice to facilitate their comparison. Additional sites which would be expected north of WS-168 and south of Warka have been deleted from the expected distribution and represent the only deviation from that model.

The expected settlement lattice would seem to represent the basic locational structure of the observed settlement distribution if irregularities of topography and watercourse distribution were removed. Note that the expected lattice has the hexagonal structure characteristic of central place–type distributions. It would appear that linear settlement distributions, highly conditioned by access to natural or artifical watercourses, are consistent with hexagonal settlement distributions. The Late Uruk settlement of the Warka area is the case in point.

It would further appear that a highly structured organization of local exchange was an important factor in determination of settlement location in the Warka area. This hypothesis was derived from a locational analysis of settlement size and distribution in the Warka area, and may be tentatively tested with independent artifactual data collected on the Warka Survey.

Local Exchange–Hypothesis Testing

The hypothesis that small Uruk sites with elaborated architecture evidenced by the presence of ceramic wall cones functioned as small specialized administrative centers in the mediation of local exchange was first developed and tested during analysis of the 1970–71 Susiana survey. We have seen that similar sites occur in the Warka area and that their

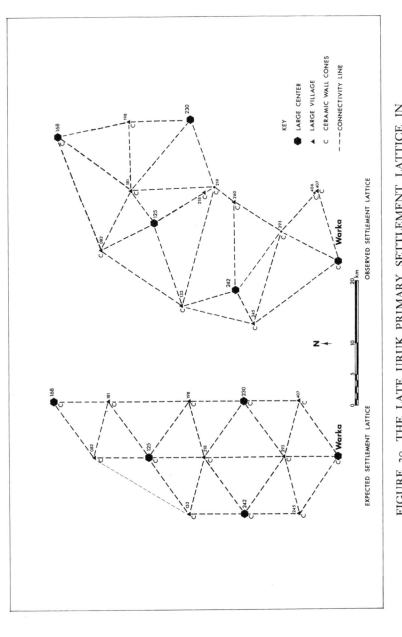

EXPECTED SETTLEMENT LATTICE

OBSERVED SETTLEMENT LATTICE

KEY
● LARGE CENTER
▲ LARGE VILLAGE
C CERAMIC WALL CONES
--- CONNECTIVITY LINE

FIGURE 30. THE LATE URUK PRIMARY SETTLEMENT LATTICE IN
THE WARKA AREA

spatial distribution is consistent with the hypothesis outlined above. Data presented by Adams and Nissen (1972) make a further test of this hypothesis possible.

If small cone sites functioned as specialized administrative centers for the mediation of local exchange, then they should also have been nodes on an exchange or transport lattice, as was discussed above. If they were nodes on a transport lattice, a greater volume of goods should have passed through these sites than through small sites located elsewhere. Assuming equal loss and/or discard rates on all sites, the greater volume of material moving through small cone sites should be reflected by a greater density of lost or discarded material. This also assumes that density of surface materials is at least proportional to the actual material density in a site.

Perishable materials are not to be expected among surface collections. This leaves nonperishable material, primarily lithics and ceramics. Ceramic vessels have already been used for chronological purposes and will be excluded from consideration. There remain a number of relatively rare artifact types recorded during the Warka survey and reported in the 1972 volume. Assuming that at least a significant proportion of craft production was carried out in centralized workshops of Large Centers, a significant proportion of these rare artifacts should be workshop products, and as such have been incorporated in the local exchange network.

Given these assumptions, the present hypothesis would then yield the prediction that small cone sites should have a significantly greater density of these other rare artifact types than should small sites without cones. Data are not available to evaluate differential artifact density. I suggest a possible substitute in artifact diversity. If this substitution is made, the prediction states that small cone sites should have a greater variety of rare artifact types on their surface than do small sites without cones. This is a testable prediction given the available data.

Adams and Nissen tabulate rare finds of the Warka survey on pages 205–17 of the 1972 report. Certain artifact types were initially excluded from consideration due to their extreme rarity. These included pot stands, clay wheels, U-shaped troughs, concentrations of flint implements, and a number of other types represented by one or two examples. Clay sickles, on the other hand, were considered too common for inclusion. Bent clay "nails" were omitted because of their primary affiliation with 'Ubaid sites.

Nine basic artifact types remained and were included in the analysis as follows. All stone vessels, mace-heads, and wall cones occurring on sites with Late Uruk occupations were included in the analysis. The two types of net weights distinguished by Adams and Nissen were combined as a single type to increase their sample size and included. Stone and clay hoes, as well as all metal objects, were combined for the same reason and included. These combinations resulted in final consideration of seven rare artifact types.

These seven types were then tabulated by the sites where they were found. As the prediction is focused on smaller sites rather than on Large Centers, the latter were excluded. The resulting data set is presented in table 11 and contains observations on the presence-absence of each of these seven rare artifact types at 52 Late Uruk sites in the Warka area.

The number of rare types occurring on each site was determined from the data table. The average number of rare artifact types present on sites where cones were present was then calculated. A similar average was calculated for those sites where cones were absent. If the prediction discussed above is correct, sites with cones should have a significantly greater average number of rare artifact types on their surfaces than should sites without cones. Although none of the types considered is temporally restricted to Late Uruk, it is assumed that their distribution is at least reflective of Late Uruk depositional patterns.

Ceramic wall cones occurred on 11 sites. These sites had an average rare artifact type count of 2.27. Cones did not occur on 41 sites. These sites had an average rare artifact type count of 1.49. Sites with cones thus do have a greater variety of rare artifacts than do sites without cones.

The significance of this difference can be evaluated with the Mann-Whitney U test (Siegel 1956:166 ff.). This is a nonparametric difference-of-means test, the results of which are given in table 12.

The prediction that small cone sites should have a significantly greater number of rare artifact types on their surfaces than do sites without ceramic wall cones is confirmed. The hypothesis that small cone sites functioned as specialized administrative centers in the mediation of local exchange is supported.

Similar tests were run for each of the six remaining rare artifact types to investigate their possible differential patterning. Table 13 presents average rare artifact type counts for sites with and without each of the

TABLE 11

PRESENCE-ABSENCE OF RARE ARTIFACT TYPES
IN SURFACE COLLECTIONS FROM LATE URUK
SITES IN THE WARKA AREA

Site	Cone	Spindle Whorl	Mace-head	Net Weight	Metal	Stone Vessel	Hoe
260	x	x	x				
218	x			x			x
133	x						
181	x	x					
219	x	x	x	x		x	
406	x				x		
082	x	x				x	
245	x						x
293	x						
407	x	x					
198	x						
137		x				x	
274		x	x		x		
109			x			x	x
152			x				
129			x				
262			x			x	
162			x		x	x	
276			x			x	
042				x			
110				x			
201				x			
020				x		x	
191				x		x	
219				x			
297				x		x	x
028				x		x	
048				x			
282				x		x	
185					x		
087					x		
285					x		
314					x	x	
272					x		
160						x	
386						x	x
193						x	x
331						x	
087						x	
144						x	

328

Site	Cone	Spindle Whorl	Mace-head	Net Weight	Metal	Stone Vessel	Hoe
163						x	
181						x	
267						x	x
292						x	x
310						x	
317						x	
334						x	
264						x	
272						x	
387						x	
051							x
460							x

TABLE 12
MANN-WHITNEY U TEST: AVERAGE RARE ARTIFACT TYPE COUNT, SMALL CONE SITES VS. OTHER SITES

Formula: $U = n_1 n_2 + \dfrac{n_1(n_1 + 1)}{2} - R_1$

where: U = the test statistic

n_1 = number of observations in the smaller of the two data sets being compared

n_2 = number of observations in the larger data set

R_1 = sum of ranks assigned to observations of set n_1 in a descending array of ranks in which both n_1 and n_2 are included

Evaluation of Significance: When dealing with large samples (n_2 = more than 20) the test statistic may be evaluated in terms of areas under a normal curve. Evaluation is made through use of a Z score.

Formula: $Z = \dfrac{U - \dfrac{n_1 n_2}{2}}{\sqrt{\dfrac{(n_1)(n_2)(n_1 + n_2 + 1)}{12}}}$

Results: $n_1 = 11$

$n_2 = 41$ $Z = -2.108$

$R_1 = 385.5$ p = ca. .018 (one tailed)

$U = 131.5$

Conclusion: The null hypothesis of no significant difference between average rare type counts is rejected. The hypothesis of significant difference between average rare type counts is supported.

seven rare artifact types under consideration. Table 14 presents the results of Mann-Whitney U tests for each artifact type.

Mace-heads, spindle whorls, and hoes, as well as cones, are significant predictors of diversity of rare artifact types in Late Uruk surface collections. A series of Chi-Square tests were made to evaluate possible redun-

TABLE 13
AVERAGE RARE ARTIFACT TYPE COUNTS:
SAMPLE DIVISION BY PRESENCE-ABSENCE
OF SEVEN RARE ARTIFACT TYPES

	Wall Cones	Mace- heads	Spindle Whorl	Hoes	Metal	Stone Vessels	Net Weights
n present	11	9	7	10	8	29	12
$\overline{X}$ types present	2.27	2.55	2.12	2.10	1.75	1.82	2.00
n absent	41	43	45	42	44	23	40
$\overline{X}$ types present	1.49	1.47	1.47	1.54	1.64	1.43	1.55

TABLE 14
MANN-WHITNEY U TESTS: AVERAGE RARE ARTIFACT
TYPE COUNTS—SAMPLE DIVISION BY PRESENCE-
ABSENCE OF SEVEN RARE ARTIFACT TYPES

	n_1	n_2	R_1	U	Z	p
Wall Cones	11	41	385.5	131.5	-2.108	.018
Mace- heads	9	43	346.0	86.0	-2.600	.005
Spindle Whorls	7	45	305.5	37.5	-3.218	.001
Hoes	10	42	355.5	119.5	-2.100	.018
Metal	8	44	227.0	161.0	-0.380	.352
Stone Vessels	23	29	552.0	391.0	1.059	.145
Net Weights	12	40	366.5	221.5	-0.402	.337

dancy in prediction. Which, if any, of these four types are significantly associated with one another? Table 15 presents the results of this associational analysis.

TABLE 15
CHI-SQUARE TESTS FOR ASSOCIATIONS OF
FOUR RARE ARTIFACT TYPES

Types	n	X²	df	p
Cones: Mace-heads	52	.130	1	greater than .70
Cones: Spindle Whorls	52	9.025	1	less than .01
Cones: Hoes	52	.104	1	greater than .70
Mace-: Spindle heads Whorls	52	.097	1	greater than .70
Mace-: Hoes heads	52	.045	1	greater than .70
Spindle: Hoes Whorls	52	do not co-occur		

The only types significantly associated with one another are wall cones and spindle whorls. Mace-heads and hoes vary independently. An explanation for the behavior of wall cones was given above. Of the types under consideration, spindle whorls would seem to have been the item most consistently involved in the Late Uruk local exchange network. The results on mace-heads and hoes suggest the presence of other important and spatially differentiated activity sets.

The major importance of this section of the analysis is that our hypothesis relative to the functional significance of small cone sites has been tested with independent data and supported. A general discussion of the Late Uruk settlement system in the Warka area is presented in the next section.

The Late Uruk Settlement System

The results of the analysis thus far are presented in figure 31, which illustrates the Late Uruk settlement system proposed for the Warka

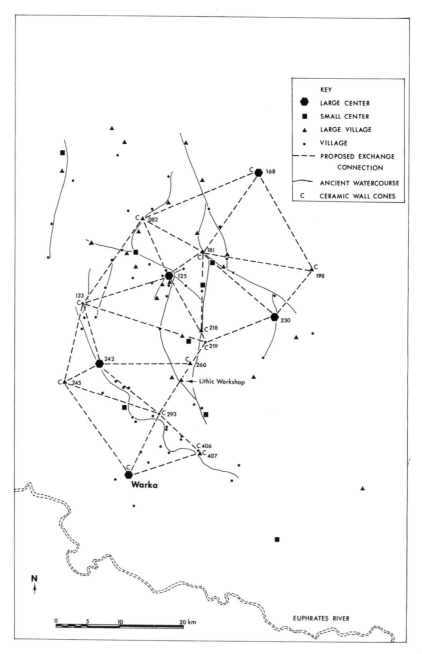

FIGURE 31. THE LATE URUK SETTLEMENT SYSTEM IN THE WARKA AREA

area. The four-level settlement hierarchy and primary settlement lattice are supplemented by the system of watercourses suggested by Adams and Nissen (1972:13, fig. 3.).

Most settlements are located on or near both watercourses and proposed exchange connections between Large Centers. This distribution would be predicted by our settlement model. There are, however, additional points of interest.

Note the location of the single lithic workshop found on the Warka survey and located on WS-264 (Adams and Nissen 1972:230). WS-264 is a predominantly Late Uruk site and is located virtually equidistant from four of the five Large Centers in the Warka area. Table 16 presents distances from this workshop site to Warka, WS-242, 125, and 230 measured along the proposed exchange connections indicated on figure 31.

TABLE 16
DISTANCES FROM THE LITHIC WORKSHOP AT WS-264
TO FOUR LATE URUK LARGE CENTERS

From	Through	To	Distance (km.)
264	293	Warka	16.70
264	260	242	16.78
264	260, 219, 218	125	18.09
264	260, 219	230	17.96

These distances are very nearly equal to one another, the difference between the shortest and longest distance being only 1.39 kilometers. This is in fact a slight improvement in uniformity over linear distances between WS-264 and these four Large Centers (see table 17).

The difference between the shortest and longest simple linear distance is thus 1.74 kilometers, or .35 kilometers greater than that for distances measured along theoretically proposed exchange connections. The proposed system of exchange connections does not impair and may even improve the centrality of this site.

The lithic workshop at WS-264 is thus located in a near maximally efficient position for distribution of its products to four of the five Late Uruk Large Centers in the Warka area. The fifth Large Center, WS-168,

TABLE 17
SIMPLE LINEAR DISTANCES BETWEEN THE
LITHIC WORKSHOP AT WS-264 AND FOUR
LATE URUK LARGE CENTERS

From	To	Distance (km.)
264	Warka	16.68
264	242	15.34
264	125	15.91
264	230	17.08

is farther removed from this workshop location. Remember, however, that we are dealing with an open system. WS-168 is located near the northern boundary of the Warka Survey and may well be associated with settlements outside of that area. An important point here is that the location of the workshop at WS-264 is consistent with, and provides additional support for, the proposed exchange relationships within the Warka area.

The location of this site is important in another respect. Examination of differential association among the rare artifact types discussed above suggested that the structure of local exchange in the area may have been considerably more complex than indicated by our Large Center–small cone site lattice. The location of a lithic workshop in a small settlement nearly equidistant from a series of Large Centers reinforces this observation. We seem to be dealing with a distinct exchange subsystem organized quite differently from the overall exchange system of the area. It is probably safe to predict that further research will reveal additional such subsystems. The structure to which I blithely refer as *the* local exchange system of the area will then appear as a complicated network of overlapping and interdigitated subsystems.

Additional features of the overall Late Uruk settlement pattern are of interest. Examination of figure 31 reveals that most of the reflexive nearest-neighbor settlement pairs noted by Adams and Nissen occur in Village-size settlements. Their interpretation of this binary pattern is consistent with the locational relationships brought out in this study.

The marked tendency for settlement agglomeration brought out by Adams and Nissen is also evident in examination of figure 31. A number

334

of these settlement clusters occur in the general area of WS-125, one of the five Large Centers defined above. Three of these clusters are of particular interest.

Note the tight group of smaller settlements in the immediate vicinity of WS-125, as well as the radial pattern of watercourses around this site. This would appear to be a case in which a Large Center directly controlled access to irrigation water by its immediately associated settlements.

Two additional clusters are located northeast and southeast of WS-125. Note that each cluster is located in the immediate area of a small cone site which marks the intersection of the complementary regions of three Large Centers. Presumably, critical nodal points such as these would be characterized by relatively intense economic activity and would thus be differentially selected for settlement location. Such hypotheses as these remain to be tested with additional fieldwork.

Though a large proportion of the variance in Late Uruk settlement location remains unexplained, the present analysis in combination with that of Adams and Nissen is able to account for a number of regularities in settlement size, settlement spacing, and differential artifact distribution. Furthermore, the results of this analysis are consistent with those obtained from an independent data set, the 1970–71 Susiana survey.

The major conclusion to be drawn from this restudy of the Warka area Late Uruk settlement pattern is that, at least by Late Uruk, the organization of local exchange was a significant factor in determination of settlement locations. The complexity of the settlement hierarchy suggests a complex administrative hierarchy, one of the functions of which was control of local exchange. It also appears that most of the settlements in the Warka area were linked in a single exchange system. Whether or not this exchange system had a political analogue is a question for future research.

SUMMARY AND CONCLUSIONS

The most striking parallels evident here are between the Middle Uruk occupation of the Susiana and the Late Uruk occupation of the Warka area. Both areas apparently contained a four-level settlement-size hierarchy. Given our assumptions, a high degree of functional complexity is indicated.

Both areas exhibit settlement distributions of the sort described by our central place model. It was proposed that the operation of a local exchange system was a major factor in the determination of these patterns.

In both areas, small sites with associated ceramic wall cones were located at apparently critical points in a local exchange network. It was proposed that these sites functioned, at least in part, as specialized administrative centers for the mediation of local exchange.

In both areas, differential artifact distributions provided a partial test of hypotheses derived from locational considerations. These distributions were consistent both with the general operation of complex local exchange systems and with the functions of small cone sites as specialized administrative centers.

Finally, the location of specialized lithic workshops on small settlements removed from Large Centers suggested the operation of distinct exchange subsystems within the overall local exchange system of both areas.

The most important differences between the settlement systems of these two areas were primarily ones of scale. The number of settlements, density of settlements, and size of settlements were all of a higher order of magnitude in the Warka area than on the Susiana. The greater regularity of patterning in the Warka area probably indicates the operation of a more complex and/or intensive local exchange system there. The presence of comparatively fewer boundary effects may also have contributed to this more regular patterning.

The Late Uruk local exchange system in the Warka area would appear to have been more complex than that operative during Middle Uruk on the Susiana. Earlier developments in the Warka area require further investigation.

I have dealt elsewhere with the problem of the apparent breakdown of the Middle Uruk settlement system on the Susiana during Late Uruk. I suggested that this breakdown was related to the inability of the Middle Uruk political organization in the area to deal with increasing administrative requirements of a newly emergent primary state. I also suggested that by Late Uruk, developments throughout Greater Mesopotamia were becoming highly interrelated, and that a portion of the expansion of the Warka system may have occurred at the expense of the Susiana system (Johnson 1973:143 ff.).

The results obtained from analysis of these independent data sets are markedly similar and mutually supportive. It is becoming increasingly clear that use of locational models can be a useful hypothesis-generating technique in the analysis of archaeological settlement patterns. It is also clear that manipulation of settlement data and surface collections must be supplemented by excavation programs designed to test much more fully the hypotheses generated by locational analysis.

This is particularly the case when dealing with the Uruk Period, for which even such basic problems as relative chronology require further work. We are, however, beginning to understand something of the complexity of this early civilization.

NOTES

1. In addition to the other contributors to this volume, I would like to thank the following persons for their comments on earlier drafts of this chapter: John Alden (the University of Michigan), Frank Hole (Rice University), Charles Sheffer (Temple University), John Speth (Hunter College), and Robert Whallon, Jr. (the University of Michigan). The Susiana survey discussed in this chapter was conducted as part of the Southwest Iran Project of the University of Michigan Museum of Anthropology, directed by Henry T. Wright and supported by National Science Foundation Grant GS-3147. Figures 18–25 are here reproduced from the University of Michigan Museum of Anthropology, Anthropological Papers No. 51.

References

ADAMS, ROBERT McC.
1972 "Patterns of Urbanization in Early Southern Mesopotamia," in *Man, Settlement and Urbanism*, ed. Peter J. Ucko, Ruth Tringham, and G. W. Dimbleby, (London: Gerald Duckworth and Co.).

ADAMS, ROBERT McC. AND HANS J. NISSEN
1972 *The Uruk Countryside* (Chicago: University of Chicago Press).

BERRY, BRIAN J. L.
1961 "City Size Distributions and Economic Development," *Economic Development and Cultural Change* 9:574–87.

BERRY, BRIAN J. L. AND WILLIAM L. GARRISON
1958 "Alternate Explanations of Urban Rank-Size Relationships," *Annals of the Association of American Geographers* 48:83–91.

CHRISTALLER, WALTER
1966 *Central Places in Southern Germany* (Englewood Cliffs, N. J.: Prentice-Hall). Translation by Carlisle W. Baskin of *Die zentralen Orte in Süddeutschland*, 1933.

CLARKE, DAVID L.
1972 "Models and Paradigms in Contemporary Archaeology," in *Models in Archaeology*, ed. David L. Clarke (London: Methuen & Co.).

GARNER, B. J.
1967 "Models of Urban Geography and Settlement Location," in *Models in Geography*, ed. Richard J. Chorley and Peter Haggett (London: Methuen & Co.).

GREMLIZA, F. G. L.
1962 *Ecology of Endemic Diseases in the Dez Irrigation Pilot Area* (New York: Development and Resources Corp.).

HAGGETT, PETER
1966 *Locational Analysis in Human Geography* (New York: St. Martin's Press).

ISARD, WALTER
1956 *Location and Space-Economy* (Cambridge, Mass.: M.I.T. Press).

JOHNSON, GREGORY A.
1973 *Local Exchange and Early State Development in Southwestern Iran*. The University of Michigan Museum of Anthropology, Anthropological Papers No. 51 (Ann Arbor).

KOCHEN, MANFRED AND KARL W. DEUTSCH
1970 "Decentralization and Uneven Service Loads," *Journal of Regional Science* 10:153–73.

LENZEN, HEINRICH J.
1968 XXXIV. *vorläufiger Bericht uber die von dem Deutschen Archäologischen Institut und der Deutschen Orient-Gesellschaft aus Mitteln der Forschungs-*

gemeinschaft unternommenen Ausgrabungen in Uruk-Warka (Berlin: Gebr. Mann Verlag).

LÖSCH, AUGUST

1954 *The Economics of Location* (New Haven: Yale University Press).

OLSSON, GUNNAR

1965 *Distance and Human Interaction: A Review and Bibliography.* Regional Science Research Institute Bibliography Series No. 2 (Philadelphia).

NISSEN, HANS J.

1970 "Grabung in den Quadraten K/L XII in Uruk-Warka," *Baghdader Mitteilungen* 5:102–91.

REDMAN, CHARLES AND PATTY JO WATSON

1970 "Systematic, Intensive Surface Collections," *American Antiquity* 25:279–91.

ROWLANDS, J. J.

1972 "Defense: A Factor in the Organization of Settlements," in *Man, Settlement and Urbanism*, ed. Peter Ucko, Ruth Tringham, and G. W. Dimbleby (London: Gerald Duckworth & Co.).

SAHLINS, MARSHALL

1972 *Stone Age Economics* (Chicago: Aldine-Atherton).

SCHACHT, ROBERT MARSHALL

1972 "Population and Economic Organization in Early Historic Southwest Iran," Ph.D. dissertation, University of Michigan, Department of Anthropology.

SIEGEL, S.

1956 *Nonparametric Statistics for the Behavioral Sciences* (New York: McGraw-Hill).

WHALLON, ROBERT JR.

1969 "Early Bronze Age Development in the Keban Reservoir, East-Central Turkey," *Current Anthropology* 10:128–33.

8

Third Millennium Modes
of Exchange and
Modes of Production

C. C. LAMBERG-KARLOVSKY

Harvard University

"Let us begin by laying the facts aside, as they do not affect the
Question."   —J. J. Rousseau

INTRODUCTION

Every dynamic system in physics that is pursued in detail is governed
by the quantum principle, which states in brief that one can never predict deterministically how a system will change in the future. To be
able to do so one must know two things: what the system is doing at
the present and how fast it is changing. The quantum principle says
that you cannot know both simultaneously in nature; hence the principle of indeterminism. Archaeologists, however, not being physicists,

believe that through the adoption of particular methods—namely, simulation models—they can define the exact role of trade in the past, as well as its evolutionary trajectory. More often than not such attempts provide classifications of assumed trade structures, each implying and often explicitly correlated with different sociopolitical structures. Such an approach is as fallacious as an attempt to classify words and derive meaning. A number of papers recently published on prehistoric trade provide an evolutionary schema for the development of exchange mechanisms (Beale 1973), a typology of trade which assumes that a certain social organization is either determined by or determines the trade mechanism. Thus, a certain type of exchange (i.e. reciprocity) is believed to be correlated with types of institutional configurations (i.e. egalitarianism); or alternatively, the sociopolitical framework (i.e. the temple-palace administration) determines the type of exchange mechanism (i.e. redistribution). It is all violently deterministic and mechanistic. Just as often the reconstructed mechanism and function of prehistoric trade are legitimized by that most circular of reasonings: ethnographic analogy. Archaeological data bearing on a trade situation are compared to a situation assumed to be historically or ethnographically analogous. The archaeological data are ordered so as to appear a perfect fit, more often than not within an evolutionary framework, and thus they enable the prehistoric condition to be reckoned as comprehensible (cf. Flannery 1968). Though ethnographic analogy is clearly helpful in providing insights, we should not be deceived into believing comforting a priori models which are set up as self-fulfilling prophecies. I am not attempting to present a catalog of errors but rather to define a certain attitude.

It is all too easy to generalize toward an appealing hypothesis, construct ideal types to which the data are made to conform, or construct research designs and test hypotheses far removed from the reality of the data. A case in point is the recent attempt to establish the rise of chiefdoms in the Near East as having first taken place during Halaf times (Watson 1973). A series of definitions and conjectures are presented—speculations on the evolution of chiefdoms in the Near East. Following this presentation of conjectural philosophy, the data of the Halaf are "tested" to fit the model, and thus the Halaf culture is supposed to represent the first chiefdom in the Near East. Even leaving aside the circularity of this reasoning, one may fairly ask why the same criteria eliminate the earlier Hassuna culture, or even seventh millennium Çatal Hüyük, from the stage of chiefdom. It seems to me that attempting to isolate self-defined attributes for the rise of the chiefdom or state is a lateral step from Childe's earlier attempt to define criteria for the stage of the urban revolution, an exercise in presenting evolutionary stages rather than in proving developmental processes. The fact that such presentations are argued as deductive tests of hypotheses does not mask the fact that the results represent, in the final determination, the type of conjectural cultural evolution and narrative history best exemplified in the works of Condorcet, Morgan, and Marx. In fact this type of historical narration is totally rejected by historians today (Hexter 1971).

Prehistoric trade is frequently perceived as a dependent variable; its supposed evolutionary development is linked to an equally hypothesized scaling of the sociopolitical order. Thus supply and demand are not believed to be operating, insofar as price is concerned, in a band, for that "type" of sociopolitical order—the band—has yet to concern itself with such formal economic matters as supply, demand, price, and the like. Such concerns are theoretically reserved for the higher rungs of the evolutionary ladder, such as the state. The presence of a formal logic of assumed aspects of cultural evolution, such as bands, correlated with equally fixed formal structures, such as reciprocity, or negatively correlated with others, such as supply and demand, has produced a rigid implicit belief that certain structures or types of social organization are to be correlated, or are not to be, with aspects of social, economic, and political organization. It is perhaps time to establish conceptions and models that address themselves to the internal structure and logic of the archaeological data and to develop categories consistent with the integrity of those data. The latter part of this chapter will discuss early third and late fourth millennium market networks between Mesopotamia and the Iranian Plateau. We will attempt to understand the market networks without resorting to analogies far removed from the data in space and time; we will not present conjectural ideas on the evolutionary development of market networks from assumed earlier or later stages. Instead, we shall attempt to penetrate the distinctive form and structure of the market networks which characterized Mesopotamia and the Iranian Plateau, a form which may be analogous to other forms or structures but which is inherently interesting because of its distinctiveness. Only an awareness of the distinctive character of the market-network structure at one time enables one to trace its development from, or contrast it with, earlier or later forms. Intensive study of one system gives us a far greater opportunity to compare or contrast comparable sets of data and ultimately to understand better the entire system at one time, as well as its development.

It is apparent that modes of exchange are generally correlated with modes of production, not in terms of one-to-one correlations but only in the sense of predominant rather than exclusive types. Thus where specialization is minimal and output restricted, group exchanges are believed to be conducted principally through reciprocity. Furthermore, in such reciprocal exchanges the flow of services, products, and labor is not usually dependent on counterflow. Supply, demand, prices, wages, and the like are considered to be of little relevance at this stage of evolutionary development. This generally accepted anthropological picture is adopted by archaeologists in discussing the evolution of trade from one of egalitarian reciprocity (with strong kinship ties) to the development of state capitalism. The adoption of such hypotheses, which are implicitly assumed without testing, has led to exclusive types of correlations, providing fuel for the belief in the rigidity of assumed evolutionary conditions. That such types of exchanges as reciprocity are not totally free from fluctuations of supply, demand, and price-fixing have only recently been acknowledged (Sahlins 1965:95–129; 1972). Thus, in the southwest Pacific, reciprocal exchanges between partners follow certain agreed ratios; in the form of mutual reciprocal exchange, for example, two spears are roughly equivalent to one axe. In one-way exchange, however, the value will change to the favor of those who pay the service of traveling. Furthermore, when the balance of supply and demand is disturbed, the less favored partner will expect to alter the exchange ratio; if he fails to do so, a new partner will be found who can fulfill the demand. And when supplies increase, producers overpay their partners without the immediate expectation of congruent increasing returns. The point is that archaeologists have adopted as valid rigidly exclusive models of economic behavior which are constructed as

344

evolutionary types directed from the simple to the complex. There are not different kinds of economies; all economies belong to a single category of human behavior: the need to exchange goods and services, which can be perceived as a continuum with market at one extreme and reciprocal exchange at the other.

In Mesopotamia, reciprocal exchange precedes the "stage" of redistribution, believed to be characterized by the nonmarket temple-palace complex. In neither reciprocity nor redistribution are profit, price-fixing, wholesaling, supply-demand, or even private ownership of land for surplus production thought to play a significant role. Our case study is but one of a number of recent studies which point to the inadequacy of this view (Adams 1972; Gelb 1969; Veenhof 1972). It is the central thesis of the second part of this chapter that all of the above existed in a market network at least by the end of the fourth millennium in Mesopotamia. By a market network I mean the processes of institutionalized transactions of commodities and services channeled from an area of high supply to one of high demand. An institutional transaction does not imply static price or definite exchange relationships but refers to the mechanism regulating the exchange relationship. Thus supplies in one area follow prescribed routes (transportation facility, profit orientation) to fulfill the demands of another area. At the same time the feedback (profit, rate, and so forth) is stimulating further productivities in opposite directions through the same network. This type of exchange may pass through a special area called a "market." The presence or absence of a physical marketplace is irrelevant, for a market exchange is but a small part of a market network. A market network is concerned not with circumscribing a marketplace but with conceptualizing a state of affairs. The question of how large an area can be circumscribed in the market network is discussed in the second part of this chapter.

The measurement of a market network involves several interdependent variables:

1. A *state of supply:* the production of a natural or artificial surplus which is transmitted to meet a demand.

2. A *state of demand:* the need for goods and services initiates the conditions of economic behavior, the reallocation of these goods and services.

3. *A state of communication:* the means of transporting commodities and transmitting goods, services, and information (the feedback).

4. *The nature and conditions of the transaction:* durability of commodities which circumscribe the area and range of the market network; aspects of storage; and political and social environment of the transaction.

All of these aspects of the market network are interdependent: Information regarding the demand stimulates supply, facility of transportation and durability of the commodity determine the range of the market network, and so forth. Our goal should be to undertake a structural analysis of the market network with a view toward constructing models that maximize the understanding of the distinctive form of the market network being studied. In their concern for evolutionary development, archaeologists have concentrated heavily on understanding developmental mechanisms of trade. They have, however, failed to understand in depth the structure of prehistoric trade at any given time. Thus we have long been interested not in what is but in what it is in the process of becoming. In order to determine how a structure changes, it is necessary first to understand the structure itself. Too often we move directly to the higher level of abstraction, simply assuming a reality to the structure itself. In this case study, we assume no developmental or evolutionary trends; we examine the structure in an attempt to provide an understanding, both synchronic and diachronic, of the complexities of a market network. In the course of our examination a number of trajectories become evident whose causes and directions will demand independent analysis. A study of the structure of a market network removes itself from functionalist empiricism, wherein groups of individuals are presumed to be integrated (to the extent that different relations are assumed to be functionally compatible). Only after studying the internal logic of a given market network can one establish theories of value, demand, profit, surplus, and the like, and their role in the total framework of social behavior. One must also be wary of the sleight of hand of the neo-evolutionists who, in adopting systemic approaches, find readily reducible the irreducibly contingent nature of historical systems.

In archaeology, a cultural-ecological approach would construct a market network as a particular system functionally bound by an ecological

346

adaptation. Instead of determination by the social system, we have determination by the environment. Such forms of ecological determinism
invoke a secret rationale of adaptive advantages to explain distinct social
organizations and occurrences such as bands or the rise of the state. This
approach quickly leads to truisms, absurdities, poor philosophy, and bad
science. Given the existence of a cultural system, it is tautological to say
that a variable is adaptive because it fulfills a function in the total system. Adaptive advantage in economic or ecological matters is indeter-
minate; it indicates what may be possible, but it renders suitable all
that is possible. Neo-evolutionary cultural ecologists have not discussed
in detail, much less observed, what happens when an economic system
goes from A to B beyond positing as explanation an adaptive change of
the culture to the environment (or the reverse). In the last analysis,
archaeological data may not allow us to uncover the mainsprings of
economic processes. Adam Smith was not far from wrong when he
wrote that only through the understanding of the psychology of man
can the drives and impulses of the economic process be uncovered. The
very thesis of *The Wealth of Nations* was derived from a fundamental,
universal element which Smith found a constant in ethnographic and
historic data: the impulse to "truck and barter," the necessity for exchange. From this necessity there arises, to some degree, a division of
labor. The archaeologist, finding it difficult to adhere to Durkheim's
dictate that "the first origins of all social processes of any importance
should be sought in the internal constitution of the social group," has
constructed an abstract evolutionary schema of mechanistic causation
built upon analogy and metaphor. The mind boggles at the thought of
encapsulating the many histories, geographies, chronologies, typologies,
and processes with which archaeologists deal in devising syntheses or
empirically drawn formulas. This cannot be done either empirically or
pragmatically. Thus archaeologists, regardless of the extent of their em-
piricisms or deductive reasonings, turn to metaphor and analogy, assuming the multiple to be the unitary, the random to be ordered, the distant
near. Achieving an understanding of the impossible is what metaphor
and analogy are all about; they provide a method of constructing a
logically ordered circular argumentation, of proving the unproven and
unprovable. What the archaeologist brings into conceptual existence he
too often believes has actual existence.

CASE STUDY: CHLORITE TRADE IN
THE THIRD MILLENNIUM

A central thesis of this chapter is that the concepts of reciprocity and redistribution are totally insufficient for an understanding of the market network in early third millennium Mesopotamia. It is my contention that the analysis of a single traded object within the Mesopotamian market network documents a far more complex economic system than previously conceived. The time has come to consider different organizing principles, to deal with a more precise and systematic examination of synchronic archaeological data so that the full complexity of a given social system can be understood and compared with other synchronic systems to determine the complexities of their change and development. The study of the structure of trade at any given point in time necessitates at a minimum: (1) close time control, enabling one to discuss comparable and contemporary sets of data; (2) contrastive and comparable sets of data within one community or area and then between two—essential in determining production, supply, demand, and the like; (3) quantitative control over the data base—an absolutely fundamental requirement in discussing trade relations, production, consumption, and the like; (4) a full contextual analysis of the data bearing on the trading situation, architectural associations on the site itself contrasted to other sites, and so forth; (5) knowledge of the modes of production and accurate definition and determination of the trade items as to geological origin, composition, and the like.

It is assumed that in Mesopotamia, at the end of the fourth and early in the third millennium, an intensification of reciprocal exchange principles resulted in coercive effects which came to supplement and eventually replace reciprocity in the form of redistribution. Though no one understands the process, it is assumed to have been part of the evolution of Mesopotamian social and economic behavior. Students of Mesopotamian redistribution exchange assume that the labor products of several individuals were brought to the administrative capital, sorted, counted, and then given to producers and nonproducers alike by the centralized authority ("Redistribution designates appropriational movement towards the centre and out of it again."—Polanyi). Such a system necessitates an organizational effort, which in Mesopotamia is believed to have been embedded in kinship relations. A significant difference in the complexity of social organization exists according to the degree of standardization of units of value. These are less standardized in reciprocal than in redistributive exchanges. Between the two a different mode of exchange is posited, but the difference, if any, in the modes of production has hardly been investigated. In fact, modes of exchange have been the subject of several archaeological studies (and of most of this volume), whereas modes of production have been all but ignored. This appears to me to be the opposite of what should be.

In Mesopotamia, in the late third millennium, there is ample evidence from textual sources that merchants specialized in the materials they traded. Thus, during Ur III times (2113–2006 B.C.) the merchant Ea-nāṣir, a member of the "group of seafaring merchants" (*alik Telmun*), received garments from Ur and took them to Dilmun (modern-day Bahrein), where he purchased large quantities of copper (Oppenheim 1954:7). Ea-nāṣir obtained capital under contractual agreements, managing the money of others as a mutual fund, while also investing his own capital in copper-trading ventures (Leemans 1960: 36–55). Customs duties were levied by city administrators on the imported copper (Oppenheim 1954:8). It would appear that by the end of the third millennium there were specialized merchants dealing with large-scale exchange of goods in a wholesaling-retailing system as defined by J. E. Vance (1970:1–33).

Turning to an even later period, in the early second millennium, it is of interest to review the conditions which were required to maintain the Old Assyrian trade:

Stable political conditions in all the areas touched by the trade were naturally essential for the merchants to succeed. This goes both for the countries where the articles of the trade originated (we hear once about a rebellion in Babylonia, from where many textiles came), the areas traversed during the journey from Assyria to Anatolia, and the local states in Asia Minor. With these authorities the Assyrians had agreements from which both parties benefited; the rulers secured the roads and received in return certain taxes on the imported goods besides enjoying the right to preemption.

The most intimate contact between the men active at the two ends of the line of transport was the other vitally important condition. Many of the best known merchants from Kanesh spent the greater part of their lives in Anatolia and they had to have their representatives in Ashur to take care of the interests there. The great bankers who financed the trade usually lived in the Assyrian capital, and for them the uninterrupted contact with the colonists in Anatolia was of the greatest importance. It is indeed remarkable to see how this intricate system was being kept through the efficient administration of the Assyrians and Anatolians (Larsen 1967:5–6).

We can see in this study, as well as in more recent ones (Veenhof 1972: 399), that the proposals put forth by Polyani (1957:12–26) about Old Assyrian moneyless markets must be rejected. Markets most certainly existed, even within a wholesale-retail format, and merchants were specialized and capitalistic. Individual profit was a prime motivation; even smuggling existed to increase profits through evading taxes and tolls (Veenhof 1972:399). I believe that a great deal of what the texts describe for the end of the third millennium already existed a millennium earlier and can be documented in the archaeological records.

We turn now to a specific case study, an analysis of trade ca. 2800 B.C., utilizing the recent evidence from Tepe Yahya and the modes of exchange and production of the resource chlorite (steatite). Chlorite has been referred to in the archaeological literature as steatite, soapstone, and talc. Our analyses of this class of stone bowls from Mesopotamian sites, as well as from Tepe Yahya, indicate the majority to be of chlorite, though several are also made of the related stone, steatite. The chlorite-steatite difference is important in terms of geological origin, area of resource production, and trade. The carved stone bowls from Mari in Mesopotamia to Moenjodaro on the Indus share an almost identical grammar of complex design motifs. In fact, these carved stone bowls represent the most widely scattered single artifact type in third millennium Mesopotamia–Iranian Plateau.

Our approach to the study of the trade in this material will be first to present a series of archaeological "facts" and then to detail the role of chlorite trade in the market network in terms of (1) access to raw materials; (2) time-space systematics; (3) supply and demand; (4) quantitative control; (5) contextual analysis; (6) physicochemical analysis; (7) work times and schedules; (8) technology of production.

These matters will be dealt with in an attempt to circumscribe the market network in the trade of this single resource.

Background "Facts"

1. Chlorite (steatite) objects have been found over a very wide distribution, on almost every site in Mesopotamia of Early Dynastic II–III date and on the contemporary sites on islands of the Persian Gulf (Tarut), the Indo-Iranian borderlands (Mehi, Yahya, etc.), and at Moenjodaro (Durrani 1964; Lamberg-Karlovsky 1970; 1971; 1972; 1973).
2. The complex design motifs carved on the stone vessels are nearly identical in style and type over the wide area of their distribution. We believe that in areas of great quantitative production and areas of great consumption there would have to be a uniform meaning in the iconography (Porada 1971).
3. Geologically, chlorite and its near relative steatite are very widely distributed throughout the Zagros Mountains (personal communication from M. Sabzehei, Geological Survey of Iran, and director of the geological surveys in the immediate vicinity of Tepe Yahya). A volume on the geology of the Tepe Yahya area, with its great abundance of chlorite, is presently being published in France.
4. The largest inventory of carved and uncarved chlorite vessels, plaques, and the like comes from Tepe Yahya, southeastern Iran. It is the only known production site in direct proximity to a source mined in antiquity and the only site known to be a production center. (See below for discussion.)
5. Neutron activation, X-ray fluorescence, and diffraction studies on chlorite, steatite, and related stone vessels from Tepe Yahya, Susa, Ur, Bismaya, Mari, Tarut, Shahr-i Sokhta, et al. have not shown the use of a single restricted resource in antiquity. Analysis indicates, within varying degrees of precision, our ability to cluster the finished products as manufactured from several different sources. To date we have analyzed over 350 samples from over a dozen sources. This pioneer study, which promises to elevate the entire discussion to a new plateau, is being undertaken by Mr. Philip

Kohl (Department of Anthropology, Harvard University) at Brookhaven Laboratories under the direction of Dr. Edward Sayre.

Access to Chlorite Resource

Though many production centers undoubtedly exist, only one is known. Geological survey of the immediate vicinity of Tepe Yahya indicates a pre-Iliassic system of granodiorite, granite, and tonalite formations, as well as serpentine and serpentinized ultrabasic rocks (chlorite) from an unknown formative system. Chlorite abounds in these latter formations, which ring the mountains within 10 miles of the site of Tepe Yahya. We have discovered to date four major localities of mining and quarrying activity, evidencing the extraction of many tons of chlorite from the face of the mountain. This evidence, combined with the recovery of finished objects, worked but unfinished objects, and thousands of waste fragments recovered over 300 square meters of excavation in Period IVB, argues for (1) local production, and (2) production quantity exceeding that needed for local consumption. Physicochemical analyses of objects from quarry sites and objects from the mound show an unequivocal identity. (Note: The complete results of these analyses, together with full quantification of chlorite and related stones at Yahya, will be published in the Ph.D. thesis of Mr. Philip Kohl.) With this information as background, we can now examine the nature and the mechanism of the market network that engaged in chlorite trade.

Time-Space Systematics

In order to understand market networks it is absolutely imperative to control the chronological and spatial framework. It simply does no good to discuss developmental mechanisms as postulated hypotheses outside of a rigorously controlled time scale. Without control over time-space systematics, one is comparing noncontrastive sets, assuming order in chaos. Several factors of time and space are pertinent in the discussion of a market network of chlorite.

Chlorite as a resource for producing bowls, beads, and mortars was utilized for the first time at Shanidar B, over 10,000 years ago (personal communication from Professor Ralph Solecki). The shape and utility of chlorite bowls varied greatly from Neolithic to Ubaid times. The technology for coring chlorite vessels was thus known from the earliest Neolithic. The great regional diversity in the use of this resource was dramatically and seemingly abruptly altered in Early Dynastic II times (2750–2600 B.C.). At this point we see a standardized series of shapes with complex designs carved on the bowls throughout Mesopotamia, the Persian Gulf, and southern Iran. The distinctive carved chlorite bowl is present in large numbers on almost every excavated Mesopotamian Early Dynastic III site and in considerable quantity outside of Mesopotamia at Yahya, Susa, Shahdad, and Malyun in southern Iran and in the Persian Gulf on the islands of Tarut and Failaka. In addition, fragments of carved bowls of this distinctive type have been found at Bampur(3), Moenjodaro(2), Sialk(1), Shahr-i Sokhta(3), and we know of a single surface find of an amulet with the common serpent motif from distant Uzbekistan SSR. The very considerable abundance of this material in identical shapes and with distinctive design elements throughout the Early Dynastic II–III period allows us considerable time control over a large geographical area. How this material was disseminated over this wide area, if indeed it was, is the topic of our case study.

Physicochemical techniques of analysis do not yet allow us to cluster areas of resource procurement (save for the site and area of Tepe Yahya). The problem is in obtaining a sufficient number of samples from known resource areas. Only a single deposit utilized in proximity to an archaeological production site is known—Tepe Yahya, located in southeastern Iran, some 800 miles distant from the Mesopotamian city-states.

Supply and Demand

Without exception, almost every site in Mesopotamia during Early Dynastic II and III times contains numerous carved chlorite bowls. The shape of the bowls and the designs carved on them are almost identical from site to site. They provide a ready parallel to the large corpus from the single site of Tepe Yahya. The natural resource for the production of chlorite bowls in southern Mesopotamia is absent. The demand for chlorite in finished form initiated its supply from outside Mesopotamia. There is not a single known site, save for Yahya, from outside of Mesopotamia, nor from Mesopotamia, that suggests the large-scale production of these bowls. The very wide distribution of the bowls with their distinctive carved designs suggests a considerable demand over a wide area. The archaeological evidence from Tepe Yahya and the results of our physico-chemical analyses support our contention that Tepe Yahya was one of the supply centers filling this demand. Three aspects of supply and demand deserve attention: (1) supply and demand competition *within* Mesopotamia; (2) supply and demand competition *between* Mesopotamia (the demand center) and known production sites (Tepe Yahya); (3) supply and demand competition *outside* Mesopotamia, i.e. between the production areas (Yahya) and the surrounding countryside.

First, we can posit from the archaeological context of carved chlorite bowls that they maintained a high value, that they were luxury items in Mesopotamia (see discussion of contextual analysis below). One can rightly assume a competition among the Mesopotamian elite for the acquisition of finished products of the luxury type. Thus the greater the quantity of this material on individual Mesopotamian sites, the more successful the competitor. If a quantitative study were possible, one might be able to indicate which Mesopotamian city-state was the most successful in long-distance trade competition with the resource area. The ability to procure luxury items and to maintain long-distance trade successfully may indicate a strong sociopolitical control over less successful neighboring city-states. We do not have the full quantitative control to document this hypothesis, but it is evident that differential quantities are found on different sites. Competition between sites in Mesopotamia would clearly have affected supply, quantity, and subsequent production rates in resource areas. The exchange value would have fluctuated according to the nature and the extent of demand in different Mesopotamian city-states and their ability to compete for the resource.

Second, it is reasonable to assume that the competition between Mesopotamian city-states and known production centers was affected by the rate of production in resource areas. The actual number of production centers is unknown. On the basis of the output at Tepe Yahya and the number of finished products found on Mesopotamian sites, we can infer that a limited number of production sites would have sufficed to fill the demand. It is very important to recognize the fact that it is extremely unlikely that Yahya, the only known production site, was under

354

the political domination of Sumerian Mesopotamia. Susa and Malyun (Anshan), the major Elamite cities, are situated between Mesopotamia and Tepe Yahya, cities which contemporary texts do not place under Sumerian domination. Furthermore, the archaeological context in which chlorite production is evident at Tepe Yahya does not support the contention that Yahya was colonized or under the authority of a foreign power. There is absolutely no evidence that internal production at Yahya, as in many mercantile systems, is politically dominated from outside as suggested by Renfrew (chap. 1 of this volume).

The rate of chlorite supply to Mesopotamia would have depended on the value of the return payment to the independent sociopolitical regime at Tepe Yahya, on the artisans producing the materials, and on the intermediate private entrepreneurs undertaking the long-distance trade. Yahya may have supplied one or more Mesopotamian cities, more likely the latter, depending on the extent of profit, the nature of the contractual relations, and the competition from other production sites. An increased demand would provide favorable conditions for higher profits to the producers and the entrepreneurs. An unfavorable return would cause a shift in trading partners, reduction in production, or contractual relations with different entrepreneurs. The above hypotheses could readily be tested with adequate quantitative, physicochemical, and contextual analyses.

Finally, we must consider the competition for carved chlorite bowls in the production zone itself. Here we are faced with a fascinating situation. There appears to have been virtually no demand for chlorite bowls on sites near the production center of Yahya, or for that matter within a wider geographical area around Yahya. Apparently the production at Yahya filled principally, if not exclusively, a distant western demand. Thus at Bampur, 300 km. to the east of Yahya, with contemporary ceramic parallels, there are but 3 fragments of carved vessels, and almost 100 ceramic copies (nonexistent in Mesopotamia). At Yahya there is a single surface find of a ceramic imitation of the carved stone vessel type. At nearby Tal-i Iblis not a single carved chlorite piece has been found, while at Shahr-i Sokhta only 3 carved chlorite pieces have been recovered. On survey, the sites located which date to this period do not indicate the presence of carved chlorite pieces on the surface. The interpretation of these limited data is inescapable: Demand was minimal within the zone of production. We note a similar phenomenon for lapis lazuli. Shahr-i Sokhta was a large production site and transshipment center for lapis, of which thousands of unworked and finished pieces have been found in the excavations (Lamberg-Karlovsky and Tosi 1973; Tosi and Piperno 1973). During the period of Shahr-i Sokhta's production of lapis lazuli, the sites of Yahya, Bampur, and Tal-i Iblis have yielded a total of under a dozen pieces. Thus neither the lapis of Shahr-i Sokhta nor the chlorite at Tepe Yahya appears to have been traded within a local sphere of economic interaction of luxury items; both must have been traded in response to Mesopotamian demand.

One final aspect of supply and demand is important. In Mesopotamia there is evidence for neither chlorite mining nor production. At Tepe Yahya no evidence exists to suggest the export of unworked chlorite in "ingots." It would appear that chlorite was exported in finished form. Such late third millennium texts as *Enmerkar and the Lord of Aratta* (Cohen 1973), said to portray activities characteristic of the Early Dynastic II period, imply that raw materials, mostly in the form of various stones (carnelian, *u*-stone, *Shumash* stone, lapis lazuli, diorite), were brought to Mesopotamia in return for Mesopotamian surplus grain. There would appear to be a contradiction here between the texts and the archaeological data. On the more than dozen sites in Mesopotamia where these characteristic stone vessels have been found, there is no direct evidence for their production. In fact, production areas have been conspicuously absent on Mesopotamian sites, but perhaps this is a reflection of areas of archaeological concentration (temple-palaces) and methodology.

Quantitative Control

A knowledge of the absolute numbers of a given commodity produced is essential to the reconstruction of a market network. Many of the hypotheses stated above can only be dealt with in substantive form when quantitative data become available. It is unfortunate that some of the important chlorite-bearing sites in the Diyala have received only preliminary publication (Delougaz 1960), if any. The attempts at synthesizing the distribution and dates of these chlorite bowls do not allow one the control to undertake a full quantitative study (Durrani 1964; Herz 1966). At Tepe Yahya we have the necessary control over the absolute numbers as well as weight of all chlorite objects, both worked and unworked. With comparable quantitative control—as well as chronological and contextual control—from a demand center, one could determine the fluctuations of supply and demand, value, and the nature of the competition between and within export and import areas. The full quantitative analysis, replete with graphs and physicochemical results, of the Yahya corpus will be presented by Philip Kohl in his dissertation.

Contextual Analysis: Place and Mode of Production Activities

Chlorite is present in artifacts from every period at Yahya, from the time of its initial settlement to its abandonment. It occurs in Period VI (4500–3900 B.C.) in the form of simple undecorated bowls, bracelets, door sockets, mortars, pestles, and even figurines (Lamberg-Karlovsky and Meadow 1970). The quantity and variety of shapes of undecorated bowls are constant throughout the early periods of Yahya V, becoming in Period VA more considerable, with the evidence of partially worked fragments. It would appear that in Period VA (ca. 3500 B.C.) at Yahya there is an increase in production. In all cases the context of the chlorite objects in Period VI and V is on floors or in fill of domestic dwellings (with the exception of an uncarved chlorite bowl in a Period VA burial). Period IVC (3200–3400 B.C.) has less than two dozen carved and uncarved chlorite fragments. The carved vessel fragments are wholly unlike the "international style" characteristic of the succeeding Period IVB. It is of interest to note that in the IVC period, characterized by a single large building in which we have found Jemdet Nasr–type cylinder seals, cylinder sealings, and ceramics, as well as Proto-Elamite tablets, there are less than twenty chlorite fragments in over 300 square meters of excavated area. This represents a lower percentage than that for Periods VI and V, and far lower than that for the following Period IVB. The Period IVC architectural complex, with its attendant features, has all the hallmarks of a Mesopotamian "redistribution center": storage rooms lined with storage jars, seals, sealings, account tablets, beveled-rim bowls (measures?), and the like. There is, however, an almost com-

357

plete absence of carved chlorite bowls, or, for that matter, of evidence for the consumption of foreign produce or export of a local produce. There can be little doubt that the tablets and sealings are *directly* related to the tablets and sealings known from Susa, almost 800 kilometers to the west. One also has the feeling—and, for a later time, the direct knowledge—that cylinder sealings and account tablets were part of the impedimenta of market networks. The material culture at Yahya is not, however, directly parallel with that of Susa. Intuitively one senses that both sites are part of a single market network, but not part of the same political entity, and that the commodities being exported and/or imported have perished from the archaeological record (Crawford 1973). Again, one senses intuitively that it would have been advantageous for a local ruler at Yahya to have exploited his countryside and population for the advantage to be gathered from participation in a wider-ranging market network. In most mercantile systems, economic motivation fosters "islands of exploitative cultures in various seas of indigenous tradition" (DiPeso 1967).

The contextual situation during Period IVB (2900–2600 B.C.) at Tepe Yahya, the period of international trade in carved chlorite bowls, is very different from the domestic context and function of chlorite in earlier times and from the "administrative" functions of the Period IVC building. Over 450 square meters of Period IVB have been exposed. The context of the Period IVB chlorite cannot be removed from a consideration of the stratigraphic situation of this period. *Directly* above the walls of the IVC building are built walls of a structure of different alignment. This building represents lowermost Period IVB. It is *sealed* by numerous surfaces within 1½ meters of deposition. The lowermost building, domestic in nature, consisting of one large two-room house with outside articulating storage bins, offered a number of chlorite objects, one Persian Gulf–type seal, and one cylinder seal, also of chlorite. (For the chlorite of Period IVB see the illustrations in Lamberg-Karlovsky 1971 and 1972, and for the stratigraphic section see Lamberg-Karlovsky and Tosi 1973.) The lower building level of Period IVB did not offer a single carved piece of the "international style." The 1½ meters of deposition, with numerous surfaces and traces of mud brick but without architectural plan, are a veritable bonanza of carved and uncarved chlorite. On these surfaces we have also recovered a considerable inventory of ceramics, metals, beads, and three chlorite cylinder seals. No identifiable clusterings of materials, types, or discernible activity areas are evident in this deposit except for areas along the surface that show dense concentrations of chlorite fragments and a number of hearths. Certain areas contain concentrations of reed matting, which may have served as shelters. All in all, it has been impossible to discern architectural or habitational plans. The remarkably rich carved chlorite assemblage of Period IVB represents the largest single collection of carved chlorite vessels in the entire area of their wide distribution. A great many of the pieces are of superb craftsmanship. What is enigmatic is their context. Had they been found in the context of Period IVC we would have been less surprised. It almost seems that we are faced with large-scale evidence for manufacture on open surfaces, with meager traces of mud brick and reed matting. The archaeological evidence appears clear: Chlorite production was not undertaken in an architectural context of specialized complexity. One might argue that we have exposed an area of industrial activity and that other areas of the mound, areas which have not been excavated, would provide the domestic and administrative complexes. This is possible, but it becomes less likely each season. The 350 square meters of exposure represent 200 meters on the south side of the mound, 100 square meters on the north side of the mound (in different step trenchs), and 50 square meters in the dead center of the mound. In all areas we find the same situation: 1 to $2\frac{1}{2}$ meters of deposition with numerous surfaces.

It would appear that chlorite was manufactured by local artisans (perhaps part time, perhaps seasonally, perhaps by a specialized encampment of exploited workers, and perhaps—least likely of all—by migrant artisans from the west; additional ethnographic analogies may more readily suit one's bias) through a demand and market network which could well have been instituted by middlemen entrepreneurs, not unlike Ea-nāṣir, discussed above. (I make this inference by ethnographic analogy and through my own bias.) Thus the demand for chlorite was not generated by a local redistributive administration, for chlorite vessels are not found in any quantity on other contemporary IVB sites in the vicinity of Tepe Yahya or for that matter in any quantity on other excavated sites in southeastern, central, or northern Iran. Nor is there any evidence of foreign colonization around the area of Yahya. In

359

summary: (1) Chlorite production for local consumption is evident at Tepe Yahya in Periods VI–IVC, where it is limited in quantity and found principally in domestic contexts. (2) In the upper levels of Period IVB there is a remarkable increase in the production of chlorite, without evidence of architectural associations. (3) There is little or no evidence to support the presence of interregional trade in chlorite vessels in the vicinity of Yahya. (4) The abundance of chlorite vessels in Mesopotamia for the first time during contemporary Yahya IVB times, the absence of chlorite as a resource in Mesopotamia, and its absence of manufacture on Mesopotamian sites provide the background for the establishment of a market network in this material based on supply and production in resource zones and demand and consumption in non-resource zones. (5) The external stimulus—namely communication—for chlorite demand was generated by entrepreneurs satisfying the desire for luxury goods among the increasingly socially stratified society of Early Dynastic Mesopotamia. Whatever profits existed in the transactions were principally in the hands of the middlemen traders and the exploitative elite of Mesopotamia (see below). The absence of any evidence of accumulated wealth at Tepe Yahya in Period IVB indicates a lack of high profit obtained and of control over the long-distance trade by the Yahya artisans. One might note that there is little evidence for accumulated wealth on any of the excavated sites of Shahr-i Sokhta, Yahya, Bampur, or Tal-i Iblis, in southern and eastern Iran. In this market network Yahya artisans worked at a set production rate, receiving goods (payment) from the middlemen, who then sold at a greater profit to the high demand centers of Mesopotamia. It is important to recall that in Mesopotamia carved chlorite bowls are found almost exclusively in elite contexts—rich burials (Royal Cemetery at Ur) and temples and palaces at Ubaid, Khafajeh, Telloh, Bismaya, Agrab, Nippur, Mari, Kish, Sippar, and elsewhere—and not in private houses or graves.

Our analysis allows us to suggest the presence of a form of economic imperialism: a degree of economic exploitation of the Iranian Plateau by the city-states of Mesopotamia. We have already indicated that there is no evidence to support the contention of direct political control over the area of Tepe Yahya by Sumerian city-states. Thus, political imperialism, evident at the end of the third millennium, seems absent.

We may profitably distinguish between political imperialism and economic imperialism, the former being a process of political control over a foreign area, the latter an economic exploitation of foreign areas without political control. The well-integrated political order in Mesopotamia, ruling over a relatively uniform geographical area, facilitated the exploitation of the politically nonintegrated, geographically disparate regions of the Iranian Plateau. The resources of the Iranian Plateau were lacking in Mesopotamia and essential to Mesopotamian society. The exploitation of the Iranian Plateau by the Mesopotamian city-states facilitated, for the first time, the rise of an elite on the plateau, evidenced by the very rich mid-third-millennium tombs of Shahdad with their lapis lazuli, chlorite, and alabaster vases, copper-bronze axes, cauldrons, and the like. It was advantageous to the elite of the Iranian Plateau to be exploited by the Mesopotamian city-states, for, in producing materials to fill Mesopotamian demand, they were better able to organize labor and establish political authority; they also obtained greater wealth in return payment from Mesopotamia, as well as enhanced prestige and information. This type of economic exploitation is to the mutual benefit of the rising elite in *both* areas, and one may suppose that political relations between the independent areas were solidified through kin-based intermarriage between the elite of Mesopotamia and the Iranian Plateau. It is possible that the Mesopotamian capacity to produce *surplus* grains, textiles, and perishables (such as fish)—the commodities which, the texts inform us, were traded for the mineral wealth of the Iranian Plateau (Crawford 1973)—assisted the Mesopotamians in their exploitation of the Iranian Plateau. It would be most informative to determine the extent of grain production in the regions with which Mesopotamia traded, for if grain production was tenuous, Mesopotamian surplus would have been of great importance in maintaining the unbalanced exploitation. Such economic exploitation and imperialism, I repeat, is different from political imperialism, in which one group takes over the political domination of another. The idea of political and economic imperialism evolved in Mesopotamia far earlier than its first historical documentation in the texts. One can surmise that rivalry between autonomous city-states over border lines and irrigation ditches led to conquest situations, that is, the conquest of one state by one or more neighboring city-states.

Textual data indicate that Lugalzagesi (ca. 2360–2335 B.C.) was the first Sumerian military leader to show signs of looking beyond the capture of a few neighboring city-states. Apart from being able to claim control over Uruk, Nippur, Umma, Ur, Larsa, and Lagash, this king boasts of even greater power:

> When the god Enlil, king of the Lands, gave to Lugalzagesi sovereignty over Sumer, caused Sumer to look directly to him (for leadership), subdued all the lands under him, made the entire region from east to west submit to him; at that time Enlil created for him a clear passage from the Lower Sea (Persian Gulf), along the Tigris and Euphrates, to the Upper Sea (Mediterranean). In the entire region from east to west Enlil made him free of opposition. He made the people of the lands lie down in peaceful pastures like cattle and supplied Sumer with water bringing joyful abundance Thureau-Dangin 1907).

One further comment before departing from considerations of the place and mode of production: The meaning of the complex iconography used by the Yahya artisans on chlorite vessels is unknown. Preliminary results of an attribute analysis suggest a great similarity in the combination of specific attributes on the different sites at which carved chlorite bowls appear. The combination of such attributes as snakes, felines, scorpions consistently identically positioned, a limited number of identically recombined geometric motifs, and elaborate and identical attributes placed on architectural scenes clearly indicates that the Yahya artisan understood the grammar of their meaning as well as did the elite Mesopotamian, who viewed them as desirable luxury items. This sharing of a symbolic ideology between the Sumerians in Mesopotamia and the cultures of the southern Iranian Plateau (Elam?) has far-reaching implications.

A related matter of shared ideology and meaning can be derived from seals. The use of the very distinctive, highly individualized styles and shapes of the seals of the Indus (square), Persian Gulf (round), Mesopotamia (cylindrical), and Turkmenistan-Seistan (compartmented) in the middle of the third millennium is, I believe, far from accidental. The seals in all of the above areas are believed to have served a similar function, namely, the sealing of goods to denote ownership. The goods then may or may not have been exchanged over long distances. Sealing, however, was not their only function. The seals made it possible to identify the mother country of the merchant and the origin of the traded commodity without opening the bundle of goods, thus facilitating storage, taxation, further shipment, and other functions. The seals, in short, provided an overt symbol of ethnic identity as well as a practical tool for trade regulation. It is of interest to note that the coincidence in the distribution of distinctive seal types is overlapped by the distribution of equally distinctive ceramic types. Such items as seals expressed a unique "cognitive set"—a collection of mental constructs that are learned, modified, and shared by members of a particular society. Thus the differences in the styles and shapes of seals over the above areas are not random or accidental but meaningful in separating areas of cultural identity. As Barth (1969:15) has observed, ethnic groups require "continued expression and validation through overt signals and signs" (symbols) and "basic value orientations" (the distinctive political-religious orientation of the seals). I believe such a concept helps to explain not only the function of the seals but their structural meaning over this wide area. One might add that seeking out the obstinately distinctive features in functional types is as informative as documenting the typological parallels which suggest the interrelations and boundary areas of archaeological cultures.

Physicochemical Analysis and Access to Raw Materials

In any discussion of the distribution of archaeological artifacts it is essential to know both the location of the natural resource and its archaeological context. Only with precise archeological, geological, and mineralogical descriptions can we proceed to map resource origins and the trade of specific resources to and from given areas. The results of X-ray diffraction and neutron activation of chlorite samples from Yahya have conclusively shown that the nearby mines provided the source for Yahya's production. The analysis of over 300 samples shows a high affinity with the chlorite of Yahya, Susa, and Mari. A plotting of these analyses will allow us to suggest a number of discrete type clusterings, suggesting distinctive production centers and preferred markets of chlorite on certain sites.

363

Work Times and Schedules

Within the market network, which includes chlorite sales, we are unable to isolate the commodity used to pay for chlorite. Nor are we able to isolate the variable profit margin of producers, entrepreneurs, and buyers. This information is fundamental to an understanding of the market network, but I rather doubt that we shall ever have a clear picture of it from the prehistoric record. We are even less able to discuss the work times and the schedules of the producers and private entrepreneurs. The great quantity of chlorite at Tepe Yahya suggests full-time specialization. This in turn implies a sufficient profit to the artisan to enable him to support himself and family, as well as a sufficient profit in further sales to support the merchants at least partially. The enigmatic context of chlorite at Yahya may even suggest a seasonal specialization. To test this hypothesis, Richard H. Meadow is undertaking a detailed analysis of the faunal materials from the many surfaces bearing chlorite.

Technology of Production

A great deal more will be said of the technology of chlorite production in Philip Kohl's thesis. The increase of production in Period IVB at Yahya is definitely not correlated with a transformation in technological development, that is, a technological breakthrough in the knowledge of carving chlorite. Already in the earlier Period VA all the techniques for mastering chlorite bowl production are evident. Thus, approximately 500–750 years prior to the production of IVB chlorite, there is evidence for the mastery of all techniques of coring, carving, lathe work, and so forth. It is impossible to support a contention that a technological breakthrough in metal implements or the introduction of new carving techniques brought about an increase of production and/or demand for carved chlorite bowls in the first third of the third millennium. Trade in chlorite was clearly brought about through a transformation in the means of production in the social organizational framework between Mesopotamia and the Iranian Plateau.

It has been our brief attempt in this all-too-preliminary paper to indicate that an analysis of a single exchanged object suggests that the early third millennium was far from characterized by a simple reciprocity-redistribution type of economic order. Selective long-distance trade, private entrepreneurship, differential exploitation, responses and stimuli to supply and demand, and other phenomena were all operative in the chlorite market network. Many of these hypotheses are undergoing rigorous analysis through quantitative, physicochemical, and contextual approaches.

The above analysis of a single market network dealing with a single commodity challenges many facile assumptions and provides many new hypotheses. I have tried to point toward the tendency of modern archaeological inquiry to conclude that, if law is anywhere, it is everywhere in the irreducibly contingent nature of historical and social systems.

References

ADAMS, R. MCC.
1972 "Anthropological Perspectives on Ancient Trade," paper read at a colloquium on "Current Themes in Anthropological Theory," Harvard University, December 1972.

BARTH, F.
1969 *Ethnic Groups and Boundaries* (Boston: Little, Brown and Co.).

BEALE, T. W.
1973 "Early Trade in Highland Iran: A View from the Source," *World Archaeology* 5(2):133–48.

COHEN, SOL
1973 "Enmerkar and the Lord of Aratta," Ph.D. dissertation, Department of Near Eastern Languages and Literature, University of Pennsylvania.

CRAWFORD, H. E. W.
1973 "Mesopotamia's Invisible Exports in the Third Millennium," *World Archaeology* 5(2):232–41.

DELOUGAZ, P.
1960 "Architectural Representations on Steatite Vases," *Iraq* 22:90–95.

DIPESO, C.
1967 "The Correlation Question in General Archaeological Perspective in Northern Mesoamerica," in *38th International Congress of Americanists*.

DURRANI, F. A.
1964 "Stone Vases as Evidence of Connection between Mesopotamia and the Indus Valley," *Ancient Pakistan* 1:51 ff.

FLANNERY, K.
1968 "The Olmec and the Valley of Oaxaca: A Model of Inter-regional Interaction in Formative Times," in *Dumbarton Oaks Conference on the Olmec*, ed. E. P. Benson (Washington, D. C.: Dumbarton Oaks Research Library and Trustees for Harvard University).

GELB, I. J.
1969 "On the Alleged Temple and State Economies in Ancient Mesopotamia," in *Studi in Onore di Eduardo Volterra*, vol. 6.

HERZ, A.
1966 "A Study of Steatite Vases of the Early Dynastic Period in Mesopotamia," M.A. thesis, Department of Fine Arts, New York University.

HEXTER, J. H.
1971 *The History Primer* (New York: Basic Books).

366

LAMBERG-KARLOVSKY, C. C.
1970   *Excavations at Tepe Yahya, 1967–1969.* American School of Prehistoric Research, Bulletin no. 27, Peabody Museum, Harvard University (Cambridge, Mass.).
1971   "The Proto-Elamite Settlement at Tepe Yahya," *Iran* 9:87–98.
1972   "Tepe Yahya 1971: Mesopotamia and the Indo-Iranian Borderlands," *Iran* 10:89–100.
1973   "Urban Interaction on the Iranian Plateau: Excavations at Tepe Yahya, 1967–1973." Albert Reckitt Archaeological Lecture, British Academy. (To be published in the *Proceedings of the British Academy.*)

LAMBERG-KARLOVSKY, C. C. AND R. MEADOW
1970   "The Neolithic at Tepe Yahya: A Unique Female Figurine," *Archaeology* 23(1):12–17.

LAMBERG-KARLOVSKY, C. C. AND M. TOSI
1973   "Shahr-i Sokhta and Tepe Yahya: Tracks on the Earliest History of the Iranian Plateau," *East and West* 23(1–2):21–57.

LARSEN, M. T.
1967   *Old Assyrian Caravan Procedures.* Uitgaven van het Nederlands historisch-archaeologisch institue te Istanbul, 22.

LEEMANS, W. F.
1960   *Foreign Trade in the Old Babylonian Period.* Studia et Documenta ad Iura Orientis Antiqui Pertinentia, 6 (Leiden: E. J. Brill).

OPPENHEIM, L.
1954   "Seafaring Merchants of Ur," *Journal of the American Oriental Society* 74:6–17.

POLANYI, K.
1957   "Marketless Trading in Hammurabi's Time," in *Trade and Market in the Early Empires,* ed. K. Polanyi, C. M. Arensberg, H. W. Pearson (New York: Free Press).

PORADA, E.
1971   "Comments on Steatite Carvings from Saudi Arabia and Other Parts of the Near East," *Artibus Asiae* 33(4):323–31.

SAHLINS, M.
1965   "Exchange Value and Diplomacy of Primitive Trade," in *Proceedings of the 1965 Annual Spring Meeting of the American Ethnological Society,* ed. June Helm (Seattle: University of Washington Press).
1972   *Stone Age Economics* (Chicago: Aldine-Atherton).

THUREAU-DANGIN, F.
1907   "Die Sumerischen und Akkadischen Konigschriften," UAB 1, p. 154, i. (Leipzig, Germany).

TOSI, M. AND M. PIPERNO
1973   "Lithic Technology behind the Ancient Lapis Trade," *Expedition* 16(1):15–23.

VANCE, J. E., JR.
1970   *The Merchant's World: The Geography of Wholesaling* (Englewood Cliffs, N. J.: Prentice-Hall).

VEENHOFF, K. R.

1972   *Aspects of Old Assyrian Trade and Its Terminology*. Studia et Documenta ad Iura Orientis Antiqui Pertinentia. (Leiden: E. J. Brill).

WATSON, PATTY-JO

1973   "Explanation and Models: The Prehistorian as Philosopher of Science and the Prehistorian as Excavator of the Past," in *The Explanation of Culture Change: Models in Prehistory*, ed. C. Renfrew (London: Gerald Duckworth & Co.). (A more extensive discussion was presented in "Excavations and Analysis of Halafian Materials from Southeastern Turkey: The Halafian Period Re-examined," presented at the 72d Annual Meeting of the American Anthropological Association, New Orleans, La., November 28–December 2, 1973.)

9

A Model of a Pre-Columbian Trading Center

JEREMY A. SABLOFF
AND
DAVID A. FREIDEL
Harvard University

"Next to the actual possession of a strategic position, the capacity to appreciate and exploit that position is most important."
—Isaac Asimov, *The Stars Like Dust*

INTRODUCTION

In recent years, we have witnessed a rapidly growing interest in the role played by trade in ancient civilizational systems. The focus of this new trend has been on the analysis of traded artifacts. This line of research has proved to be productive, as highly sophisticated research strategies, aided by a whole new armory of scientific techniques, have produced many new and significant data and theories. Understandably, much less attention has been paid to investigating trade facilities themselves and attempting functionally to identify the makeup of the facilities, since such research is difficult and has less obvious potential.[1]

We believe, however, that this second line of research is a necessary complement to the first and that it can be quite rewarding in the testing of hypotheses about the changing economic and political functions of trading centers or ports. Even on the Mexican island of Cozumel, where the architectural remains are often scanty and many of the traded items perishable, we feel that exercises such as the one attempted in this chapter form an essential part of our study of the role of trade in the development of Maya civilization. A combination of studies of traded goods and studies of the facilities that expedited the transfer of the goods, when used to test general hypotheses about the role of trade in ancient civilizations, will do much to help advance the frontiers of our knowledge.

Are there structural and artifactual remains which are peculiar to trading centers? If so, is there a cross-cultural regularity in such features? Are there consistent physical and cultural types of trading centers? Can the special features of trading centers be tied to behavioral regularities? Can the presence, absence, groupings, or changes in features be consistently linked to developmental regularities in trading centers? These questions and many others of similar ilk can be broached only after archaeologists have come to grips with the question of the physical and behavioral makeup of trading centers.

The Cozumel Archaeological Project was undertaken in order to study the material structure of a trading center as a means of better understanding the operation of the larger system of which it was a part.[2] The general hypotheses and objectives governing our research have been carefully detailed elsewhere, as have some of our preliminary data.[3] We will limit ourselves here to looking at Cozumel at one period of time, the Decadent or Late Postclassic Period, which lasted from about A.D. 1250 to the time of the Spanish Conquest.[4] This is the period when Cozumel, an island off the east coast of the Yucatán Peninsula, acted not only as a trading port but also as a pivotal node in the pre-Columbian Maya long-distance trading network.

The purpose of this chapter is to examine one trading center at one time (Cozumel in the Decadent Period) as the first step in testing a general model in which trading centers are related to the larger sociopolitical systems of which they are a part. In other words, we wish to construct a low-level-culture historical model which helps us understand

370

how the varied sites of Cozumel together functioned as one trading center. This specific model, we hope, will resolve some apparent contradictions in the archaeological data and allow us to proceed with the testing of our general model.

COZUMEL AS TRADING CENTER: SOME GENERAL COMMENTS ON MODEL BUILDING

Ethnohistoric sources clearly indicate that Cozumel was an important link in the long-distance trading routes during the period immediately preceding the Spanish Conquest (see especially Scholes and Roys 1948; also see Chapman 1957). Cozumel was also a major pilgrimage shrine during this period (Scholes and Roys 1948). Accepting these sources as valid and presuming that the trading pattern existed for at least 250 years (that is, for the duration of the Decadent Period),[5] we may proceed to suggest both general and specific models which we feel best explain the data we have collected on Cozumel.

In testing these models, we face a problem on Cozumel—an important problem because it is prevalent in Mesoamerican archaeology: Our primary source of positive evidence concerning trade is artifactual. With exotic materials in hand, it is relatively easy to argue the existence of trade, but a broader data base is required to characterize the institutions that move such materials. Certain obvious trade-related facilities, such as permanent docking construction, storage structures, and marketplaces, are lacking on Cozumel. Ethnohistoric information on the nature of transportation and important trade items can partially account for the absence of these features. For example, it has been reported that canoes were beached in sheltered locations and did not require permanent docks; markets were seen to have been located in open plazas (of which we have found a number on Cozumel), but they have left few distinctive material remains. The important trade items (including salt, honey, cacao, and textiles) require certain warehousing, packaging, and transport facilities, but the requirements are so general as to make positive identification of these activities difficult.

If we can solve the problem of identifying these economic activities, we will be able to build a stronger, more explanatory model of Cozumel as a trading center. Since facilities—as opposed to artifacts—have proved most difficult to analyze in terms of trade models, one of the goals of this chapter will be to concentrate on certain lines of evidence concerning the appearance and organization of trading facilities on Cozumel. We believe that identification of trading activities is possible and necessary because, as more and more data have been collected and analyzed, we have become increasingly convinced that a model of Cozumel as a trading center will ultimately integrate the bulk of the data better than any alternative model.

Solution of this problem through examination of the settlement pattern also helps us formulate a specific model of Cozumel in Decadent times which we will link to a more general model proposed by Rathje and Sabloff (1973).

COZUMEL AS TRADING CENTER: THE GENERAL MODEL VERSUS THE SPECIFIC DATA

Elsewhere, Rathje and Sabloff (1972; 1973) have shown in detail how models based on the historically known trading patterns on Classic Rhodes and Delos can be used to predict changing patterns on Cozumel. Of particular interest here is their prediction that a centralization of control of the resources in a given trading area will lead to the decentralization of administrative control of trading ports associated with that area. On the other hand, a decentralization of resource control will lead to a centralization of control of the various trading ports. Furthermore, the organizations of trading ports will emphasize information and capital procurement, flexibility of cultural norms, and the minimization of cultural conflict.

As regards Cozumel, Rathje and Sabloff (1973) predicted that during the Modified Florescent Period (A.D. 900–1250), when the Toltecs and their Putún allies controlled the greater Yucatán area, Cozumel itself should have lacked tight local control of its port facilities. With the collapse of the Toltec capital at Chichén Itzá and the concomitant decline of Toltec power (the events marking the transition between the Modified Florescent and Decadent Periods [A.D. 1250]), control of the procurement and distribution of resources from the greater Yucatán area became fragmented, or localized. Major centers at Mayapán,

Tulum, and in the Tabasco-Campeche Lowlands arose at this time and became controlling centers of the long-distance trading network. Rathje and Sabloff predicted that during this same transition period Cozumel should have asserted administrative control of its major resource, its port facilities.

A number of test expectations for the predictions of early decentralization versus later centralization on Cozumel were noted by Rathje and Sabloff. We hope that artifact analyses currently in progress will allow us to test the general model adequately in the near future. At present, however, some preliminary observations can be made by examining the location of sites on the island and inquiring into their probable functions.

Looking at the geography of Cozumel, we would expect the bulk of the island's trading activities and population to have been concentrated around the natural harbors of San Miguel on the protected leeward coast. Comparisons to other trading ports would lead us further to expect trading facilities, warehouses, and administrative offices to have been located in or immediately adjacent to the port. But such was not the case on Cozumel in Decadent times. Although there was an important population concentration in San Miguel, there was apparently a major storage area at the site of Buena Vista, as well as smaller storage areas at sites such as La Expedición and Chen Cedral. In addition, the administrative and religious center of the island apparently was located in the San Gervasio zone (see figure 32 for the locations of all the Cozumel sites mentioned in this chapter).

How can we account for this unexpected distribution, especially in light of Rathje and Sabloff's (1973) prediction that the Decadent Period, a time of decentralization of resource control in the greater Yucatán area, should see a centralization of control of the island and its trading activities?

To answer this question we must first examine our concept of trade and then the available data in light of this concept. As is the case with many archaeological concepts which have been borrowed from other fields, the concept of *trade* is a loaded one. The term often is used to describe a multitude of differing activities. In many cases, the definitional intent of the term is clear enough to avoid confusion. In some instances, however, the term can be used to cover related but functionally differing

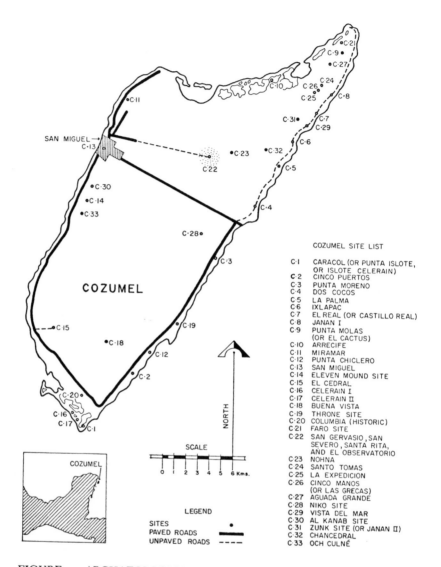

COZUMEL SITE LIST

C·1	CARACOL (OR PUNTA ISLOTE, OR ISLOTE CELERAIN)
C·2	CINCO PUERTOS
C·3	PUNTA MORENO
C·4	DOS COCOS
C·5	LA PALMA
C·6	IXLAPAC
C·7	EL REAL (OR CASTILLO REAL)
C·8	JANAN I
C·9	PUNTA MOLAS (OR EL CACTUS)
C·10	ARRECIFE
C·11	MIRAMAR
C·12	PUNTA CHICLERO
C·13	SAN MIGUEL
C·14	ELEVEN MOUND SITE
C·15	EL CEDRAL
C·16	CELERAIN I
C·17	CELERAIN II
C·18	BUENA VISTA
C·19	THRONE SITE
C·20	COLUMBIA (HISTORIC)
C·21	FARO SITE
C·22	SAN GERVASIO, SAN SEVERO, SANTA RITA, AND EL OBSERVATORIO
C·23	NOHNA
C·24	SANTO TOMAS
C·25	LA EXPEDICION
C·26	CINCO MANOS (OR LAS GRECAS)
C·27	AGUADA GRANDE
C·28	NIKO SITE
C·29	VISTA DEL MAR
C·30	AL KANAB SITE
C·31	ZUNK SITE (OR JANAN II)
C·32	CHANCEDRAL
C·33	OCH CULNÉ

SCALE

0 1 2 3 4 5 6 Kms.

NORTH

LEGEND

SITES	●
PAVED ROADS	━━━
UNPAVED ROADS	- - - -

FIGURE 32. ARCHAEOLOGICAL SITE LOCATIONS ON THE ISLAND OF COZUMEL, MEXICO. A preliminary map (1972 field season).

activities and can hence lead to the burying of significant factors which are essential to an understanding of "trade" in a particular area. We believe that this has happened on Cozumel, where the use of the cover term *trade* helped hide from us, until recently, at least two different kinds of exchange activities.

One type is a regular, nonseasonal trade; the other is a seasonal trade. We will argue below that the factor of different kinds of trade along with local ecological factors and the general historical change in Yucatán from centralized to noncentralized control of resources combined to produce the settlement and trading pattern on Cozumel in Decadent times.

Applying the distinction between seasonal and nonseasonal trade to the items traded on Cozumel, we are better able to understand the physical separation between storage facilities and the principal port zone. Among the important traded goods were salt, honey, and cacao. These goods were not available all year round. Salt, for instance, was collected on the nearby east coast on a seasonal basis (Roys 1943:53). Logically speaking, it would have economically behooved Cozumel to stockpile such goods during the limited time of the year at which they were available, so that they would be able to sell them throughout the year. Other materials, such as obsidian and various hard stone items, would probably have been available at all times. Goods such as these would have flowed through the continuously active San Miguel port all year round.

The seasonally available items had to be stored, but San Miguel was not the logical place because of its great vulnerability to attack from the sea. It must be recalled that the Decadent Period was a time of decentralization of resource control, with no one power dominating the scene such as the Toltec/Putún had done in the preceding Modified Florescent Period (900–1250 A.D.). There was raiding on the long-distance trade routes and the ever-present danger of attack (Roys 1933: 142, 156; 1943: 53, 70). It is for this reason, we believe, that Tulum, for example, was built on such a defensible position and was surrounded by a large wall, as were the defensible sites of Xcaret and Ichpaatún on the east coast.[6]

On Cozumel, it would have been defensibly sound to locate the storage areas inland, where they would not have been readily vulnerable to seaborne pirates. Furthermore, a system of defensively placed shrines on the opposite side of the island from San Miguel could have provided a complete warning system against attack on the unprotected windward coast of the island. The need for defensive storage locations would have outweighed the inefficiency of locating long-term warehousing far from the port of San Miguel and would account for the inland location of the major storage site of Buena Vista.

But can we say anything more about the particular location of Buena Vista, about five hours' walking time from San Miguel? Two additional factors need to be considered. One is that there are two other excellent docking areas in addition to the leeward coastal harbors. These are the lagoons on both the north and south coasts of Cozumel which would have provided excellent harbors for the large-length but small-draft dugout canoes utilized in the long-distance trade of the area. The southern lagoons might have been used by traders traveling with the strong coastal current from the south who brought such seasonal goods as cacao, while the northern ones could have been used by traders bringing goods such as salt from the north. In the northern part of the island, a series of raised causeways lead south away from the lagoons; these would have allowed passage to storage areas over flooded low-lying zones during the rainy season, a time when many seasonal goods would not be available.

Buena Vista is relatively near, but not *too* close to, the southern lagoons. In addition, it is situated in one of the richest agricultural zones, if not the richest, of the island (as determined by Paula L. W. Sabloff's historical research). Archaeological evidence indicated that prior to the Decadent Period a population center of some importance existed there but did not have the later huge storage platforms. The controllers of the Buena Vista zone would have had considerable economic power and wealth due to their marketing of agricultural produce. It is possible that when and if sociopolitical power on the island was centralized at San Gervasio in the Decadent Period, the ruling family from Buena Vista would have had enough clout to have the major storage facility on the island situated on their lands in the southern part of the island. It also should be noted that there is only one elite residence complex at Buena Vista. On the basis of historical analogy, it is possible that the owners of Buena Vista might have maintained a residence between Buena Vista and San Gervasio (Paula L. W. Sabloff, personal communication; also see Sabloff et al. in press for a discussion of other evidence for private property on Cozumel). The site would have been run by a manager who lived in a house unit in the elite complex throughout the year. A similar situation of only one elite residence complex adjacent to important storage zones was found at both La Expedición and San Gervasio in the north.

The other important question that we would like to consider is why the political center of Cozumel apparently was located at the inland San Gervasio zone. As in the case of the storage areas, defensive protection may have been a significant factor. Tradition and history may also have been important, since San Gervasio, situated like Buena Vista in a rich agricultural area, had been a major center since the time of the first large occupation of the island. Moreover, San Gervasio is well placed, being within several hours' walking distance from San Miguel and the northern lagoons.

Another factor in the separation of the administrative and major population centers of the island may have been the environmental one of ready access to fresh water. Over one hundred cenotes can be found in the interior of the island, including some in the San Gervasio zone, but few are known in the immediate vicinity of San Miguel. Although over 10,000 people live in and around San Miguel today, much of the water is pumped in from wells located in the center of the island, and a new desalinization plant was recently built to handle the load. Thus, ready access to water and food may have helped dictate the location of Cozumel's major center at San Gervasio.

Finally, there is the factor of the location of the Ix Chel shrine. There is some evidence to suggest that this important "talking" oracle may originally have been situated in the San Gervasio zone, although it may have been moved to San Miguel just prior to the conquest (Freidel n.d.). The elite of Cozumel may have wished to keep their residences and administrative work near the shrine that helped legitimize their power and lent importance to Cozumel's role in the long-distance trading system. Moreover, the shrine may have enhanced the elite's stature and solidified their economic position by making the foreign traders come to them, away from the ordinary transactions of the port and the lodgings and activities of the seamen and porters. As Scholes and Roys (1948:33–34) point out, the merchants probably visited the Ix Chel shrine in addition to attending to their economic concerns. Furthermore, the aura of religious sanctity in the San Gervasio zone might have helped to dampen potential conflict between merchants from diverse backgrounds and smooth the economic transactions among these people (also see Rathje and Sabloff 1972 for a full discussion of the necessity for trading ports to minimize cultural conflict). Of course, this line of reasoning still begs the questions of why the Ix Chel shrine might have originally been located at San Gervasio and of whether it preceded the economic center or was created later to help justify it.

To conclude, although one initially might have expected that centralization of trading facilities and centralization of administration would go hand in hand, we believe that decentralization of facilities is not incompatible with administrative centralization. In fact, it could be argued that the separation of functionally differentiated facilities, such as appears in Decadent times on Cozumel, would require a strong centralized administration to coordinate the island's trading activities. If archaeological analyses now under way could show, for instance, artifactual and architectural conformity among Cozumel's varied sites during Decadent times, then support could be provided for the project's general model. Such support would be further strengthened if such a situation could be contrasted with artifactual and architectural differentiation among sites during the earlier Modified Florescent Period.

FUNCTIONAL IDENTIFICATIONS IN THE SPECIFIC MODEL: THE DATA BASE AND ITS PROBLEMS

We now turn to an examination of the data that allowed us to make the functional identifications of trading port and storage facilities. Specifically, how can we identify Buena Vista as a major storage site and San Gervasio as the politico-religious center of Cozumel? It should be stressed that our discussion is based principally on settlement and comparative data, since the detailed laboratory analyses of the archaeological finds from Cozumel have not yet been made. Final reports by William L. Rathje and David A. Gregory, in preparation now, will consider the Buena Vista and San Gervasio data, respectively, in full detail. However, it is only through preliminary working hypotheses, such as the ones proposed here and in all the other preliminary publications of the project, that our knowledge of Cozumel and its makeup as a trading center will be advanced. Finally, we have attempted to present the data in some detail, with all their inconsistencies and unevenness, so as to give the reader some appreciation of the numerous difficulties involved in functional identifications in a trading center. We feel the effort involved is worthwhile and hope that the reader will come to a similar conclusion. Before turning to a consideration of the differing features of Buena Vista and San Gervasio, some general data must be discussed.

Domestic Architecture

Stone foundations of perishable domestic structures, tentatively dated to the Decadent period on the basis of ceramic evidence, have been positively identified at six sites on Cozumel. Owing to the considerable range of variation in both size and form, these structures can be grouped into several types. Implicit in the following analysis is the assumption that a similarity in form reflects a similarity in the inhabitants' organization and conception of domestic space.

The most common of these dwelling types is a single-roomed rectangular structure with clearly defined bench areas along the back and side walls. Examples of this type range from diminutive (3 m. by 4 m.) rural homesteads, far from major settlement zones, to fairly imposing (6 m. by 12 m.) centrally located elite residences. The type occurs on the northeast coast and in the north interior and south interior parts of the island. Given the assumption that the amount of labor invested in the construction of a domestic facility covaries with the economic resources of the residents, the fact that there is a wide range in size and elaborateness of the structures within this type indicates that it cannot be associated with a particular economic class. If the assumption is made that a particular organization and conception of domestic space can be correlated with a particular sociocultural group, then the wide spatial distribution of this type, unmatched by any other type, reflects the wide distribution of such a group.

Remaining domestic foundations fall into three categories, each with a small representative sample: (1) rectangular single-roomed structures without bench areas, (2) rectangular multiroomed structures with bench areas and medial walls, and (3) apsidal single-roomed structures. The first type is limited in known distribution to the northwest coast and the northern interior region of the island; the second is found only at the major northern interior settlement of San Gervasio; the third is found only at the major southern interior settlement of Buena Vista.

While the first type is not particularly distinctive with respect to regional distribution, the second and third types are. Two-roomed rectangular structures with benches and medial walls are the typical form of house found at Decadent Mayapán. However, they are rarely found outside the immediate vicinity of that site (Ruppert and Smith 1957; Smith 1962). One notable exception is the Decadent site of Tulum, on the mainland south of Cozumel, where several structures of this type have been identified. Apsidal structures, on the other hand, are a widely distributed modern Maya house type (Wauchope 1934; 1940; Kurjack 1972) of demonstrable antiquity in northern Yucatán. With reference to the correlation of form with a particular sociocultural group, it is interesting that while two examples of this type were found to date to the Decadent at Dzibilchaltún, a large site in northwestern Yucatán, the apsidal structure is not represented at Mayapán (Kurjack 1972, table 5).

Despite survey work in the area (Sanders 1955; 1960; E. W. Andrews IV and A. Andrews in press), practically nothing is known of domestic architecture on the central coast of Quintana Roo opposite Cozumel. Hence it is difficult to place our data in local perspective. It has been noted that Mayapán-style structures are found at Tulum and San Gervasio. It might therefore be argued that the Mayapán-type houses at San Gervasio simply reflect the influence of a formidable east coast neighbor. But this is clearly not the case, for our Mayapán-type structures are found associated with outbuildings in elite residential complexes that are typical of Mayapán. Such complexes are not found at Tulum, nor is our single-roomed benched type.

In summary, we seem to have a predominant local house type with a fairly wide range of variation and no clear affiliations with nearby regions. There are also two exotic house types represented, one specifically correlated with Mayapán and Tulum, the other found at Dzibilchaltún in the Decadent period. We have, then, exotic facilities as well as exotic materials in the Decadent period on Cozumel.

Substructures

Substructures characterized by stone rubble, trash fill, and roughly dressed retaining walls are the most common architectural feature on Cozumel. They occur in a wide variety of shapes, sizes, and patterns. Stone foundations of perishable houses, such as those discussed above, are frequently found on such substructures but may also occur on natural rises without them. Nonetheless, the vast majority of substructures lack surface indications of identifiable superstructures. In such cases, it is very difficult to characterize the function of the substructures.

This problem, a common one in the area, has been handled by different students in different ways. Sanders (1960), for example, found many such substructures at Tancah (on the mainland opposite Cozumel) and speculated that they were used for priestly residences and houses of the elite. He considered terraced areas at Tulum to be substructures for houses. A. L. Smith (1962) faced a similar problem at Mayapán, where there were a thousand substructures whose function was unknown. He suggested that they might have supported perishable structures used as guesthouses, storage facilities, kitchens, or workshops.

Intensive excavation of such substructures revealed that they were often plastered on the surface, expanded and rebuilt, and contained trash in the fill that can most easily be identified as domestic. Furthermore, "chultúns," or storage pits, which are also associated with houses that have stone foundations, are occasionally found built into these substructures. Thus it seems safe to speculate that at least some of our many substructures did indeed support completely perishable houses. How many, and which ones, it is impossible to determine, as some of these platforms lack all of the above characteristics. Yet the patterns that these substructures form in settlements on the island, and their associations with other identifiable facilities, may yield some clues as to their use. Before we discuss these patterns, we must describe the general class of structures composed of masonry architecture.

Masonry Architecture

The superstructures on Cozumel with standing masonry walls generally include types that have been considered civil-religious in function.

Although our typology is still in the preliminary stages of formulation, and although distinctive forms grade into one another, there are strong similarities in form between Decadent masonry architecture on Cozumel and that reported from the east coast and Mayapán. These similarities constitute a substantial body of information providing possible approaches to a functional interpretation of masonry-walled structures.

In terms of the established typology for the Decadent, general forms include: (1) small square or rectangular buildings with altars, called "shrines"; (2) larger rectangular buildings, often with colonnaded front doors and medial partitions, called either "temples" or "palaces"; and (3) long, open-sided, colonnaded rectangular buildings.

Debris associated with these types has supported the following functional generalizations. The trash recovered from "shrines" on Cozumel includes quantities of censer ware and cache offerings. Here and elsewhere the function of these objects seems to be primarily religious. Although little debris was associated directly with "temples" or "palaces" on Cozumel, that which was excavated seemed nondomestic, consisting of religious sculpture, dedicatory caches, and the like. In cases where domestic middens were found near "temples" or "palaces," these structures were juxtaposed with clearly domestic facilities. Therefore the association does not lead to any clear functional interpretation.

Colonnaded structures, the third category, were not intensively excavated by our project. But what little was found supports the general picture at Mayapán, where a number of these buildings were investigated. The associated trash was religious in orientation, including evidence of sacrifice, incense, censer ware, and idols (Shook and Irving 1955). By analogy with known institutions at the time of the conquest, Proskouriakoff (1962) holds that these were public residences for unmarried men. If most domestic activities were relegated to nearby structures, colonnaded buildings might be considered dwellings, but the associated debris indicates a function other than that of residence.

Relative location can also shed some light on the function of masonry structures on Cozumel. The "temples" or "palaces" and the colonnaded structures are consistently associated with compact plaza arrangements, in contrast to "shrines" and pyramid substructures surmounted by "shrines," which may or may not be found in such association. The imposing size of these plaza complexes and their relative scarcity on the island give the impression that they were public, central locations for a variety of community and supracommunity activities, despite the frequent occurrence of domestic structures in them. With noted exceptions, such plaza groups are hereafter termed "elite residence complexes," following the terminology used at Mayapán (Smith 1962).

Problems are raised, however, in the functional interpretation of the above categories of structures when ethnohistorical information is taken into account. "Shrines" on Cozumel, for example, were described by the Spanish as "chapels," a term which supports the idea that these buildings had a religious function. On the other hand, Bernal Díaz described those "shrines" along the coast of the island as "towers" (Roys 1943). Early descriptions of "temples" likewise fit known features on the island, but a clear distinction between "temples" and "palaces" on the basis of form cannot be derived from the ethnohistorical materials. Similarly, the Spanish noted many "stone houses" on Cozumel, so it is likely that at least some of the large masonry structures were used as residences. But undoubtedly a number of other activities were carried out in the masonry structures, although these are rarely described. Roys (1943), for example, notes that at the important commercial center of Cachí, in northeastern Yucatán, there was a masonry structure which housed a market court in one corner of a large open plaza. At Chauacha, in the same region, part of the market was inside stone buildings with thatched roofs.

Unlike analysis of the general class of perishable houses with stone foundations, a consideration of masonry structures does not yield a clear intersection of the various lines of evidence that would allow an ideal correlation of form with function. A number of alternatives—based upon patterns of association between the formal properties of the structures, associated debris, relative and absolute location, and ethnohistorical analogies—must be considered in assigning a function to any particular structure. This analysis will be attempted in the final report.

Settlement Patterns

Although the Decadent Period in the northern Maya lowlands is not well understood, it does seem to mark some notable departures from earlier norms in settlement organization. The nucleated, walled settlements of Mayapán, Tulum, and Ichpaatún stand in sharp contrast to the dispersed settlements the Maya seem generally to have preferred throughout their history in the lowlands. Nevertheless, dispersed settlements continued during the Decadent Period and were found later by the Spanish. Hence the nucleated settlements have been interpreted as indicating that there was some shift in social organization or settlement function at a few locations. Settlements on Cozumel reflect this situation.

Eight settlements, defined as the loci of distinct communities, were found on Cozumel. Despite previous work on the island (Escalona Ramos 1946; Fernández 1940; Sanders 1960) and the extensive nature of our survey, other settlements undoubtedly remain undiscovered. Each of the known settlements will now be briefly described.

Aguada Grande

Aguada Grande is the smallest settlement investigated by the survey, with an occupation zone of less than 10 hectares. This settlement, as the name implies, is located next to a large seasonal limestone sink, or *aguada*, at the northeasternmost extension of the island. It consists of the following features: (1) a group of four small "shrines" associated with a unique multiroomed perishable structure with stone foundations; (2) a number of fairly large rubble substructures (the largest measuring 30 m. on a side); and (3) two benched, single-roomed, domestic structures. These features are interconnected by a grid of stone field walls (such walls cover all but a fraction of the island) to which they are precisely oriented, giving the impression that the grid and the features were built at the same time.

A functional interpretation of this settlement must take into consideration, first, that Aguada Grande had a very small resident population, despite the presence of a ceremonial precinct, indicated by the "shrine" group. Second, the fact that a raised stone path or *sacbe* runs north-south through the *aguadas* to the north and south of the settlement indicates that an important route, used during the rainy season, ran through the settlement. Third, only one of the rubble substructures yielded debris of any kind. It was domestic in nature. The lack of trash associated with any of the other substructures points to the possibility that their function was other than domestic. Finally, the fact that the multiroomed structure associated with the four "shrines" fits no known formal, functional, or ethnohistorical category implies that it had some specialized function. We suggest on the basis of the number and small size of the rooms that it might have served as a storage facility.

Taking the above into consideration, we have tentatively interpreted Aguada Grande as a relay station on the overland transport route from the northern lagoons to settlements located on the windward coast and the interior further south.

La Expedición

Located on the northeast coast, four kilometers south of Aguada Grande, La Expedición is a larger, more complex, dispersed settlement. The site contains: (1) an elite residence complex composed of three "palaces" or "temples" and two single-roomed, benched, domestic structures arranged on a raised plaza; (2) a number of positively identifiable domestic structures scattered to the north and south of the plaza; (3) a number of low, rectangular, rubble substructures dispersed to the south and west of the plaza; (4) one large, agglutinated rubble substructure; and (5) several smaller agglutinated substructures.

As agglutinated substructures have not been considered previously, we will discuss them now. They are seen today as large single features with multiple discrete rectilinear areas that are defined by variation in height. It appears from excavation that at one time these structures consisted of clustered, single substructures which later were attached to one another and functioned as a unit.

In the functional interpretation of these substructures, a deductive argument is perhaps most fruitful. If it is assumed that the substructures were constructed primarily as raised and leveled areas for dwellings, the facts that several of the more elaborate domestic structures at the settlement are found without substructures and that the largest and most elaborate agglutinated substructure has only a single domestic structure seem incongruous. Likewise, the general expectation that the amount of effort invested in a support substructure should vary positively with that invested in a superstructure is not realized in this case. Furthermore, a group of houses on a large, shared platform without plaza arrangement would in itself be an unusual departure from the surrounding pattern. Although the vagaries of preservation may play some role in this situation, identifiable domestic foundations always consist of walls made of dressed stone. While the pattern of the structure may be destroyed, such stone should remain on the surface despite slumping and root action. Apart from the single known domestic structure, no cut stone was located on the surface or in the immediate vicinity of the large agglutinated substructure at La Expedición.

In light of the above evidence, two explanations are possible: (1) we are dealing with a group of people who organized themselves spatially in sharp contrast to their neighbors within the settlement and who had very different ideas about the appropriate labor investment in domestic construction; or (2) the one known domestic structure was in fact the only such structure on the large agglutinated substructure, while the other areas on it were built to support structures with a different function. These alternatives will be discussed further below.

Zuuk

The settlement of Zuuk is located about four kilometers south of La Expedición on the northeast coast. The site is composed of: (1) an elite residence complex with two masonry "temples" or "palaces" and two perishable benched domestic structures arranged on a raised plaza; (2) a zone of low rubble substructures next to and east of the above complex, on top of which were found another elaborate benched domicile, a masonry shrine, and fragments of several nonbenched perishable structures; (3) a group of two shrines next to a cenote 150 meters west of the above zone and connected to the elaborate benched domicile by a *sacbe*; (4) a zone of large, discrete substructures with a few wall fragments of nonbenched perishable structures south of the elite residence complex; and (5) two masonry "temples" or "palaces" on the eastern edge of the above zone of substructures.

Our control of features at Zuuk is minimal. The zone of large substructures, situated in a large field, was only briefly explored after a burning. More intensive investigation might reveal more information concerning superstructures in this zone. With this qualification, we offer the following general observations. Zuuk seems to have a cluster of

386

more elaborate domestic facilities near the elite residence complex to the north, and a zone of dispersed residences to the south. However, other functions cannot be precluded for this southern zone. Aside from its smaller size, Zuuk contrasts with La Expedición primarily in the lack of agglutinated substructures.

Chen Cedral

This settlement is located about six kilometers south of Zuuk and about four kilometers inland from the northeast coast. The settlement consists entirely of massive agglutinated rubble substructures arranged in a compact, nucleated pattern with accessways and courtyard areas interspersed among or defined by them. These substructures are precisely the same type as those found at La Expedición.

Only two masonry structures were found at the site. The first of these is a completely destroyed "shrine" located about two hundred meters from the nearest substructures on the western edge of the settlement zone next to a cenote. The second structure, also a "shrine," is located on top of a large agglutinated substructure within the settlement. This fairly well preserved "shrine" is on the edge of a dressed stone enclosure which forms a large rectangle on top of the substructure. The only other superstructural remains are a small number of fragments of foundation walls on the substructures west of the "shrine." No complete foundations of any structural type were discovered. Because the retaining walls of the substructures themselves are the best preserved on the island, it is doubtful that this absence of foundations can be completely attributed to the factor of poor preservation.

It is difficult to conceive of a settlement of this size (approximately twenty hectares) not having a resident population, so undoubtedly there were dwellings here. The few wall fragments found may well relate to the known rectangular, nonbenched house type, but it is obvious that people were investing relatively little effort in the construction of buildings and great effort in the construction of substructures at Chen Cedral. In fact, it has fewer identifiable structures than any other settlement on the island. Masonry architecture is limited to a centrally located "shrine" and its sacred enclosure. An elite residence complex is notably absent.

387

Again, either we are dealing with a segment of Decadent Period society with distinctive ideas about the arrangement of living space and the appropriate investment of labor in construction related to it, or such substructures had a predominant function other than domestic. If this is the case, the entire site was oriented toward some other function.

San Miguel

Very little is known about the settlement of San Miguel, which is situated on the northwest coast of Cozumel. It has been almost completely destroyed by the one modern town on the island. All the ancient masonry structures have been razed in this century to provide building materials for modern construction projects. Some of these structures, however, were recorded before they disappeared (see, for example, Holmes 1895). They appear to be buildings of the "temple" or "palace" type. We did find a number of scattered, small substructures (approximately ten meters by ten meters) to the north of the present town behind a natural rise about two hundred meters inland. This rise transects the town and parallels the shore. Some additional small substructures were found behind the same rise, to the south of the zone of modern construction. These scanty data leave us with the impression of a fairly long, narrow, dispersed settlement paralleling the beach.

San Miguel would have made a fine port facility in antiquity, as it faces a small protected *caleta*, or bay, on the leeward side of the island. Spanish sources indicate that it was probably a large settlement in the sixteenth century (Lothrop 1924:14, 154). Test pitting in one of the northern substructures revealed a series of plastered floors but no foundation walls. It is frustrating that so little can be said of the facilities here, because surface collections yielded a representative sample from a number of periods and a rich assortment of trade wares, in addition to exotic materials such as copper and obsidian.

El Cedral

To a degree, El Cedral suffers from the same problem as San Miguel in that a modern community is superimposed upon it. The modern community is quite small, however, and, despite considerable stone theft,

388

much of the site remains intact. El Cedral is a dispersed settlement covering about forty hectares. It consists of: (1) masonry "temples" or "palaces" and "shrines" in plaza groups sharing rectangular support substructures; (2) isolated "shrines" on substructures; and (3) domestic structures on support substructures. There are only a few rubble substructures at the site. These lack remains of identifiable structures and are not particularly large.

Compared with other settlements on Cozumel, El Cedral is unusual in that it contains a large number of "temple" or "palace" structures. Similarly, the ratio of structures to substructures is high, and the investment of labor in the substructures seems more or less in balance with that in the structures on top of them. Furthermore, two of the "shrines" at this site have beveled vault stones which give the soffit a smooth, even surface in contrast to other vaults on the island, which are stepped.[7] (This was noted by Fernández 1940 and its significance pointed out to us by E. W. Andrews IV and A. Andrews, personal communication.)

El Cedral, located on a fertile land base about four kilometers inland from the southwest coast, seems to have been a rather prosperous and socioculturally homogenous or unspecialized community.

San Gervasio

Located in the north-central part of Cozumel, San Gervasio is the largest settlement on the island, with an occupation zone of more than a hundred hectares. The settlement pattern is basically dispersed, composed of four subzones or districts separated by areas of scattered features. The first of these zones includes five groups of structures but has as its focus a large plaza complex of four "temples" or "palaces" and three colonnaded structures. All seven rest on long, narrow support substructures, which are located on three sides of the rectangle. On the fourth side of the plaza is an empty, long substructure that supported some kind of perishable structure with a plastered floor. In contrast to similar complexes found elsewhere on the island, this group shows no evidence of identifiable domiciles. No domestic trash was recovered in or around the empty substructure or elsewhere in the group. Associated materials included censer ware, dedicatory caches, and religious sculpture. Keeping in mind the problematic interpretation of "palaces" or "temples" and colonnaded structures discussed above, we may conclude that the associated debris, central location, and monumentality of the features supports an exclusively civil-religious, nondomestic function for this complex.

The second group of structures in this first district, located to the south of the first group, is in poor condition. It is composed of a large, rectangular, nonbenched, multiroomed structure, a second, badly preserved, rectangular structure with two massive columns (possibly door jambs), and a small, square, plaster-floored substructure with a retaining wall of very finely cut, reused, Puuc-style veneer stone dating to the Florescent Period. This may have supported a perishable "shrine." Several low, rectangular, rubble substructures without clear features and another possible perishable "shrine" are scattered in the immediate vicinity of this group. The group appears to have been a residence with associated perishable structures arranged around a plaza.

The third group, east of the first group, is a typical Mayapán-style elite residence group, consisting of a large, multiroomed, benched house and a specialized ceremonial structure, called an oratory at Mayapán. It was interpreted there as a private "shrine." These structures are on opposite sides of a single substructure. They form a plaza group with a platform altar.

Immediately south of the Mayapán group is another more complex one. This fourth group consists of the following features: In the first case, there are two structures arranged on a plaza at right angles to each other, sharing one end of a large, low substructure. The first building is a perishable, anomalous, multibenched structure on an elaborate individual support substructure. The second building is a combination "shrine-palace" or "complex shrine"—a shrine enclosed within a large masonry structure, according to the east coast typology (A. Andrews, personal communication). Secondly, to the east of, but associated with, this plaza group, is another complex shrine. Finally, there are large, low, rubble substructures with some evidence of perishable structures in the form of cut stone. These extend to the east, beyond the main plaza of this fourth group.

This group, as a whole, has been interpreted as a religious focus, represented by the two complex shrines, associated with a nonelite residential zone as evidenced by the low rubble substructures and the high concentration of domestic trash in the area.

The fifth and final group in this district is a second Mayapán-style elite residence complex located next to, and immediately west of, the first group.

In interpreting the settlement pattern of this district, the following evidence must be considered: First, the district is composed predominantly of plaza groups. Not only is this particular arrangement of structures relatively rare on the island, but the clustering of complexes of this kind is unique to District 1. Second, as outlined above, the large plaza complex termed Group 1 appears to have had an exclusively civil-religious function. Third, the elite residential complexes here contrast with those at Expedición, Zuuk, Buena Vista, and District 4 San Gervasio in that they lack "palaces," "temples," and colonnaded structures, the presence of which indicates a civil-religious and/or administrative function. While we cannot preclude the presence of such a function, it is clearly not emphasized architecturally in these residential complexes. Third, Groups 2, 3, and 4 are connected to Group 1 by *sacbes*. Finally, rubble substructures in Group 4 and the domestic trash in its vicinity suggest that the nonelite population was small. Therefore the pattern of this district may be seen as a more complex version of the single plaza, elite residence complexes found as the focus of La Expedición, Zuuk, Buena Vista, and District 4 at San Gervasio. In this case, however, the residential function is found separated from the central focus, which has taken on a purely civil-religious and/or administrative function.

Having established the civil-religious focus of the district, we can further interpret it in three ways. District 1 could have functioned as an administrative center for an archaeologically invisible, largely nonelite surrounding population. The presence of an invisible population is necessarily problematic, but it seems unlikely given the pattern of other settlements on the island. Elite residence complexes, for example, at the other sites are found inside distinct settlement zones made up of a large number and variety of observable features. If the first district were merely a grander version of these elite residence complexes with the same general function, one would expect to find a large zone of observable features in association with it. This clearly does not occur.

Secondly, District 1 might have functioned as an administrative center for the settlement of San Gervasio as a whole. This possibility could be refuted by the fact that other districts have elite residence complexes and civil-religious plaza groups associated with them. These other central places, however, do not compare to the first district in terms of the size and elaborateness of Decadent Period "temples" or "palaces" and colonnaded structures. Therefore it may indeed be postulated that District 1 served as a civil-religious center for the entire settlement. But this does not appear to have been its only function, as the first district is separated from the other three districts of San Gervasio by a distance of approximately one kilometer. Hence it is not centrally located with regard to the settlement as a whole. In fact, it seems quite isolated. Centrality of location for civil-religious centers is a hallmark of Maya lowland settlement pattern. Therefore if the first district is solely a civil-religious center for the entire settlement, it stands in sharp contrast to this general pattern.

This leads us to the third alternative. In addition to serving as a civil-religious center for San Gervasio as a whole, the district could have functioned as an administrative center at the supracommunity level, coordinating institutional activities involving resident populations at a number of other settlements on the island. Supporting this hypothesis is the presence of a particularly large *sacbe* running from the first group in the first district toward the northeast coast. Unfortunately, only five kilometers of this road could be mapped because within four kilometers of the coast it disappeared into a small ancient settlement. Given its unusual size and the fact that it is punctuated by four shrines at one-kilometer intervals and a freestanding arch at the entrance into San Gervasio, it seems unlikely that the road would have ended in this obscure settlement. It appears far more probable that this particular *sacbe* continued through the settlement and ran all the way to the coast. As the northeast coast is a region of dense settlement including the known sites of Aguada Grande, La Expedición, Zuuk, and Chen Cedral, it would appear that this *sacbe* was an intersite transportation route.

In conclusion, District 1 appears to have served not only as a civil-religious center for the site of San Gervasio as a whole, but also as an administrative center coordinating institutional activities involving resident populations elsewhere on the island.

North and west of the first district there is an isolated group consisting of two masonry "temples" or "palaces," a perishable "temple," and two "shrines," one of which is round and placed on a round terraced substructure. These structures form an irregular, nonrectangular plaza and rest on a single substructure. The associated debris, including caches and censer ware, and the lack of identifiable domestic features point to an exclusively civil-religious function for this group.

Three discontinuous *sacbes* run off this group. This first spans a small *aguada* next to the group and heads in the general direction of District 1. The *sacbe* ends at the other side of the *aguada*, covering a distance of less than twenty meters. The second *sacbe* runs west toward District 2, which is approximately one kilometer away. This *sacbe* was deliberately destroyed about halfway between the group and District 2. The third *sacbe* runs toward the northern lagoons. If these *sacbes* were operating at the same time, the group formed a nexus of the routes they defined. Because of the complicated problems involved in further functional interpretation of this group, which can best be dealt with from a broad comparative perspective, we will return to it in the summary.

The second district, located about a kilometer west of the first, is situated on a natural rise, one of the highest points on the island. This district consists of the following features: (1) a massive plaza group with long, high substructures on four sides; (2) a second plaza sharing one side with the first plaza group, with a "temple" or "palace" structure along another side and a low rubble substructure on a third; (3) a large (60-by-100-meter) empty rectangular enclosure with walls formed of massive (3-by-2-by-2-meter) slabs of bedrock south of the plazas; (4) five large, low agglutinated rubble substructures with no clear superstructural remains, situated south and west of the rectangular enclosure; and finally (5) several "shrines," one on a pyramidal substructure, and one elite residence group scattered to the west of the abovementioned features.

District 2 presents us with an interesting situation. The two plaza groups share a massive low substructure. There are remains of only two standing masonry structures in these plazas: the abovementioned "palace" and another "temple" or "palace" located in the first plaza group. Despite the lack of below-floor ceramics associated with the "palace" in the second plaza, it can be clearly dated, on the basis of architectural style and construction technique, to the Early Period, many hundreds of years before the Decadent. The other "temple" can be dated to the Florescent Period on the basis of sealed below-floor ceramics. Test excavations in the massive substructures and plaza floors yielded material dating predominantly to periods prior to the Decadent. The impression given by this information is that little or no construction was taking place in these plaza groups during the Decadent Period.

The large size, plaza arrangements, and associated "temples" or "palaces" indicate that these plazas functioned during some periods as a civil-religious center. The lack of construction activity and the general sparsity of occupation debris dating to the Decadent indicate that the function of these groups had changed dramatically by Decadent times. However, the fact that Decadent censer ware was found directly on top of the well-preserved floor of the first "palace" indicates that the "palace" was still being used during the Decadent and that this use cannot be clearly interpreted as postoccupational.

While no date can be assigned to the rectangular enclosure or the agglutinated substructures, circumstantial evidence points to the use of the former during the Decadent. A *sacbe* was found running from one corner of the enclosure to the staircase of the pyramidal substructure and "temple" located about 150 meters west of it. This "temple" clearly dates to the Decadent. The other "shrines" and the elite residence in the vicinity also date to the Decadent.

It can be argued, then, (1) that the vicinity of the plaza groups was not abandoned during the Decadent; (2) that one of the ancient structures associated with the plazas was being maintained and that the enclosure was being used during this period; and (3) that the choice elevated location and available substructures were not being exploited for construction of monumental buildings during the Decadent.

Our preliminary interpretation of this situation is that during Decadent times these plaza groups and the associated rectangular enclosure were maintained as important sacred space for ritual activities. Although construction was being scrupulously avoided within the "sacred precinct" it was being carried out in its vicinity. The "shrines" and elite residence further indicate the importance of this district during the Decadent and generally support its characterization as a ceremonial center.

The disposition of the five agglutinated substructures remains problematical. The fact that they join the outside walls of the rectangular enclosure on two sides and do not continue into it indicates that they were built sometime after the enclosure. While they may have supported a resident population associated with the plaza groups when these groups were an active administrative center, they fall into the general pattern of construction found at Chen Cedral, District 4 at San Gervasio, and Buena Vista (as discussed below). These agglutinated patterns date primarily to the Decadent, although they may have begun earlier. As we will argue in the summary, such agglutinated rubble substructures served purposes other than residential.

The third district at San Gervasio is situated in a large (25 hectares) open field about 400 meters west and south of the second district. This field was burned clear just before our first exploration of it in 1972, but in 1973 it was thickly covered with tall fodder grass. This made a survey of the superstructural remains on all but a few of the substructures impossible. The following description and analysis are based upon selectively cleared substructures and exploration notes from 1972.

The district consists of twenty large (20 by 30 meters average) discrete substructures with rectangular or L-shaped plan. These substructures are dispersed over about 20 hectares, the majority forming a cluster in the 10 easternmost hectares of the field. One positively identifiable elite residence complex was found. Another probable elite residence complex and a number of domestic structures were located on substructures in the district. Fragments of unidentifiable superstructures were found on still other substructures. In the center of the district was a group consisting of an elaborate support substructure for a perishable "temple" or "palace" with balustraded staircase and a running stucco facade around the base, and a perishable, single-room benched structure. These features shared a larger substructure and faced each other and a small plaza between them. There was a tomb in the plaza with an above-surface stone roof resembling a table altar.

Our functional interpretation of District 3 is based upon: (1) the presence of elite residence complexes resembling those of District 1 in that they lack clear evidence of civil-religious or administrative function in the form of "temples," "palaces," or colonnaded structures; (2) the presence of a variety of other domestic structures; (3) the fact that, despite their clustered pattern, the substructures are clearly discrete, unconnected features which are not close enough to each other to define accessways, and which thus form a pattern other than which we are calling agglutinated or nucleated; and (4) the relatively small size of

395

the central civil-religious "temple" or "palace" group. From this evidence we surmise that District 3 functioned primarily as an important residential zone, although other functions cannot be ruled out.

The fourth district of San Gervasio, located about 250 meters south and west of the third district, is made up of these features: First, there is an elite residence complex consisting of a long, large, single-room benched structure with columns, a smaller single-room benched structure, a masonry shrine, and fragments of a large single-room structure arranged on a plaza and sharing a large substructure. Second, four very large substructures form a compact cluster around this central plaza. One of these substructures is of the irregular agglutinated type, the other three are roughly rectangular. One of the rectangular substructures is attached directly to the main plaza complex, the second is connected to this first one by a short (10-meter) raised *sacbe*, and the third is two meters distant from the second, thus forming an accessway between the first two. Remains of two definite single-room benched domiciles and fragments of a possible third one were discovered on these substructures.

The connected and agglutinated nature of the substructures, the sparsity of domestic structures on them, and the civil-religious features of the elite residence complex relate District 4 to patterns found elsewhere on Cozumel. Like Expedición, Zuuk, and Buena Vista, it has an elite residence complex with possible administrative functions. Like Chen Cedral, the agglutinated substructure at La Expedición, and like Buena Vista, it has a compact, connected arrangement with some agglutinated features and few remains of domestic structures.

We tentatively conclude that: (1) District 4 was to some degree administratively self-sufficient; (2) its distinctive pattern may reflect some specialized function other than residential for the district as a whole.

East of District 4 and south of Districts 2 and 3, there is a large zone of low-density dispersed substructures. These substructures, generally smaller than those in the above districts, are located in two large, open fields (about 10 and 5 hectares). While no excavation was carried out in this zone, surface collections yielded utility wares in quantity, some luxury wares, and obsidian blades. Such debris may be generally characterized as domestic, and gives us a tenuous identification of the function of these substructures.

The zone is lacking in features with a relatively high potential for functional identification, such as elite residences and standing masonry architecture. Two nonbenched rectangular domestic structures were located on substructures in the first field, and one benched domestic structure was observed in the second field. This evidence leaves us with the unsatisfactory conclusion that the zone was nonelite and possibly residential in function.

In conclusion, the large size of San Gervasio (over one hundred hectares) and the high frequency of elite and civil-religious features indicate that it was the major settlement on Cozumel. Our tentative functional analysis would lead us to consider it an administrative center with supracommunity responsibilities, and an important ceremonial and population center. However the data are ultimately interpreted, the variety of settlement patterns represented at the site reflects a complexity of spatial organization unequalled on the island.

Buena Vista

Located about a kilometer and a half inland from the southeast coast, Buena Vista is the most intriguing settlement on Cozumel. The following features are found at the site: (1) an artificially raised and leveled area or massive substructure covering approximately five hectares on which are clustered substructures of varying sizes and shapes; (2) a particularly large plaza group situated at the northern end of the raised and leveled area consisting of two colonnaded structures, a large rectangular nonbenched perishable structure, and a large benched domestic structure; (3) a group of two shrines and a "temple" or "palace" located about two hundred meters north of the abovementioned plaza group; (4) another group of shrines and a "temple" or "palace" located about one hundred meters to the south of the southern edge of the raised and leveled area; (5) a scattering of shrines to the east and west of the raised area; and (6) a scattering of substructures to the west of the raised area.

Given the size of the raised and leveled area, superstructural remains on it are surprisingly sparse. They consist of two positively identified single-room benched structures, two more tentatively identified structures of the same type, several apsidal structures, wall fragments of several more rectangular structures that were probably not benched, and one small shrine. A second shrine is located next to the raised and leveled area.

Debris found in excavations on substructures in this area may be generally characterized as domestic. Such debris and the features identified above indicate that one of the functions of these massive substructures was that of supporting residences. Substructural forms, such as the large pyramid, and arrangements, such as the large open plaza, which might indicate a civil-religious function are absent. While the general observation can be made that the raised and leveled area appears to exploit a natural ridge running north-south, the organization of substructures upon it is apparently haphazard, the result of continuous construction over a long period of time. The simplest generalized inference, the one for which we have some positive evidence, is that this raised and leveled area is a particularly large nucleated residential zone.

However, a number of interpretive problems are raised if we accept this inference. The nucleated area is clearly the central focus of the settlement. Monumental architecture in the form of shrines and other masonry structures is dispersed around this focus. Dispersed among these shrines and beyond them are substructures to the west, south, and east. The settlement is more or less concentrically organized. Concentric organization itself is not unusual in the Maya Lowlands as observed archaeologically and substantiated ethnohistorically. The usual pattern, however, is to have facilities associated with community-level administrative and ceremonial activities as the focus, with residential districts dispersed around them. The plaza group at the northern end of the nucleated area probably functioned as an administrative center. Thus its location at the focus conforms to our expectations. But otherwise the pattern is a reversal of those found elsewhere in the Maya Lowlands and on Cozumel, as in the case of District 1 at San Gervasio. If Buena Vista were not concentrically organized, the dispersion of presumably community-level facilities might not strike us as so peculiar. But concentric organization generally implies that the activities pertaining to the center are the focus of community attention. Given our initial inference that the nucleated area functioned primarily for residential purposes, it is difficult to explain why domestic activities should attain such prominence and civil-religious activities should be relegated to the periphery. This problem is aggravated by the presence of dispersed sub-structures in the settlement zone. Surface samples of ceramics, though small, indicate that these substructures were occupied contemporane-ously with the nucleated zone. Furthermore, the presence of storage pits in some of the substructures indicates that they may also have been domestic in function. With the given inference, we are confronted with a residential pattern that is partially nucleated, partially dispersed. Only excavation in the dispersed substructures could reveal any significant differences between the associated debris in them and that in the nu-cleated zone, but the general expectation might be that such differences are present.

The problems outlined above might be resolved by a variety of con-clusions: (1) the residents of the nucleated area were members of a socially distinct class—an elite group; (2) the residents of the nucleated area were members of a culturally distinct group; or (3) the residents of the nucleated area participated in nonsubsistence service activities for a surrounding population. In this last case, Buena Vista might be charac-terized as a multifunctional "town."

Negative evidence is only as strong as the associated sample of positive data, and our excavation sample from Buena Vista is relatively limited, so inferences concerning the nature of the settlement pattern are quite tentative and should be tested with further investigation in the field. At present, the following observations can be made: (1) the domestic debris found at Buena Vista is not qualitatively different from that found at other settlements on Cozumel; (2) no evidence of occupa-tional specialization in the form of workshop areas or specialized mid-dens was found; (3) specialized districts in the form of plaza groups or concentrations of particular types of superstructures were not identified; and (4) investment of labor in superstructures was negligible in com-parison to that invested in substructures in the nucleated area. Although significant patterns in the distribution of artifacts and debris may even-tually be identified as analysis progresses, none of the three suggested possibilities are currently supported by our data.

We propose a fourth possibility as a working hypothesis: that the nucleated area at Buena Vista was indeed a residential district, but that it was also a major storage area for perishable commodities being trans-shipped through Cozumel in its role as a trading port. In a sense, this is a modification of our third suggestion. We see the residents of the nucleated area at Buena Vista as active in nonsubsistence service, but, rather than servicing a local population, they were serving the elite of Cozumel by maintaining storage facilities.

This hypothesis accounts for our negative evidence in the following manner: (1) members of the resident maintenance population were recruited from the surrounding rural population and thus were culturally indistinguishable and not members of the elite; (2) the resident population was specialized only in that its members maintained warehouses and guarded and possibly transported commodities; (3) distinctive districts are absent because the nucleated area as a whole was specialized, and all the residents were participating in the same activities; and (4) the advantage of substructures—namely, their elevation above damp and inundated terrain in the rainy season—would be particularly important in the storage of perishables like salt and cloth. The last point explains why so much labor was invested in substructures while that invested in superstructures serving such a storage function could have been quite modest. The wall fragments of nonbenched structures at Buena Vista might pertain to such features.

But dealing with negative evidence is a little like designing new clothes for the emperor. The advantage we see in our hypothesis is that it also accounts for the positive data at hand. If the nucleated area served an important function other than residential, such as large-scale storage, its location as the focus of the settlement seems more reasonable. According to this theory, the nucleated area and associated plaza did not serve as a central place of civil-religious importance to the local surrounding populace. Civil-religious activities took place at the civil-religious structures on the periphery of the settlement; this arrangement not only defined the boundaries of local access to the central place but focused local attention away from the nucleated area. Thus nucleation of storage facilities could have served two purposes simultaneously. It would have allowed greater accessibility to and control of the facilities by a largely nonresident elite while making the facilities more inaccessible to and isolated from a local population.

Our basic argument then, is that nucleation did not develop on Cozumel as a response to localized factors such as demographic pressure on the land, increasing need for elite control of the support population, or adaptation to a local resource that allowed or encouraged centripetal movement of residence location. Instead, we see nucleation as a response on the part of the elite on Cozumel to external economic factors— namely, the development of a commercial network passing through the island.

The disposition of nucleated features elsewhere on Cozumel seems to support this hypothesis. District 4 at San Gervasio is nucleated, has its own plaza group, and is found in the context of a dispersed settlement. Likewise, the agglutinated substructures at La Expedición are found in the context of dispersed features. Therefore, we see nucleation not as an overall response on the part of Cozumel's population to local conditions but rather as an aspect of the total settlement pattern. Superstructures and debris associated with these nucleated areas indicate that their occupants had the same material culture as the occupants of the dispersed features. Therefore we identify the nucleated areas as functionally rather than culturally distinctive. We feel that they were not constructed to service local residents in a religious or civil-administrative capacity, for we have other facilities that fit these functions better.

Although we have no positive corroborating evidence for the presence of storage facilities, we suggest that this is the best interpretation of the information available to us at the present time.

Discussion

Our preliminary analysis of settlements on Cozumel during the Decadent Period yields several general inferences. First of all, Cozumel appears to have been a single sociocultural and political unit. A characteristic administrative center is found in a majority of the settlements, consisting of civil-religious and domestic architecture arranged around a plaza. The feature types in these plaza groups, with the exception of San Gervasio, have an island-wide distribution. A considerably more elaborate version of this administrative center is found at San Gervasio, incorporating features typical at Mayapán. Therefore we believe that the administrative elite on Cozumel was a unified group whose leadership was centered at San Gervasio. This leadership had strong ties with

Mayapán. The existence of a generally homogeneous material culture characterizing the period and the presence at that time of a network of field walls covering the island support our inference.

While the settlement patterns during the Decadent may be generally characterized as dispersed, we have discovered nucleated features at four sites on the island. From the information available to us we cannot attribute these instances of nucleation to distinctive sociocultural groups or to an adaptation to localized resources. Furthermore, in three cases these features occur in the context of dispersed settlement patterns. Therefore we hypothesize that such features were functionally specialized. Working from our first inference and from the wide distribution of nucleated facilities over the island (though they are absent at several settlements), we argue that these nucleated features were constructed to serve the purposes of the elite rather than the local populace.

Our identification of these nucleated features as storage facilities is based upon negative and circumstantial evidence. As the former has already been considered, only the latter will be considered now. From historical documents we know that Cozumel was situated on a major trade route from the northwest provinces of Yucatán to Honduras. The major commodities moving north to south on this route were salt, cotton fabrics, slaves, honey, and copal incense. The major commodities moving south to north were cacao and various exotic imperishables including gold, jade, and obsidian (Scholes and Roys 1948). We also know that Cozumel was regularly visited by pilgrims from Tabasco and the west coast of Yucatán, major commercial centers at the time of contact. From this evidence we infer that traders were stopping regularly at Cozumel during the Decadent Period. The wide distribution of the aforementioned exotic imperishables over the island during the Decadent demonstrates that these merchants were carrying on active trade with the islanders.

The merchants established factories and warehouses at a number of nodes in the trade network, notably Naco in Honduras and Xicalango in Tabasco (Scholes and Roys 1948). It is reasonable to suppose that such facilities were constructed at a number of other nodes on the route. Unfortunately, we have been unable to discover a clear description of warehouses in the historical literature. Apparently the Spanish explorers did not pay a great deal of attention to them. Since Cozumel was a node on the route, with the added attractions of being an important pilgrimage center, having the only leeward coast on the eastern side of the peninsula, and being highly defensible, we postulate that Cozumel was a likely location for warehouses and factories.

It is worthwhile to reemphasize the defensibility of the island's sites. The locations of Cozumel's hypothesized storage facilities indicate that they were relatively inaccessible. Some other aspects of the settlement pattern potentially support the notion of defense. We have already mentioned that a grid of field walls datable to the Decadent Period covers most of Cozumel. On the seaward side of Chen Cedral and Buena Vista, this wall system is unusual. The typical wall was a single course of dry laid rubble standing about one and a half meters high. In the vicinities of these two sites, the walls of the grid are much more massive, standing at a preserved height of two and a half meters in some places, and two meters wide. Such massive walls are combined in an apparently random fashion with smaller walls. Given their location, it is possible that such walls performed a defensive function, lending some protection to the nucleated sites on their seaward sides. It should be noted in this regard that the walls surrounding Tulum and Ichpaatún probably performed a defensive function also. Unlike the smaller walls, such walls could have supported palisades of perishable materials.

Members of the Grijalva expedition in 1518 described the lighting of bonfires at shrines all along the western coast of Cozumel as they proceeded north toward the port at San Miguel. These shrines no longer exist, but this description and our observation of shrines all along the eastern coast of the island make it clear that the entire coast of Cozumel was dotted with these erstwhile lookout posts (Wagner 1942). They seem to have been distributed in a consistent pattern, with one or more located on the coast directly in front of settlements situated farther inland. The observations of the members of the Grijalva expedition indicate that such shrines along the coast served both as ritual centers and as watchtowers.

In terms of our theory about the economic importance of Buena Vista and its disposition as a storage area, it is interesting to note that the structure on the east coast of the island in front of the settlement is not a shrine at all, but a long, rectangular, three-roomed masonry structure. This structure is unique on the island and is not apparently religious in function. Situated next to it is a large substructure without superstructural remains. We infer that despite the difficulties of landing on the windward side of the island, Buena Vista's attractiveness as a storage center and its vulnerability on this side required that a small garrison rather than a simple shrine be located at this spot.

SUMMARY

In order adequately to test general hypotheses about ancient trading systems through the archaeological data uncovered on Cozumel, we must come to grips with some specific cultural, historical, and ecological factors. In particular, we have to understand the seasonality of trade, the necessity of defense, the availability of water, and the requirements of an important religious shrine. By taking these and other factors into account when examining the location of sites and the settlement pattern on Cozumel, we have produced a preliminary model of how Cozumel could have functioned as a trading entity in Decadent times. In addition, we have seen how decentralization of facilities is compatible with a centralization of administration, as one of the Cozumel Project's general hypotheses has predicted (although the hypothesis has yet to be proven).

We have presented the settlement data "warts and all." Too often, all the false starts in the testing of hypotheses are concealed after the fact and the inconsistencies in the data are smoothed out, leaving the adequacy of the data unclear in the reader's mind. As Jeffrey Parsons (1973:647) has so cogently pointed out, "Many of the archaeological data we now possess are inadequate for the kinds of questions we now wish to ask about process in history." Yet much useful information can be gleaned if our hypotheses and their test expectations are sharp enough and if maximum effort is made to squeeze the information for all it is worth.

Finally, we hope that we have shown how the study of the material and behavioral correlates of trading facilities can and should be a useful companion to studies of traded artifacts. The potential feedback between these two lines of study should prove to be most fruitful to archaeologists interested in understanding the role of trade in ancient trading systems.

NOTES

1. In Mesoamerica, the important and illuminating research of Flannery and his associates on the nature of trade in Oaxaca in Early Preclassic times (see especially Flannery 1968) is an exception to this generalization and is just one example of the potential of studying both traded items and trade facilities.

2. The Cozumel Project was sponsored by the Peabody Museum, Harvard University and the University of Arizona, with J. A. Sabloff and W. L. Rathje as codirectors. The project conducted field investigations on Cozumel, Quintana Roo, Mexico, from February to July 1972 and February to July 1973. The project has been generously supported by the National Geographic Society, the Ford Foundation, the Ford Motor Company, the American Can Company, the Harvard Graduate Society, the Clark and Milton funds of Harvard University, Mrs. Charles Ayling, and Mr. Landon Clay. Its work was conducted with the cooperation and authorization of the Instituto Nacional de Antropología e Historia of Mexico. Important contributions by students from the University of Arizona, Harvard University, New England College, Wesleyan University, and Stanford University helped make the project possible, as did our many friends and colleagues in Cambridge, Tucson, Mexico City, Mérida, and Cozumel. We particularly wish to thank Paula L. W. Sabloff, the project's social anthropologist, for her aid in the preparation of this paper. The critical advice of C. C. Lamberg-Karlovsky and Stephen Williams has also been of great help to us, as has the intellectual stimulation of W. L. Rathje.

3. See Rathje and Sabloff 1972; Sabloff et al. in press; Sabloff and Rathje 1973; Rathje and Sabloff 1973; Rathje, Sabloff, and Gregory in press.

4. See Andrews (1965) for a discussion of the chronological terminology of northern Yucatán.

5. In our final reports, we will argue that Cozumel, was in fact, a trading center as early as A.D. 800 (also see Rathje, Sabloff, and Gregory in press).

6. Scholes and Roys (1948:37) note that the commercial town of Potonchán in Tabasco—one of the few such centers described by early Spanish explorers—was protected from attack by "a palisade of thick timbers."

7. This is a type marker of Puuc and related architectural styles dating to the Late Classic and Early Postclassic periods. Ceramics found under a sealed plaster floor on the substructure of one of these shrines date to the Florescent and Modified Florescent periods exclusively while Decadent censer ware was found above the floor. Sherds dating earlier than the Decadent Period were also found under three sealed floors in one of the "palaces" or "temples." Therefore it seems likely that the pattern observed at El Cedral was established before the Decadent and remained unmodified by continued occupation.

References

ANDREWS, E. WYLLYS
1965 "Archaeology and Prehistory in the Northern Maya Lowlands: an Introduction," in *Handbook of Middle American Indians*, vol. 2, ed. R. Wauchope and G. R. Willey (Austin: University of Texas Press).

ANDREWS, E. W. IV AND ANTHONY P. ANDREWS
in press A *Preliminary Study of the Ruins of Xcaret, Quintana Roo, Mexico*, Middle American Research Institute, Tulane University.

CHAPMAN, ANNE M.
1957 "Port of Trade Enclaves in Aztec and Maya Civilizations," in *Trade and Market in the Early Empires*, ed. K. Polanyi, C. M. Arensberg, and H. W. Pearson (New York: Free Press).

ESCALONA RAMOS, ALBERTO
1946 "Algunas ruinas prehispánicas en Quintana Roo," *Boletín de la Sociedad Mexicana de Geografía y Estadística* 61:(3):513–628.

FERNÁNDEZ, MIGUEL ANGEL
1940 "Exploraciones Arqueológicas en la Isla Cozumel, Quintana Roo," *Anales de Instituto Nacional de Antropología e Historia* 1:107–20.

FLANNERY, KENT V.
1968 "The Olmec and the Valley of Oaxaca: A Model of Interregional Interaction in Formative Times," in *Dumbarton Oaks Conference on the Olmec*, ed. E. P. Benson (Washington, D. C.: Dumbarton Oaks Research Library and Trustees for Harvard University).

FREIDEL, DAVID A.
n.d. "The Ix Chel Shrine." Unpublished manuscript.

HOLMES, WILLIAM H.
1895 *Archaeological Studies among the Ancient Cities of Mexico*, part I, Field Columbian Museum Publication 8.

KURJACK, EDWARD
1972 "Prehistoric Lowland Maya Patterns of Settlement and Culture Change: A Case Study," Ph.D. dissertation, Ohio State University.

LOTHROP, SAMUEL K.
1924 *Tulum, An Archaeological Study of the East Coast of Yucatán*. Carnegie Institution of Washington Publication 335.

406

PARSONS, JEFFREY R.
1973 "Review of *Man, Settlement and Urbanism,* ed. P. J. Ucko, R. Tringham, and G. W. Dimbleby," *Science* 181:646–47.

PROSKOURIAKOFF, TATIANA
1962 *Civic and Religious Structures of Mayapán.* Carnegie Institution of Washington Publication 619, pp. 87–164.

RATHJE, WILLIAM L. AND JEREMY A. SABLOFF
1972 "A Model of Ports-of-trade," paper read at the Annual Meeting of the Society for American Archaeology, Miami.
1973 "A Research Design for Cozumel, Mexico," *World Archaeology* 5:(2):221–31.

RATHJE, WILIAM L., JEREMY A. SABLOFF,
AND DAVID A. GREGORY
in press "El descubrimiento de un jade olmeca en la isla de Cozumel, Quintana Roo, México," *Estudios de Cultura Maya* 9.

ROYS, RALPH L.
1933 *The Book of Chilam Balam of Chumayel.* Carnegie Institution of Washington Publication 438.
1943 *The Indian Background of Colonial Yucatán.* Carnegie Institution of Washington Publication 548.

RUPPERT, KARL AND A. LEDYARD SMITH
1957 "House Types in the Environs of Mayapán and at Uxmal, Kabáh, Sayil, Chichén Itzá, and Chacchob," Carnegie Institution of Washington *Current Reports* 39.

SABLOFF, JEREMY A. AND WILLIAM L. RATHJE
1973 "A Study of Changing Precolumbian Commercial Patterns on the Island of Cozumel, Mexico," *Acts of the XL International Congress of Americanists,* Rome 1:455–63.

SABLOFF, JEREMY A., WILLIAM L. RATHJE, DAVID A. FREIDEL,
JUDITH G. CONNOR, AND PAULA L. W. SABLOFF
in press "Trade and Power in Postclassic Yucatán: Initial Observations," in *Mesoamerican Archaeology, New Approaches,* ed. N. Hammond (Austin: University of Texas Press).

SANDERS, WILLIAM T.
1955 "An Archaeological Reconnaissance of Northern Quintana Roo," Carnegie Institution of Washington *Current Reports* 24.
1960 *Prehistoric Ceramics and Settlement Patterns in Quintana Roo, Mexico.* Carnegie Institution of Washington Publication 606, contribution 60, pp. 155–264.

SCHOLES, FRANCE V. AND RALPH L. ROYS
1948 *The Maya Chontal Indians of Acalán-Tixchel.* Carnegie Institution of Washington Publication 560.

SHOOK, EDWIN M. AND W. N. IRVING
1955 "Colonnaded Buildings at Mayapán," Carnegie Institution of Washington *Current Reports* 22.

407

SMITH, A. LEDYARD
1962   *Residential and Associated Structures at Mayapán*. Carnegie Institution of Washington Publication 619, pp. 165–320.

WAGNER, HENRY R. (translator and editor)
1942   *The Discovery of New Spain in 1518 by Juan de Grijalva* (Berkeley, Calif.: Cortés Society, Bancroft Library).

WAUCHOPE, ROBERT
1934   *House Mounds of Uaxactún, Guatemala*. Carnegie Institution of Washington Publication 436, contribution 7.
1940   "Domestic Architecture of the Maya," in *The Maya and Their Neighbors*, ed. C. Hay et al. (New York: Appleton-Century).

10

The Last Tango in Mayapán
A Tentative Trajectory of
Production-Distribution Systems[1]

WILLIAM L. RATHJE

University of Arizona

"The age was materialistic . . . personal comfort and glory came ahead of religious devotion."—H. E. D. Pollock

"There seems to be little striving for permanence, just window dressing and false fronts. In spite of this, however, Mayapán must have presented an impressive picture. . . . A coat of paint will hide many faults, and the ample use of plaster at Mayapán undoubtedly accomplished the same purpose."—A. L. Smith

GENERAL SYSTEMS THEORY AND
THE ISLAND OF COZUMEL

The initial goals of the Cozumel Archaeological Project[2] required the retrieval of specific, limited sets of data. Archaeological data are not separately packaged, and the project has now excavated and catalogued a wide variety of the remnants of a long-term cultural system. The systematic reporting of such a collection requires a research design general enough to organize the analyses of all of the materials excavated on the island of Cozumel and relate these analyses to the extant record of the development of Maya civilization.

General Systems Theory was developed to study the shared behavioral properties of all systems (Boulding 1956a). It provides a set of definitions and principles that can be applied to the description and analysis of any system or set of material components interrelated by the transfer of energy and information (Buckley 1968; Miller 1965). Although archaeological materials are for the most part only fossils of the completed matter, energy, and information transformations of long-extinct cultural systems, concepts from General Systems Theory can be used to reconstruct the behavior of extinct cultural systems at a highly abstract level (cf. Clarke 1968; Flannery 1968; 1972; Glassow 1972; and others).

Cultural systems are open systems which extract matter, energy, and information from their environments. One of the most obvious properties of an open system in a temporal matrix is that the dynamics of the system's internal matter-energy-information structures change. General Systems Theory can be viewed as a concern with deriving directional trajectories, general principles which describe replicated long-term trends in the internal restructuring of the matter-energy-information interaction within systems. To archaeologists, the most directly observable results of change are measurable modifications in the form and distribution of cultural systems' material components. At a basic General Systems Theory level, then, archaeology must be concerned with: (1) quantifying the significant changes in resource management behavior by measuring changes in the form and distribution of material culture components through time, and (2) deriving the trajectories which succinctly describe these changes.

The construction and testing of *material culture* trajectories may serve several useful functions:

1. As blatant as some material culture trajectories may be, they will provide data relevant to the question of whether the long-term behavior of cultural systems is patterned (cf. Kroeber 1962; Clarke 1968; Glassow 1972; and others).

2. The evaluation of material culture trajectories can be effected through objective measures so that analysis results from diverse time-space proveniences will be comparable.

3. If the trajectories are substantiated, they will not become an end in themselves. They will form the basis for questions about general patterns in the organization of human behavior which produce, and

410

are affected by, patterned changes in the form and distribution of material culture through time.

This chapter is a preliminary exercise in the applicability of highly abstract concepts of General Systems Theory to the specifics of archaeological analysis of resource management, as reflected in the artifacts excavated on the island of Cozumel, Quintana Roo, Mexico.

ASSUMPTION BASE FOR THE PRODUCTION-DISTRIBUTION TRAJECTORY

One of the most general trajectories of cultural systems is growth and decline. Homeostatic feedback mechanisms are obviously important to cultural systems; for the purposes of a long-term view of cultural systems, however, it will be assumed here that the growth rates of open cultural systems either accelerate or decelerate and that open systems do not exhibit the kind of equilibrium typical of closed systems (cf. Boulding 1956b; Meadows et al. 1972).

In defining the trajectories of growing systems, one useful concept, which will be accepted as a given in this paper, is the "principle of nonproportional change" (Boulding 1956b:71): "As any structure grows, the proportions of its parts and of its significant variables *cannot* remain constant."[3] For example, if the linear measurements of a physical structure are doubled, the area increases four times and the volume eight times. One corollary of this principle is that growth "always involves a compensatory change in relation to the original proportion and requirements" of the expanding system (Boulding 1956b:71). A second corollary holds that "if the process of compensation for structural organization has limits, as in fact seems to be the case, the size of the structure itself is limited by its ultimate inability to compensate for non-proportional changes" (Boulding 1956b:71). A final corollary states that nonproportional changes are most drastic as a system's growth rate first begins to accelerate and as that growth rate slows down (Boulding 1956b:74).

Every system must face certain general types of nonproportional change:

An increase in the number of components in a system requires a disproportionately larger increase in the number of information

411

processing and deciding components (Boulding 1956b:74; cf. Miller 1965:392, hypothesis 3.3.4.2–8; Bertalanffy 1968:48).

This creates strain which may lead to at least three modes of compensation:

1. The most obvious, but least practical, method of compensation for an expanding system is to "increase the proportion of the organization which is devoted to the communication system" (Boulding 1956b:72). Cultural systems, however, cannot long afford a "disproportionately larger" investment of personnel and resources in communications if other facilities continue to expand rapidly at the same time. Thus, additional compensatory behavior may be expected through time as growth continues. Such behavior requires the introduction of cost-control techniques which decrease the human and material resources invested in the production and distribution of information-processing and -deciding components.

2. One possible method of compensation in information processing is suggested by a hypothesis of general systems behavior:

Over time a system tends to decrease the amount of recoding necessary within it by developing more and more common system-wide codes (Miller 1965:392, hypothesis 3.3.4.2–8).

Thus, a viable alternative to compensation based on simple increase in investment in components is partially to diminish the need for communications by decreasing internal variety. This is accomplished by developing "rigid ritualistic [standardized] patterns of behavior" (Boulding 1956b:74) and by using standardization as a means to decrease the costs of production of information-processing components.

3. A third method of communication compensation may also develop. As systems expand they develop increased internal differentiation and often spread into a variety of differentiated environments. Because variety is necessary to organize variety (Ashby 1968), standardization and diminished internal variety may no longer be sufficient in compensating for an increasing variety in the quantity and diversity of communication needs in different parts of a growing system. At this point Boulding (1956b:72) suggests that as a supplement to "rigid ritualistic patterns," an increase in "local autonomy" in establishing these standardized patterns may develop to increase system-wide variety.

412

The whole set of compensatory changes may be summarized as a three-phase development of *Progressive Mechanization:*

At first, systems are governed by dynamic interaction of their components; later on, fixed arrangements and conditions of constraint are established which render the system and its parts more efficient, but also gradually diminish and eventually abolish its equipotentiality (Bertalanffy 1968:44).

THE TENTATIVE PRODUCTION-DISTRIBUTION TRAJECTORY

The General Systems Theory principle of nonproportional growth and its result, progressive mechanization, is a base upon which an archaeological research design can be built to analyze long-term cultural development. In order to define an area of application, the nature of archaeological data must be considered. Energy and information are not directly observable in the archaeological record. Matter is observable, and from it previous energy and information transformations can be reconstructed. This chapter will attempt to limit its data base to directly measurable material objects[4] and limit its specific focus to a trajectory that defines resource management changes through time in the material attributes of production and distribution systems.[5]

No proposals are made in this chapter as to where, when, or why the manufacture of certain products begins or ends. Nor are propositions presented for the cessation of certain cultural patterns and the "rise" of new cultural systems as they are traditionally defined. The trajectory presented below is simply a device for describing limited aspects of the transformation of the internal matter-energy-information structure of systems, however they are arbitrarily bounded in time and space, during their operational history.

Hypothesized production-distribution system trajectories can be derived by referring back to nonproportional change in communication demands caused by system growth. I propose that compensations for increased demands occur in the following order: (1) by a disproportionately large investment of system resources into information processing components; (2) by rigid patterning of sets of interactions among components; and (3) by increasing low-level autonomy for the form of

413

sets of interacting components. It is implicit in this hypothesis that throughout the sequence the absolute number of information-processing components and the social and physical space through which components are distributed will increase.

Since forms of matter are here assumed to be critical components of cultural communication systems as counters, symbols, facilities, and tools, material culture should be affected in a patterned way by compensations for nonproportional changes as systems grow and communication needs and solutions develop. Nonproportional changes in past production-distribution procedures cannot be directly observed. They must be inferred from objective measures of differences in the composition, form, and location of contrasting sets of artifacts. For this chapter a statistical trajectory based on Boulding's hypothesized communication system compensations can be proposed for material items:

1. During a system's initial phase of development, human and material resources will be heavily concentrated into craft production which turns out a small number of commodities whose distribution is highly constrained within social and/or physical space. *Assumption Base:* This action represents disproportionately large investments in research and development of communication-processing components that will function to move the communication within a system through centralized, highly controlled foci. Such resource concentration may be a critical attribute of processes of growth and centralization which are based not on expanding local communication networks but on superimposing whole new communication structures founded on supralocal control of investment of human and material resources.

2. After the initial research and development phase, human and material resources will be invested in the process of mass replication and distribution of standardized sets of products.[6] *Assumption Base:* As the growing system faces new communication demands, it will place increasing emphasis upon rigid patterning of sets of interactions among components. One way to develop standardized behavior patterns is through the use of standardized sets of associated material items. Just as our current system produces new forms of material culture like telephones and computers to meet communication needs, past systems modified production procedures as an important means of meeting such needs. The

414

introduction of mass replication and distribution techniques transforms the focus of social integration based on production-distribution systems from elite reinforcement through high-investment products loaded with psychological and ideological values toward a more direct form of economic integration in which local small-scale production units are superseded by an overarching production and distribution system.

3. Through time, standardized mass-production and -distribution techniques will be modified to meet increasingly specialized local requirements by investing human and material resources in an increase in the variety of specific products. *Assumption Base:* As the system expands and meets local variety, it will retool its techniques to produce variety on a local level in its communication system. Such modifications can only be expected to characterize commodities which have sufficient local "economies of scale" (i.e. sufficiently high local demand) to make mass production and distribution methods efficient as a form of controlling costs. This expectation does not imply that the actual physical control of production-distribution systems is either centralized or decentralized, only that final products show an increasing variety in form and distribution produced by modifications in established cost control techniques of mass production and dispersion (cf. Netting 1972).

Thus at the beginning of growth, high investment of human and material resources characterizes those components which participate significantly in a system's initial expansion. As workable components are produced, however, human and material resource investment shifts from research and development of new components to research and development of new techniques to maintain the functioning of, and effect the replication and distribution of, increased numbers of components at lower and lower costs/object.[7]

Trajectory Summary: "At first, systems are governed by dynamic interaction of their components; later on, fixed arrangements and conditions of constraint are established which render the system and its parts more efficient" (Bertalanffy 1968:44).[8] *Or:* Research and development in production-distribution components and products is followed by cost-control mass replication and distribution of commodities within the constraints of an expanding cultural system.

The trajectory at its simplest holds that *cost-control devices will be*

*increasingly applied as a form of compensation for the exponentially
expanding communication needs of a system growing at a more linear
rate.*

The term *cost-control*, as I use it in this chapter, means that the
human and material resources invested per commodity in production
and distribution decrease, while the numbers of commodities and their
range of distribution increase (figure 33). Cost-control is the means by
which volume replaces value in specific products and economic interdependence replaces psychological-ideological interdependence among social units in a cultural system. It is implicit within the trajectory that
cost-control techniques will produce an increase in the absolute number
of information-processing components and in the spatial distribution of
components through time.

THE TRAJECTORY AND
THE ANCIENT MAYA

The history of Maya society on the Yucatán Peninsula is repeatedly
disrupted by collapse, economic and physical invasion, and "resurgence."
The first fault line in Maya history is the Classic/Postclassic transition.
Between 400 B.C. and A.D. 800 the physical center of the peninsula was
also the demographic center (see figures 34 and 35). During the Preclassic and Classic periods, in this and surrounding areas, the Maya
built large ceremonial centers like Tikal, Mirador, Calakmul, Yaxchilán,
Piedras Negras, and Copán. Between A.D. 800 and 850 the central region
of the Yucatán Peninsula was drastically depopulated and its large ceremonial centers and those of many neighboring areas were abandoned to
the jungle (Culbert 1973). Both new and old centers in the north of
the peninsula and along its coasts were the major foci of a restructuring
of the population.

The second disruption was either concurrent with or followed shortly
after (depending on the dating system) the "Classic" Maya demographic collapse. This disjunction in Maya society was created by the
physical and economic movement of the "Putún," "Mexicanized Maya,"
or "Toltec" from Tabasco and/or Veracruz onto the peninsula (Thompson 1970; Sabloff and Willey 1967; Rathje and Gregory in press). This
"invasion" was a prelude to a third fault line in Maya history, the "con-

416

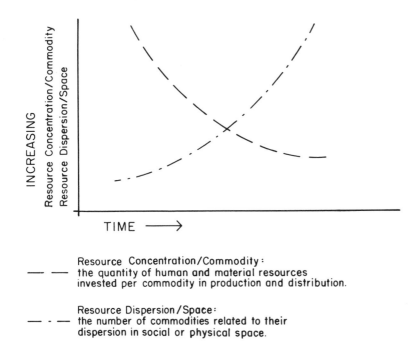

Resource Concentration/Commodity:
— — the quantity of human and material resources
invested per commodity in production and distribution.

Resource Dispersion/Space:
— · — the number of commodities related to their
dispersion in social or physical space.

FIGURE 33. PROPOSED COST-CONTROL TRAJECTORY

quest" of the peninsula by the "Toltec" and their hegemony centered at
Chichén Itzá between A.D. 1000 and 1200. Following the "fall" or ex-
pulsion of the Toltecs came a Maya "resurgence" centered on the construction of the walled town of Mayapán around A.D. 1250. This site
became the political focus of much of the peninsula, and its sack by
dissident noble families was the final jolt in Maya cultural development
before the arrival of the Spanish.

This compressed sequence is chaotic and presents a good testing
ground for a trajectory that proposes to describe the general direction of
changes within Maya production and distribution resource management
systems through time. For the purposes of this chapter the Yucatán
Peninsula will serve as the arbitrary boundary of a "growing" Maya cultural system. Changes in cost-control procedures in past production-

417

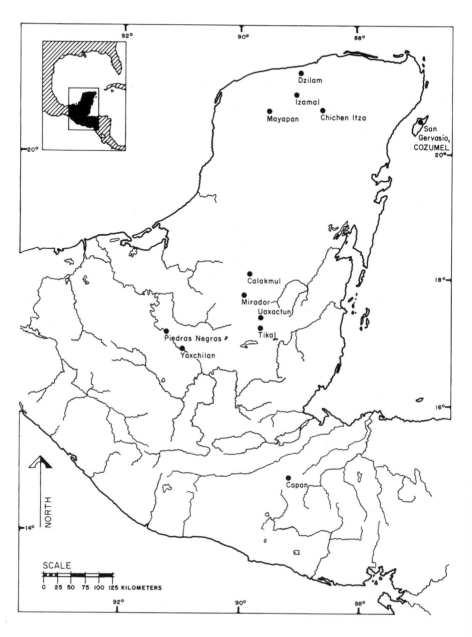

FIGURE 34. THE MAYA LOWLANDS

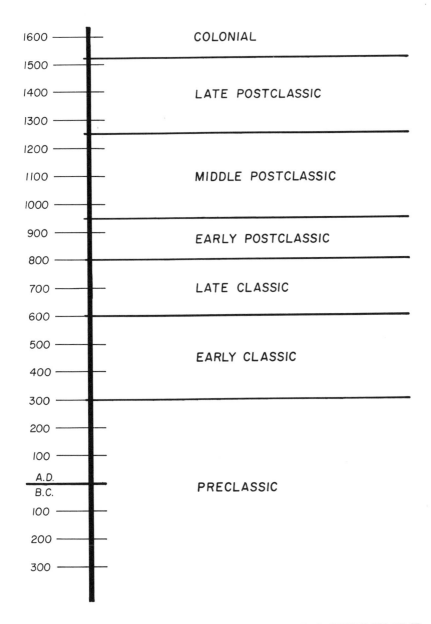

FIGURE 35. A CHRONOLOGY FOR MAYA CULTURAL DEVELOPMENT

distribution systems cannot be directly observed. I will assume here that differential emphasis on cost-control may be directly described as a function of differences in the composition, form, and location of contrasting sets of artifacts deposited by Maya civilization. The following test implications are phrased in terms of specific architecture, cache, and pottery data, so that their potential to be implemented through quantitative methods can be evaluated. Because this is only a preliminary research design for the study of archaeological data from Cozumel and other Maya material culture, statements which will be tested through objective methods are presented below as subjective evaluations and should be taken only as indicators of the attributes by which data will be described. In addition, only the opposite ends of the Maya spectrum, the Classic and the Late Postclassic, will be examined in this study. Many of the contrasted data will be drawn from the reported remains of Classic Tikal and Late Postclassic Mayapán. These sites were selected because both were major political, population, and material culture foci during their respective occupations.

The following test implications are designed to demonstrate only two aspects of change through time: (1) that cost-control techniques were increasingly applied through time to the production process of specific types of artifacts and/or functional sets of artifacts measured (for this chapter) by quantification of the resource concentration for a given commodity and resource dispersion over a given space; (2) that through time, cost-control techniques led to a replication of the basic sequence proposed by Boulding for information-processing components—research and development to centralized mass replication to increased local variety as a product of the use of mass replication and other cost-control techniques.

Trajectory Test Implication 1

Resource concentration per commodity should decrease through time as a part of cost-control, probably both in terms of the proportion of resources in specific commodities relative to the resources in the whole system and in terms of absolute resources per commodity. Resource concentration per commodity can be measured (a) by difficulty of resource procurement for the manufacture of a given item and (b) by the sheer quantity of material and human resources, as well as the amount of skill in organization or execution of production, invested in specific commodities.

Architecture: Resource Procurement. In the Preclassic, Classic, and Early Postclassic periods huge quantities of stone were quarried, transported, and finished for temple and palace fill, walls, and facades. Over the thousand-year history of Maya architecture, a reservoir of construction materials was produced at great cost in human effort (cf. Erasmus 1965). It has been suggested that Late Postclassic builders, unlike their predecessors, reused large quantities of cut stone, even thin veneer slabs. "Carved stone, other than these reused fragments, disappeared from architecture" (Andrews 1965:323). This process, seen by some archaeologists as decadence and cultural deterioration, from the perspective of this chapter is recycling, a form of cost-control which decreased the cost of resource procurement per commodity in the Late Postclassic. Human energetics studies of stone cutting (cf. Saraydar and Shimada 1971; 1973) and estimates of quantity of construction during given time periods can be used to evaluate the cost-control significance of "recycling" activities. Even without such quantification, however, it is clear that the effect of recycling upon cutting costs of resource procurement in the Late Postclassic must have been significant.

Architecture: Quantity of Material and Quantity and Skill of Human Resources. Resource concentration/commodity ratios, measured by quantity of resources invested for housing, changed between the Classic and Late Postclassic. In the Classic, in both the southern and northern lowlands, the building of temple and palace structures entailed skill in executing block masonry and functional corbeling. Masonry blocks were well cut and fitted and sometimes beautifully carved; in addition, structures were covered with a coat of plaster and often sculpted stucco. Human labor and materials were concentrated not only in care and detail of construction, but also simply in size of construction. The two largest Maya buildings are temples built during the Classic Period at Izamal and Dzilam (Andrews 1965:299). The Izamal pyramid is 700,000 cubic meters of rubble (Segovia personal communication, June 1973), almost ten times the size of the largest Late Postclassic pyramid. As a result of the quantity of invested materials and human labor and skill, many large Classic construction units, such as palace A-V at Uaxactún (cf. A. L. Smith 1950) and the North, Central, and South acropoli at Tikal (figure 36; cf. Coe 1967 and Culbert 1974) were foci of tremendous resource concentration.

One example of Late Postclassic ("Decadent" Period) architecture, comparable to Tikal in many functional respects, is Mayapán, a walled city of perhaps ten thousand residents, measuring about four square kilometers. The main temple in the ceremonial precinct at Mayapán was small, about eighty thousand cubic meters. No other structure was the focus of large-scale resource concentration of the type found in Classic structures and construction units (figure 36). Not only did size of structures decrease, but so did demands for expertise in organization and concentration. The quantities of stone and human labor and skill needed for corbeled roofs were replaced by the simpler requirements of thatch and beam-and-mortar roofing. The need for careful cutting and sculpting of stone was replaced by reuse of previously cut stone (with a decrease in precision of fit) and heavy application of plaster. The result of this cost-control implementation is the critique that Mayapán's "monuments were thrown together with a minimum of skill" (Andrews 1968).

Comparisons between Classic and Postclassic construction may not be simple to quantify in detail. The differences, however, are clearly significant in controlling costs per commodity. A good example may be found in contrasting Classic and Postclassic "palace" or "elite residence" structures. At Mayapán and San Gervasio (Cozumel), there are rectangular low masonry platforms which support low walls on several sides. Any structure incorporating the low walls would have been part stone and plaster (no hearting was used; the masonry walls were usually only one stone thick) and part wood and thatch. The combination of stone wall and traditional house construction would have resulted in a living-working area which was wider, higher, drier, cooler, and certainly less costly in resources and skill than rooms in "palaces" built solely of stone and mortar and constrained by the limitations of corbeled arches. Compare palace reconstructions from Uaxactún (Classic) and Mayapán (Late Postclassic) for a rough cost per structure estimate (figure 37).[9]

Trajectory Test Implication 2

Resource dispersion/space should increase through time as cost-control is applied to production and distribution procedures. One method of evaluating this implication is by measuring the distribution of a set of items within a physical or cultural space and/or the degree of accessibility to those resources.

Architecture: Resource Dispersion/Space. There should be an increase through time in the distribution of ceremonial loci (temples or shrines), administrative loci (palaces and the like), and other functionally specific structure types as a result of production cost-control techniques. Given current data on settlement, this assertion is difficult to test over broad regions. Not the least of the problems is the identification of functionally similar structures; a few gross contrasts can be specified, however. Classic sites are characterized by resource concentration in imposing ceremonial precincts such as the large temple-plaza North and South acropoli at Tikal (figure 36). Extant evidence from Late Postclassic sites indicates that resources were not concentrated in a few imposing ceremonial precincts within centers, but were dispersed among large numbers of ceremonial loci in the form of "private" *oratorios* (figure 36).[10] The dispersion of resources into small shrines was so great at Mayapán that many "private" shrines were "at least as opulently furnished as any found in the ceremonial district of the city" (Proskouriakoff 1962:428).

Trajectory Test Implication 3: Boulding's Communication Compensation Sequence

The tentative data on both resource concentration per commodity and commodity dispersion over space are quantifiable and will represent a test of the trajectory. These data must also be supplemented in any evaluation with data that relate these changes to the three-part communication compensation sequence proposed by Boulding: in contrast to those of the Classic Period, Late Postclassic communication-processing components should display an increased variety adapted to local conditions.

Architecture: Boulding's Communication Compensation Sequence. One of the major new techniques that can be viewed as an aspect of

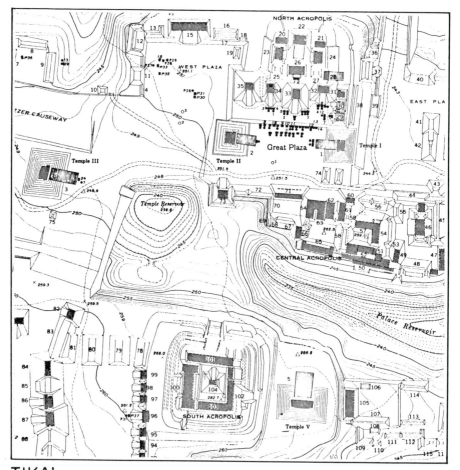

TIKAL

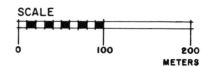

SCALE

0   100   200

METERS

MAYAPAN

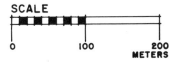

0   100   200
        METERS

FIGURE 36. MAPS OF THE CENTER OF THE CLASSIC SITE OF TIKAL AND THE POSTCLASSIC SITE OF MAYAPAN. Map of Tikal reproduced from Carr and Hazard (1961). Map of Mayapán reproduced from Pollock et al. (1962).

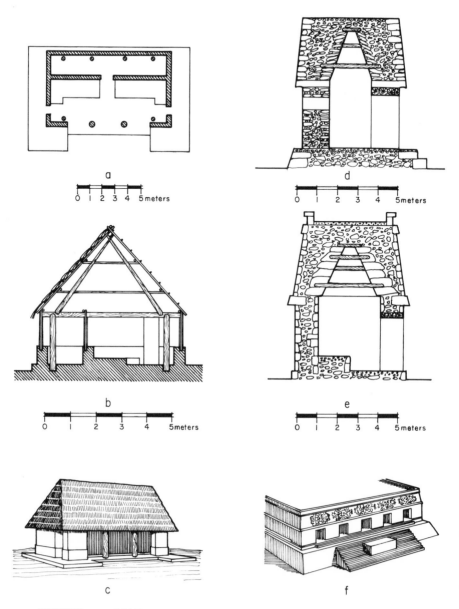

FIGURE 37. CONSTRUCTION AND RECONSTRUCTION OF A POST-CLASSIC "ELITE" STRUCTURE AND A CLASSIC "ELITE" STRUCTURE. *a-c* reproduced from A. L. Smith (1962: fig. 9); *d* and *e* reproduced from Pollock (1965: fig. 16); *f* after Proskouriakoff.

cost-control in the Late Postclassic is the replacement of corbeled roofing with mortar-and-beam or thatch roofing. This change in the use of materials and human labor also changed potential room size. The effect can be seen by comparing room sizes measured by floor space at Uaxactún (51 rooms from the latest construction phase of palace A-V and Group E) (A. L. Smith 1950: figs. 69–70; Ricketson and Ricketson 1937) and at Mayapán (132 rooms) (A. L. Smith 1962: figs. 2–8). Comparisons show that there was a change in the average size of room from the Classic Uaxactún figure of 13.9 square meters to the Late Postclassic Mayapán figure of 20.4 square meters (cf. also Weaver 1972: fig. 24). In addition, there was a more even distribution of rooms of different sizes at Mayapán than at Uaxactún (figure 38). If these rooms are assumed to have had communication and administrative functions and if size of room is related to communication ability, then the Mayapán structures which were the result of a high level of cost-control may have been more effective as communication facilities. Even if these assumptions will not hold, it is clear that because of a change in construction techniques, there was more variety in potential room forms and sizes to choose from at the local level in the Late Postclassic at Mayapán than in the Classic Period at Uaxactún.

The wide distribution of resources in numerous "private" ceremonial loci in the Late Postclassic also facilitated efficient information processing by establishing increased local (intrasite) autonomy in relation to (1) investment in ceremonial structures and (2) fulfillment of personal religious functions. This pattern contrasts with the Classic one, in which a great amount of community capital was concentrated into a small number of "public" ceremonial loci.

A few other examples of potential test implications and possible indicative measures can be mentioned.

Caches: Resource Concentration/Commodity. Caches of objects from Classic sites have been found in abundance in major ceremonial and palace structures. Jade, shell, eccentric flints and obsidians, other "valuables," and pottery were common Classic cache contents (Coe 1965; cf. Longyear 1952; Kidder 1947; A. L. Smith 1950; and others). Some of the stashed items are truly extraordinary. The Early Classic mosaic idols from Tikal are one example (Moholy-Nagy 1965). Through time, caches tended to become more standardized in their positioning and

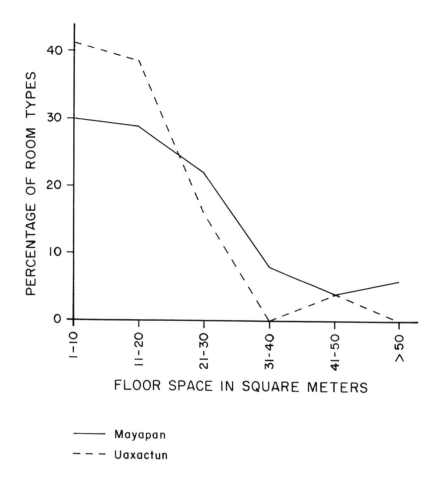

FIGURE 38. DISTRIBUTION OF DIFFERENT-SIZED ROOMS AT CLASSIC
UAXACTUN AND POSTCLASSIC MAYAPAN

contents, but they continued to be characterized by permanent burial
of "objects of beauty and value" (Proskouriakoff 1962:429; Coe 1965).

The picture from the Late Postclassic stands in stark contrast to that
from the Classic. The variety and quantity of whole functional cache
items were much smaller. When "valuables" were cached, they were
often broken or otherwise inferior and useless. To elaborate this contrast
with the Classic pattern, interesting aspects of the celt data from Cozu-

428

mel can be usefully quantified. Eighty-seven celts were intentionally deposited during the Postclassic in one cache (C-22, Group IV, Operation
183) and one altar (C-22, Group IV, Operation 185) excavated at the
site of San Gervasio. Thirty-six items, over 40 percent of the total, were
only celt fragments. The fragments do not represent the pieces of a few
broken celts, but rather single pieces from 36 broken celts. Fragments
compose nearly one-half of the celts in the altar (11 of 24) and over
one-third (25 of 63) of those in the cache. Most of the additional celts
were badly chipped and would have had to be reground before reuse.
Thus Late Postclassic caches, in contrast to Classic caches, may have
formed a cost-control repository for broken or battered items rather
than serving as loci of significant wealth investments in architectural
constructions.

Caches: Resource Dispersion/Space. Unlike those of preceding periods, many Late Postclassic caches came from dispersed "palaces" and
"elite" house mounds (not mainly from major ceremonial structures);
and although few Late Postclassic caches contained articles of "value,"
at Mayapán there was little disparity in contents between ceremonial
precinct caches and those from "private" structures (A. L. Smith 1962;
Proskouriakoff 1962). Proskouriakoff notes that "the reclaim of such
caches was common practice when structures were being rebuilt" or
abandoned (1962:429); here too Postclassic patterns differ from Classic.
This reclamation meant that items placed in Postclassic caches were
not necessarily permanently buried, but could be recycled spatially
through time.

Caches: Boulding's Communication Compensation Sequence. Proskouriakoff concluded that "however we interpret the religious implications of the shallow placement and recovery of such offerings, there is
surely a significant difference between this practice and the permanent
burial of objects of beauty and value that was customary in Classic
times" (1962:429). The basic trend seems to have moved from lavish
community investment in patterns of little direct economic return to
individual-based disbursement of items into "safe-deposit boxes" from
which they were recoverable. This behavior change between the Classic
and Late Postclassic meant that far less capital was taken irretrievably
from the Late Postclassic system and that multiple locations were possible for commodities over a period of time. The result of the trend in

the Late Postclassic was increased individual local autonomy (as opposed to Classic community-wide participation) in investment in caches or, as Proskouriakoff put it (1962:428), "intensive development of private ceremonial."

Pottery: Resource Concentration/Commodity. Mass production cost-control techniques make possible the cheap and efficient production of large quantities of goods by instituting the principles of specialization, standardization (or routinization), and simplification. Pottery constitutes a good example for an investigation of mass replication cost-control techniques because it is easily amenable to mass production, owing to the fact that it is manufactured in a number of distinct steps. The ramifications of mass production manufacture of ceramics for controlling costs are numerous. The division of labor specializes information and routinizes tasks, resulting in less dependence on skilled labor than is necessary when single artisans individually produce finished pots. Yet because each specialist becomes an expert in his specific task, "economies of skill" are attained in mass production systems, and products acquire at least certain aspects of technical superiority. In addition, large quantities of standardized vessels can consistently be turned out. Routinization of production activities works to minimize risks and reduce loss caused by technical error. In terms of transport, production of standardized shapes and sizes makes possible efficient packaging. The production of vessels which can be uniformly stacked conserves space in transport and at the same time reduces the danger of loss through breakage. Finally, simplification both in the production process and in the products themselves reduces production costs and, in conjunction with specialization and standardization, results in increased output and distribution per unit of labor and material (cf. Connor and Rathje 1973).

Decorated Late Classic pottery was surely made through specialization (in this case division of labor). Production at individual sites was definitely standardized, but neither the standards in sizes, decoration, or basic techniques, nor the pottery itself seems to have been shared between major sites (cf. Willey, Culbert, and Adams 1967:310; R. E. Smith and Gifford 1965:533). Classic pottery was definitely not a product of simplification. A large majority of decorated pottery was painted and a significant percentage of painted pots were decorated with complicated figural scenes or glyphic inscriptions or both. The production

430

of these pots required skilled craftsmen. Other less complicated painted pottery also required skill, for few designs were extremely simple (figure 39; cf. R. E. Smith 1955). The Postclassic brought an end to this kind of "craft production" for high turnover commodities such as pottery and instituted mass replication systems.

Many Postclassic wares evidence significant division of labor in production and show widely shared standardization in material composition, form, firing, design, and design techniques (cf. R. E. Smith 1971; Rathje and Gregory in press). Although some types were made continuously for 600 years or more, there are few good stylistic or technological attributes to divide pottery types like Puuc Slate or Fine Orange into chronologically meaningful units. Many types were decorated with different techniques, but most of the techniques show a concern for labor-saving simplification over Classic methods. For example, the difference between Fine Orange and Fine Gray pottery was merely a matter of firing. Modes of surface treatment which require little skill were emphasized. Complicated designs, especially human figures, involved mold-made modeled carving. Painted designs were often limited to easily reproduced geometric or natural forms. The painting on Late Postclassic Peto Cream Ware was simplified to "dribbles" (figure 39; Proskouriakoff 1965:495; R. E. Smith 1958; 1971).

Preliminary test implications based on objective measures[11] have been formulated for measuring the effect of cost-control procedures on ceramic production (Connor and Rathje 1973). Standardization has been the major focus for test implications and will measure the difference in degree of consistency in physical, structural, and stylistic attributes between Classic and Postclassic wares. Means of quantifying simplicity are also being developed; however, some contrasts are so obvious that such measures may not be required (figure 39).

Pottery: Resource Dispersion/Space. Decorated Late Classic pottery was made in several large centers in the Petén and traded to smaller surrounding centers, but never in large quantities. This pattern may have changed after the transition to Late Postclassic. From Cozumel settlement data and other evidence (Rathje and Gregory in press; Connor and Rathje 1973; Rathje, Sabloff, and Gregory in press), it has been suggested that during the Classic/Postclassic transition a regional trade system based on land transport was largely supplemented by an external

431

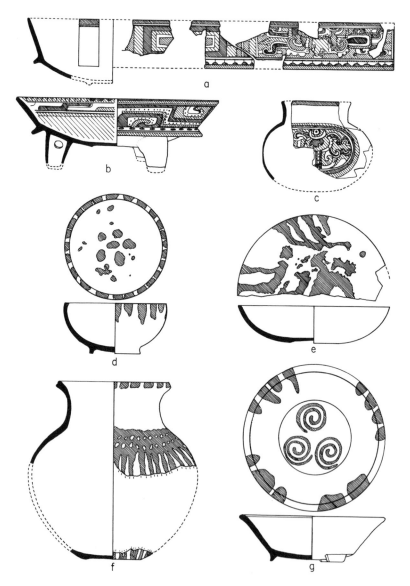

FIGURE 39. CLASSIC AND POSTCLASSIC PAINTED POTTERY. *a-c* reproduced from R. E. Smith (1955: figs. 27b4, 13c, 24a7); *d-g* reproduced from R. E.
Smith (1971: figs. 26-23, 13d, 10g, 19).

large-scale commercial system utilizing marine transport. Such a sea transport system would have been capable of moving goods more cheaply and in greater quantities than a system hauling goods overland by human carriers.[12] In fact, Fisk (1967:23) reports that "after 20 centuries of development, seaborne trade is still the cheapest method of transporting bulky, low-value goods over great distances."

With such a shift in the technology of physical distribution of goods, changes would be expected in other aspects of the trade system (Vance 1971). Sea transport in the Postclassic would have made feasible the transport of such bulky and inexpensive goods as pottery and textiles. At the same time, a wide-scale trade network based on marine transport would have created a new mass market potential for all varieties of trade items. One reaction to the creation of mass markets is the mass distribution of pottery produced in quantity by cost-control techniques.

Fine Orange pottery is the only Postclassic ceramic marker that has been analyzed with a spatial variable in mind. Unlike many earlier pottery types, it was produced for over six centuries and, according to neutron-activation test data, was widely distributed throughout Yucatán and neighboring areas from a limited set of production centers in Tabasco (Sayre, Chan, and Sabloff 1971; cf. Adams 1971). The standardization and simplification of Puuc Slate and Peto Cream ("Dribble") Ware suggest that they might have been widely distributed from a few centers, probably by sea; however, the required material tests have not yet been performed.

Pottery: Boulding's Communication Compensation Sequence. A new element of the Late Postclassic ceramic complex seems to have continued trends toward cost-control mass replication, but with increased local variety as an end result, through the use of interchangeable parts. This new element comprised the Chen Mul Modeled Type full-figure effigies.

> The combined modeling and molding techniques are primarily concerned with effigy censers, effigy vessels, and figurines, most of which are embellished with applique adjuncts. . . . Many are part modeled and part moldmade; often the head is moldmade, less frequently the body. The head may be made in a mold and then have features (a long nose, a beard, whiskers and tusks) or other devices added (R. E. Smith 1971:40).

433

The results of this ability to create massive variety at a local level amazed the conquest chronicler Fray Diego de Landa: "They have such a great quantity of idols that even those of their gods were not enough; for there was not an animal or insect of which they did not make a statue" (Tozzer 1941:110). The economic attributes of the mass replication system were not lost on Bishop Landa; he records that almost every ceremony required new pottery figurines (Tozzer 1941:147) and as a result "[the Indians] earned a great deal by making idols of clay" (Tozzer 1941:94).

Fragments from over six thousand effigy vessels were recovered from Mayapán and led R. E. Smith to conclude his pottery analysis with the statement that

> the most revealing change indicated by this ceramic study was that from a generalized god and nature worship to idol worship as manifested in the vast accumulation of full-figure effigy censers and effigy vessels (1971:256).

Once again variety seems to have been the result of mass replication systems in the Late Postclassic.

The preceding "subjective" evaluations of cost-control seem to indicate that, following the proposed test implications of the trajectory, cost-control procedures were applied differentially throughout the development of Maya civilization. The potential of objective description of critical changes in the matter-energy-information structure of cultural systems suggests that quantifiable measures of cost-control should be implemented in future studies of Cozumel and ancient Maya material culture.

IMPLICATIONS OF THE PROPOSED TRAJECTORY: THE END

The development of Maya civilization, from the "Classic" at A.D. 300 to the final "Decadent" Period terminated by the Spanish in the sixteenth century, has fascinated scholars of cultural growth and collapse. The Classic/Postclassic transition especially has long occasioned debate over whether the Maya were headed toward cultural decay or a new renaissance. Although there are many views, the majority seem to hold that the transition led downhill from a pinnacle (Erasmus 1968 and Andrews 1965 and 1973 are exceptions).

According to many Maya archaeologists, the Late Postclassic was "born when civilization was in eclipse" (Pollock et al. 1962:15–16) and the signs of decay are as "unmistakable as they [are] pitiable." At the core of these evaluations is the evidence of Late Postclassic manufactured commodities. For example, R. E. Smith observes that Peto Cream Ware "clings to most of the vessel shapes and decorative devices of the [preceding] Sotuta Ceramic Complex while using a new crude method of manufacture" and "may be considered the opening wedge of a new and certainly decadent era" (1971:154).

Although all these characterizations are aesthetically justifiable, the first implication of the proposed trajectory is that Late Postclassic material culture may be viewed as a logical outcome of previous patterns. Late Postclassic remains can be described by quantitative measures of cost-control without using loaded "decadent" terminology to illustrate the obvious contrast between Late Postclassic and earlier production-distribution techniques and results. In fact, while the Postclassic system was functioning, the differences may not have been so obvious. For example, because of cost-control techniques, Late Postclassic buildings are not as structurally sound or as large and impressive as earlier buildings. Often they are not as well preserved after 500 years as many Classic structures after more than 1000. However, as A. L. Smith, one of the excavators of Mayapán, observed:

> There seems to be little striving for permanence, just window dressing and false fronts. In spite of this, however, Mayapán must have presented an impressive picture. . . . A coat of paint will hide many faults, and the ample use of plaster at Mayapán undoubtedly accomplished the same purpose (1962:269).

This Classic/Postclassic contrast raises an interesting question: How did material culture differ in its relation to the power bases of Tikal and Mayapán? The trajectory suggests a tentative answer. Viewed from a (presently) "subjective" evaluation of material culture, the interdependence of Classic populations must have been based to a large extent upon resource concentration foci which formed a critical part of ideological integration systems. In the Classic/Postclassic transition, the role of material culture seems to have changed in relation to population integration. Over a period of time, the cost-control trajectory is proposed to have led to lower production costs per item and greater resource dispersion over social and geographical space. By the Postclassic, these trends in material culture production-distribution may have fostered interdependence among populations through an expanding social and economic (rather than ideological) order (cf. McVicker in press), while at the same time they produced variety in response to local information-processing and -deciding needs (cf. Tozzer 1941:94; Webb 1973; Erasmus 1968). Thus while Classic populations were to a large extent integrated through the costly maintenance of an elite minority, Postclassic populations were most probably integrated through a rising standard of living locked into large-scale population participation in a commerce which emphasized economic efficiency and mass consumption. From this viewpoint, transformations within material culture production-distribution systems may hold one important key to describing and understanding the nature of the difference between Classic and Postclassic Maya cultural systems.

IMPLICATIONS OF THE PROPOSED TRAJECTORY: THE BEGINNING

The speculative trajectory also suggests that regardless of the "oscillations" in many aspects of material production-distribution systems (cf. Clarke 1968:224–25), there is a statistical validity to some few trajectories, specifically cost-control in the sequence from research and development to mass replication to local variety resulting from modified processes of mass replication of material culture.

This suggestion is not limited to the Classic Maya. It is applicable to other cultures in time and space. It can even be applied to early "pristine" civilizations. The sequence of 35 large Egyptian pyramids built between 2700 and 1700 B.C. (Edwards 1961) provides a good example of hypothesized production-distribution cost-control.

Resource Procurement

The kinds of resources used in pyramid construction changed several times in the course of the sequence. In the Fourth Dynasty, near the

436

beginning of pyramid construction, the brick cores of earlier step pyramids were replaced in the Cheops pyramid with large (up to 15-ton) Tura limestone blocks, cut and transported from the cliffs across the Nile from Giza. By the Fifth Dynasty, pyramids were often made with a core of small cut stones (locally mined) cased in Tura limestone blocks; problems with fit were solved with mud brick and mortar. In the Sixth Dynasty, the core of small stones in some pyramids was simply coated with a mortar of Nile mud, usually available in quantity close to pyramid construction sites.

Quantity of Material and Human Resources

Accurate figures on total volume of pyramids (assumed to be proportional to the quantity of material and human resources consumed in construction) are available for only 11 out of the 34 pyramids (figure 40). These figures certainly illustrate a curve of decreasing material and human resource concentration, plummeting from over 90 million cubic feet of limestone to less than 10 million cubic feet of rubble and Nile mud. A curve utilizing the base measurements of 30 pyramids illustrates the same trend (figure 41). Base measurements are used because height measures are not available; however, base lengths are of value as a resource concentration measure because the height of a pyramid (and thus its total volume) was usually a set proportion of its base (Edwards 1961).

Skill In Execution and Organization

Skill in organization certainly decreased with time and the change in the size of pyramids, but so did the skill needed for execution. Late in the dynastic cycle of the Old Kingdom, when Neb-hepet-Re-Mentuhotep revived pyramids (around 2130–2080 B.C.), an interesting change took place. The architects of Mentuhotep's pyramid solved the technological and labor problems of inner chamber construction by making the structure solid. The pharaoh's body was placed in the associated mortuary complex.

Over time, then, (1) resources changed from multiton Tura limestone blocks to small rubble and mud brick, which were much easier to pro-

437

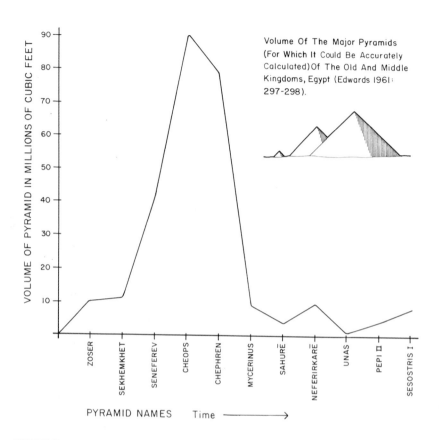

FIGURE 40. EGYPTIAN PYRAMID VOLUMES THROUGH TIME

cure; (2) quantity of resources and labor and organizational requirements decreased from the mammoth Giza pyramids to the diminutive later ones; and (3) skill needs were reduced by making the pyramid a solid mass instead of including a mortuary chamber and intricate passageways. This example is given not as a support for the hypothesized trajectory, but merely as an example of how its implications can be explored.

The emphasis of this chapter has been upon material culture and quantifiable aspects of its form and distribution. Our approach, how-

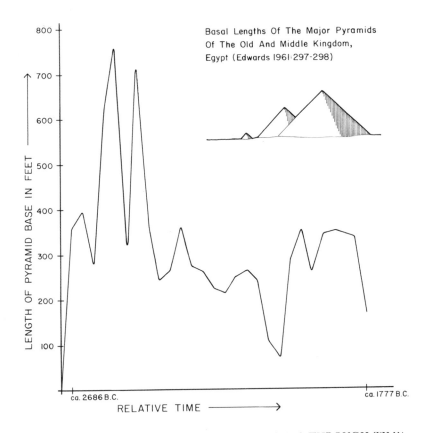

FIGURE 41. EGYPTIAN PYRAMID BASAL LENGTHS THROUGH TIME

ever, does have significance for the analysis of human behavior through time. Just as material culture is an intricate part of systems today, so it was in the past an integral component of the origin, development, and decline of complex civilizations. One aspect of the importance of the cost-control trajectory is summed up in two statements:

> The overwhelming need [in large-scale system formation] is not to expand existing political mechanisms (they are in certain respects radically inelastic) but literally to transcend them. The new grouping must be united, not by kinship or territory alone, but by belief, by the infinite extendibility of common symbols, shared cosmology

439

and the overarching unity of fears and hopes made visible in ritual (Netting 1972:233).

As pyramid building started a profound change had to take place in the living conditions of the population, affecting more and more people as the work proceeded. They and their families became completely dependent on the central administration which employed and fed them. At the same time the administration must have made annual levies to obtain the grain needed to supply their workers. These deliveries had to be increased steadily, until in the end an entirely new system of supply and distribution was established. This system, operating for a period of years, would have made a complete break with the previous isolated village economy, ushering in a basically different phase in the life of the whole country (Mendelssohn 1971:216).

These quotations suggest that in the development of large-scale cultural systems the concentration of resources in material components with heavy ideological values is a key ingredient. The resulting ideological and material focal points (foci based upon a combination of material form, the economic and personnel integration that produced them, and their ideological significance) may be critical in opening up the potential for economic integration based upon local production-distribution units being superceded by large-scale supralocal production-distribution units.

CONCLUSIONS

Material culture is a critical component in the understanding of any cultural system. From the earliest known pebble tools, material culture has proliferated until today our economic, social, and ideological existence depends upon it and we find ourselves literally encapsulated in it. Our present precarious position makes it increasingly apparent that material culture is not a static or even passive system component; it is a dynamic component that changes rapidly in ways which both are affected by and affect our patterns of behavior. Yet most anthropological models of the long-term development of civilizations employ material culture only as a passive indicator of other aspects of system structure or change. They often make little or no effort to identify regular patterns in changes in the form and distribution of material culture or to determine the role these critical changes in energy and information transformation played in cultural development. If may be time to supplement the few processual models of cultural development (such as White 1949; Quigley 1961; and Flannery 1972) by constructing dynamic and quantified descriptions of the development of material culture.

This chapter is a plea not for material culture as superorganic, but for a clearer definition of material culture's role in matter-energy-information systems (cf. Clarke 1968; Gorman 1972; 1973; Justeson 1973). The hypothesized trends in resource management and production-distribution systems provide a series of test implications that require quantitative answers. As these materialist hypotheses are tested, they can be expanded to include significant nonmaterial correlates. For example:

Does the shift from craft production to mass replication always include a shift from public ritual to more individualized social interactions (concentration to dispersion in the social realm)? Are mass replication techniques of production correlated directly with centralized or decentralized political control or are they workable under either?

Considering the new view that population pressure may lead to intensification of agricultural production systems (Boserup 1965) and that many cost-control techniques of production and distribution require a basic population threshold, what is the relation of product demand, mode and efficiency of production, and work force needs to population growth? Do the crossing of demand thresholds and the resultant job openings and increased product availability lead to further population increase?

Can different rates of change in production-distribution trajectories (Teotihuacán and the Valley of Mexico versus the Maya of Yucatán) be correlated with basic differences in types of energy extraction systems and related social-material interactions?

The proposed trajectory has many steps to go from its initial statement here to its test against Cozumel data. Not the smallest steps are defining system boundaries and growth and transforming test implications into empirical, quantifiable tests. Once the tests are made, however, no matter what they show they will be useful in systematically and quantitatively describing the material correlates of cultural development.

Whether the resource management cost-control trajectory proposed

441

here withstands quantitative testing is not important.[13] Beginning a quantitative analysis of material attributes of long-term sociomaterial systems is!

NOTES

1. The major stimulus for this paper was five months of daily discussions and archaeological discoveries with the staff, students, and workmen of the 1973 Cozumel Archaeological Project. For that opportunity thanks are due to all the institutions and friends in Mexico City who made our work possible. The joint Harvard University–University of Arizona project was accomplished by financial contributions from the National Geographic Society, the Ford Foundation, Mrs. Charles Ayling, Mr. Landon Clay, the Ford Motor Company, and the American Can Company and by the dedication of participating students.

The interest in growth models and General Systems Theory of T. P. Culbert, D. A. Phillips (cf. Phillips and Sessions n.d.), D. A. Freidel (cf. Freidel n.d.), I. Shimada (cf. Shimada n.d.), and F. J. Gorman has been a constant source of discussions and constructive criticisms. Also of great value were the encouragement, ideas, and commonsense evaluations contributed by J. A. Sabloff, D. A. Gregory, T. A. Lee, Jr., M. E. Harlan, E. W. Andrews, V. A. Andrews, and J. M. Andrews.

In addition, this paper has benefited from detailed criticisms by J. Connor, R. Cunningham, S. Graham, J. Justeson, E. Kurjack, W. Longacre, J. Hill, J. Rosenthal, B. Voorhies, S. Whittlesey, G. Willey, N. Yaffee, and Col. R. F. B. Driftwood (Royal Bengal Lancers, Ret.). The title was suggested by J. Justeson. The figures were drawn by Charles Sternberg.

2. These goals are presented in Rathje and Sabloff (1973); Sabloff et al. (1973); Sabloff and Rathje (1973 and in press).

3. This concept is similar to "deviation amplification" as presented by Maruyama (1963).

4. Interesting views on patterns of economic and social organization changes, similar to the nonproportional growth compensations suggested by Boulding, are presented in Quigley (1961); Flannery (1972); Gibson (1972); Lees (1972); Jacobs (1969); and Meadows et al. (1972).

5. In a paper on the general properties of production systems, Shimada (n.d.) observes that of the two basic components of such systems, material and human resources, the human resources are the most significant. His focus is on the types of social organization that structure human resources into production systems. This critical transformation of potential human energy into kinetic energy will not be considered in this paper. The aim here is to describe replicated temporal patterning in the form and distribution of the products that result from this transformation, regardless of the human behavioral means by which the transformation is achieved.

Also it should be noted that while the interests of Leslie White (1949) were useful in developing this paper, the trajectory is concerned not with the quantity of energy extracted but with the way the use of that energy changes through time.

6. It is important to note that system growth may be necessary to develop the

"economies of scale," or demand thresholds, required for mass production to work, even on a preindustrial level.

7. For somewhat similar statements see Quigley's model (1961) of the transformation from an "institution" into an "instrument," and Jacob's model (1969) of "developmental" capital becoming "working" capital.

8. Taagapera uses a similar concept in describing the "logistic growth curves of empires." He defines "autocatakinetic growth" as a process in which a "substance or structure itself acts as a nucleus for the formation about it of further quantities of the same substance or structure" (Taagapera 1968:174; cf. also Simon 1962 and his concept of "near decomposibility").

9. A. L. Smith was not joking when he used the term "false front" to describe Late Postclassic architecture (1962; see opening quotation). At San Gervasio (Cozumel), there is one rectangular platform which supports just one wall on the long side facing onto the plaza. Thorough searching for back walls showed that they were not made of stone. Thus, any structure made from the single wall would have been one front wall of stone and plaster, possibly with side walls of wood and a thatch roof. Compare the resemblance of the San Gervasio remains to an ethnohistoric description of elite houses at the time of the conquest: "They build a wall in the middle dividing the house lengthwise, leaving several doors in the wall into the half which they call the back of the house, where they have their beds; and the other half they whitened very nicely with lime. And the lords have their walls painted with great elegance; and this half is for the reception and lodging of their guests" (Tozzer 1941:85).

10. The *oratorios* dispersed among "elite residences" at Late Postclassic Mayapán are called "private shrines" after ethnohistoric descriptions of the following conquest period: "And besides the community temples, the lords, priests and the leading men had also oratorios and idols in their houses, where they made their prayers and offerings in private" (Tozzer 1941:108).

11. The tests include resistance to impact, resistance to chipping, compressive and flexural strength, surface hardness, water absorption, and specific gravity and degree of vitrification (cf. Connor and Rathje 1973). These measures were selected because they relate to the specific functions that ceramics are designed to perform.

12. One indicator of a new transport system in the Postclassic is relevant to the discussion of resource dispersion over space. Peter Urban has recently compared obsidian distribution patterns between the Postclassic and Classic. Although obsidian sources are located twice as far from selected Postclassic (average: 815 km.) as Classic (average: 420 km.) sites, the ratio of obsidian to flint in Postclassic centers and house mounds (2.1:1) is double that in Classic centers (.9:1) (Urban n.d.).

13. In fact, the points in system development at which the trajectory does not work will be especially significant, as these seem to be the points at which new internal matter-energy-information structurings lead to a new acceleration of growth.

References

ADAMS, R. McC.
1971   *The Ceramics of Altar de Sacrificios, Guatemala.* Peabody Museum Papers 63, no. 1.

ANDREWS, E. W., IV
1965   "Archaeology and Prehistory in the Northern Maya Lowlands: An Introduction," in *Handbook of Middle American Indians*, 2:288–330 (Austin: University of Texas Press).
1968   "Dzibilchaltún: A Northern Maya Metropolis," *Archaeology* 21:36–47.
1973   "The Development of Maya Civilization after Abandonment of the Southern Cities," in *The Classic Maya Collapse*, ed. T. P. Culbert (Albuquerque: University of New Mexico Press).

ASHBY, W. R.
1968   "Variety, Constraint and the Law of Requisite Variety," in *Modern Systems Research for the Behavioral Scientist*, ed. W. Buckley (Chicago: Aldine Publishing Co.).

BERTALANFFY, L. VON
1968   *General Systems Theory: Foundations, Development, Applications* (New York: George Braziller).

BOSERUP, E.
1965   *The Conditions of Agricultural Growth: The Economics of Agrarian Change under Population Pressure* (Chicago: Aldine Publishing Co.).

BOULDING, K.
1956a   "General Systems Theory—The Skeleton of Science," *General Systems* 1:11–17.
1956b   "Toward a General Theory of Growth," *General Systems* 1:66–75.

BUCKLEY, W. (ed.)
1968   *Modern Systems Research for the Behavioral Scientist* (Chicago: Aldine Publishing Co.).

CARR, R. F. AND J. E. HAZARD
1961   *Tikal Report No. 11: Map of the Ruins of Tikal, El Petén, Guatemala* (Philadelphia: University Museum).

CLARKE, D. L.
1968   *Analytical Archaeology* (London: Methuen & Co.).

COE, W. R.
1965   "Caches and Offertory Practices of the Maya Lowlands," in *Handbook of Middle American Indians*, 2:462–68 (Austin: University of Texas Press).

1967 *Tikal: A Handbook of the Ancient Maya Ruins* (Philadelphia: University Museum).

CONNOR, J. G. AND W. L. RATHJE

1973 "Mass Production and the Ancient Maya: Experiments in Cracking Maya Pots," paper read at the Society for American Archaeology Meeting, San Francisco.

CULBERT, T. P.

1973 *The Classic Maya Collapse* (Albuquerque: University of New Mexico (ed.) Press).

1974 *The Lost Civilization: The Story of the Classic Maya* (New York: Harper and Row).

EDWARDS, I. E. S.

1961 *The Pyramids of Egypt* (Harmondsworth, Eng.: Penguin Books).

ERASMUS, C. J.

1965 "Monument Building: Some Field Experiments," *Southwestern Journal of Anthropology* 21:277–301.

1968 "Thoughts on the Upward Collapse: An Essay on Explanation in Anthropology," *Southwestern Journal of Anthropology* 24:170–94.

FISK, G.

1967 *Marketing Systems: An Introductory Analysis* (New York: Harper and Row).

FLANNERY, K. V.

1968 "Archaeological Systems Theory and Early Mesoamerica," in *Anthropological Archaeology of the Americas*, ed. B. J. Meggers (Washington, D. C.: Anthropological Society of Washington).

1972 "The Cultural Evolution of Civilizations," *Annual Review of Ecology and Systematics* 3:399–426.

FREIDEL, D. A.

n.d. "A Model for Culture Change," manuscript in the Peabody Museum Library, Harvard University.

GIBSON, M.

1972 "Hydraulic Systems, River Shifts, and Population Adjustment in Mesopotamia," paper read at the Southwestern Anthropological Association Meeting, Long Beach.

GLASSOW, M. A.

1972 "Changes in the Adaptations of Southwestern Basketmakers: a Systems Perspective," in *Contemporary Archaeology*, ed. M. P. Leone (Carbondale: Southern Illinois University Press).

GORMAN, F. J. E.

1972 "Prehistoric Cultures as Information Processing Systems: A Partial Example from Hay Hollow Valley, East Central Arizona," paper read at the American Anthropological Association Meeting, Toronto.

1973 "An Investigation of Degradation Trends in Natural and Prehistoric Cultural Systems," paper read at the American Anthropological Association Meetings, New Orleans.

JACOBS, J.

1969 *The Economy of Cities* (New York: Random House).

445

JUSTESON, J. S.
1973 "Limitations of Archaeological Inference: An Information Theoretic Approach with Applications in Methodology," *American Antiquity* 38:131–49.

KROEBER, A. L.
1962 *A Roster of Civilizations and Cultures: An Essay on the Natural History of the World's Cultures, Living and Ancient* (Chicago: Aldine Publishing Co.).

KIDDER, A. V.
1947 *The Artifacts of Uaxactún.* Carnegie Institution of Washington Publication 576.

LEES, S. H.
1972 "The State's Use of Irrigation in Changing Peasant Society," paper read at the Southwestern Anthropological Association Meeting, Long Beach.

LONGYEAR, J. M., III
1952 *Copan Ceramics: A Study of Southeastern Maya Pottery.* Carnegie Institution of Washington Publication 597.

McVICKER, D. E.
in press "Variation in Protohistoric Maya Settlement Pattern," *American Antiquity.*

MARUYAMA, M.
1963 "The Second Cybernetics: Deviation Amplifying Mutual Causal Processes," *American Scientist* 51:164–79.

MEADOWS, D. H., D. L. MEADOWS, J. RANDERS, AND W. W. BEHRENS III
1972 *The Limits to Growth: A Report for The Club of Rome's Project on the Predicament of Mankind.* (New York: Universe Books).

MENDELSSOHN, K.
1971 "A Scientist Looks at the Pyramids," *American Scientist* 59:210–20.

MILLER, J. G.
1965 "Living Systems: Cross-level Hypotheses," *Behavioral Systems:* 380–411.

MOHOLY-NAGY, H.
1965 "Tikal Mosaic Statuettes," *Archaeology* 19:84–89.

NETTING, R. M.
1972 "Sacred Power and Centralization: Aspects of Political Adaptation in Africa," in *Population Growth: Anthropological Implications,* ed. B. Spooner (Cambridge, Mass.: M.I.T. Press).

PHILLIPS, D. AND S. SESSIONS
n.d. "Mesoamerica and the Cyclical Nature of Civilization," manuscript in the Arizona State Museum Library.

POLLOCK, H. E. D.
1965 "Architecture of the Maya Lowlands," *Handbook of Middle American Indians,* 2:378–440 (Austin: University of Texas Press).

POLLOCK, H. E. D., R. L. ROYS, T. PROSKOURIAKOFF, AND A. L. SMITH
1962 *Mayapán, Yucatán, Mexico.* Carnegie Institution of Washington Publication 619.

PROSKOURIAKOFF, T.
1962   *The Artifacts of Mayapán*, Carnegie Institution of Washington Publication 619, pt. 4.
1965   "Sculpture and Major Arts of the Maya Lowlands," *Handbook of Middle American Indians*, 2:469–97 (Austin: University of Texas Press).

QUIGLEY, C.
1961   *The Evolution of Civilizations: An Introduction to Historical Analysis* (New York: Macmillan Co.).

RATHJE, W. L.
1973   "Classic Maya Development and Denouement," in *Classic Maya Collapse*, ed. T. P. Culbert (Albuquerque: University of New Mexico Press).

RATHJE, W. L. AND D. A. GREGORY
in press   "Trade Models and Archaeological Problems: Classic Maya Examples," in *Ancient Mesoamerican Commercial Systems*, ed. T. A. Lee, Jr. (Provo, U.: New World Archaeological Foundation).

RATHJE, W. L. AND J. A. SABLOFF
1973   "Ancient Maya Commercial Systems: A Research Design for the Island of Cozumel," *World Archaeology* 5:221–31.

RATHJE, W. L., J. A. SABLOFF AND D. A. GREGORY
in press   "An Olmec Jade Head from the Island of Cozumel," *Estudios de Cultura Maya* 9.

RICKETSON, O. G., JR., AND E. B. RICKETSON
1937   *Uaxactun, Guatemala, Group E—1926–1931.* Carnegie Institution of Washington Publication 477.

SABLOFF, J. A. AND W. L. RATHJE
1973   "A Study of Changing Precolumbian Commercial Patterns on the Island of Cozumel, Mexico," *Atti Del XL Congresso Internazionale Degli Americanisti*, 455–63.
in press   *A Study of Changing Precolumbian Commercial Systems: The 1972–1973 Seasons at Cozumel, Mexico*, Peabody Museum Papers.

SABLOFF, J. A., W. L. RATHJE, D. A. FREIDEL,
J. G. CONNOR, AND P. L. W. SABLOFF
in press   "Trade and Power in Postclassic Yucatán: Initial Observations," in *Mesoamerican Archaeology: New Approaches*, ed. N. Hammond (London: Gerald Duckworth & Co.).

SABLOFF, J. A. AND G. R. WILLEY
1967   "The Collapse of Maya Civilization in the Southern Lowlands: A Consideration of History and Process," *Southwestern Journal of Anthropology* 23: 311–36.

SARAYDAR, S. C. AND I. SHIMADA
1971   "A Quantitative Comparison of Efficiency between a Stone Axe and a Steel Axe," *American Antiquity* 36:216–17.
1973   "Experimental Archaeology: A New Outlook," *American Antiquity* 38:344–50.

SAYRE, E. V., L. CHAN, AND J. A. SABLOFF
1971   "High Resolution Gamma Ray Spectroscopic Analyses of Fine Orange Pot-

tery," in *Science and Archaeology*, ed. R. H. Brill (Cambridge, Mass.: M.I.T. Press).

SHIMADA, I.
n.d. "The Structural Relationship between Local and State Economies in *Tahuatinsuyu*: An Examination of a State Revenue Production Model," manuscript in the Arizona State Museum Library.

SIMON, H. A.
1962 "The Architecture of Complexity," *Proceedings of the American Philosophical Society* 106:467–82.

SMITH, A. L.
1950 *Uaxactún, Guatemala: Excavations of 1931–1937*. Carnegie Institution of Washington Publication 588.
1962 *Residential and Associated Structures at Mayapán*. Carnegie Institution of Washington Publication 619, pt. 3.

SMITH, R. E.
1955 *Ceramic Sequence at Uaxactún, Guatemala*. Middle American Research Institute Publication 20, 2 vols. (New Orleans: Tulane University).
1958 "The Place of Fine Orange Pottery in American Archaeology," *American Antiquity* 24:151–60.
1971 *The Pottery of Mayapán*. Peabody Museum Papers 66, 2 vols.

SMITH, R. E. AND J. C. GIFFORD
1965 "Pottery of the Maya Lowlands," in *Handbook of Middle American Indians*, 2:498–534 (Austin: University of Texas Press).

TAAGAPERA, R.
1968 "Growth Curves of Empires," *General Systems* 8:171–75.

THOMPSON, J. E. S.
1970 *Maya History and Religion* (Norman: University of Oklahoma Press).

TOZZER, A. M. (ed.)
1941 *Landa's Relación de las Cosas de Yucatán*. Peabody Museum Papers 18.

URBAN, J. J., JR.
n.d. "A Proposed Method to Measure the Efficiency of Long-distance Trade of the Maya," manuscript in the Arizona State Museum Library.

VANCE, J.
1971 *The Merchant's World* (Englewood Cliffs, N. J.: Prentice-Hall).

WEAVER, M. P.
1972 *The Aztecs, Maya, and Their Predecessors: Archaeology of Mesoamerica* (New York: Seminar Press).

WEBB, M. C.
1973 "The Peten Maya Decline Viewed in the Perspective of State Formation," in *The Classic Maya Collapse*, ed. T. P. Culbert (Albuquerque: University of New Mexico Press).

WHITE, L. A.
1949 *Science of Culture*. (New York: Farrar Skaus).

WILLEY, G. P., T. P. CULBERT AND R. E. W. ADAMS
1967 "Maya Lowlands Ceramics: A Report from the 1965 Guatemala City Conference," *American Antiquity* 32:289–315.

PART IV

OVERVIEW
AND
PROSPECT

11

The Emerging Place of Trade
in Civilizational Studies

ROBERT McC. ADAMS

University of Chicago

An assembly of individual contributions like the foregoing would be ill served by straightforward synthesis or summary, useful as such an effort might seem at first glance for the casual peruser of this volume. Its strength lies in diversity, not cohesiveness. The specialized regional orientation of several chapters eludes easy or accurate abstraction by anyone less specialized than their authors. Perhaps the only common characteristic, in fact, is the search for new formulations, new analytical approaches with which to revive an old and, until recently, rather neglected field of inquiry. A variety of more or less difficult and problematical routes are proposed toward a still-remote but rewarding objective. This is a time to encourage the pursuit of all of them, not to seek prematurely to harmonize them or to nit-pick about unexamined premises and contradictory assumptions.

A personal formulation that speaks to some of the positions taken by contributors to this volume, and in particular that of Polanyi and Dalton, is appearing elsewhere (Adams 1974); a restatement of it here accordingly would be redundant. I cannot forebear interjecting an occasional reservation or alternative hypothesis at points, but in general I am persuaded by the totality of the effort that a preliminary period of syncretistic faith will serve us better than immediate, corrosive skepticism. Things are moving again on trade, unevenly but excitingly. A fundamentally new direction has been set, in which patterns in the diffusion of archaeologically recognizable commodities are no longer the end of study but one of a battery of means by which we seek to identify trade as a complex interactive, adaptive, and in part consciously directed process. Hence it was the right time and setting for a highly exploratory symposium on the subject. This was surely the most important consensus discernible among the contributors.

Renfrew's wide-ranging introduction plots the formal layout of the field for us, largely in terms of alternative possibilities for spatial interaction. Detailed testing and application will require many separate undertakings, and comments at this juncture on the apparent fit of his categories to data offered by other contributors would be insubstantial and premature. Our concern ought to be less with fashioning, or criticizing, a comprehensive approach than with identifying underlying issues that remain to be dealt with before any such approach is likely to succeed.

An issue of growing importance is adumbrated by Renfrew's brief comment on the complexity of communication accompanying trade. He suggests that we must learn to distinguish "different categories of information, conveyed by different channels." In a later, equally concise observation, he characterizes spatial distributions of artifacts as the relics of an "information flow" that may bring us closer to the strategic importance of trade for an understanding of complex early societies.

A recent paper by Kent Flannery develops a similar position more fully, within the context of a formal, systems approach to cultural evolution. Declaring that "everything which transmits information is within the province of ecology" (1972:400), Flannery maintains that "one of the main trends in the evolution of bands into tribes, chiefdoms, and states must be a gradual increase in capacity for information processing,

tion and political centralization as constituting the vital, central axis of development toward statehood. My strategy of research therefore calls, for example, for substantial emphasis on the distribution of wealth—the correspondence between classes of luxury commodities in tombs, private houses, and ritual contexts; the correspondence of wealth in tombs with skeletal indicators of health and stature; the distribution of such wealth by sloping curve or disjunctive step function. Both Johnson and Wright, in the course of a very rewarding discussion at the symposium, opted instead for a more constrained and formal view of the evolution of the state, in terms of an increasing number of tiers in the hierarchy of information channeling. One substantive outcome of this difference is that they, identifying the state with the emergence of an apparent three-tiered hierarchy, place its advent in the Near East a minimum of several centuries earlier than a primary concern for a stratified social order with "disembedded" political institutions allows me to do. It would be futile to try to resolve our differences here, since they probably touch on differing assessments of the core processes by which civilizations came into being or of how they are to be distinguished from all lesser levels of sociocultural integration. But at least this suggests how lively an issue information channeling is likely to be during the years immediately ahead.

Mention of "disembedded" political institutions recalls Eisenstadt's (1963) identification of the historical bureaucratic societies on the basis of their rulers' pursuit of autonomous goals with a sufficient level of "free-floating," potentially mobilizable resources. I would buttress my identification of the first appearance of the state with the observation that neither of these features can be identified before the emergence of militaristic Mesopotamian urban polities in the Early Dynastic period. Earlier patterns of control, at least in that region (and Webb joined my argument during discussions at the symposium that there were probably close analogies elsewhere), then tend to be identified according to this schema by their theocratic overtones and the apparent absence of a secularized elite. Wright, on the contrary, seemingly finds the hypothesis of a theocratic society incommensurate with analytical distinctions based on features of social organization that are used for later phases, and perhaps also objectionable on the grounds that it is fuzzy and non-falsifiable.

This is another set of knotty issues, not to be resolved quickly if at all. But my earlier discussion of fungibility at least suggests a path toward its more productive study. Whatever else the earliest states imply, they seem to have been accompanied by the "disembedding" of functionally specialized institutions. Is that the only context in which "secularization" can be operationally defined? Can secularization occur other than as an aspect of ongoing functional and occupational specialization within a larger social entity? And what of specialization itself? Can it occur other than in the context of heightened fungibility of commodities and services, and hence a widening exchange economy, that is increasingly open to all classes of a society? If all of these speculations have any substance, then, again, the systematic study of fungibility would appear to be a rewarding avenue for future investigation.

At this point, an at least temporarily insurmountable methodological problem looms with which the symposium regrettably had little time to deal. Let us concede that, except in instances of family archives, tomb inscriptions, and the like, we cannot identify wealth or status in terms of formal rank, administrative positions held, and differential access to productive resources such as agricultural lands. In order to proceed at all, therefore, we must often simply assume that wealth and status covary not only with one another but with available archaeological indicators: private house size and embellishments, tomb furnishings, and the like. But was this really so? A convincing test of the proposition that wealth in daily accoutrements or grave furnishings correlates closely with functional wealth and socially recognized status would appear to be highly desirable. At issue, in the broadest terms, is the adequacy of the stock of privately held commodities that archaeologists can recover as an index of circulating wealth and recognized status and authority. This is an issue thoughtfully adumbrated in Renfrew's contribution also.

The same ambiguity with respect to the proportionality of archaeological remains to the activity that engendered them has still another effect on the study of trade. Johnson assumes that trade routes can be identified from the concentrations of rare or luxury commodities found at settlements along them which presumably served as warehousing or break-of-bulk centers, necessarily presupposing that archaeologically observed debris will be heaviest in the vicinity of the heaviest traffic in the articles. But with seemingly equal plausibility, one might suppose instead that dealers in valuable commodities packaged and shipped them with far lower unit losses than among ultimate consumers, or that virtually all of the luxury goods we encounter on surface reconnaissance derive not from ordinary loss and breakage but from the exposure by erosion or disturbance of graves or other loci of final consumption. Something like the first of these latter alternatives may well be implied for Cozumel, in fact, by the paucity of recognizable trading debris that Sabloff and Freidel can identify at what they postulate as major storage and transshipment facilities. One interpretation does not disprove the other, of course, because the settings are so different. But both reinforce the impression that we tend to rely heavily and somewhat uncritically on assumptions about the regular relationship between behavior and the archaeological relics of behavior that need much closer scrutiny.

A further methodological problem can be identified in those cases in which the archaeological study of trade must proceed unaided by documentary sources. Trade and exchange are time-bound phenomena, the character of which is best understood when the standards of exchange value governing individual transactions can be related directly to those transactions. Moreover, if trade is generally the dynamic, unstabilizing force that the ethnohistoric record seems to suggest (cf. Adams 1974), wide fluctuations over short intervals are to be expected in the geographic range of trade, in the extent of local participation in trading networks, and in the selection of trading partners. Yet the archaeological record is characteristically an aggregative one, difficult to connect with short or precise time intervals.

Attempts have been made to rectify this on the basis of a microstratigraphic approach to the deposition of measured quantities of raw materials or other commodities (Winters 1968; Wright 1972), and one may only hope that they will continue and prosper. But knowledge that archaeologists can work with briefer intervals than heretofore does not advance us very far toward specifying what the chronological intervals really are. Nor, if we disaggregate gross levels and deal with the necessarily small quantities of goods or resources that are to be found in individual microstratigraphic components, have we yet found a way to discriminate between random variation, the influence of exogenous variables, and genuine fluctuations in trading activity. While the record of archaeological progress during recent years suggests that these difficulties will not prove as intractable as they seem at present, at the very least it would appear that important conceptual advances in the study of trade are more likely to emerge and be adequately tested in fields in which the archaeological remains can be joined to a historical chronology and written economic records.

Let us shift from matters of methodology to unanswered questions directed more toward the substance of trade, while noting that methodologically rigorous, innovative studies contribute decisively to the need and possibility for such a shift. Johnson, for example, suggestively traces out hierarchically organized, putatively hexagonal networks of "local exchange," using that term only in "a very general sense denoting reciprocal movement of goods or services or both within a single settlement system" (pp. 285–86). That the spatial distributions he documents reflect a "highly structured organization" having something to do with local exchange seems only reasonable. But does this kind of generalized, elusive "local exchange," subsuming a great range of possible institutions, interactions, and interrelationships, really permit us to identify some tangible entity as "a significant factor in determination of settlement locations" (p. 335), or only to discern what might equally well be a consequence or correlate of some other set of systemic requirements for settlement location than Christaller's "Marketing Principle"? I would suggest that, until we can specify the content of the particular exchange relationships with which he deals more closely, elaborate "tests" of some of Johnson's propositions may lend a spurious sense of precision and corroboration to an ambitious, plausible, but still very largely conjectural series of hypotheses.

Let me illustrate how little we really know with a casually offered alternative explanation for the "small cone sites" to which considerable importance is attached by his analysis. Everything he records about their spatial distribution and artifact content seems equally consistent with the *"imams"* that are still to be found in the region today. These are shrine structures housing the tomb of a locally venerated saint; generally they lack attendants and are maintained by sporadic, voluntary labor. At least in the Warka region, they are often on long-abandoned mounds in the open desert (e.g., Adams and Nissen 1972: WS-444, 449). Yet their sanctity is such that travelers can leave unneeded valuables—plows, shovels, iron pails, clothing, firewood, bicycles, even portable radios—in their close proximity with assurance that they will not be molested.

458

Imams not infrequently adjoin disputed tribal boundaries, and hence often serve as places of assured personal refuge and as settings within which feuds or disputes can be negotiated without fear of treachery or violence. Clearly, they have little or nothing to do with "administered" movement of anything, nor with routes of "local exchange," since the individual bundles are all differentiated personal belongings and not trade wares. Ultimately they may well display the kind of geometrical regularity of spacing that Johnson is at pains to demonstrate, perhaps serving as nodes in an information and transport network even in the total absence of any resident population. But how far can we go in speaking of a "highly structured organization of local exchange" in the fourth millennium B.C. when our systematic fieldwork is still so limited that something along the lines of the modern *imam* is within the range of alternative explanations that must be considered?

Quite apart from the "small cone sites," to be sure, Johnson assembles cumulatively impressive evidence of distributional regularities in the deposition of goods. But again, how wide is the range of interpretation for such regularities? Johnson argues for the "administered movement of centrally produced craft items" (p. 304), but the evidence for even this very vague and cautious formulation seems comparatively slight. Do "relatively standardized" (and the variance deserves more scrutiny) bowls really argue for "an administered redistribution or ration system" (p. 304), or are standardized volume measures a prerequisite for almost any relatively large and complex system of exchange—kin-based reciprocity, market, or whatever—in which grain is a principal measure? The hypothesis of an administered system introduces the state as an effective agent in the transaction and in that sense is consistent with Johnson's stress on equating formal levels of settlement hierarchy with emerging strata of political authority. But the alternative possibilities are many, and the evidence for excluding most of them remains quite unconvincing.

Consider some other possibilities. Goods could have been carried from central craft workshops by those who were thus recompensed for temple building or other services. What are the limits within which a theocratic center (permit me that characterization once more for the sake of the argument) could have been supported through voluntary offerings brought in by pilgrims, combined in some measure with acts of reci-

459

procity or exchanges for subsistence products on the part of the inhabitants of a holy place like Uruk? Or, at the other extreme, what Johnson views (as I have also, on other occasions) as "near capacity production" by the "resident agricultural population" of a center like Uruk also could have involved dependent agricultural labor in the ring of fields surrounding a city, performed by those living in villages outside that ring. This could well have been the outcome of those "asymmetries" of wealth or political power mentioned earlier, and would have left the inhabitants of the central place free to intensify their specialization in the crafts, in military pursuits, and in cosmological speculations. To repeat, however, my point is not to rebut Johnson's challenging hypotheses and innovative approach to testing them, but only to stress how wide the realm of virtually uncontrolled plausibility yet remains.

Another important group of substantive questions concerning trade can best be outlined in terms of the spatial aspects of exchange patterns, although for the most part they do not fall within the framework of Renfrew's discussion. A number of them concern the relationship of different sizes and kinds of units to different analytical objectives, and perhaps may be subsumed under the rubric of "boundary problems."

Renfrew, if I understand him rightly, takes a "civilization" as the primary unit of his analysis. Within it, at least in many cases, he is able to identify a number of "autonomous central places," and his discussion of the articulation of their patterns of exchange with their overall geometrical arrangement goes on from there on the assumption that they are all more or less equivalent social groupings. That may be, indeed, the only way to proceed if the geographical limits of study are those we have traditionally observed: the Aegean world, the lower Mesopotamian plain, or similar "natural" units from a geographic viewpoint. But Lamberg-Karlovsky's paper persuasively argues—demands, in fact, as Renfrew readily acknowledges—that we recognize the significance of much wider and more diverse patterns of interaction. And if we are to do so, we must somehow take into account the probable nature of contacts between social units that were in no sense equivalent—in subsistence patterns, in level of sociocultural complexity, in military potential, in technological capabilities and requirements, and in many other respects. It is this kind of "asymmetrical" contact and interaction that, except in the rather limited terms of a typology of information flow, appears in Renfrew's paper only as a considered rejection of the older, Childean model that saw "secondary" state growth as a result of trade-induced "emulation," and that was not taken up systematically at the symposium itself.

Complex as this problem is when approached on a single time-level, the contributors all share the common, added difficulty that they must deal with it through a temporal sequence. Surely the regional or spatial units of analysis that are appropriate at one stage in the evolution of urban, state society are not a priori appropriate at another. Early villages, for example, conceivably may be dealt with within a system bounded by the limits of their own subsistence-sustaining area. To be sure, a wider set of boundaries drawn to include symbiotic or competitive relations with similar, neighboring settlements, as well as to take into account the interaction of zones of optimal and marginal subsistence potentiality (Binford 1968), seems inherently more productive if we propose to work with truly explanatory rather than descriptive objectives. But in either case the geographical range is likely to be relatively small and the differences in sociocultural content and complexity fairly subtle. How does this change when, at a later point in the evolutionary sequence, we must deal with systems whose subordinate settlements focus centripetally on central urban places, separated from other such systems by increasingly disjunctive barriers of conflicting allegiance and political or military rivalry? Yet if trade is approached as a process of intercommunal exchange in the broadest sense, which it was surely the consensus of the symposium that we must do, the potentialities and conditions of contact obviously change profoundly as sociocultural development continues along these lines.

At what point—responsive to what degrees of religious integration, political centralization, or advancement in the technology of transport—does it become useful to speak, for example, of the "central Mexican symbiotic region" (Sanders 1956), or a "macro-adaptation" dominated by a key central area of "massed power" rather than an unranked mosaic of "micro-adaptations" (Palerm and Wolf 1957:29)? At what different point, and in what fashion, did lines of territorial consolidation associated with the formation of urban polities begin to crosscut and transform the nascent patterns of symbiotic interchange? To what extent can institutional developments in subordinated or peripheral regions have been imposed along lines that were congruent with the needs of the central power but that were either mutually contradictory or locally dysfunctional in their secondary, derived setting? Obviously some asymmetrical, more or less forcibly imposed interrelationships may have led to bizarre combinations and local inconsistencies. (Even dispensing with smooth, functional integration in the outlying region as a requirement, however, Lamberg-Karlovsky's attempt to identify "market networks" in early southeastern Iran in the apparent absence of "marketing" or "market places" seems somewhat confusing.) Finally, for many later, historically documented periods, we know that political frontiers and the limits of geographical regions or culture areas often were not at all coterminous. Was this merely a consequence of the growth of conquest-oriented societies, or does it suggest a deep-rooted flux and indeterminacy in the interaction of political and economic or subsistence variables that may have originated much earlier? Simply to raise these questions is to indicate not merely the intellectual direction in which the revived study of trade will take us but also the relative paucity of significant findings that we can claim to have achieved thus far.

The foregoing considerations lead me to return once more to the debate during the symposium over whether or not it was useful to characterize a major epoch during the evolution of civilizations as "theocratic." Webb's contribution notes that one of "the two most characteristic features of chiefdoms . . . especially those whose size and complexity approach the maximum for the type," is that they "are almost invariably theocracies" (p. 162). Using all the archaeological or protohistorical evidence known to me for a surely "primary" region of civilizational emergence like lowland Mesopotamia (down to at least the end of the Uruk period), however, it is the theocratic character that seems assured while the existence of a corresponding, secular organization that may be termed a chiefdom seems wholly speculative. It is only when we turn to the peripheries of the Mesopotamian plain that the appurtenances of rank and wealth, in a framework of predominantly secular controls that Jawad (1965) describes as an "era of townships," give focus to a form of social organization for which the term *chiefdom* may well be appropriate.

Recalling Renfrew's hesitancy to accept any of the criteria that heretofore have been offered for distinguishing "primary" from "secondary" or "derived" civilizations, it is thus tempting to speculate that the term *chiefdom* conflates phases in the evolutionary development of two distinguishable types of society precisely by neglecting important differences in this "theocratic" dimension. One could argue, for example, that the relations of "primary" civilizations with their outliers were, for a significant transitional period during their growth, characterized by patterns of interaction and superordination that took predominantly peaceful, theocratic forms. "Secondary" civilizations, on the other hand, would have been precociously exposed to essentially secular politico-military institutions and better organized, more dangerous forms of intersocietal predation, and might well have begun to emulate them after a much briefer and more attenuated phase of theocratic integration.

The case of "secondary" state formation that emerges most convincingly in these chapters—and quite possibly anywhere—is that outlined by Wheatley for Southeast Asia. I do not think I was alone among anthropologically trained archaeologists and culture historians in my prior general ignorance of the evocatively rich historical material on the region. While he is at pains to describe the religious and administrative bias of his sources, the strategic role of exogenous maritime trade in the process of state development and urban generation there nonetheless emerges very strikingly. Hence this chapter is a critical contribution to the symposium as a whole.

Wheatley's account visualizes the expansion of the ecumene of Malayan chieftains in response to seasonal visits of Indian traders, leading to the borrowing of alien perceptions, roles, and organizational skills oriented toward Indian models of divine kingship that were somewhat dysfunctional in their new setting. Such individuals, he argues, "would have manipulated the new alternatives or inconsistencies thus created in the indigenous scheme of values in an effort to strengthen their own prestige and ultimately to achieve some degree of freedom from the restrictive bonds of tribal custom" (p. 242). Divine kingship was apparently crucial in this respect, so that the cultural form by which the ongoing process can be detected is one of brahmanization. Particularly important for our understanding of economic processes in other regions is his description of mobilizative, redistributive and market subsystems

463

not as "inexorably fixed, established for all time by divinely ordained structural necessity" (p. 228), but rather as blending into one another with parallel changes and mutual adjustments.

As Wheatley notes, the earliest stages of literacy in most of the "primary" civilizations were exactly contemporaneous with pristine state development. Hence it may be that only in "secondary" cases like his can we ever hope for the kind of broadly based, organizational understanding that voluminous written records alone provide. That does not mean we should uncritically join "primary" and "secondary" into a single civilizational type if the evidence warrants separating them—I certainly concede, with Renfrew, that that issue is still open—but it does imply persisting in a comparative approach and remaining optimistic about the potentialities of new evidence from many unexpected quarters.

It thus becomes clear that another area of consensus emerged at the symposium, in addition to the recognition that trade has become a rapidly changing and highly productive focus for research on the development of ancient complex societies. The conceptual and methodological problems are staggering, but we concluded with a sense of optimism that much progress can be made toward solving them. And we are aware that in order to achieve this progress we will need to remain in active communication, which is the least formal but most effective means of maintaining a comparative perspective.

References

ADAMS, ROBERT McC.
1974 "Anthropological Reflections on Ancient Trade," *Current Anthropology* (in press).

ADAMS, ROBERT McC., AND HANS J. NISSEN
1972 *The Uruk Countryside* (Chicago: University of Chicago Press).

ARROW, KENNETH J.
1974 "Limited Knowledge and Economic Analysis," *American Economic Review* 64:1–10.

BINFORD, LEWIS R.
1968 "Post-Pleistocene Adaptations," in *New Perspectives in Archaeology*, ed. L. R. and S. R. Binford (Chicago: Aldine Publishing Co.).

EISENSTADT, SHUMEL N.
1963 *The Political Systems of Empires* (London: Collier-Macmillan; New York: Free Press of Glencoe).

FLANNERY, KENT V.
1972 "The Cultural Evolution of Civilizations," *Annual Review of Ecology and Systematics* 3:399–426.

JAWAD, ABDUL JALIL
1965 *The Advent of the Era of Townships in Northern Mesopotamia* (Leiden: E. J. Brill).

PALERM, ANGEL, AND ERIC R. WOLF
1957 "Ecological Potential and Cultural Development in Mesoamerica," in *Studies in Human Ecology*, Panamerican Union Social Science Monograph 3.

SANDERS, WILLIAM T.
1956 "The Central Mexican Symbiotic Region: A Study in Prehistoric Settlement Patterns," in *Prehistoric Settlement Patterns in the New World*, ed. Gordon R. Willey. Viking Fund Publications in Anthropology 23.

WINTERS, HOWARD D.
1968 "Value Systems and Trade Cycles of the Late Archaic in the Midwest," in *New Perspectives in Archaeology*, ed. L. R. and S. R. Binford (Chicago: Aldine Publishing Co.).

WRIGHT, HENRY T.
1972 "A Consideration of Interregional Exchange in Greater Mesopotamia: 4000–3000 B.C.," in *Social Exchange and Interaction*, ed. Edwin N. Wilmsen. University of Michigan Museum of Anthropology Anthropological Papers 46 (Ann Arbor).

Index*

Compiled by Elizabeth Hart and Martha Prickett

* Names of scholars mentioned as references in the text have not been indexed. Readers are referred to the individual reference lists at the end of each chapter.

Index

Index

Index

Index

Index

Pacific peoples: trade among, 39, 344, chiefdoms among, 167
Padlĕgan, Java, 268
Pagan (site, Burma), 241, 249
Pakistan, 172, 173
palace, 96, 247, 256
Palĕbuhan (Goreng Gareng), Java, 267
Palembang, Sumatra, 267
Palĕpangan (Barabudur), Java, 270–71
Pali, 232, 260
Pāṇḍya Dynasty, India, 241
Pañji narrative cycle (Javanese), 241
P'an-p'an (state, Southeast Asia), 243
pasar (market, Javanese), 271–72
patriarchalism, 247
patterning, of a cultural system, 410, 412, 413, 414
payments: noncommercial, 88; redistributive, 88; price, 253
pearls, 252
Pearson, Harry, 116
peasantries, 76, 91, 96
Peisistratids (Greek family), 138
Periplus Maris Erythraei, 231, 232, 233, 234–35, 259–60
Persia, Persians, 243, 259, 264. See also Iran
Persian Empire, 192
Persian Gulf, 233, 351, 353, 358, 362
Peru, 54, 87, 114, 168, 171, 174, 176, 177, 181, 183, 188, 189, 194
Petén, Guatemala, 14, 431
petrological microscope, 39
Phnom Penh, Cambodia, 259, 265
Phoenicians, 104, 134, 191
physiochemical analyses, 353, 354, 355, 363, 369, 443
Piedras Negras (site, Mexico), 416
pigs, 97; tusks of, 86, 96
pilgrims, 235, 371, 402, 403, 459
Pillars of Hercules, 140
piracy, 108
Plumbangan, Java, 271
plaza complexes, 382, 383, 385, 386, 389, 390, 391, 392, 393, 394, 395, 396, 397, 398, 400, 401, 423, 443
Pliny, 234
plow, 264
Podoukê, India, 235
Polanyi, Karl, 63–123 passim
political institutions, 453
polyculture. See agriculture
Polynesia, 12, 167, 176, 178, 179, 194
Pondicherry, India, 235

population, 184, 186, 288, 292, 293, 305, 307, 309; growth, 188; mass, 248; ports, 370, 372, 373; pressure, 441
port: facilities, 150; identification of, 375, 378, 388; of trade, 11, 43, 45, 74, 79, 80, 83, 100, 102, 122, 152, 153, 372–73, 379
Portuguese, as colonizers, 77, 148
Postclassic Period (Mesoamerica), 160, 189, 422, 424, 425, 427, 429, 431, 432, 433, 435, 436, 443; Early, 405, 421; Late, 370, 371, 372, 373, 375, 376, 378, 380, 382, 383, 384, 387, 392, 393, 394, 395, 401, 402, 403, 405, 420, 421, 422, 423, 427, 428, 429, 430, 431, 433, 434, 435, 443
post-Neolithic Europe, 178
potlatch, 96, 113, 120
Potonchán (site, Mexico), 405
poultry products, 9
power: concentration of, 157; division of, 180; hierarchical aspects of, 453
Práḥ Khăn (temple, Southeast Asia), 252, 253, 254, 255
Práḥ Viḥar (temple, Southeast Asia), 256
Preclassic Period (Mesoamerica), 416, 421; Early, 405
pre-Columbian Period (Mesoamerica), 370
predynastic period (Egypt), 171
prestige, 239, 253; sector, 82
price, 228, 343, 344, 345; differentials, 150; fixing, 256; theory, 73, 75, 85, 115
priesthood, 245, 246, 251, 252, 265
production, 86; centralized, 299; distribution system, 413, 414, 415, 417, 418, 420, 423, 436, 440, 441; modes of, 344, 348, 349, 350, 362, 364, 421, 430, 436, 441
profit, 233, 345, 350, 364; motive, 136, 137
property, private, 377
Protoclassic Period (Mesoamerica), 168, 171, 188
Proto-Elamite tablets, 357
Ptolemaic astronomers, 52
Ptolemy, 235
public works, 158, 163, 182, 185, 220, 298
Pura Bukit Indrakila, Bali, 272
purchasing power, 288
Pūrvatatathāgata (temple, Southeast Asia), 254
Putún (Mesoamerican people), 372, 375, 416

Index

Sanskrit: language and literature, 232, 240, 241, 244, 250, 251, 256, 260, 265; word derivation, 240, 250, 266, 268; Sanskritization, 240, 241
sārdhakāra (state official, Southeast Asia), 249
satyānṛta: defined, 259
Sayre, Edward, 352
seafaring, 244, 260, 261
seals, 121; forms of, 303, 362; use of, 362–63
secularism, 455, 456, 462, 463
Seistan (region, Iran), 362
Sĕluyut (Southeast Asia), 256, 265
Sembiran, Bali, 268, 272
services, 86, 89, 162, 214, 344; redistribution of, 299; ritual, 245, 249
sesame, 252
settlement: agglomeration, 334; archaeology, 213; distribution, 52, 183, 290, 291, 293, 296, 298, 299, 307, 309, 324, 333, 335, 336; hierarchy, 17, 292, 293, 296, 297, 304, 309, 314, 317, 318, 319, 333, 335–36, 459; intrusive, 239; location, 322, 335, 383, 390, 404, 458; organization, 395, 396, 397, 398, 399, 400; pattern, 286, 291, 294, 298, 299, 307, 310, 311, 317, 321, 322, 375, 392, 397, 398, 399, 401, 402, 403, 404; primary, 324, 333; size, 293, 298, 315, 319, 324, 335
Shahdad (site, Iran), 353, 361
Shahr-i Sokhta (site, Iran), 351, 353, 355, 356, 360
shamans, 245, 247
Shang China, 18, 173, 192, 218, 219
Shanidar B (site, Iraq), 352
Shansi, China, 217, 219
Shantung, China, 219
Sharafabad (Uruk site), 303
Shensi, China, 219
sheep, 216
shells, 65, 222; cowrie, 28, 86, 216–17, 220, 221; marine, 39; pearl, 97; tambu, 28; as trade commodity, 427; turtle, 217, 220
Shilluk (group in sub-Saharan Africa), 160, 161
ships: captains of, 267, 268; pilots of, 268
shrine, 230, 243, 249, 251, 252, 254, 255, 256, 371, 375, 377–78, 404; building type, 382, 383, 384, 385, 386,

387, 389, 390, 392, 393, 394, 396, 397, 398, 403, 404; distribution of, 423, 427; imams, 458–59
Shumash stone, 356
Sialk (site, Iran), 353
Siamo-Malay Peninsula, 217, 241, 242, 243, 245, 250
Siassi-Gomlongon market, 8
Siberia, 233
Sicily, 105
Sīhaḷavatthuppakaraṇa (Pali text), 232, 260
silk, 135, 145, 252, 263
silver, 252, 255
Siṁhaladvīpa. See Ceylon
Singhalese, in Java, 267
Sippar (site, Mesopotamia), 360
site-to-site distance, 314
Śiva (Hindu god), 240, 263, 265
Śīwagĕrha, Java, 267
skulls, 151
slaves, 98, 121, 135, 142, 145, 147, 148, 151, 217, 402
Smith, Adam, 347
Smrti canon, 236, 244, 245
social control, 165
society: complex, 257, 452, 460; evolution of, 343, 344, 348, 452, 454–55, 461, 463, 464; segmentary, 238, 253; stratification of, 360, 454, 455; tribal, 159, 232, 235, 236, 238, 240, 242, 247, 250, 257. See also tribe
Society Islands, chiefdoms in, 159–60
Sogdian people (Central Asia), 243, 264
Solecki, Ralph, 352
Solomon, King, 138
Solon, 138
Sōpatma, India, 235
Souppara, India, 235
South Africa, 77
South America, 76, 77, 178
South China Sea, 231, 238
Southeast Asia, 192, 227–72 passim, 463
Southwest Asia, 229, 234
Southwest Iran Project, 294
Soviet Union, 91
space, 211
Spanish: as colonizers, 77; in Mesoamerica, 108, 370, 371, 383, 384, 388, 402–3, 405, 417, 434, 443
spatial distribution, 40, 52; of materials, 218; of natural resources, 215; organization of, 289, 379, 383, 386,